Theories of International Relations

Theories of International Relations

Third edition

Scott Burchill, Andrew Linklater, Richard Devetak, Jack Donnelly, Matthew Paterson, Christian Reus-Smit and Jacqui True

First edition 1996
Second edition 2001

Published 2005 by
PALGRAVE MACMILLAN
Houndmills, Basingstoke, Hampshire RG21 6XS and
175 Fifth Avenue, New York, N.Y. 10010
Companies and representatives throughout the world.

PALGRAVE MACMILLAN is the global academic imprint of the Palgrave
Macmillan division of St. Martin's Press, LLC and of Palgrave Macmillan Ltd.
Macmillan® is a registered trademark in the United States, United Kingdom
and other countries. Palgrave is a registered trademark in the European
Union and other countries.

ISBN-13: 978–1–4039–4865–6 hardback
ISBN-10: 1–4039–4865–8 hardback
ISBN-13: 978–1–4039–4866–3 paperback
ISBN-10: 1–4039–4866–6 paperback

This book is printed on paper suitable for recycling and made from fully
managed and sustained forest sources.

A catalogue record for this book is available from the British Library.

Library of Congress Cataloging-in-Publication Data
    Theories of international relations / Scott Burchill ... [et al.]. – 3rd ed.
        p. cm.
    Includes bibliographical references and index.
    ISBN-13: 978–1–4039–4865–6 (cloth)
    ISBN-10: 1–4039–4865–8 (cloth)
    ISBN-13: 978–1–4039–4866–3 (pbk.)
    ISBN-10: 1–4039–4866–6 (pbk.)
        1. International relations – Philosophy. I. Burchill, Scott, 1961–

JZ1242.T48 2005
327.1'01—dc22   2005043737

10 9 8 7 6 5 4 3 2 1
14 13 12 11 10 09 08 07 06 05

Printed in China

Contents

Preface to the Third Edition   viii

List of Abbreviations   ix

Notes on the Contributors   x

1 **Introduction**   1
   Scott Burchill and Andrew Linklater

   Frameworks of analysis   1
   Diversity of theory   2
   Contested nature   5
   The foundation of International Relations   6
   Theories and disciplines   9
   Explanatory and constitutive theory   15
   What do theories of international relations
       differ about?   18
   Evaluating theories   23

2 **Realism**   29
   Jack Donnelly

   Defining realism   30
   Hobbes and classical realism   32
   Waltz and structural realism   34
   Motives matter   40
   Process, institutions and change   44
   Morality and foreign policy   48
   How to think about realism (and its critics)   52

3 **Liberalism**   55
   Scott Burchill

   After the Cold War   55
   Liberal internationalism: 'inside looking out'   57
   War, democracy and free trade   58
   Economy and terrorism   70
   Conclusion   81

4   **The English School**   **84**
    Andrew Linklater

    From power to order: international society   89
    Order and justice in international relations   93
    The revolt against the West and the expansion of
        international society   98
    Progress in international relations   103
    Conclusion   108

5   **Marxism**   **110**
    Andrew Linklater

    Class, production and international relations in
        Marx's writings   112
    Nationalism and imperialism   120
    The changing fortunes of Marxism in
        International Relations   124
    Marxism and international relations theory today   132
    Conclusion   135

6   **Critical Theory**   **137**
    Richard Devetak

    Origins of critical theory   137
    The politics of knowledge in International Relations theory   140
    Rethinking political community   146
    Conclusion   159

7   **Postmodernism**   **161**
    Richard Devetak

    Power and knowledge in International Relations   162
    Textual strategies of postmodernism   167
    Problematizing sovereign states   171
    Beyond the paradigm of sovereignty: rethinking the political   181
    Conclusion   187

8   **Constructivism**   **188**
    Christian Reus-Smit

    Rationalist theory   189
    The challenge of critical theory   193
    Constructivism   194

Constructivism and its discontents 201
The contribution of constructivism 205
Constructivism after 9/11 207
Conclusion 211

9 **Feminism** 213
Jacqui True

Empirical feminism 216
Analytical feminism 221
Normative feminism 228
Conclusion 232

10 **Green Politics** 235
Matthew Paterson

Green political theory 237
Global ecology 238
Ecocentrism 238
Limits to growth, post-development 239
Green rejections of the state-system 242
Objections to Green arguments for decentralization 246
Greening global politics? 248
Conclusions 254

Bibliography 258

Index 289

Preface to the Third Edition

Like its predecessors, the third edition is intended to provide upper-level undergraduates and postgraduates with a guide to the leading theoretical perspectives in the field.

The origins of the project lie in the development by Deakin University of a distance-learning course in 1995: early versions of several chapters were initially written for the course guide for this. The first edition of this book brought together substantially revised versions of these with new chapters on Feminism and Green Politics. The second edition added a further chapter on Constructivism. None of those involved in the project at the outset guessed that the result would be quite such a successful text as this has turned out to be, with course adoptions literally all over the world.

The third edition has again been substantially improved. For this edition, Jack Donnelly has written a new chapter on the varieties of Realism. Jacqui True has produced what is virtually a new chapter on Feminism. Andrew Linklater's chapter on the English School replaces the one on Rationalism which he contributed to the first and second editions. All chapters, however, have been revised and updated to reflect developments in the literature and to take account, where appropriate, of the significance of '9/11' for theories of world politics. The third edition also includes a significantly revised introduction on the importance of international relations theory for students of world affairs. Last but not least, the whole book has been redesigned, consistency between chapters in style and presentation has been improved, and a consolidated bibliography has been added with Harvard references replacing notes throughout.

As with the earlier editions, our publisher, Steven Kennedy has been keenly involved in every stage of the production of this book. We are grateful once again for his unfailing commitment and wise counsel. Thanks also to Gary Smith of Deakin University and Dan Flitton for their contributions to earlier editions. Above all we would like to thank our co-authors for their hard work and forbearance.

SCOTT BURCHILL
ANDREW LINKLATER

List of Abbreviations

APEC	Asia Pacific Economic Cooperation
CND	Campaign for Nuclear Disarmament (UK)
FDI	Foreign direct investment
GAD	Gender and development
GPT	Green political theory
ICC	International Criminal Court
ICJ	International Court of Justice
IO	International organization
ILO	International Labour Organization
IMF	International Monetary Fund
IPE	International Political Economy
IUCN	International Union for the Conservation of Nature and Natural Resources
MAI	Multilateral Agreement on Investments
MNC	Multinational corporation
NAFTA	North American Free Trade Agreement
NATO	North Atlantic Treaty Organization
NGO	Non-governmental organization
NTB	Non-trade barrier
OECD	Organization for Economic Cooperation and Development
SAP	Structural adjustment policy (IMF)
TNC	Transnational corporation
UNCED	United Nations Conference on Environment and Development
UNDP	United Nations Development Programme
WCED	World Commission on Environment and Development
WHO	World Health Organization
WMD	Weapons of mass destruction
WTO	World Trade Organization
WID	Women in international development

Notes on the Contributors

Scott Burchill is Senior Lecturer in International Relations, Deakin University, Australia.

Richard Devetak is Lecturer in Politics, Monash University, Australia.

Jack Donnelly is Andrew W. Mellon Professor of Political Science, University of Denver, USA.

Andrew Linklater is Woodrow Wilson Professor of International Politics, University of Wales, Aberystwyth, UK.

Matthew Paterson is Associate Professor of Political Science, University of Ottawa, Canada.

Christian Reus-Smit is Professor of International Relations, Australian National University, Australia.

Jacqui True is Lecturer in International Politics, University of Auckland, New Zealand.

Chapter 1

Introduction

SCOTT BURCHILL AND ANDREW LINKLATER

Frameworks of analysis

The study of international relations began as a theoretical discipline. Two of the foundational texts in the field, E. H. Carr's, *The Twenty Years' Crisis* (first published in 1939) and Hans Morgenthau's *Politics Among Nations* (first published in 1948) were works of theory in three central respects. Each developed a broad framework of analysis which distilled the essence of international politics from disparate events; each sought to provide future analysts with the theoretical tools for understanding general patterns underlying seemingly unique episodes; and each reflected on the forms of political action which were most appropriate in a realm in which the struggle for power was pre-eminent. Both thinkers were motivated by the desire to correct what they saw as deep misunderstandings about the nature of international politics lying at the heart of the liberal project – among them the belief that the struggle for power could be tamed by international law and the idea that the pursuit of self-interest could be replaced by the shared objective of promoting security for all. Not that Morgenthau and Carr thought the international political system was condemned for all time to revolve around the relentless struggle for power and security. Their main claim was that all efforts to reform the international system which ignored the struggle for power would quickly end in failure. More worrying in their view was the danger that attempts to bring about fundamental change would compound the problem of international relations. They maintained the liberal internationalist world-view had been largely responsible for the crisis of the inter-war years.

Many scholars, particularly in United States in the 1960s, believed that Morgenthau's theoretical framework was too impressionistic in nature. Historical illustrations had been used to support rather than demonstrate ingenious conjectures about general patterns of international relations. In consequence, the discipline lagged significantly behind the study of Economics which used a sophisticated methodology drawn from the natural sciences to test specific hypotheses, develop general

1

laws and predict human behaviour. Proponents of the scientific approach attempted to build a new theory of international politics, some for the sake of better explanation and higher levels of predictive accuracy, others in the belief that science held the key to understanding how to transform international politics for the better.

The scientific turn led to a major disciplinary debate in the 1960s in which scholars such as Hedley Bull (1966b) argued that international politics were not susceptible to scientific enquiry. This is a view widely shared by analysts committed to diverse intellectual projects. The radical scholar, Noam Chomsky (1994: 120) has claimed that in international relations 'historical conditions are too varied and complex for anything that might plausibly be called "a theory" to apply uniformly' (1994: 120). What is generally know as 'post-positivism' in International Relations rejects the possibility of a science of international relations which uses standards of proof associated with the physical sciences to develop equivalent levels of explanatory precision and predictive certainty (Smith, Booth and Zalewski 1996). In the 1990s, a major debate occurred around the claims of positivism. The question of whether there is a world of difference between the 'physical' and the 'social' sciences was a crucial issue, but no less important were disputes about the nature and purpose of theory. The debate centred on whether theories – even those that aim for objectivity – are ultimately 'political' because they generate views of the world which favour some political interests and disadvantage others. This dispute has produced very difficult questions about what theory is and what its purposes are. These questions are now central to the discipline – more central than at any other time in its history. What, in consequence, is it to speak of a 'theory of international politics?

Diversity of theory

One purpose of this volume is to analyse the diversity of conceptions of theory in the study of international relations. Positivist or 'scientific' approaches remain crucial, and are indeed dominant in the United States, as the success of rational choice analysis demonstrates. But this is not the only type of theory available in the field. An increasingly large number of theorists are concerned with a second category of theory in which the way that observers construct their images of international relations, the methods they use to try to understand this realm and the social and political implications of their 'knowledge claims' are leading preoccupations. They believe it is just as important to focus on how we approach the study of world politics as it is to try to explain global phenomena. In other words the very process of theorizing itself becomes a vital object of inquiry.

Steve Smith (1995: 26–7) has argued that there is a fundamental division within the discipline 'between theories which seek to offer *explanatory* (our emphasis) accounts of International Relations' and perspectives which regard 'theory as *constitutive* (our emphasis) of that reality'. Analysing these two conceptions of theory informs much of the discussion in this introductory chapter.

The first point to make in this context is that constitutive theories have an increasingly prominent role in the study of international relations, but the importance of the themes they address has long been recognized. As early as the 1970s Hedley Bull (1973: 183–4) argued that:

> the reason we must be concerned with the theory as well as the history of the subject is that all discussions of international politics ... proceed upon theoretical assumptions which we should acknowledge and investigate rather than ignore or leave unchallenged. The enterprise of theoretical investigation is at its minimum one directed towards criticism: towards identifying, formulating, refining, and questioning the general assumptions on which the everyday discussion of international politics proceeds. At its maximum, the enterprise is concerned with theoretical construction: with establishing that certain assumptions are true while others are false, certain arguments valid while others are invalid, and so proceeding to erect a firm structure of knowledge.

This quotation reveals that Bull thought that explanatory and constitutive theory are both necessary in the study of international relations: intellectual enquiry would be incomplete without the effort to increase understanding on both fronts. Although he wrote this in the early 1970s, it was not until later in the decade that constitutive theory began to enjoy a more central place in the discipline, in large part because of the influence of developments in the cognate fields of social and political theory. In the years since, with the growth of interest in international theory, a flourishing literature has been devoted to addressing theoretical concerns, much of it concerned with constitutive theory. This focus on the process of theorizing has not been uncontroversial. Some have argued that the excessive preoccupation with theory represents a withdrawal from an analysis of 'real-world' issues and a sense of responsibility for policy relevance (Wallace 1996). There is a parallel here with a point that Keohane (1988) made against post-modernism which is that the fixation with problems in the philosophy of social science leads to a neglect of important fields of empirical research.

Critics of this argument maintain that it rests on unspoken or undefended theoretical assumptions about the purposes of studying international relations, and specifically on the belief that the discipline should be concerned with issues which are more vital to states than to civil society actors aiming to change the international political system (Booth 1997; Smith 1997). Here it is important to recall that Carr and Morgenthau were interested not only in explaining the world 'out there' but in making a powerful argument about what states could reasonably hope to achieve in the competitive world of international politics. Smith (1996: 113) argues that all theories do this whether intentionally or unintentionally: they 'do not simply explain or predict, they tell us what possibilities exist for human action and intervention; they define not merely our explanatory possibilities, but also our ethical and practical horizons'.

Smith questions what he sees as the false assumption that 'theory' stands in opposition to 'reality' – conversely that 'theory' can be tested against a 'reality' which is already 'out there' (see also George 1994). The issue here is whether what is 'out there' is always theory-dependent and invariably conditioned to some degree by the language and culture of the observer and by general beliefs about society tied to a particular place and time. And as noted earlier, those who wonder about the point of theory cannot avoid the fact that analysis is always theoretically informed and likely to have political implications and consequences (Brown 2002). The growing feminist literature in the field discussed in Chapter 9 has stressed this argument in its claim that many of its dominant traditions are gendered in that they reflect specifically male experiences of society and politics. Critical approaches to the discipline which are discussed in Chapters 6 and 7 have been equally keen to stress that there is, as Nagel (1986) has argued in a rather different context, 'no view from nowhere'.

To be fair, many exponents of the scientific approach recognized this very problem, but they believed that science made it possible for analysts to rise above the social and political world they were investigating. What the physical sciences had achieved could be emulated in social-scientific forms of enquiry. This is a matter to come back to later. But debates about the possibility of a science of international relations, and disputes about whether there has been an excessive preoccupation with theory in recent years, demonstrate that scholars do not agree about the nature and purposes of theory or concur about its proper place in the wider field. International Relations is a discipline of theoretical disagreements – a 'divided discipline', as Holsti (1985) called it.

Contested nature

Indeed it has been so since those who developed this comparatively new subject in the Western academy in the aftermath of the First World War first debated the essential features of international politics. Ever since then, but more keenly in some periods than in others, almost every aspect of the study of international politics has been contested. What should the discipline aim to study: Relations between states? Growing transnational economic ties, as recommended by early twentieth-century liberals? Increasing international interdependence, as advocated in the 1970s? The global system of dominance and dependence, as claimed by Marxists and neo-Marxists from the 1970s? Globalization, as scholars have argued in more recent times? These are some examples of how the discipline has been divided on the very basic question of its *subject matter*.

How, in addition, should international political phenomena be studied: by using empirical data to identify laws and patterns of international relations? By using historical evidence to understand what is unique (Bull 1966a) or to identify some traditions of thought which have survived for centuries (Wight 1991)? By using Marxist approaches to production, class and material inequalities? By emulating, as Waltz (1979) does, the study of the market behaviour of firms to understand systemic forces which make all states behave in much the same way? By claiming, as Wendt (1999) does in his defence of constructivism, that in the study of international relations it is important to understand that 'it is ideas all the way down?' These are some illustrations of fundamental differences about the appropriate *methodology* or *methodologies* to use in the field.

Finally is it possible for scholars to provide neutral forms of analysis, or are all approaches culture-bound and necessarily biased? Is it possible to have objective knowledge of facts but not of values, as advocates of the scientific approach argued? Or, as some students of global ethics have argued, is it possible to have knowledge of the goals that states and other political actors should aim to realize such as the promotion of global justice (Beitz 1979) or ending world poverty (Pogge 2002) These are some of the *epistemological* debates in the field, debates about what human beings can and cannot know about the social and political world. Many of the 'great debates' and watersheds in the discipline have focused on such questions.

In the remainder of this introductory chapter we will examine these and other issues under the following headings:

- The foundation of the discipline of International Relations
- Theories and disciplines

- Explanatory and constitutive theory
- What do theories of international relations differ about?
- What criteria exist for evaluating theories?

One of our aims is to explain the proliferation of theories since the 1980s, to analyse their different 'styles' and methods of proceeding and to comment on a recurrent problem in the field which is that theorists often appear to 'talk past' each other rather than engage in productive dialogue. Another aim is to identify ways in which meaningful comparisons between different perspectives of International Relations can be made. It will be useful to bear these points in mind when reading later chapters on several influential theoretical traditions in the field. We begin, however, with a brief introduction to the development of the discipline.

The foundation of International Relations

Although historians, international lawyers and political philosophers have written about international politics for many centuries, the formal recognition of a separate discipline of International Relations is usually thought to have occurred at the end of the First World War with the establishment of a Chair of International Relations at the University of Wales, Aberystwyth. Other Chairs followed in Britain and the United States. International relations were studied before 1919, but there was no discipline as such. Its subject matter was shared by a number of older disciplines, including law, philosophy, economics, politics and diplomatic history – but before 1919 the subject was not studied with the great sense of urgency which was the product of the First World War.

It is impossible to separate the foundation of the discipline of International Relations from the larger public reaction to the horrors of the 'Great War', as it was initially called. For many historians of the time, the intellectual question which eclipsed all others and monopolized their interest was the puzzle of how and why the war began. Gooch in England, Fay and Schmitt in the United States, Renouvin and Camille Bloch in France, Thimme, Brandenburg and von Wegerer in Germany, Pribram in Austria and Pokrovsky in Russia deserve to be mentioned in this regard (Taylor 1961: 30). They had the same moral purpose, which was to discover the causes of the First World War so that future generations might be spared a similar catastrophe.

The human cost of the 1914–18 war led many to argue that the old assumptions and prescriptions of power politics were totally discredited. Thinkers such as Sir Alfred Zimmern and Philip Noel-Baker came to prominence in the immediate post-war years. They believed that peace would come about only if the classical balance of power were replaced by a system of collective security (including the idea of the rule of law) in which states transferred domestic concepts and practices to the international sphere. Central here was a commitment to the nineteenth-century belief that humankind could make political progress by using reasoned debate to develop common interests. This was a view shared by many liberal internationalists, later dubbed 'idealists' or 'utopians' by critics who thought their panaceas were simplistic. Carr (1939/1945/1946) maintained that their proposed solution to the scourge of war suffered from the major problem of reflecting, albeit unwittingly, the position of the satisfied powers – 'the haves' as opposed to the 'have-nots' in international relations. It is interesting to note that the first complaint about the ideological and political character of such a way of thinking about international politics was first made by a 'realist' such as Carr who was influenced by Marxism and its critique of the ideological nature of the dominant liberal approaches to politics and economics in the nineteenth century. Carr thought that the same criticism held with respect to the 'utopians', as he called them.

The war shook the confidence of those who had invested their faith in classical diplomacy and who thought the use of force was necessary at times to maintain the balance of power. At the outbreak of the First World War few thought it would last more than a few months and fewer still anticipated the scale of the impending catastrophe. Concerns about the human cost of war were linked with the widespread notion that the old international order, with its secret diplomacy and secret treaties, was plainly immoral. The belief in the need for a 'clean break' with the old order encouraged the view that the study of history was an imperfect guide to how states should behave in future. In the aftermath of the war, a new academic discipline was thought essential, one devoted to understanding and preventing international conflict. The first scholars in the field, working within universities in the victorious countries, and particularly in Britain and the United States, were generally agreed that the following three questions should guide their new field of inquiry:

1. What were the main causes of the First World War, and what was it about the old order that led national governments into a war which resulted in misery for millions?
2. What were the main lessons that could be learned from the First World War? How could the recurrence of a war of this kind be prevented?
3. On what basis could a new international order be created, and how could international institutions, and particularly the League of Nations, ensure that states complied with its defining principles?

In response to these questions, many members of the first 'school' or 'theory' of international relations maintained that war was partly the result of 'international anarchy' and partly the result of misunderstandings, miscalculations and recklessness on the part of politicians who had lost control of events in 1914. The 'idealists' argued that a more peaceful world order could be created by making foreign policy elites accountable to public opinion and by democratizing international relations (Long and Wilson 1995; see also Chapter 2 in this volume). According to Bull (quoted in Hollis and Smith 1990: 20):

> the distinctive characteristic of these writers was their belief in progress: the belief, in particular, that the system of international relations that had given rise to the First World War was capable of being transformed into a fundamentally more peaceful and just world order; that under the impact of the awakening of democracy, the growth of the 'international mind', the development of the League of Nations, the good works of men of peace or the enlightenment spread by their own teachings, it was in fact being transformed; and that their responsibility as students of international relations was to assist this march of progress to overcome the ignorance, the prejudices, the ill-will, and the sinister interests that stood in its way.

Bull brings out the extent to which normative vision animated the discipline in its first phase of development when many thought the First World War was the 'war to end all wars'. Only the rigorous study of the phenomenon of war could explain how states could create a world order in which the recurrence of such a conflict would be impossible. Crucially, then, the discipline was born in an era when many believed that the reform of international politics was not only essential but clearly achievable. Whether or not the global order can be radically improved has been a central question in the study of international relations ever since.

The critics' reaction to this liberal internationalism dominated the discipline's early years. Carr (1939/1945/1946: Chapter 1), who was one of the more scathing of them, maintained that 'utopians' were guilty of 'naivety' and 'exuberance'. Visionary zeal stood in the way of dispassionate analysis. The realist critique of liberal internationalism launched by Carr immediately before the Second World War, and continued by various scholars including Morgenthau in the United States in the 1940s and 1950s led to the so-called first 'great debate'. Whether this debate actually occurred has been contested by recent scholars (Wilson 1998); however the myth of a great debate between the realists and the idealists gave the discipline its identity in the post-Second World War years. Interestingly Carr (1939/1945/1946), who criticised the utopians for their 'naivety' also turned his guns on the realists, accusing them of 'sterility' and 'complacency'. Theories acquire dominance in any discipline for different reasons, such as the extent to which they prevail in debates with their adversaries (sometimes more imagined than real). They can also be the beneficiary of widespread beliefs that they are right for the times or more relevant to the dominant events of the day than are other perspectives. The 'twenty years' crisis' culminating in the Second World War and followed by the Cold War era led in any case to the dominance of realism.

The purpose of theory in the early years of the discipline was to change the world for the better by removing the blight of war. A close connection existed between theory and practice: theory was not disconnected from the actual world of international politics. This was true of the liberal internationalists who believed 'the world to be profoundly other than it should be' and who had 'faith in the power of human reason and human action' to change it so 'that the inner potential of all human beings [could] be more fully realised' (Howard 1978: 11). It was no less true of the realists who thought that theory had a stake in political practice, most obviously by trying to understand as dispassionately as possible the constraints on realizing the vision which the 'utopians' had been too anxious to embrace. It was the realist position in the dispute about what could and could not be achieved in a world of competing states which gave the discipline its identity in the 1950s and 1960s.

Theories and disciplines

Some forty years ago, Wight (1966a) posed the question, 'Why is there no International Theory?'. His reason for the absence of traditions of international theory ('speculation about the society of states, or the family of nations, or the international community') which even begin to match the achievements of political theory ('speculation about the state') was as follows. Domestic political systems had witnessed extraordinary developments over the centuries including the establishment of public education and welfare systems. But in terms of its basic properties, the international political system had barely changed at all. Wight called it 'the realm of recurrence and repetition' which was 'incompatible with progressivist theory'. Whereas political theory was rich in its characterizations of 'the good life', international theory was confined to questions of 'survival'. The language of political theory and law which was a language 'appropriate to man's control of his social life' had no obvious use for analysts of international affairs (Wight 1966a: 15, 25–6, 32).

At first glance Wight sided with the realists in their debate with those with a utopian temperament. But in an influential set of lectures given at the London School of Economics in the 1950s and 1960s, Wight (1991) protested against the reduction of thinking about international relations to two traditions of thought. What was lost in the division of the field into 'realism' and 'idealism' was a long tradition of inquiry (the 'rationalist' or 'Grotian' tradition) which regarded the existence of the society of states as its starting point. This perspective which has come to be known as The English School (see chapter 4 in this volume) has been influential especially in Britain, and also in Australia and Canada to some extent. Its distinguishing quality is that international relations are neither as bleak as realists suggest nor as amenable to change as utopians ('revolutionists', in Wight's language) believe. There is, members of the English School argue, a high level of order and cooperation in the relations between states, even though they live in a condition of anarchy – a condition marked by the absence of a power standing above and able to command sovereign states.

Four decades on, we can no longer refer, as Wight did, to the 'paucity' of international theory. As this volume will show, there are now many rich strands of international theory, many of which are not constrained by the problem of state survival or by the apparent absence of a vocabulary with which to theorize global politics. How did this change come about, and where does it leave earlier discussions about the possibility or impossibility of progress in international relations?

We can begin to answer these questions by noting that the 1960s and 1970s saw the rapid development of the study of International Relations as new academic departments and centres appeared not only in the United States and Britain but in several other places. This period also saw the rapid proliferation of approaches to the field. The preoccupation with war and conflict remained, the nuclear age leading to the rise of a new sub-field of strategic studies in the 1950s and 1960s. However, the boundaries of the discipline expanded in the period now under discussion to include foreign policy analysis (itself divided into several divisions, one aiming for a predictive science of foreign policy behaviour which might lead to better 'crisis management' (Hill 2003). The 1970s witnessed the rise of study of international interdependence – or, rather, its re-emergence, because liberal internationalists such as Zimmern had identified the expansion of international trade as a crucial level of analysis. Liberal theories of interdependence and the later 'neo-liberal institutionalist' analysis of international regimes argued that the economic and technological unification of the human race required new forms of international cooperation. To those influenced by the socialist tradition, however, international interdependence was a misnomer. The reality was a system of global dominance and dependence which divided the world between 'core' and 'periphery'. The phrase, 'the inter-paradigm debate' was used in the 1970s and 1980s to show that an early consensus about the nature of the discipline (which was always incomplete) had been replaced by a broad spectrum of contending approaches, a condition that survives to this day (Banks 1985; Hoffman 1987). Only some of these approaches (neo-realism being by far the most important – see chapter 3 in this volume) continue to regard the international system as a unique 'anarchic' domain which can be analysed in isolation from social and economic developments within and across societies. The influence of other disciplines and cognate fields is now pronounced in the subject, and many strands of International Relations theory deny that the subject has a distinctive subject matter or can proceed without borrowing heavily from languages of inquiry in other fields of investigation. The import of various ideas from social and political theory is one development which has become increasingly prominent in the 1980s and 1990s (see chapters 6 and 7 in this volume).

In the course of this volume we will examine a number of the more influential theories, including liberal internationalism, realism, neo-realism and the English School, as well as less influential approaches such as Marxism and newer perspectives such as constructivism, feminism and green political thought. In this way, we hope to provide a snapshot of contemporary debates about the nature and purposes of International Relations theory. We have chosen to call them 'theories', but in the literature over the years they have also been referred to as 'paradigms', 'perspectives', 'discourses', 'schools of thought', 'images' and 'traditions'. What they are called is less important than what they set out to do, and how they differ from one another. The following descriptions of theory capture some of their diverse purposes:

- Theories explain the laws of international politics or recurrent patterns of national behaviour (Waltz 1979)
- Theories attempt either to explain and predict behaviour or to understand the world 'inside the heads' of actors (Hollis and Smith 1990)
- Theories are traditions of speculation about relations between states which focus on the struggle for power, the nature of international society and the possibility of a world community (Wight 1991)
- Theories use empirical data to test hypotheses about the world such as the absence of war between liberal-democratic states (Doyle 1983)
- Theories analyse and try to clarify the use of concepts such as the balance of power (Butterfield and Wight 1966)
- Theories criticise forms of domination and perspectives which make the socially constructed and changeable seem natural and unalterable (critical theory)

- Theories reflect on how the world ought to be organized and analyse ways in which various conceptions of human rights or global social justice are constructed and defended (normative theory or international ethics)
- Theories reflect on the process of theorizing itself; they analyse epistemological claims about how human beings know the world and ontological claims about what the world ultimately consists of – for example, whether it basically consists of sovereign states or individuals with rights against and obligations to the rest of humanity (constitutive theory).

This list shows that practitioners in the field do not agree about what is involved in theorizing international relations. When we compare theories we are comparing different and seemingly incommensurable phenomena. There is no agreement about what counts as the best line of argument in any theory, and no agreement about whether their principal achievements can be combined in a unified grand theory. Postmodernist theory – or theories, since its advocates would deny there is a single approach to which all faithfully adhere (see Chapter 7 in this volume) – rejects the possibility of one total theory of international relations. More basically, and as already noted, there is a good deal of overlap between different theories but no consensus about what the term, 'International Relations', actually signifies. Its most obvious meaning is the analysis of relations between nations – more accurately, states, but this is the approach taken by realists and neo-realists and rejected or substantially qualified by exponents of competing perspectives, some of whom think the term 'global politics' or 'world politics' is a better term for describing what the subject should study in the contemporary age (Baylis and Smith 2005).

Though far from exhaustive, the following list summarises some disciplinary preoccupations in recent times:

- *Dominant actors* – traditionally this was the sovereign state but the list now includes transnational corporations (TNCs), transnational classes and 'casino capitalists', international organizations such as the World Trade Organization (WTO), international non-governmental organizations (NGOs) such as Amnesty International, new social movements including women's and ecological movements and international terrorist organizations such as Al-Qaeda
- *Dominant relationships* – strategic relations between the great powers traditionally, but also in recent years trade relations between the advanced industrial societies, the 'liberal peace', relations of dominance and dependence between the core and periphery in the capitalist world economy and forms of solidarity within 'global civil society'
- *Empirical issues* – the distribution of military power, arms control and crisis management but also globalization, global inequality, identity

politics and national fragmentation, the universal human rights culture, the plight of refugees, gender issues, environmental conservation, transnational crime and the global drugs trade and HIV/AIDS
- *Ethical issues* – the just war, the rights and wrongs of humanitarian intervention, the case for and against the global redistribution of power and wealth, duties to nature, to future generations and to non-human species, respect for cultural differences and the rights of women and children
- *Issues in the philosophy of the social sciences* – methodological disputes about the possibility of a science of international politics, competing epistemological and ontological standpoints, the nature of causation and the idea of historical narrative
- *The prospects for multidisciplinarity* – recasting the discipline by using liberal and radical approaches to develop international political economy was the most significant shift towards interdisciplinarity in the 1980s and 1990s. Building links with social theory, historical sociology and 'world history', and dismantling barriers between International Relations, Political Theory and Ethics have been leading developments since the 1990s.

Quite how to deal with such a rich diversity of themes is one of the central questions every theory of international relations must address. Theories have to rely on some principles of selection to narrow their scope of inquiry; they discriminate between actors, relationships, empirical issues and so forth which they judge most important or regard as trivial. Waltz's neo-realist theory is one of the most debated illustrations of this process of selectivity. Waltz (1979) maintained that theory must abstract from the myriad forces at work in international politics while recognizing that in reality 'everything is connected with everything else'. But theory must 'distort' reality – and Waltz offers a complex argument about the philosophy of social sciences and the achievements of Economics to explain this – if it is to explain what Waltz regards as the central puzzle of world politics: the 'dismaying persistence' of the international states-system and the recurrence of the struggle for power and security over several millennia. Waltz argued that international economic relations, international law and so forth are undoubtedly interesting phenomena but they must be ignored by a theory with the purposes he sets for it.

It is useful to compare this argument with Cox's (1981, 1983) claim – influenced by Marxism – that a theory of International Relations has to deal with social forces (including class relations), states and world order if it is to understand the nature of global hegemony and identify 'counter-hegemonic' movements which are working to promote realizable visions of a better form of world order. In this approach, the question of what is most important in world politics is not answered by providing a list of the most powerful actors and relationships but by inquiring into the causes of inequalities of power and opportunities between human beings and by identifying the political movements which are spearheading the struggle against these asymmetries – movements which are not as powerful as states but, in Cox's analysis, more important than them *because of the values they are trying to realize* (for further discussion, see Chapters 5 and 6 in this volume).

In Cox's argument – and this is a position common to the various strands of radical scholarship in the field (see Chapters 5–10 in this volume), the question of what is important in international relations is not an empirical problem which can be solved by looking at what is 'out there' in the 'real world'; it is fundamentally a political question, one that begins with the issue of whose interests are protected and whose are disadvantaged or ignored by the dominant political and economic structures. Such matters are not resolved by empirical inquiry – first and foremost they are ethical matters which have crept to the centre of the field over the last twenty or so years.

This raises important issues about how theories acquire disciplinary dominance or hegemony. The post-positivist turn has made such matters prominent in the field, but they have a more ancient lineage. Since the 1960s, for example, radical scholars in the United States such as Yergin (1990) and Chomsky (1969) have analysed the close connections which have often existed between the academic study of International Relations and the world of government, especially in the United States (for an appraisal of Chomsky's work, see the Forum on Chomsky, *Review of International Studies* 2003). They have stressed how the dominant political needs of the time, as defined by government, have favoured some theories over others so that one perspective acquires hegemony while others make dissenting claims on the margins of the field. Strategic studies was regarded as a case in point, and many radical scholars stressed its close connections with the 'military–industrial complex' in the 1960s. Realism was the dominant ideology of the US political establishment in the late 1960s and early 1970s when the Nixon Administration broke with the Cold War ideology which had impeded the development of amicable relations with the Soviet Union and China (Henry Kissinger, Nixon's National Security Advisor and later Secretary of State had been a leading realist academic prior to 1968). Since the 1980s, the dominant ideology has been neo-liberal economics, which has had enormous influence through the 'Washington Consensus' in promoting the deregulation of world markets (see Chapter 2 in this volume). A fascinating illustration of the changing political fortunes of academic theories is that realism has come to have a dissenting role with respect to recent US foreign policy while remaining one of the dominant traditions in the American academy. The phenomenon of 'realists against the war' (many leading realist scholars published their opposition to the war against Iraq in *The New York Times* in 2002) is an example of how dominance in one domain may not be converted into dominance in the other.

It is necessary to stress the politicized nature of the discipline because the politics of International Relations can determine how broad the spectrum of 'legitimate theoretical opinion' can actually be. For example, Marxist scholars have highlighted the limits of expressible dissent in the discipline's attempt to uncover the cause of the First World War. They have pointed to the conceptual and ideological parameters beyond which the investigators into war causes could not, or would not, proceed. For opinion to be considered legitimate it had to fall between the poles of 'idealism' at one end of the spectrum and 'realism' at the other. According to these Marxists, certain facts were axiomatically excluded as not belonging to the inquiry at all. Tensions within society, such as class struggles and economic competition between colonial powers – during this period a popular Marxist explanation of the origins of war – were not considered seriously within the discipline at this time. One commentator has suggested that the theory of imperialism was deliberately excluded because, by locating the causes of war within the nature of the capitalist system, it posed a direct threat to the social order of capitalist states: 'this false doctrine had to be refuted in the interest of stabilising bourgeois society ... the [historians] acted and reflected within the social context of the bourgeois university, which structurally obstructed such revolutionary insights' (Krippendorf 1982: 27). Feminists have made a similar claim about the exclusion of their presence and perspectives from the concerns of International Relations, arguing that the organization of the academy was designed in ways that occluded inquiry into masculine power.

Explanatory and constitutive theory

One aim of studying a wide variety of International Relations theories is to make international politics more intelligible – to make better sense of the actors, structures, institutions, processes and particular episodes mainly, but not only, in the contemporary world. At times theories may be involved in testing hypotheses, in proposing causal explanations with a view to identifying main trends and patterns in international relations – hence the claim that they are *explanatory* theories.

But why study international relations in this way? Is it obvious that the student of international relations needs theory at all? Is it not more centrally important to investigate the facts which are already out there? Halliday's three answers to this last question are instructive:

> First, there needs to be some preconception of which facts are significant and which are not. The facts are myriad and do not speak for themselves. For anyone, academic or not, there needs to be criteria of significance. Secondly, any one set of facts, even if accepted as true and as significant, can yield different interpretations:the debate on the 'lessons of the 1930s' is not about what happened in the 1930s, but about how these events are to be interpreted. The same applies to the end of the Cold War in the 1980s. Thirdly, no human agent, again whether academic or not, can rest content with facts alone: all social activity involves moral questions, of right and wrong, and these can, by definition, not be decided by facts. In the international domain such ethical issues are pervasive: the question of legitimacy and loyalty – should one obey the nation, a broader community (even the world, the cosmopolis), or some smaller sub-national group; the issues of intervention – whether sovereignty is a supreme value or whether states or agents can intervene in the internal affairs of states; the question of human rights and their definition and universality. (Halliday 1994: 25)

In this view, theories are not 'optional extras' or interesting 'fashion accessories'. They are a necessary means of bringing order to the subject matter of International Relations. Theories are needed to conceptualize contemporary events. As Doyle (1983) argues in his writings on the liberal peace, an explanation of the absence of war between liberal states for almost two centuries has to begin by discussing what it means to describe a state as 'liberal' and what it means to claim there has been 'no war'. As Suganami (1996) has argued, an explanation of what causes war or what makes peace possible between societies, will be unsatisfactory unless it deals with the question of what it means to say that '*x*' causes '*y*'. Conceptual analysis – an inherently philosophical activity – is a necessary part of any attempt to explain or understand world politics.

International relations comprise a plethora of events, issues and relationships which are often enormous in scale and bewildering in their complexity. Theories can help the observer to think critically, logically and coherently by sorting these phenomena into manageable categories so that the appropriate units and level of analysis can be chosen and, where possible, significant connections and patterns of behaviour identified.

To the scholar of the 'international', theories are unavoidable. After all, the interpretation of 'reality' is always contingent on theoretical assumptions of one kind or another. To reiterate the point, the events and issues which comprise international relations can be interpreted and understood only by reference to a conceptual framework. The theory of international relations provides us with a choice of such frameworks.

The process we undertake when theorizing is also in dispute and, as Bull insisted, critical, reflective examination is always required. Gellner (1974: 175) asks whether it is possible or meaningful to distinguish 'between a world of fact "out there" and a cognitive realm of theory that *retrospectively* (our emphasis) orders and gives meaning to factual data'. If, as some postmodernists maintain, there is no Archimedean standpoint which makes objective knowledge about an external reality possible, then the very process of separating 'theory' from 'practice', or the 'subject' from the 'object' it seeks to comprehend, is deeply problematical. Indeed, the very process of using positivist social science to acquire 'objective knowledge' may be deeply ideological. Far, then, from rising above the 'particular' to produce 'universal' truths about the social world, analysis may simply reflect specific cultural locations and sectional interests and reproduce existing forms of power (George and Campbell 1990).

These questions lead to a second category of theory, *constitutive* international theory. Everyone comes to the study of international relations with a specific language, cultural beliefs and preconceptions and with specific life-experiences which affect their understanding of the subject. Language, culture, religion, ethnicity, class and gender are a few of the factors which shape world views. Indeed it is possible to understand and interpret the world only within particular cultural and linguistic frameworks: these are the *lenses* through which we perceive the world. One of the main purposes of studying theory is to enable us to examine these lenses to discover just how distorted and distorting any particular worldview may be. This is why it is important to ask why, for example, realists focus on specific images which highlight states, geopolitics and war while remaining blind to other phenomena such as class divisions and material inequalities.

As noted earlier, in the theory of international relations it is important to be as concerned with how we *approach* the study of world politics as we are with events, issues and actors in the global system. It is necessary to examine background assumptions because all forms of social analysis raise important questions about the moral and cultural constitution of the observer. It is important to reflect upon the cognitive interests and normative assumptions which underpin research. The point here is to become acutely aware of hidden assumptions, prejudices and biases about how the social and political world is and what it can be. According to various 'critical' perspectives, it is futile or unrealistic to attempt to dispense with these assumptions. Indeed, postmodern approaches have called for the celebration of diverse experiences of the world of international relations while maintaining that all standpoints should be subject to forms of critical analysis which highlight their closures and exclusions (George and Campbell 1990). We can best do this by developing an awareness of the diversity of images of international relations. The task of constitutive international theory is to analyse the different forms of reflection about the nature and character of world politics and to stress that these forms of knowledge do not simply mirror the world, but also help to shape it.

What do theories of international relations differ about?

Although this volume identifies major perspectives, the authors do not want to give the impression that schools of thought are monolithic and homogeneous theoretical traditions. Although they may share some basic assumptions, the exponents of any perspective can have widely differing and even conflicting positions on the issues raised earlier. Feminism and Marxism are examples of very broad 'churches' which display great diversity – and can on occasion seem as different from each other as the main perspectives in the field. Realism has its internal variations; so has the English School, the many branches of critical theory and so on. To someone who is new to the field, this diversity can be frustrating but there is nothing abnormal about differences of perspective within the same broad theoretical tradition. Heterogeneity is a strength and an obstacle to ossification.

It is possible to compare and contrast and sub-schools of International Relations because they do have much in common. It is possible to focus on what they generally agree are the issues worth disagreeing about, on what they think are the principal stakes involved in understanding the world and in creating more sophisticated modes of analysis. Here is it necessary to proceed with great caution because no account of the main stakes can do justice to the many debates and controversies in the field. There is bound to be some arbitrariness in any attempt to make sense of the discipline as a whole. However, with that caveat, we believe it is useful to consider what the main perspectives have concluded about the following four issues: certainly a brief summary of where these theories stand on these issues may enable newcomers to chart a path through the thicket of major controversies in the field.

Object of analysis and scope of the enquiry

The first is the *object of analysis and the scope of the enquiry*. Debates about the object of analysis have been especially important in the discipline since the 'level of analysis' debate (Singer 1961; Hollis and Smith 1990: 92–118). One of the best illustrations of what is at stake here is Waltz's discussion of the causes of wars. In *Man, the State and War*, Waltz (1959) argued that three different levels of analysis (or three 'images') had been explored in the literature on this subject: (a) human nature, (b) the structure of political systems and (c) the nature of the international system. Waltz showed how many psychologists have tried to explain war by looking at the innate aggressiveness of the species; many liberals and Marxists maintained that war is the product of how some political systems are organized. Liberals maintained that war was the result of autocratic government; Marxists saw it as a product of capitalism. From each standpoint, war was regarded as a phenomenon which could be abolished – by creating liberal regimes in the first case and by establishing socialist forms of government in the second. According to students of the third level of analysis, war is a product of the anarchic nature of international politics and the unending competition for power and security. Waltz argued for the primacy of this 'third image of international politics', which stressed that war is inevitable in the context of anarchy (while claiming that the other two levels of analysis also contribute to the study of war origins).

Thinking back to an earlier part of the discussion, we can see that the dominance of realism was in large part a consequence of its argument about the most important level of analysis for students of the field. We can also see that some of the main changes in the discipline have been the result of discontent with the realists' concentration on the problem of anarchy and its virtual exclusion of all other domains of world politics. When feminists argue for bringing women within the parameters of discussion, or the English School argues for focusing on international society, when constructivists urge the importance of understanding the social construction of norms and so on, they are involved in fundamental disciplinary debates about the correct *object* (or level) of analysis.

Purpose of social and political enquiry

They are also involved in crucial debates about the *purpose of social and political enquiry*. Returning to Waltz, in his account of the causes of war (and later in his classic work, *Theory of International Politics, 1979*), he maintained that the purpose of analysis is to understand the limits on political change, more specifically to show that states are best advised to work with the existing international order rather than to try to change it radically. Above all else, they should ensure as far as they can the preservation of a *balance of power* which deters states from going to war although it cannot always prevent it. Ambitious projects of global reform are, on this analysis, destined to fail. Members of the English School do not deny the importance of the balance of power but they stress the need to attend to all the phenomena that make international order possible including the belief that the society of states is legitimate and, in the aftermath of Western colonialism, willing to be responsive to claims for justice advanced by 'Third World' states. Other perspectives include the liberal argument that the purpose of analysis is to promote economic and social interdependence between individuals across the world and, in the case of many radical approaches to the field, to create new forms of political community and new forms of human solidarity.

For the neo-realist, the purpose of the analysis is defined by the fact that international anarchy makes many of these visions utopian and dangerous. For many opponents of neo-realism, its purpose of inquiry is too quick to resign to what it regards as unchangeable; one of the main purposes of international political inquiry is to resist the fatalism, determinism and conservatism of this position. In this context, the emergence of critical approaches to international relations (whether derived from Marxism and the Frankfurt School or located within developments in French social theory) have been especially important. Their purpose is to criticise neo-realist claims about the 'knowable reality' of international politics. Postmodernists, for example, maintain that 'reality' is discursively produced (that is, constructed by discourse): it is 'never a complete, entirely coherent "thing", accessible to universalized, essentialist or totalized understandings of it ... [it] is always characterized by ambiguity, disunity, discrepancy, contradiction and difference' (George 1994: 11). It can never be contained, in other words, within one grand theory or reduced to one set of forces which are judged more important than all others. For the postmodernist, neo-realism is just another construction of the world, one that should be challenged because it does 'violence' to reality and because it has the obvious political consequence of maintaining that efforts to change that world are futile.

Critiques of the neo-realist purpose of inquiry have had huge implications for the scope of inquiry mentioned earlier. One consequence has been to make questions of ontology more central to the field. As Cox (1992b: 132) argues, 'ontology lies at the beginning of any enquiry. We cannot define a problem in global politics without presupposing a certain basic structure consisting of the significant kinds of entities involved and the form of significant relationships among them.' He adds that 'ontological presuppositions [are] inherent in ... terms such as "International Relations", which seems to equate nation with state and to define the field as limited to the interactions among states' (Cox 1992b: 132). Cox displays a preference for focusing on how domestic and international dominant class forces, states and powerful international institutions combine to form a global hegemonic order. Debates about the 'basic structure of international politics' are not just about what is 'out there' and how we come to know 'reality' (more on this later); they are also inextricably tied up with different views about the purposes of political inquiry. Cox (1981: 128) emphasized this point in the striking claim that 'theory is always *for* someone and *for* some purpose'.

In one of the most influential distinctions in the field, Cox claims that neo-realism has a 'problem-solving' purpose, its main task being to ensure that existing political arrangements 'function more smoothly' by minimizing the potential for conflict and war. Of course, Cox does not underestimate the importance of this endeavour, but he challenges its sufficiency. The main problem, as he sees it, is that neo-realism assumes that the world is frozen in particular ways and ultimately unchangeable through political action. But the consequence of taking 'the world as it finds it ... as the given framework for action' is that neo-realism confers legitimacy on that order and the forms of dominance and inequality which are inherent in it. (There is a direct parallel here with one of the central themes in postmodernism – ultimately derived from Foucault's writings – on how forms of knowledge are connected with forms of power (see chapter 7 in this volume). On the other hand, critical theory, Cox (1981, 1992b) maintains, has a broader purpose which is to reflect on how that order came into being, how it has changed over time and may change again in ways that improve the life-chances of the vulnerable and excluded. A broadly similar critical purpose runs through all the main radical approaches to the field, including feminism, green political theory and 'critical constructivism'. All are actively libertarian in that they are broadly committed to the normative task of exposing constraints upon human autonomy which can in principle be removed.

Appropriate methodology

Debates about the purpose of international political enquiry lead to a third point of difference between approaches which revolves around the *appropriate methodology* for the discipline. Key questions here are best approached by recalling that politically motivated scholarship is deeply controversial and often anathema to many scholars. The main issue is the status of normative claims. Is it possible to provide an objective account of why human beings should value autonomy and rally around a project of promoting universal human emancipation? Exponents of scientific approaches have argued that objective knowledge about the ends of social and political is unobtainable; postmodernists have argued that the danger is that any doctrine of ideal ends will become the basis for new forms of power and domination. In the 1990s, debates about what constitutes the 'knowable reality' of International Relations (ontological questions) were accompanied by increasingly complex discussions about how knowledge is generated (epistemological questions). Of course, the 'great debate' in the 1960s was very much concerned with epistemological issues, with the advocates of science such as Kaplan and Singer supporting quantificationist techniques and hypothesis-testing while 'traditionalists' such as Bull defended the virtues of history, law, philosophy and other classical forms of academic inquiry as the best way to approach international politics. As noted earlier, this was a debate (with its origins in the late eighteenth century) about the extent to which the methods of the natural sciences can be applied the study of society and politics. It was also a debate about the possibility of a neutral or 'value-free' study of international relations.

Such debates are far from being resolved – or, at least, there is no consensus in the field as to how to resolve them. Various forms of critical theory joined the critique of scientific approaches, claiming (as Horkheimer and Adorno had done in the 1940s) that they are inseparable from efforts to create new forms of social and political power. However, scientific approaches continue to have the upper hand in the American study of International Relations. They have been central to studies of the liberal peace (see Doyle 1983), and one analyst has claimed that the observation that there has been no war between liberal states for nearly two centuries is the nearest thing to a law in world politics (Levy 1989). It is also important to note the increasing prominence in the United States of 'rational choice' or 'game-theoretical' approaches as applied to studies of cooperation between 'rational egoists' (see Keohane 1984).

Distinct area of intellectual endeavour

A fourth point of difference between perspectives revolves around the issue of whether the discipline should be conceived as a *relatively distinct area of intellectual endeavour* or considered as a field which can develop only by drawing heavily on other areas of investigation, such as historical sociology and the study of world history (see Buzan and Little 2001). The more the analyst sees international politics as a realm of competition and conflict, the stronger the tendency to regard it as radically different from other academic fields. Here, its anarchic character is often seen as separating the study of International Relations from other social sciences, and the relevance of concepts and ideas drawn from outside the discipline is assumed to be limited. We have already encountered this theme in Wight's (1966) paper, 'Why is there no International Theory?'.

Neo-realism is also associated with the view that, like most of the states it studies, International Relations has sharply defined boundaries. Waltz (1979) is explicit on this point, claiming that the international political system should be regarded as a 'domain apart' – although he looks beyond the field to Economics and to developments in the philosophy of science to develop his thesis about international anarchy. The more dominant tendency in recent international theory has been to embrace multidisciplinarity as a way of escaping the perceived insularity of the field. Many theorists have looked to developments in European social theory, postcolonial thinking and Sociology more generally to explore new areas of investigation; some look to studies of ethics and political theory for insight. Many of the questions which have fascinated feminist scholars – about patriarchy, gender identity, etc. – can be answered only by going outside classical disciplinary boundaries. This is also manifestly true of much recent thinking about green politics which necessarily looks beyond the conventional discipline (see Chapter 10 in this volume). The most recent phase in the history of globalization has led many to deepen this move towards multidisciplinarity (Scholte 2000). The upshot of these developments is that the boundaries of International Relations have been keenly contested and in many sub-fields substantially redrawn. This does not mean the end of International Relations as an academic discipline, although the extent to which it borrows from other fields without having much influence on the wider humanities and social sciences is, for some, a real cause for concern (see Buzan and Little 2001). All theories of international relations have to deal with the state and nationalism, with the struggle for power and security, and with the use of force, but they do not deal with these phenomena in the same way. Different conceptions of the scope of the inquiry, its purpose and methodology mean that issues of war and peace which formed the classical core of the subject are conceptualized and analysed in increasingly diverse ways.

Evaluating theories

We probably should not expect too much from any empirical theory. No single theory identifies, explains or understands all the key structures and dynamics of international politics. International historians such as Gaddis (1992–3) stressed that none of the major traditions of international theory predicted the collapse of the Soviet Union and its immediate consequences for Europe and the rest of the world. But many theorists do not believe that their purpose is prediction or concede that theories should be assessed by how well they can predict events. An assessment of different theories cannot begin, then, by comparing their achievements in explaining international political reality 'out there'.

What we have tried to show in this Introduction, and the other chapters demonstrate, is that some of the most interesting debates revolve around the question of *what it means to provide a good account* of any dimension of international politics. We do not claim that this volume provides an exhaustive survey of the field at the current time, and we do not deny the claims of other perspectives which lack representation here. But we do believe that a comparison of the nine main theories considered in this volume will show why the nature of a good account of international political phenomena is keenly contested and why *debates about this matter are important*. This is why the great proliferation of theoretical approaches should be applauded rather than lamented as evidence that the discipline has lost its way or has collapsed into competing 'tribes'. One can begin to decide if one has a good account of any international political phenomenon only by engaging with different theories. In this way, analysts of international relations become more self-conscious about the different ways of practising their craft and more aware of omissions and exclusions which may reflect personal or cultural biases. This theme is crucially important if those of a critical persuasion are broadly right that all forms of inquiry have political implications and consequences, most obviously by creating narratives which privilege certain standpoints and experiences *to some degree*.

There is one final point to make before commenting briefly on the chapters that follow. Here, it is necessary to return to a comment made at the start of this Introduction, namely that the realists and the liberal internationalists have been involved in a major controversy about the forms of political action that are most appropriate in a realm in which the struggle for power and security is pre-eminent. It is also worth recalling Steve Smith's claim that theories 'do not simply explain or predict, they tell us what possibilities exist for human action and intervention; they define not merely our explanatory possibilities, but also our ethical and practical horizons' (see p. 4). Now the analyst of any dimension of international politics may not be concerned with the possibilities for 'human action and intervention'; and many theorists of international relations would deny that this is what theory is essentially about. There is no reason to suggest an agenda that all good theories should follow. But to look at the main perspectives and at the debates between them is to see that the issue of whether or not the international political system can be reformed is *one* recurrent question which concerns all of them. For those who think global reform is possible, other questions immediately follow. How are different visions of international political life to be assessed, and what are the prospects for realizing them? We suggest these questions provide one measure of a good account of world politics. Others will disagree. To decide the merits of different positions on the possibilities for 'human action and intervention' – whether large or small – one needs to be familiar with at least the perspectives which are considered in this volume.

In Chapter 2, Jack Donnelly analyses classical realism which dominated the field for at least the first fifty years of its existence and which remains highly influential in the discipline today. The writings of early realists such as Carr and Morgenthau remain key reference points in contemporary debates more than five decades after their first publication. Interestingly, as explained in Chapter 2, neo-realism which emerged in the late 1970s and which was at the heart of most debates during the following two decades, was one of the main challenges to classical realism. However, neo-realism is largely concerned with the critique of liberal approaches (as well as Marxist and other radical approaches to the field) which it thinks guilty of exaggerating the ability of global economic and social processes to change the basic structure of international politics. In Chapter 3, Scott Burchill discusses the development of the liberal tradition, noting in particular how many contemporary neo-liberal accounts of the world market and the defence of free trade resonate with ideas promoted by economic liberals in the nineteenth century. However, contemporary liberalism contains much more than a particular conception of how freeing trade and global markets from the hands of the state can promote material prosperity and establish the conditions for lasting peace. Other features of the perspective which have been influential in recent years include the defence of the universal human rights culture and the development of international criminal law, the study of 'cooperation under anarchy' associated with neo-liberal institutionalism and the immensely important discussion of the liberal peace. These features of recent liberal thinking about international relations will also be discussed in Chapter 3.

In Chapters 4 and 5, Andrew Linklater analyses the English School and Marxism. Neither has enjoyed the global influence of realism/neo-realism and liberalism/neo-liberalism, although the English School has been particularly influential in British International Relations. The years since 1998 have seen renewed interest in the English School theory of international society and in its position as a 'third way' between the pessimism of realism and the more idealistic forms of liberalism and various radical perspectives including Marxism. Chapter 4 pays particular attention to the contribution of Wight, Vincent and Bull to the discipline, and notes their special relevance for contemporary discussions about human rights, humanitarian intervention and the use of force in international affairs. Chapter 5 turns to Marxism, which has often been criticized by neo-realists and members of the English School although neither anchored its critique in a careful interpretation of one of its main theoretical adversaries. Whether the rejection of Marxism overlooked its ability to make a significant contribution to the field is a question that Chapter 5 considers in detail. Particular attention will be paid to

Marx's writings on globalization, to Marxist analysis of nationalism and internationalism, and to reflections on the importance of forms of production – and specifically the development of modern capitalist forms of production – for global politics. The 'critical' dimensions of Marxism – its interest not only in explaining the world, but in changing it – will also be noted in this chapter.

Marxism provided the intellectual background for the development of critical theory as developed by members of the Frankfurt School such as Horkheimer and Adorno in the 1930s, and by Habermas, Honneth and others in more recent times. In Chapter 6, Richard Devetak explains the central aims of critical theory and their impact on various theorists such as Ashley in the early 1980s, and on Ken Booth (1991a, b) and Cox who have defended a version of international politics committed to the idea of human emancipation. Although the term 'critical theory' was initially associated with the Frankfurt School which derived many of its ideas from a dialogue with orthodox Marxism, it is also strongly associated with postmodernism, a perspective which is deeply suspicious of the emancipatory claims of classical Marxism. In Chapter 7, Richard Devetak explains the postmodern turn in the social sciences by considering the writings of Derrida, Foucault and Lyotard, and analyses its influence on International Relations since the 1980s. Its critique of the 'Enlightenment project' of universal human emancipation is an important element of this chapter, as is the stress on the critique of 'totalizing' perspectives which are judged to be a threat to the flourishing of human differences.

Constructivism, which Christian Reus-Smit discusses in Chapter 8, has emerged as a powerful challenge to orthodox perspectives in the field, most crucially to theories which assume that states derive certain interests from their location in an anarchic condition. In a famous challenge to those approaches, Alexander Wendt (1992) argued that 'anarchy is what states make of it'. The claim was that anarchy is socially constructed, that it is shaped by the beliefs and attitudes of states; it is not an unchanging structure which imposes certain constraints on states and compels all to participate in an endless struggle for power and security. Constructivism which has focused particularly on the relationship between interests and identities encompasses several competing approaches. Some are influenced by postmodernism, others by critical theory in the Frankfurt School tradition; some share the neo-realist focus on analysing relations between states in isolation from other processes (systemic constructivism) whereas others see the states-system in connection with a range of national and global cultural and political phenomena (holistic constructivism).

In Chapter 9, Jacqui True sheds light on a subject which first came onto the International Relations agenda in the mid-1980s, namely feminism. This perspective is not reducible to a study of the position of women in the global order, although many feminists such as Cynthia Enloe did set out to explain how women are affected by war and by developments in the global economy, including structural adjustment policies (SAPs) in the 1980s and 1990s. The invisibility of women in mainstream approaches and in many critical alternatives was one reason for the development of the feminist literature. However, feminist perspectives have been no more homogeneous than other theoretical standpoints. Some feminists, such as Christine Sylvester (1994a, 2002), have used postmodern approaches to question 'essentialist' accounts of women, their interests and rights. One concern has been to question claims that the dominant Western conceptions of 'woman' are valid for women everywhere. Other feminists, such as Steans (1998), have been influenced by the Marxist tradition. It is important to stress that feminism is not simply interested in the place of women in the global political and economic order. It is also preoccupied with constructions of gender including constructions of masculinity, and with how they affect forms of power and inequality and, at the epistemological level, knowledge claims about the world.

Matthew Paterson discusses developments within green political thinking in Chapter 10. Environmental degradation, transnational pollution and climate change have had a significant impact on the study of global politics. These issues have featured in studies of 'international regimes' with responsibility for environmental issues. Questions of global justice have been at the heart of discussions about the fair distribution between rich and poor and about moral responsibilities to reverse environmental harm. Obligations to non-human species and to future generations have been important themes in environmental ethics. Green political thought has criticised the dominant assumptions until the 1960s about infinite economic growth and the faith in the virtues of unbridled capitalism. Questions about the prospects for 'ecologically responsible' states and global environmental citizenship which have been discussed in recent green political thought have special relevance for students of International Relations. These are some of the ways in which green political thought and practice have tried to reconfigure the study of International Relations so that more attention is devoted to the long-term fate of the planet and the different lifeforms which inhabit it.

Most of the authors in this volume identify with one or other of the perspectives analysed in this book, but none argues that any one theory can solve the many problems which arise for theorists of international relations. We see merit in all the approaches surveyed below, and we certainly believe it is essential to engage with all theoretical perspectives from the 'inside', to see the world from different theoretical vantage-points, to learn from them, to test one's own ideas against them and to think carefully about what others would regard as the vulnerabilities of one's perspective, whatever it may be. Those who teach the theory of international relations are sometimes asked 'what is the correct theory?'. We hope our readers will conclude there is no obviously correct theory which solves all the problems listed in this Introduction and considered in more detail in the pages below. Some may concur with Martin Wight (Wight 1991) that the truth about international relations will not be found in any one of the traditions but in the continuing *dialogue and debate* between them. This is almost certainly the right attitude to adopt when approaching the study of international theory for the first time, and it may still be the best conclusion to draw from one's analysis.

Chapter 2

Realism

JACK DONNELLY*

'Realism' is a term that is used in a variety of ways in many different disciplines. In philosophy, it is an ontological theory opposed to idealism and nominalism. 'Scientific realism' is a philosophy of science opposed variously to empiricism, instrumentalism, verificationism and positivism. 'Realism' in literature and cinema is opposed to romanticism and 'escapist' approaches. In International Relations, political realism is a tradition of analysis that stresses the imperatives states face to pursue a power politics of the national interest. This is the only sense of realism that we will address here, other than to note that these various senses, despite their clear family resemblances, have no necessary connections. Many political realists, for example, are philosophical nominalists and empiricists.

Political realism, *Realpolitik*, 'power politics', is the oldest and most frequently adopted theory of international relations. Every serious student must not only acquire a deep appreciation of political realism but also understand how her own views relate to the realist tradition. To lay my cards on the table at the outset, I am not a realist. Normatively, I rebel against the world described in realist theory and I reject realism as a prescriptive theory of foreign policy. Analytically, however, I am no more an anti-realist than I am a realist. Realism, I will argue, is a limited yet powerful and important approach to and set of insights about international relations.

This chapter highlights some of realism's characteristic forms, strengths and weaknesses. I also use the discussion of realism to address broader issues of the nature of theories of international relations, and how to evaluate them.

---

* Smith (1986) and Donnelly (2000) provide book-length introductions that focus exclusively on realism. Doyle (1997) and Wight (1991) consider realism in relation to two alternative traditions. Donnelly (1992), Forde (1992), Grieco (1997), and Jervis (1998) are representative single-chapter introductions. On the place of realism in the academic discipline of international studies see Donnelly (1995), Kahler (1997), Guzzini (1998), Schmidt (1998) and Vasquez (1998).

Theory is artful abstraction. It draws our attention away from the welter of 'confusing details', directing it towards what is 'most important' to the case at hand. Theories are beacons, lenses or filters that direct us to what, according to the theory, is essential for understanding some part of the world.

The theories considered in this volume have two important dimensions. They are general orientations rooted in a central substantive focus or insight: for example, gender for feminism, international society for the English School, power for realism. They also include particular explanatory theories, models, or propositions: for example, patriarchalism and hegemonic masculinity or anarchy and the balance of power. This chapter begins and concludes by looking at the general character of the realist approach. In between we focus on particular realist explanations.

Defining realism

Although definitions of realism differ in detail (see Cusack and Stoll 1990: chapter 2; Donnelly 2000: 6–9), they share a clear family resemblance, 'a quite distinctive and recognizable flavour'. (Garnett 1984: 110). Realists emphasize the constraints on politics imposed by human selfishness ('egoism') and the absence of international government ('anarchy'), which require 'the primacy in all political life of power and security' (Gilpin 1986: 305). Rationality and state-centrism are frequently identified as core realist premises (e.g. Keohane 1986: 164–5). But no (reasonably broad) theory of international relations presumes irrationality. And if we think of 'states' as a shorthand for what Gilpin calls 'conflict groups' (1996: 7) or what Waltz (1979) calls 'units', state-centrism is widely (although not universally) shared across international theories. The conjunction of anarchy and egoism and the resulting imperatives of power politics provide the core or realism. Emblematic twentieth-century figures include George Kennan, Hans Morgenthau, Reinhold Niebuhr and Kenneth Waltz in the United States and E. H. Carr in Britain. In the history of Western political thought, Niccolo Machiavelli and Thomas Hobbes are usually considered realists. Thucydides is sometimes seen as a realist, but that is a minority reading today.

Realists, although recognizing that human desires range widely and are remarkably variable, emphasize 'the limitations which the sordid and selfish aspects of human nature place on the conduct of diplomacy' (Thompson 1985: 20). As Machiavelli puts it, in politics we must act as if 'all men are wicked and that they will always give vent to the malignity that is in their minds when opportunity offers' (1970: Book I, Chapter 3).

'It is above all important not to make greater demands on human nature than its frailty can satisfy' (Treitschke 1916: 590).

A few theorists (e.g. Niebuhr 1932; Tellis 1995/6: 89–94) adopt realism as a general theory of politics. Most, however, treat realism as a theory of *international* politics. This shifts our attention from human nature to political structure. 'The difference between civilization and barbarism is a revelation of what is essentially the same human nature when it works under different conditions' (Butterfield 1949: 31). Within states, egoism usually is substantially restrained by hierarchical political rule. In international relations, anarchy allows, even encourages, the worst aspects of human nature to be expressed.

Statesmanship thus involves mitigating and managing, not eliminating, conflict; seeking a less dangerous world, rather than a safe, just, or peaceful one. Ethical considerations must give way to 'reasons of state' (*raison d'état*). 'Realism maintains that universal moral principles cannot be applied to the actions of states' (Morgenthau 1948/1954/1973: 9).

Many realists, especially in recent decades, have given near-exclusive emphasis to anarchy, the absence of hierarchical political rule. For example, John Herz argues that anarchy assures the centrality of the struggle for power 'even in the absence of aggressivity or similar factors' (1976: 10; compare Waltz 1979: 62–3). 'Structural realism' is the standard label for such theories. 'Neo-realism' is the other standard term, distinguishing this rigorous structural emphasis from earlier, more eclectic realists. The two terms are usually used interchangeably.

Other realists, without denying the centrality of anarchy, also emphasize human nature. For example, Morgenthau argues that 'the social world [is] but a projection of human nature onto the collective plane' (1962: 7; compare Niebuhr 1932: 23). Such realists 'see that conflict is in part situationally explained, but ... believe that even were it not so, pride, lust, and the quest for glory would cause the war of all against all to continue indefinitely. Ultimately, conflict and war are rooted in human nature' (Waltz 1991: 35). 'Classical realism' is the most common label for this position. (I prefer the label 'biological realism', which identifies a distinguishing substantive feature of this style of realism. Few others, however, endorse this preference.)

Realists can be further distinguished by the intensity and exclusivity of their commitment to core realist premises. Here we can think of a continuum of positions.

'Radical' realists exclude almost everything except power and self-interest from (international) politics. The Athenian envoys to Melos in Thucydides' *History* (1982: Book V, Chapter 85–113) express such a view, but it is held by few if any international theorists.

'Strong' realists stress the predominance of power, self-interest and conflict but allow modest space for politically salient 'non-realist' forces and concerns. Carr, Morgenthau and Waltz, the leading realists of their generations, all lie in this range of the continuum. As Carr puts it, 'we cannot ultimately find a resting place in pure realism' (1939/1945/1946: 89).

'Weak' or 'hedged' realists accept the realist analysis of the 'problems' of international politics but are open to a wider range of political possibilities and see more important elements of international relations lying outside the explanatory range of realism. Weak realism gradually shades into something else. At some point (non-realist) 'hedges' outweigh the (realist) 'core'. Conversely, analysts operating from other perspectives may appeal to characteristically realist forces and explanations that 'hedge' their own theories.

Hobbes and classical realism

Chapter 13 of Thomas Hobbes' *Leviathan*, originally published in 1651, imagines politics in a pre-social state of nature. The result is an unusually clear classical realist theory that gives roughly equal weight to human nature and international anarchy and is almost universally agreed to offer important insights into some perennial problems of international relations.

The Hobbesian state of nature

Hobbes makes three simple assumptions.

1. *Men are equal*. (The gendered language reflects standard seventeenth-century usage. We might, however, see the analysis – particularly Hobbes' assumptions about the overriding motives of 'men' – as more deeply gendered, reflective of a particular masculinist perspective. See Tickner 1988 and Chapter 9 in this volume.)
2. They interact in *anarchy*.
3. They are driven by *competition, diffidence and glory*.

The conjunction of these conditions leads to a war of all against all.

Men are equal in the elemental sense that 'the weakest has strength enough to kill the strongest, either by secret machination or by confederacy with others' (para. 1). 'From this equality of ability ariseth equality of hope in the attaining of our ends' (para. 3). I'm as good as you are and thus ought to have (at least) as much as you. But scarcity prevents each from having as much as he desires – which makes men enemies.

Enmity is exacerbated by competition, diffidence and glory. 'The first maketh men invade for gain; the second, for safety; and the third, for reputation' (para. 7). Even where one is not seeking gain, fear of others leads to defensive war, for 'there is no way for any man to secure himself so reasonable as anticipation' (para. 4). And every man's desire 'that his companion should value him at the same rate he sets upon himself' (para. 5) leads to conflict over reputation.

Add the absence of government and the mixture becomes volatile and vicious. 'During the time men live without a common power to keep them all in awe, they are in that condition which is called war; and such a war as is of every man against every man' (para. 8). Although fighting is not constant, any dispute may quickly degenerate into violence. As a result, human industry has little scope for operation 'and the life of man [is] solitary, poor, nasty, brutish, and short' (para. 10).

This logic of conflict can be evaded only if one or more of the model's assumptions either does not hold or is counter-balanced by other forces. Fundamental power inequalities typically lead to imposed hierarchical order, substantially mitigating conflict and violence. Establishing international government would go even further, ending (at least formally) the state of war. Even in anarchy, the frequency and intensity of conflict could be dramatically reduced by constraining competition, diffidence and glory. Containing the pursuit of gain and glory would be particularly efficacious, for diffidence leads to war primarily through fear of predation.

Among countervailing forces, Hobbes stresses 'the passions that incline men to peace' and reason, which 'suggesteth convenient articles of peace upon which men may be drawn to agreement' (para. 14). But he has little confidence in the power of these forces to overcome the more egoistic passions, especially in the absence of government to enforce rules of cooperation.

Assessing Hobbesian realism

Hobbes acknowledges (para. 12) that such a savage state never existed across the entire globe. I would suggest that we go further and abandon any pretence at history or comparative anthropology. Hobbes, in this reading, identifies a *logic of interaction*, an ideal-type model of pressures and tendencies. When equal actors interact in anarchy, driven by competition, diffidence and glory, generalized violent conflict can be predicted.

Theory requires radical simplification. Much as a good caricature selects, exaggerates and willfully distorts in order to capture the defining features of its subject, a good theory intentionally oversimplifies in order to highlight forces that typically control behaviour. Rather than ask whether Hobbes accurately describes the world – of course, he doesn't: much, even most, of politics lies outside his scope – we should ask whether his theoretical assumptions help us to understand important elements of international political reality.

Hobbes, like most realists, is sceptical of altering human nature. Analysts may reasonably disagree about the variability and malleability of human nature or the interests of states. Most, however, would agree that Hobbes' emphasis on competition, diffidence and glory represents a penetrating, if one-sided, caricature that deserves serious consideration.

Anarchy has been replaced by hierarchical political rule within most states. Even vicious and inefficient governments usually provide considerable security for the lives and property of their citizens, dramatically reducing the pressures to replace the international state of nature with international government. International anarchy can therefore be expected to persist, even without taking into account the strong desire of states and their citizens for autonomy.

Material inequality reduces the number of effective players. But unless one is clearly superior to all others, the Hobbesian logic will reassert itself in relations among the strong. 'Great powers' – states with the capacity to inflict punishing damage, even the threat of death, on any other power in the system – are Hobbesian equals. In passing, we should note that this suggests that (Hobbesian) realism is a theory of great power politics, rather than a general theory of international relations. Relations between fundamentally unequal powers would be governed by another logic of interaction.

Each of Hobbes' assumptions would seem to be applicable to important parts of international relations. The crucial question is the extent to which other factors and forces push in different directions. How much of international relations, in what circumstances, is governed by the Hobbesian conjunction of anarchy, egoism and equality? To use social scientific jargon, what are the relative forces of 'endogenous variables' (factors included within the theory) and 'exogenous variables' (those not included)? We will return, recurrently, to this question as we proceed.

Waltz and structural realism

Hobbes' 'classical' realism gives roughly equal emphasis to anarchy and egoism. Although 'neo-classical' realism (Rose 1998) has recently made a modest comeback, most realist work since the 1970s has been more or less rigorously structural, largely as a result of the influence of Kenneth Waltz.

Waltzian structuralism

Structural realism attempts to 'abstract from every attribute of states except their capabilities' (Waltz 1979: 99) in order to highlight the impact of anarchy and the distribution of capabilities. 'International structure emerges from the interaction of states and then constrains them from taking certain actions while propelling them toward others' (1991: 29). Therefore, despite great variations in the attributes and interactions of states, there is a 'striking sameness in the quality of international life through the millennia' (1979: 66).

Political structures are defined by their ordering principle, differentiation of functions and distribution of capabilities. How are units related to one another? How are political functions allocated? How is power distributed?

Hierarchy and anarchy are the two principal political ordering principles. Units either stand in relationships of authority and subordination (hierarchy) or they do not (anarchy). Waltz argues that striking qualitative differences exist 'between politics conducted in a condition of settled rules and politics conducted in a condition of anarchy' (1979: 61). Some of those differences are the focus of the following sub-sections.

'Hierarchy entails relations of super- and subordination among a system's parts, and that implies their differentiation' (1979: 93). Consider the separation of legislative, executive and judicial powers. Anarchic orders, however, have little functional differentiation. Every unit must 'put itself in a position to be able to take care of itself since no one else can be counted on to do so' (1979: 107). Differences between states 'are of capability, not function' (1979: 96). 'National politics consists of differentiated units performing specified functions. International politics consists of like units duplicating one another's activities' (1979: 97).

If all international orders are anarchic, and if this implies minimal functional differentiation, then international political structures differ only in their distributions of capabilities. They are defined by the changing fates of great powers. More abstractly, international orders vary according to the number of great powers.

Balancing

The central theoretical conclusion of structural realism is that in anarchy states 'balance' rather than 'bandwagon' (1979: 126). In hierarchic political orders, actors tend to 'jump on the bandwagon' of a leading candidate or recent victor, because 'losing does not place their security in jeopardy' (1979: 126). 'Bandwagoners' attempt to increase their gains (or reduce their losses) by siding with the stronger party. In anarchy, however, bandwagoning courts disaster by strengthening someone who later may turn on you. The power of others – especially great powers – is always a threat when there is no government to turn to for protection. 'Balancers' attempt to reduce their risk by opposing the stronger party.

Weak states have little choice but to guess right and hope that early alignment with the victor will bring favourable treatment. Only foolish great powers would accept such a risk. Instead, they will balance, both internally, by reallocating resources to national security, and externally, primarily through alliances and other formal and informal agreements. (Randall Schweller 1994, 1997, however, has argued for the potential rationality of bandwagoning in the face of a rising revolutionary power.)

Structural pressures to balance explain important yet otherwise puzzling features of international relations. Consider Soviet–American relations. The United States opposed the Russian Revolution and for two decades remained implacably hostile to the Soviet Union. Nonetheless, a common enemy, Hitler's Germany, created the American–Soviet alliance in the Second World War. Notwithstanding their intense internal differences and history of animosity, they balanced against a common threat. After the war, the United States and the Soviet Union again became adversaries. In this version of the story, though, internal and ideological differences did not cause renewed rivalry (although they may have increased its virulence and influenced its form). Enmity was *structurally induced*. In a bipolar world, each superpower is the only serious threat to the security of the other. Each, whatever its preferences or inclinations, must balance against the other.

The Cold War, in this account, was not 'caused' by anyone but was the 'natural' result of bipolarity. Soviet expansion into Central and Eastern Europe arose from neither vicious rulers in the Kremlin nor rabid anti-communists in Washington. It was the normal behaviour of a country that had been invaded from the west, with devastating consequences, twice in twenty-five years, and once more a century earlier. Cold War conflicts in Vietnam, Central America and Southern Africa likewise were not part of a global communist conspiracy but rather ordinary efforts by a great power to increase its international influence.

This example suggests a very important interpretative point. Realism is a *theoretical account of how the world operates*. It can be used as easily for peaceful purposes – there are a number of Quaker realists – as for war. For example, hundreds of thousands of lives might have been saved, and millions of casualties avoided, had the United States pursued a realist bipolar rivalry with the Soviet Union rather than an ideological Cold War. Leading realists such as Niebuhr and Morgenthau (1970: 33) were not merely strong but early critics of the war in Vietnam.

Robert Tucker (1985) opposed the Reagan Administration's support of armed counter-revolution in Nicaragua. A striking fact about the list of supporters of the American invasion of Iraq in 2003 is the almost complete absence of prominent realists.

Prisoners' dilemma, relative gains and cooperation

Anarchy and egoism greatly impede cooperation. The Prisoners' Dilemma offers a standard formal representation of this logic. Imagine two criminals taken in separately by the police for questioning. Each is offered a favourable plea bargain in return for testimony against the other. Without a confession, though, they can be convicted only of a lesser crime. Each must choose between cooperating (remaining silent) and defecting (testifying against the other). Imagine also that both have the following preference ordering: (1) confess while the other remains silent; (2) both remain silent; (3) both confess; (4) remain silent while the other confesses. Assume finally that their aversion to risk takes a particular form: they want to minimize their maximum possible loss.

Cooperating (remaining silent) rewards both with their second choice (conviction on the lesser charge). But it also leaves the cooperator vulnerable to the worst possible outcome (serving a long prison term – and knowing that your partner put you there). Each can assure himself against disaster by confessing (defecting). The rational choice thus is to defect (confess) *even though both know that they both could be better off by cooperating*. Both end up with their third choice, because this is the only way to assure that each avoids the worst possible outcome.

Conflict here does not arise from any special defect in the actors. They are mildly selfish but not particularly evil or vicious. Far from desiring conflict, both actually prefer cooperation. They are neither ignorant nor ill informed. In an environment of anarchy, even those capable of mastering their own desires for gain and glory are pushed by fear towards treating everyone else as an enemy.

Anarchy can defeat even our best intentions – which realists see as rare enough to begin with. Without insurance schemes that reduce the risk of cooperating, and without procedures to determine how to divide the gains, even those who want to cooperate may remain locked in a vicious cycle of mutually destructive competition. For example, states may engage in costly and even counter-productive arms races because arms control agreements cannot be independently verified.

Herbert Butterfield calls this 'Hobbesian fear'. 'If you imagine yourself locked in a room with another person with whom you have often been on the most bitterly hostile terms in the past, and suppose that each of you has a pistol, you may find yourself in a predicament in which both of you would like to throw the pistols out of the window, yet it defeats the intelligence to find a way of doing it' (1949: 89–90). The 'security dilemma' (Jervis 1978; Glaser 1997) has a similar logic. 'Given the irreducible uncertainty about the intentions of others, security measures taken by one actor are perceived by others as threatening; the others take steps to protect themselves; these steps are then interpreted by the first actor as confirming its initial hypothesis that the others are dangerous; and so on in a spiral of illusory fears and "unnecessary" defenses' (Snyder 1997: 17).

Anarchic pressures towards balancing and against cooperation are reinforced by the relativity of power. Power is control over outcomes, 'the ability to do or effect something' (*Oxford English Dictionary*). It is less a matter of absolute capabilities – how much 'stuff' one has – than of relative capabilities. Facing an unarmed man, a tank is pretty powerful. The same tank facing a squadron of carrier-based attack jets is not very powerful at all.

The relativity of power requires states to 'be more concerned with relative strength than with absolute advantage' (Waltz 1979: 106). Bandwagoning seeks absolute gains, aligning early with a rising power to gain a share of the profits of victory. Balancing pursues relative gains.

Relative gains concerns dramatically impede cooperation. One must consider not only whether one gains but, more importantly, whether one's gains outweigh those of others (who, in anarchy, must be seen as potential adversaries). Even predatory cooperation is problematic unless it maintains the relative capabilities of the cooperating parties. In fact, states may be satisfied with conflicts that leave them absolutely worse off – so long as their adversaries are left even worse off.

Polarity

The preceding two sub-sections have considered some of the theoretical implications of anarchy, the first element of structure (ordering principle). If, following Waltz, we see minimal functional differentiation in anarchic orders, the other principal contribution of structural realism should lie in its analysis of the impact of the distribution of capabilities. How does polarity, the number of great powers in a system, influence international relations?

Unipolarity has become a hot topic since the end of the Cold War. Structural logic (Layne 1993; Mastanduno 1997) suggests that unipolarity is unstable. Balancing will facilitate the rise of new great powers, much as a rising hegemon (e.g. Napoleonic France) provokes a 'grand coalition' that unites the other great powers. (Wohlforth 1999, however, rejects this argument. More generally, see Kapstein and Mastanduno 1999.) But whatever the resilience of unipolarity, while it persists hegemony (and resistance to it) will give international relations a very different character from systems with two or more great powers.

Schweller (1998) has shown that tripolar systems have a distinctive structural logic. And systems with very many or no great powers – the two are effectively equivalent – have a different structural logic than multipolar systems with a few (four, five, or a couple more) great powers. Systems with a one, two, three, or a few great powers are monopolistic or oligopolistic. Those with many or no great powers are more like competitive markets.

Most of the attention, however, has focused on the differences between bipolar and multipolar orders. For example, conflicts in the periphery pose little threat to the general bipolar balance. In multipolar systems, where power is divided among more actors, a change in the periphery of the same absolute magnitude may have a noticeable impact on the general balance.

The significance of such a difference, however, is obscure. Should peripheral conflicts be more frequent in bipolar systems because they are less destabilizing and thus 'safer' (for the great powers)? Or should they be less frequent because there are no compelling reasons to become involved? There is thus considerable disagreement over the relative stability of bipolar and multipolar systems. Deutsch and Singer (1964), Waltz (1964) and Rosecrance (1966) argue, respectively, for bipolarity, multipolarity, and 'bi-multipolarity' (both/neither). More sophisticated accounts try to incorporate, for example, the impact of different forms of alignment (Christensen and Snyder 1990) and changes across time in the distribution of capabilities (Copeland 1996). Unfortunately, empirical tests are constrained by the fact that in 2,500 years of Western history there have been as few as four bipolar systems (Athens–Sparta in the fifth century BCE, Carthage–Rome in the third century BCE, the Hapsburg–Bourbon rivalry in the sixteenth century and the United States–Soviet Union in the twentieth century) (Copeland 1996).

The nature of structural predictions

Part of the problem with the debate on the relative stability of bipolar and multipolar orders is that the question itself, posed as it is in structural terms, is probably misguided. For example, a rising 'revisionist' or 'revolutionary' power with a high propensity for risk poses very different problems than risk-averse, satisfied 'status quo' powers. Such considerations fall outside the scope of Waltz' structural theory (although they are important to many classical realist theories, e.g. Kissinger 1957; Morgenthau 1948/1954/1973: Chapters 4, 5). If their effects characteristically are as great or greater than those of polarity, there can be no answer to the (structural) question of the relative stability of bipolar and multipolar orders.

Structure pushes states in certain directions. It does not mechanically determine outcomes. States are also subject to numerous other pressures and influences. Sometimes 'exogenous variables' are decisive in determining outcomes. This does not make polarity or anarchy unimportant. It just happens that other forces are sometimes more powerful.

The predictions of structural realism are, as Waltz repeatedly notes, 'indeterminate' (1979: 124, 122, 71; 1986: 343). Theories in the social sciences typically identify law-like regularities rather than exceptionless deterministic laws. They identify forces that press in a particular direction. It is the job of the analyst, not the theorist, to determine where a particular theoretical logic applies in the real world. Whether a 'good theory', in the sense of a rigorous logic of interaction, is a 'good' theory to apply in any particular case depends not on the theory but on contingent facts about the world.

If a theoretically predicted outcome does not occur because the assumptions of the theory are not satisfied in the case under consideration, such a 'failure' is entirely attributable to the analyst. If the underlying assumptions are satisfied but the predicted results do not occur, the failure is attributable to the theory. The most interesting situation, however, is when the theoretically predicted pressures operate but are overwhelmed by other forces.

The significance of this third type of theoretical 'failure' depends on which exogenous variables prevail, how often and in what kinds of cases. We will also want to know how powerful those exogenous forces must be to overcome the effects of the endogenous variables. If endogenous variables almost always hold up against all but the strongest expressions of a few exogenous variables, the theory is extremely powerful. If a wide range of relatively weak exogenous variables regularly swamp the effects of the endogenous variables, the theory is not exactly 'wrong' – the predicted pressures do still operate – but neither is it very useful.

Every theory must make simplifying assumptions. Fruitful assumptions abstract from factors that are typically less important to determining outcomes than those highlighted by the theory. Many of the disagreements between realists and their critics can be seen as, in effect, disputes about the frequency and significance of realism's failures of the third type.

Motives matter

How far we can go with purely structural theories – that is, with anarchy, the distribution of capabilities and nothing else? Not very far, I will argue. State motives are essential, as suggested by their centrality to the Prisoners' Dilemma and the security dilemma.

Abstracting from or assuming motives

Waltz claims to 'abstract from every attribute of states except their capabilities' (1979: 99), as suggested by his talk of 'units', abstract, characterless concentrations of capabilities. In fact, however, his theory, by his own admission, 'is based on assumptions about states', 'built up from the assumed motivations of states' (1979: 118; 1996: 54). But there is a huge difference between abstracting from all particulars and assuming certain ones. And the substance of realist assumptions about states accounts for much of the distinctive character of the theory.

Anarchy alone does not produce Hobbes' war of all against all. It arises from equal individuals driven by competition, diffidence and glory interacting in anarchy. Homeric heroes seeking glory through great deeds, Hobbesian egoists driven by a fear of violent death, Nietzschean individuals driven by a will to power and *homo economicus* may behave very differently in the same anarchic structure. As Butterfield puts it, 'wars would hardly be likely to occur if all men were Christian saints, competing with one another in nothing, perhaps, save self-renunciation' (McIntire 1979: 73).

Even Waltz, despite repeated claims to the contrary, admits this. 'Structurally we can describe and understand the pressures states are subject to. We cannot predict how they will react to the pressures without knowledge of their internal dispositions' (1979: 71). To abstract from all attributes of states (other than capabilities) leaves the theory no predictive or explanatory power. Thus in practice Waltz, like other realists, relies heavily on knowledge of or assumptions about the interests and intentions of states.

If assumptions about state motivation are simple, clear, and coherent, and if they apply to all units in the system, the resulting theory will still be very strongly structural. The easiest way to do this would be to assume a single motive. States 'are unitary actors with a single motive – the wish to survive' (Waltz 1996: 54; compare Spykman 1942: 18; Morgenthau 1948/1954/1973: 9; Kissinger 1977: 46).

But if states seek only survival – as they must if survival is the sole motive assumed in the theory – there will be no aggression. Introducing acquisitive motives makes the theory more 'realistic'. But allowing that 'some states may persistently seek goals that they value more highly than survival' (Waltz 1979: 92) admits that such states may rationally choose *not* to balance. And in practice Waltz introduces many additional motives that fatally undermine the logical coherence of his theory.

Waltz claims that states 'at minimum, seek their own preservation and, at maximum, drive for universal domination' (1979: 118). Survival, however, is not a small quantity of domination, nor is domination a surplus of survival. And the area 'between' them involves neither a lot of survival nor a little domination but something else – actually, many other things.

'The first concern of states is … to maintain their positions in the system' (Waltz 1979: 126). Preserving one's relative position, however, is neither survival nor domination. It is obviously inconsistent with domination (except for hegemons) and may require risking survival. And the risk to survival may be even greater if, as Mearsheimer argues, states 'aim to maximize their relative power position over other states' (Mearsheimer 1994/5: 11).

But Waltz does not stop here. He also claims that states seek wealth, advantage and flourishing (1993: 54; 1986: 337; 1979: 112), peaceful coexistence (1979: 144) and peace and prosperity; (1979: 144, 175) that they want to protect their sovereignty, autonomy and independence; (1979: 204, 107, 104) and that they act out of pride and the feeling of being put upon (1993: 66, 79). Predicted behaviour, however, will vary dramatically among states seeking to survive, maintain their relative position, improve their welfare, respond to slights, or achieve universal domination. Yet Waltz, despite his reputation for rigour, shifts between these motives entirely without theoretical justification, and with no appreciation of the deep incoherence it introduces into the theory.

But even if states seek only survival, without knowing who holds which particular capabilities and their intentions – as well as who we are and what we value – we simply cannot say whether there is a threat against which to balance. Thus Stephen Walt (1987), one of Waltz's leading students, has introduced balance of threat theory: states balance not against (all) external capabilities but against threats, which are defined as much by intentions as by capabilities. Compare American behaviour towards British, French and Chinese (or Israeli, Indian and North Korean) nuclear arsenals, which weigh about equally in the global distribution of capabilities.

Unfortunately, realism has had very little to say about threats. And structural realism in principle can have has nothing to say about threat (as opposed to capabilities), leaving the crucial explanatory variable completely outside the scope of the theory. Thus John Vasquez (1998: 254–7) argues that balance of threat is theoretically degenerative, an ad hoc addition to the theory inconsistent with its basic propositions but necessary to 'rescue' it from the theoretical failures inherent in those basic premises.

Offensive and defensive realism

Predictions based solely on anarchy and polarity are so indeterminate that they are rarely of significant value. If realist theories are to be of substantial utility to analysts and policy makers, additional variables must be included – not in the ad hoc and incoherent way that Waltz appeals to multiple motives, but rigorously integrated into one or more theoretical models.

Survival and domination can be seen as extreme statements of defensive and expansive orientations. The literature on offensive and defensive realism (see, e.g., Lynn-Jones 1995; Labs 1997: 7–17; Zakaria 1998: 25–42; Taliaferro 2000/1; Snyder 2002) in effect revives the classical realist distinction between status quo and revolutionary or revisionist powers and develops two different realist theories from these contrasting orientations. For example, Michael Mastanduno (1991) argues that 'realists expect nation-states to avoid gaps that favor their partners, but not necessarily to maximize gaps in their own favor. Nation-states are not "gap maximizers." They are, in Joseph Grieco's terms, "defensive positionalists." ' (Mastanduno 1991: 79, n. 13). John Mearsheimer, by contrast, argues that 'states seek to survive under anarchy by maximizing their power relative to other states' (1990: 12). His states are 'short-term power maximizers' (1994/5: 82); that is, *offensive* positionalists. As Fareed Zakaria puts it, 'the best solution to the perennial problem of the uncertainty of international life is for a state to increase its control over that environment through the persistent expansion of its political interests abroad' (1998: 20).

This internal debate among realists is often presented (e.g. Labs 1997) as a matter of choosing 'the best' or most truly realist assumption/ theory. We saw above, though, that a world of defensive positionalists would be unrealistically peaceful. Yet unless most states are defensive positionalists, international relations would be a Hobbesian war of all against all – which it simply is not. Realism would seem to need *both* assumptions to retain the scope to which most realists aspire.

There are at least two ways to proceed. Offensive and defensive realism could be seen as abstract logics of interaction rather than substantive claims about the nature of states (compare Snyder 2002: 172). The contrasting predictions of the two models can be used both to guide policy or analysis and to facilitate further inquiry into the objectives of the parties (by inferring intentions from theoretically predicted behaviour). The other alternative would be to include offensive and defensive motives in a single theory that explains when each orientation should be expected to prevail. Mearsheimer's *The Tragedy of Great Power Politics* (2001) might be read as an effort to explain when, why, and how, offensive motivations characteristically take priority in the behaviour of great powers.

Process, institutions and change

Explicitly introducing state motives is only one of many possible strategies for improving the determinacy and range of realist theories. In this section, we examine Glenn Snyder's introduction of what he calls 'process variables' into structural realist theorizing. We then turn to institutions, norms and identities, variables that have traditionally been denigrated by realists. This section concludes by addressing the issue of change in international relations, a topic of considerable importance that arises out of a discussion of the importance of process and institutions in the discipline.

Process variables

Snyder tries to produce more determinate realist explanatory theories by introducing a series of 'process variables'. This in effect involves rethinking the nature of system-level theorizing and expanding it from Waltz's extraordinarily narrow structuralism.

A system is a bounded space defined by (a) units that interact with each other much more intensively than they interact with those outside the system; (b) the structure within which they interact; and (c) the characteristic interactions of the units within that structure. Process variables focus on patterns of interaction that are neither structural nor at the level of the unit – that is, are systemic but not structural.

Consider *alignment*. States may stand in relations of amity or enmity, seeing themselves as allies or adversaries. (Other relationships – most obviously, neutrality – are regular features of international relations, but allies and adversaries is a useful preliminary simplification.) States rarely fear all external concentrations of power, nor is their fear based solely on material capabilities. States, for example, are more likely to balance against adversaries than allies. Conversely, relative gains considerations may be substantially muted among allies, as illustrated by US support for European integration in the 1950s and 1960s.

Both allies and adversaries may have common or competing interests, which also help to make predictions more determinate. Common interests facilitate cooperation – although, of course, anarchy and relative gains always work against successful cooperation. Conversely, competing interests may be impede or prevent balancing against a common enemy.

Waltzian structural realism allows us only to predict *that* balances will form. Taking alignment, interests and other process variables into account allows us to predict which particular balances are likely or unlikely to develop. 'If, as Waltz says, system structures only "shape and shove", [process variables] give a more decided push' (Snyder 1997: 32).

The cost, however, is greater complexity and less generality. Greater depth typically requires a sacrifice in breadth. The additional variables that add depth, richness and precision produce a theory with a narrower range. Structure influences all states. Particular process variables influence only some parts of the system.

Parsimony and scope are great theoretical virtues; to explain everything with a single variable is the theorist's utopia. It is important that we appreciate the attractions of Waltz's ability to say some very important things about international relations, more or less anywhere and any time, based only on anarchy and the distribution of capabilities. Such a theory, within the domain of its operation, has considerable power. Snyder, however, argues – correctly, in my view – that Waltz is guilty of 'excessive parsimony, in the sense that the explanatory gain from some further elaboration would exceed the costs in reduced generality' (1996: 167).

This does not, however, sacrifice system-level theorizing. Alignment, for example, is about the *distribution* of amity and enmity and thus no less systemic than the distribution of capabilities. The system level of theorizing is not restricted to structure (which is only one of the defining elements of a system). Similarly, offensive and defensive realists usually treat motives by assumption or stipulation, identifying abstract kinds of actors and thus still functioning at the level of the system. To the extent that anarchy or distribution of capabilities shapes the choice of offensive or defensive objectives, the theory may even be rigorously structural.

Norms, institutions and identities

Snyder also identifies what he calls structural modifiers, 'system-wide influences that are structural in their inherent nature but not potent enough internationally to warrant that description' (1996: 169). He looks at military technology and norms and institutions. On the role of military technology, consider, for example, the special character of nuclear weapons, which Waltz (however inconsistently) uses to explain the Cold War peace (1990), or the impact of the relative advantage of offensive or defensive forces on conflict and the propensity to war (e.g. Glaser and Kaufmann 1998; Van Evera 1998). Here I will briefly consider norms and institutions.

Norms and institutions are clearly structural in domestic society. 'They create the hierarchy of power and differentiation of function that are the hallmarks of a well-ordered domestic polity, but that are present only rudimentarily in international society. In principle, they are also structural internationally' (Snyder 1996: 169).

As both this quote and the earlier reference to potency make clear, the actual international impact of norms and institutions is an empirical, not a theoretical question. Shared values and institutions may in particular cases shape and shove actors even more strongly than (Waltzian) structure. Consider not only the European Union but also the Nordic countries and the US–Canadian relationship. The literature on pluralistic security communities (e.g. Adler and Barnett 1998) emphasizes the potential impact of institutions, values and identities even in the high politics of international security. In a somewhat different but largely complementary vein, see the discussion of regional security relations in (Buzan and Waever 2003).

Even at the global level, norms and institutions can have considerable influence. Sovereignty and other rights of states are a matter of mutual recognition, not capabilities. Power alone will not even tell us which of their rights states actually enjoy. It simply is untrue that, as the Athenians at Melos put it, 'the strong do what they can, the weak suffer what they must' (Thucydides 1982: Book V, Chapter 89). The strong are often constrained by the rights of even weak states. They may, of course, violate the rules of sovereignty. But predictions based on, say, the norm of non-intervention are no more 'indeterminate' than those based on anarchy or polarity. And it is an empirical not a theoretical question whether the logic of rights or the logic of power more frequently accounts for international behaviour.

Consider also the principle of self-determination, which played a central role in creating scores of new, usually weak, states. Most postcolonial states have survived not through their own power or the power of allies but because of international recognition. Their survival – which offensive realists in particular must find inexplicable – was further enhanced by the effective abolition of aggressive war in the second half of the twentieth century.

Pursuing this line of analysis (see also Buzan, Jones and Little 1993) leads us well into the 'weak' or 'hedged' range of the realist spectrum – or off the scale altogether. Snyder clearly is a realist: he emphasizes anarchy and the struggle for power and is sceptical of the relative power of norms and institutions. But his approach to institutions and norms is unusually open, suggesting interesting conversations with convergent non-realist analyses.

For example, Alexander Wendt (1999: Chapter 6) shows that anarchic orders function very differently when actors see each other as 'enemies' out to destroy each other, 'rivals' who compete but do not threaten each others' survival and 'friends' who have renounced force in their relations. Realism in effect becomes a special case; what Wendt calls the 'Hobbesian' anarchy of enemies. Sovereignty, understood as rights to territorial integrity and political independence, transforms relations into those among 'Lockean' rivals, with the rivalry having been substantially moderated by the abolition of aggressive war.

Most realists, however, downplay the significance of institutions, as suggested in titles such as 'The False Promise of International Institutions' (Mearsheimer 1994/5) and *Sovereignty: Organized Hypocrisy* (Krasner 1999). Institutions and norms are treated as largely reducible to the material interests of the powerful. They are at best 'intervening variables' that can be expected to have independent effects only in minor issue areas far removed from the struggle for power. (An interesting, and little explored, alternative is represented by the effort of Schweller and Priess 1997 to theorize institutions from within a realist framework.)

Realists are a bit less reluctant to talk about identities – although usually this seems to be done unwittingly. This is most evident in the classical realist distinction between status quo and revisionist powers or the parallel split between offensive and defensive structural realists. But there are many other examples. 'Great power' signifies not merely unparalleled material capabilities but also a managerial role in international society (Bull 1977: Chapter 9; Simpson 2004) and an identity type. Balance of power is also a complex set of institutions (Gulick 1967; Bull 1977: Chapter 4; Cronin 1999: Chapter 1). The sovereign territorial state is a particular system-wide construction of 'unit' identity (Compare Cronin 1999; Reus-Smit 1999). To take a simple example, the attitude towards territory is very different among early modern dynastic sovereigns and late nineteenth- and twentieth-century national/territorial sovereigns. (On the general importance of identity in international political thought see Keene (2005).)

Structural realists, however, have no theoretical basis for incorporating identity. Like Waltz on state motivation, identity conceptions are implicitly, and illicitly, incorporated into an analysis that presents itself in different terms. (Neo-)classical realists do have theoretical space for identity and institutional roles, but few have pursued the issue systematically. One notable exception is Schweller's work on revisionist powers (1994, 1999: 18–23), which aims to meld structural, motivational, and identity elements into a coherent and rigorous realist account.

Constancy and change

Identities, institutions and norms are important for our purposes here not so much because they are central concerns of most realists but because they represent the principal points of substantive divergence between realist and other approaches in contemporary international theory. They also indirectly raise the issue of change. A standard complaint about realism is its inability to comprehend fundamental change in international relations. The implications of this charge, however, are less damning than critics often imagine.

Realism is a theory 'tuned' to explaining constancy. Realists are more impressed by the repeated occurrence of certain patterns across time than by the undeniable historical and cultural diversity of actors and interactions in international relations. They emphasize constancy not accidentally but by self-conscious theoretical choice. Although others may not share this judgement, it is one about which reasonable people may reasonably disagree.

The failure of realism to account for the end of the Cold War is a large part of the explanation of its declining popularity over the past fifteen years. Ironically, though, realists can fairly claim that they never attempted to explain change. They can even note, with a certain smugness, that no other theory of international relations did a better job. Everyone was caught by surprise.

It is understandable that dramatic change is held up against a theory that emphasizes constancy. But whatever kind of failure it represents is shared by all other prominent theories of international relations. It is a failing of the discipline as a whole rather than realism in particular.

Morality and foreign policy

In popular and foreign policy discussions, 'realist' most frequently refers to arguments against pursuing moral objectives in international relations. Although in principle simply a special case of the broader issue of norms and institutions, the place of morality in foreign policy has been a central concern of the classical realist tradition, not only in canonical texts such as Thucydides' Melian Dialogue and Machiavelli's *The Prince* but also in the work of major twentieth-century realists such as Carr, Morgenthau and Niebuhr. It is also an issue of vital substantive importance. Therefore, it is well worth discussion here, even though it has been a peripheral concern of academic realists since the 1970s, whose concerns have been more scientific and scholarly than directly policy oriented.

The subordination of morality to power often is presented as a descriptive statement of the facts of international political life. 'The actions of states are determined not by moral principles and legal commitments but by considerations of interest and power' (Morgenthau 1970: 382).

'States in anarchy cannot afford to be moral. The possibility of moral behavior rests upon the existence of an effective government that can deter and punish illegal actions' (Art and Waltz 1983: 6).

Such claims, however, are obviously false. Just as individuals may behave morally in the absence of government enforcement of moral rules, states often can and do act out of moral concerns. Consider, for example, the outpouring of international aid in the wake of the Indian Ocean tsunami and other natural and political disasters.

It simply is not true, of either men or states, that they 'never do good unless necessity drives them to it', that 'all do wrong to the same extent when there is nothing to prevent them doing wrong' (Machiavelli 1970: Book I, Chapter 2, 58). States sometimes – I would suggest frequently – value compliance with ethical and humanitarian norms for reasons that have little or nothing to do with the threat of coercive enforcement. And even when states do violate norms because of the absence of enforcement, the independent ethical force of an infringed norm frequently is a significant part of the normative calculus of both the state acting and those who judge it.

We should also remember that even in anarchy coercive enforcement is sometimes possible, most obviously through self-help. Furthermore, various mechanisms exist to induce, even when they cannot compel, compliance. Public opinion, both national and international, can be a powerful force. In some cases, the power and authority of intergovernmental institutions may be significant. More generally, international law, which includes some obligations that are also moral obligations, is no more frequently violated than domestic law. In any case, violations typically do have costs for states (although not always sufficiently high costs to compel compliance).

Realists, with good cause, emphasize that a state, especially a powerful state, bent on violating a moral norm usually can get away with it – and that when it can't, it usually is because the power of others states has been mobilized on behalf of the moral norm. Nonetheless, states do sometimes comply with moral norms both for their own sake and out of consideration of the costs of non-compliance. As a matter of fact, states regularly conclude that in some instances they *can* afford to be moral, despite international anarchy.

For example, humanitarian interventions in Kosovo, East Timor and Darfur, however tardy and limited, simply cannot be understood without the independent normative force of the anti-genocide norm and humanitarian principles. Such normative concerns rarely are the sole motive behind foreign policy action. But they often are an important element of the calculus. And few significant foreign policy actions reflect just a single self-interested motive either. Foreign policy is driven by the intersection of multiple motives, some of which are ethical in a large number of countries.

Pursuing moral objectives such as spreading democracy or combating preventable childhood diseases certainly may be costly. But no political goals can be achieved without cost. Just as the cost of pursuing economic objectives is no basis for excluding economic interests from foreign policy, the costs of pursuing moral objectives do not justify categorically excluding them from foreign policy agendas. The proper course is to weigh the costs and benefits of pursuing all relevant interests, moral and non-moral interests alike. Moral values are indeed values and therefore must be taken into account in any truly reasonable and realistic political calculus. Thus even Mearsheimer allows that 'there are good reasons to applaud the 1978 Vietnamese invasion of Cambodia, since it drove the murderous Pol Pot from power' (1994/5: 31).

Realists often suggest that ordinary citizens and even politicians, especially in democracies, tend to underestimate the costs of – and thus over-estimate the space available for – the pursuit of moral interests. But to the extent this is true, most non-realists would offer the same criticisms. There is nothing distinctively realist about insisting that foreign policy should be based on a rational calculation of costs and benefits.

Notice that as this discussion has progressed, we have moved towards more prescriptive arguments against the wisdom of pursuing moral objectives. Along similar lines, realists often stress the constraints on foreign policy imposed by the special office of the statesman. For example, Kennan argues that the 'primary obligation' of any government 'is to the *interests* of the national society it represents' and that therefore 'the same moral concepts are no longer relevant to it' (1954: 48; 1985/6: 206). Morgenthau talks about the special demands of statesmanship in terms of 'the autonomy of politics.' (1948/1954/1973: 12; 1962: 3)

Kennan claims that an overriding concern for the national interest is a matter of 'unavoidable necessit[y]' and therefore 'subject to classification neither as "good" or "bad" ' (1985/6: 206). But if the national interest is not merely good but a very high good, there is no reason to accept it as a standard for judging international political behaviour. The 'necessity' here is ethical, not a matter of physical or logical compulsion.

Many realists thus explicitly present pursuit of the national interest, and realist power politics, as a matter of ethical obligation. Joel Rosenthal's social history of post-war American realists is nicely titled *Righteous Realists* (1991). Morgenthau goes so far as to speak of 'the moral dignity of the national interest' (1951: 33–9).

A few realists adopt a radically nationalist ethic that holds that 'the State is not to be judged by the standards which apply to individuals, but by those which are set for it by its own nature and ultimate aims'

(Treitschke 1916: 99). Most, however, show varying degrees of discomfort with the fact that 'the great majority persists in drawing a sharp distinction between the welfare of those who share their particular collective and the welfare of humanity' (Tucker 1977: 139–40). Many use the language of tragedy, for example, in titles such as *Truth and Tragedy* (Thompson and Meyers 1977) and *The Tragedy of Great Power Politics* (Mearsheimer 2001). Niebuhr (1932) bemoans the severe attenuation of our moral sentiments and resources in social life in general and in international politics in particular. Carr goes so far as to claim that 'the impossibility of being a consistent and thorough-going realist is one of the most certain and most curious lessons of political science' (1939/1945/1946: 89).

The special ethical demands of statesmanship certainly deserve emphasis. The statesman has an ethical obligation to protect and further the national interest, much as lawyers, especially in adversarial legal systems, have an ethical obligation to pursue the interests of their clients, often even when they conflict with justice or truth. We rightly expect national leaders to give special weight to national interests. It would be not only politically irresponsible but ethically derelict to consult only religious precepts, universal moral principles, international law, or a broader human interest in formulating and implementing foreign policy.

Survival in particular is such an overriding priority that even most moralists would agree with Machiavelli that 'when the safety of one's country wholly depends on the decision to be taken, no attention should be paid either to justice or injustice' (1970: Book 1, Chapter 41). But such an argument applies no less against non-moral objectives, such as pursuing economic interests and supporting an ally. And survival rarely is at stake in international relations.

It simply is not true that 'the struggle for power is identical with the struggle for survival' (Spykman 1942: 18). Neither is it true that 'the system forces states to behave according to the dictates of realism, or risk destruction' (Mearsheimer 1995: 91). Many moral foreign policy objectives pose no risk to national survival. And other national interests simply do not have the ethical priority of survival. Much as a lawyer who learns that her client is planning to commit a murder ordinarily is required to breach client confidentiality, the ethical obligations of the statesman to the national interest must sometimes be balanced against other norms and values.

Realists certainly are correct to criticize 'moralism', the belief that international relations can appropriately be judged *solely* by conventional moral norms. But few if any serious theorists or activists have actually held such a view. Even the inter-war peace activists that realists pejoratively dismiss as idealists in fact usually held far more sophisticated views (Lynch 1999).

To the extent that there is a tendency toward moralism in foreign policy, especially in the United States, realists may offer a healthy corrective. Five hundred years ago, it might have been scandalous for Machiavelli to argue that a good statesman must 'learn to be able not to be good, and to use this and not use it according to necessity' (1985: Chapter 15). Today, however, almost all students of international relations agree that sometimes the good statesman ought to act in ways inconsistent with the principles of private morality – for example, to give greater consideration to preserving the lives of her own soldiers than the soldiers of her adversary.

Controversy arises over when, where and how frequently violating moral norms is truly necessary. Realists suggest that anarchy and egoism so severely constrain the space for the pursuit of moral concerns that it is only a small exaggeration to say that states in anarchy cannot afford to be moral. This, however, is a contingent empirical claim about which reasonable people may reasonably disagree. And even if we accept it, it provides no grounds for categorically excluding morality from foreign policy. Even if the primary obligation of the statesman is to the national interest, that is not her exclusive obligation. States not only are free to, but in fact often do, include certain moral objectives in their definition of the national interest.

How to think about realism (and its critics)

Time after time we have identified an unfortunate tendency among realists to push an important insight well beyond the breaking point. Not only are they prone to rhetorical exaggerations, such as Nicholas Spykman's claim that 'the search for power is not made for the achievement of moral values; moral values are used to facilitate the attainment of power' (1942: 18). Even more moderate statements regularly lack the necessary qualifications. Note the absence of an adverb like 'often', 'frequently', or even 'usually' in Kennan's claim, quoted above, that non-moral considerations 'must be allowed to prevail'. Likewise, Mearsheimer, on the same page that he argues that institutions 'matter only on the margins' – a controversial but plausible empirical claim rooted in a standard realist analysis of the impact of anarchy – also asserts the obviously false claim that institutions that 'have no independent effect on state behavior' (1994/5: 7).

Strong adherents of a theory often unthinkingly slide from (justifiable) theoretical simplifications to (unjustifiable) descriptive claims. As I have noted repeatedly, theories must abstract, simplify and thus exaggerate. The danger arises when these simplified theoretical ideal-types are presented as categorical empirical claims. That realists are no less prone to this confusion than adherents of other theories is ironic but not particularly surprising.

Waltz nicely captures the contribution of realism: it tells us 'a small number of big and important things' (1986: 329). Were realists, and Waltz himself, always this modest, the discipline, especially in the United States, would be much better off – particularly if realists took to heart the negative implication that there are a large number of big and important things about which realism is necessarily silent. Realism simply fails to explain most of international relations. Anarchy, egoism and the distribution of capabilities cannot explain the vast majority of what happens in such relations.

The realist response that they explain 'the most important things' is a contentious normative judgement. Furthermore, given the 'indeterminacy' of most realist predictions, it is by no means clear that realism offers deep or satisfying explanations of even the things to which it applies (compare Wendt 1999: 18, 251–9). But even if realism does adequately explain the few most important things, there is no reason to restrict the discipline to those. The resulting impoverishment would be equivalent to restricting medicine to studying and treating only the leading causes of death.

That realism cannot account for substantial swathes of international relations is no reason to denigrate or marginalize it. Realists, though, must allow the same for other theories. Realism must be an important, even essential, part of a pluralistic discipline of international studies. No less. But no more.

The familiar question 'Are you a realist?' may be appropriate if we understand realism as a moral theory or world-view. A few realists, particularly Augustinian Christians such as Niebuhr (1941, 1943) and Butterfield (1953) have treated realism in such terms. Among contemporary academic realists, Robert Gilpin (1986, 1996) perhaps borders on holding such a view. But world-views – natural law, Islam, Kantianism, Christianity, Aristoteleanism, humanism – are not usually what we have in mind by 'theories of international relations'. If we are talking about analytical or explanatory theory, 'being' (or 'not being') a realist makes little sense.

Unless realist predictions or explanations are almost always correct across something like the full range of international relations – and neither realism nor any other theory of international relations even approximates this – no serious student or practitioner would want to 'be' a realist in the sense of always applying or acting upon realist theory. But unless realism never provided valuable insights or explanations – and even its strongest critics do not suggest this – no reasonable person would want to 'be' an anti-realist in the sense of never using realist theories.

The proper questions are how regularly, in what domains and for what purposes does realism help us to understand or act in the world. My general answer is 'a lot less often than most realists claim, but a lot more frequently than most anti-realists would like to allow'. But more important than this general answer is the fact that, depending on one's political interests and substantive concerns, one might appropriately use realism regularly, occasionally, or almost never in one's analyses or actions.

Realism *must* be a part of the analytical toolkit of every serious student of international relations. But if it is our only tool – or even our primary tool – we will be woefully underequipped for our analytical tasks, our vision of international relations will be sadly impoverished, and, to the extent that theory has an impact on practice, the projects we undertake in the world are liable to be mangled and misshapen.

Chapter 3

Liberalism

SCOTT BURCHILL

As one of the two great philosophical products of the European Enlightenment, liberalism has had a profound impact on the shape of all modern industrial societies. It has championed limited government and scientific rationality, believing individuals should be free from arbitrary state power, persecution and superstition. It has advocated political freedom, democracy and constitutionally guaranteed rights, and privileged the liberty of the individual and equality before the law. Liberalism has also argued for individual competition in civil society and claimed that market capitalism best promotes the welfare of all by most efficiently allocating scarce resources within society. To the extent that its ideas have been realized in recent democratic transitions in both hemispheres and manifested in the globalization of the world economy, liberalism remains a powerful and influential doctrine.

There are many strands of liberal thought which influence the study of international relations. The chapter will begin with an analysis of the revival of liberal thought after the Cold War. It will then explain how traditional liberal attitudes to war and the importance of democracy and human rights continue to inform contemporary thinking. The influence of economic liberalism, in particular interdependency theory and liberal institutionalism, will then be assessed before liberal arguments for globalization and the impact of non-state terrorism on liberal thought is measured. The conclusion will judge the contribution of liberalism to the theory of international relations.

After the Cold War

The demise of Soviet Communism at the beginning of the 1990s enhanced the influence of liberal theories of international relations within the academy, a theoretical tradition long thought to have been discredited by perspectives which emphasize the recurrent features of international relations. In a confident reassertion of the teleology of

55

liberalism, Fukuyama claimed in the early 1990s that the collapse of the Soviet Union proved that liberal democracy had no serious ideological competitor: it was 'the end point of mankind's ideological evolution' and the 'final form of human government' (1992: xi–xii). It is an argument that has been strengthened by recent transitions to democracy in Africa, East Asia and Latin America.

For Fukuyama, the end of the Cold War represented the triumph of the 'ideal state' and a particular form of political economy, 'liberal capitalism', which 'cannot be improved upon': there can be 'no further progress in the development of underlying principles and institutions' (1992: xi–xii). According to Fukuyama, the end of the East–West conflict confirmed that liberal capitalism was unchallenged as a model of, and endpoint for, humankind's political and economic development. Like many liberals he sees history as progressive, linear and 'directional', and is convinced that 'there is a fundamental process at work that dictates a common evolutionary pattern for *all* human societies – in short, something like a Universal History of mankind in the direction of liberal democracy' (Fukuyama 1992: xi–xii, 48).

Fukuyama's belief that Western forms of government and political economy are the ultimate destination which the entire human race will eventually reach poses a number of challenges for orthodoxy within International Relations. First, his claim that political and economic development terminates at liberal-capitalist democracy assumes that the Western path to modernity no longer faces a challenge of the kind posed by communism, and will eventually command global consent. Secondly, Fukuyama's argument assumes that national and cultural distinctions are no barrier to the triumph of liberal democracy and capitalism, which face little if any serious resistance. Thirdly, Fukuyama's thesis raises vital questions about governance and political community. What are the implications of globalization for nation-states and their sovereign powers?

Most importantly, Fukuyama believes that progress in human history can be measured by the elimination of global conflict and the adoption of principles of legitimacy that have evolved over time in domestic political orders. This constitutes an 'inside-out' approach to international relations, where the behaviour of states can be explained by examining their endogenous arrangements. It also leads to Doyle's important claim that 'liberal democracies are uniquely willing to eschew the use of force in their relations with one another', a view which rejects the realist contention that the anarchical nature of the international system means states are trapped in a struggle for power and security (Linklater 1993: 29).

Liberal internationalism: 'inside looking out'

Although he believes that his 'hypothesis remains correct', the events of 9/11 have subsequently caused Fukuyama to reflect on resistance to political and economic convergence in the modern world and the reaction in many societies against the dominance of the West (Fukuyama 2002: 28). The path to Western modernity in 2005 does not look as straight or inevitable as it did a decade or more ago. The rise of Islamic militancy may only be a transient and disproportionately influential revolt against Western cultural authority, but from the perspective of the 1990s it was as unexpected as it was violent.

Nonetheless, in the 1990s Fukuyama revived a long-held view among liberals that the spread of legitimate domestic political orders would eventually bring an end to international conflict. This neo-Kantian position assumes that particular states, with liberal-democratic credentials, constitute an ideal which the rest of the world will emulate. Fukuyama is struck by the extent to which liberal democracies have transcended their violent instincts and institutionalized norms which pacify relations between them. He is particularly impressed by the emergence of shared principles of legitimacy among the great powers, a trend which he thought would continue in the post-Cold War period. The projection of liberal-democratic principles to the international realm is said to provide the best prospect for a peaceful world order because 'a world made up of liberal democracies ... should have much less incentive for war, since all nations would reciprocally recognise one another's legitimacy' (Fukuyama 1992: xx).

This approach is rejected by neo-realists who claim that the moral aspirations of states are thwarted by the absence of an overarching authority which regulates their behaviour towards each other. The anarchical nature of the international system tends to homogenize foreign policy behaviour by socializing states into the system of power politics. The requirements of strategic power and security are paramount in an insecure world, and they soon override the ethical pursuits of states, regardless of their domestic political complexions.

In stressing the importance of legitimate domestic orders in explaining foreign policy behaviour, realists such as Waltz believe that liberals are guilty of 'reductionism' when they should be highlighting the 'systemic' features of international relations. This conflict between 'inside-out' and 'outside-in' approaches to international relations has become an important line of demarcation in modern international theory (Waltz 1991a: 667). The extent to which the neo-realist critique of liberal internationalism can be sustained in the post-Cold War era will be a major feature of this chapter.

Fukuyama's argument is not simply a celebration of the fact that liberal capitalism has survived the threat posed by Marxism. It also implies that neo-realism has overlooked 'the foremost macropolitical trend in contemporary world politics: the expansion of the liberal zone of peace' (Linklater 1993: 29). Challenging the view that anarchy conditions international behaviour is Doyle's argument that there is a growing core of pacific states which have learned to resolve their differences without resorting to violence. The likely expansion of this pacific realm is said to be the most significant feature of the post-Communist landscape. If this claim can be upheld it will constitute a significant comeback for an international theory widely thought to have been seriously challenged by Carr in his critique of liberal utopianism in the 1940s. It will also pose a serious challenge to a discipline which until recently has been dominated by assumptions that war is an endemic feature of international life (Doyle 1986: 1151–69).

War, democracy and free trade

The foundations of contemporary liberal internationalism were laid in the eighteenth and nineteenth centuries by liberals proposing preconditions for a peaceful world order. In broad summary they concluded that the prospects for the elimination of war lay with a preference for democracy over aristocracy and free trade over autarky. In this section we will examine these arguments in turn, and the extent to which they inform contemporary liberal thought.

Prospects for peace

For liberals, peace is the normal state of affairs: in Kant's words, peace can be perpetual. The laws of nature dictated harmony and cooperation between peoples. War is therefore both unnatural and irrational, an artificial contrivance and not a product of some peculiarity of human nature. Liberals have a belief in progress and the perfectibility of the human condition. Through their faith in the power of human reason and the capacity of human beings to realize their inner potential, they remain confident that the stain of war can be removed from human experience (Gardner 1990: 23–39; Hoffmann 1995: 159–77; Zacher and Matthew 1995: 107–50).

A common thread, from Rousseau, Kant and Cobden, to Schumpeter and Doyle, is that wars were created by militaristic and undemocratic governments for their own vested interests. Wars were engineered by a 'warrior class' bent on extending their power and wealth through territorial conquest. According to Paine in *The Rights of Man*, the 'war system' was contrived to preserve the power and the employment of princes, statesmen, soldiers, diplomats and armaments manufacturers, and to bind their tyranny ever more firmly upon the necks of the people' (Howard 1978: 31). Wars provide governments with excuses to raise taxes, expand their bureaucratic apparatus and increase their control over their citizens. The people, on the other hand, were peace-loving by nature, and plunged into conflict only by the whims of their unrepresentative rulers.

War was a cancer on the body politic. But it was an ailment that human beings, themselves, had the capacity to cure. The treatment which liberals began prescribing in the eighteenth century had not changed: the 'disease' of war could be successfully treated with the twin medicines of *democracy* and *free trade*. Democratic processes and institutions would break the power of the ruling elites and curb their propensity for violence. Free trade and commerce would overcome the artificial barriers between individuals and unite them everywhere into one community.

For liberals such as Schumpeter, war was the product of the aggressive instincts of unrepresentative elites. The warlike disposition of these rulers drove the reluctant masses into violent conflicts which, while profitable for the arms industries and the military aristocrats, were disastrous for those who did the fighting. For Kant, the establishment of republican forms of government in which rulers were accountable and individual rights were respected would lead to peaceful international relations because the ultimate consent for war would rest with the citizens of the state (Kant 1970: 100). For both Kant and Schumpeter, war was the outcome of minority rule, though Kant was no champion of democratic government (MacMillan 1995). Liberal states, founded on individual rights such as equality before the law, free speech and civil liberty, respect for private property and representative government, would not have the same appetite for conflict and war. Peace was fundamentally a question of establishing legitimate domestic orders throughout the world. 'When the citizens who bear the burdens of war elect their governments, wars become impossible' (Doyle 1986: 1151).

The dual themes of domestic legitimacy and the extent to which liberal-democratic states exercise restraint and peaceful intentions in their foreign policy have been taken up more recently by Doyle, Russett and others. In a restatement of Kant's argument that a 'pacific federation' (*foedus pacificum*) can be built by expanding the number of states with republican constitutions, Doyle claims that liberal democracies are unique in their ability and willingness to establish peaceful relations among themselves. This pacification of foreign relations between liberal states is said to be a direct product of their shared legitimate political orders based on democratic principles and institutions. The reciprocal recognition of these common principles – a commitment to the rule of law, individual rights and equality before the law, *and* representative government based on popular consent – means that liberal democracies evince little interest in conflict with each other and have no grounds on which to contest each other's legitimacy: they have constructed a 'separate peace' (Doyle 1986: 1161; Fukuyama 1992: xx). This does not mean that they are less inclined to make war with non-democratic states, and Doyle is correct to point out that democracies maintain a healthy appetite for conflicts with authoritarian states, as recent conflicts in the Middle East and Central Asia attest to. But it does suggest that the best prospect for bringing an end to war between states lies with the spread of liberal-democratic governments across the globe. The expansion of the zone of peace from the core to the periphery is also the basis of Fukuyama's optimism about the post-Communist era (Doyle 1986, 1995, 1997; Russett 1993).

There are both structural and normative aspects to what has been termed 'democratic peace theory'. Some liberals emphasize the institutional constraints on liberal-democratic states, such as public opinion, the rule of law and representative government. Others stress the normative preference for compromise and conflict resolution which can be found in liberal democracies. A combination of both explanations strengthens the argument that liberal-democratic states do not resolve their differences violently, although realist critics point to definitional problems with the idea of liberal democracy and the question of covert action, and argue that at best democratic peace theory identifies a correlation in international politics rather than an 'iron law' or theory (Maoz and Russett 1993; Owen 1994).

The argument is also extended by Rawls, who claims that liberal societies are also 'less likely to engage in war with nonliberal outlaw states, except on grounds of legitimate self-defence (or in the defence of their legitimate allies), or intervention in severe cases to protect human rights' (Rawls 1999: 49). Recent US-led wars in Afghanistan and Iraq pose significant challenges to the claim that only self-defence and humanitarianism incline liberal-democratic states to war.

A related argument by Mueller (1989) claims that we are already witnessing the obsolescence of war between the major powers. Reviving the liberal faith in the capacity of people to improve the moral and material conditions of their lives, Mueller argues that, just as duelling and slavery were eventually seen as morally unacceptable, war is increasingly viewed in the developed world as repulsive, immoral and uncivilized. That violence is more widely seen as an anachronistic form of social intercourse is not due to any change in human nature or the structure of the international system. According to Mueller, the obsolescence of major war in the late twentieth century was the product of moral learning, a shift in ethical consciousness away from coercive forms of social behaviour. Because war brings more costs than gains and is no longer seen as a romantic or noble pursuit, it has become 'rationally unthinkable' (Mueller 1989).

The long peace between states of the industrialized world is a cause of profound optimism for liberals such as Fukuyama and Mueller, who are confident that we have already entered a period in which war as an instrument of international diplomacy is becoming obsolete. But if war has been an important factor in nation-building, as Giddens, Mann and Tilly have argued, the fact that states are learning to curb their propensity for violence will also have important consequences for forms of political community which are likely to emerge in the industrial centres of the world. The end of war between the great powers may have the effect of weakening the rigidity of their political boundaries and inspiring a wave of sub-national revolts, although the new wave of anti-Western terror may complicate matters in this regard by encouraging states to solidify their boundaries and make greater demands on the loyalty of citizens. If war has been a binding as well as destructive force in international relations, the problem of maintaining cohesive communities will be a major challenge for metropolitan centres.

Far from sharing the post-Cold War optimism of liberals, realists such as Waltz and Mearsheimer argue that the collapse of bipolarity in the early 1990s was a cause for grave concern. Mutual nuclear deterrence maintained a stabilizing balance of power in the world, whereas unipolarity would not last, eventually leading to volatility and war. As Waltz argues, 'in international politics, unbalanced power constitutes a danger even when it is American power that is out of balance' (Waltz 1991a: 670). Accordingly, the expansion of a zone of peace is no antidote to the calculations of raw power in an anarchical world.

Recent conflicts in the Balkans, Central Asia and the Persian Gulf – all involving major industrial powers – are a reminder that the post-Cold War period remains volatile and suggest that war may not yet have lost its efficacy in international diplomacy. None of these constitutes conflicts between democratic states but they are no less important to the maintenance of world order. These and other struggles in so-called 'failed states' such as Afghanistan, Somalia and possibly Indonesia and Papua New Guinea, highlight the fact that the fragmentation of nation-states and civil wars arising from secessionist movements have not been given the same attention by liberals as more conventional inter-state wars.

They also remind us of the limitations of democratic peace theory, which provides few guidelines for how liberal states should conduct themselves with non-liberal states. Rawls, on the other hand, is concerned with the extent to which liberal and non-liberal peoples can be equal participants in a 'Society of Peoples'. He argues that principles and norms of international law and practice – the 'Law of Peoples' – can be developed and shared by both liberal and non-liberal or decent hierarchical societies, without an expectation that liberal democracy is the terminus for all. The guidelines and principal basis for establishing harmonious relations between liberal and non-liberal peoples under a common Law of Peoples, takes liberal international theory in a more sophisticated direction because it explicitly acknowledges the need for utopian thought to be realistic (Rawls 1999: 11–23).

As the number of East Asian and Islamic societies which reject the normative superiority of liberal democracy grows, doubt is cast on the belief that the non-European world is seeking to imitate the Western route to political modernization. This has also been graphically illustrated in the current wave of anti-Western Islamist terror. Linklater suggests that it is not so much the spread of liberal democracy *per se* which has universal appeal, 'but the idea of limited power which is present within, but not entirely synonymous with, liberal democracy' (Linklater 1993: 33–6; Rawls 1999). The notion of limited power and respect for the rule of law contained within the idea of 'constitutionalism' may be one means of solving the exclusionary character of the liberal zone of peace. It is a less ambitious project and potentially more sensitive to the cultural and political differences among states in the current international system. It may avoid the danger of the system bifurcating into a privileged inner circle and a disadvantaged and disaffected outer circle (Linklater 1993: 33). The greatest barrier to the expansion of the zone of peace from the core is the perception within the periphery that this constitutes little more than the domination of one culture by another.

The spirit of commerce

Eighteenth- and nineteenth-century liberals felt that the spirits of war and commerce were mutually incompatible. Many wars were fought by states to achieve their mercantilist goals. According to Carr, 'the aim of mercantilism ... was not to promote the welfare of the community and its members, but to augment the power of the state, of which the sovereign was the embodiment ... wealth was the source of power, or more specifically of fitness for war'. Until the Napoleonic wars, 'wealth, conceived in its simplest form as bullion, was brought in by exports; and since, in the static conception of society prevailing at this period, export markets were a fixed quantity not susceptible of increase as a whole, the only way for a nation to expand its markets and therefore its wealth was to capture them from some other nation, if necessary by waging a trade war' (Carr 1945: 5–6).

Free trade, however, was a more peaceful means of achieving national wealth because, according to the theory of comparative advantage, each economy would be materially better off than if it had been pursuing nationalism and self-sufficiency (autarky). Free trade would also break down the divisions between states and unite individuals everywhere in one community. Artificial barriers to commerce distorted perceptions and relations between individuals, thereby causing international tension. Free trade would expand the range of contacts and levels of understanding between the peoples of the world and encourage international friendship and understanding. According to Kant, unhindered commerce between the peoples of the world would unite them in a common, peaceful enterprise. 'Trade ... would increase the wealth and power of the peace-loving, productive sections of the population at the expense of the war-orientated aristocracy, and ... would bring men of different nations into constant contact with one another; contact which would make clear to all of them their fundamental community of interests' (Howard 1978: 20; Walter 1996). Similarly Ricardo believed that free trade 'binds together, by one common tie of interest and intercourse, the universal society of nations throughout the civilised world' (Ricardo 1911: 114).

Conflicts were often caused by states erecting barriers which distorted and concealed the natural harmony of interests commonly shared by individuals across the world. The solution to the problem, argued Adam Smith and Tom Paine, was the free movement of commodities, capital and labour. 'If commerce were permitted to act to the universal extent it is capable, it would extirpate the system of war and produce a revolution in the uncivilised state of governments' (Howard 1978: 29). Writing in 1848, John Stuart Mill also claimed that free trade was the means to bring about the end of war: 'it is commerce which is rapidly rendering war obsolete, by strengthening and multiplying the personal interests which act in natural opposition to it' (Howard 1978: 37). The spread of markets would place societies on an entirely new foundation. Instead of conflicts over limited resources such as land, the industrial revolution raised the prospect of unlimited and unprecedented prosperity for all: material production, so long as it was freely exchanged, would bring human progress. Trade would create relations of mutual dependence which would foster understanding between peoples and reduce conflict. Economic self-interest would then be a powerful disincentive for war.

Liberals have always felt that unfettered commercial exchanges would encourage links across frontiers and shift loyalties away from the nation-state. Leaders would eventually come to recognize that the benefits of free trade outweighed the costs of territorial conquest and colonial expansion. The attraction of going to war to promote mercantilist interests would be weakened as societies learn that war can only disrupt trade and therefore the prospects for economic prosperity. Interdependence would replace national competition and defuse unilateral acts of aggression and reciprocal retaliation.

Interdependence and liberal institutionalism

Free trade and the removal of barriers to commerce is at the heart of modern interdependency theory. The rise of regional economic integration in Europe, for example, was inspired by the belief that the likelihood of conflict between states would be reduced by creating a common interest in trade and economic collaboration among members of the same geographical region. This would encourage states, such as France and Germany, which traditionally resolved their differences militarily, to cooperate within a commonly agreed economic and political framework for their mutual benefit. States would then have a joint stake in each other's peace and prosperity. The European Union is the best example of economic integration engendering closer economic and political cooperation in a region historically bedevilled by national conflicts.

As Mitrany argued, initially cooperation between states would be achieved in technical areas where it was mutually convenient, but once successful it could 'spill over' into other functional areas where states found that mutual advantages could be gained (Mitrany 1948: 350–63). In a development of this argument, Keohane and Nye have explained how, via membership of international institutions, states can significantly broaden their conceptions of self-interest in order to widen the scope for cooperation. Compliance with the rules of these organizations not only discourages the narrow pursuit of national interests, it also weakens the meaning and appeal of state sovereignty (Keohane and Nye 1977). This suggests that the international system is more normatively regulated than realists would have us believe, a position further developed by English School writers such as Wight and Bull (see Chapter 4 in this volume).

A development of this argument can be found in liberal institutionalism which shares with neo-realism an acceptance of the importance of the state and the anarchical condition of the international system, though liberal institutionalists argue that the prospects for cooperation, even in an anarchical world, are greater than neo-realists would have us believe (Young 1982; Nye 1988; Powell 1994). Liberal institutionalists believe that cooperation between states can and should be organized and formalized in institutions. 'Institutions' in this sense means sets of rules which govern state behaviour in specific policy areas, such as the Law of the Sea.

Accepting the broad structures of neo-realism, but employing rational choice and game theory to anticipate the behaviour of states, liberal institutionalists seek to demonstrate that cooperation between states can be enhanced even without the presence of a hegemonic player which can enforce compliance with agreements. For them, anarchy is mitigated by regimes and institutional cooperation which brings higher levels of regularity and predictability to international relations. Regimes constrain state behaviour by formalizing the expectations of each party to an agreement where there is a shared interest. Institutions then assume the role of encouraging cooperative habits, monitoring compliance and sanctioning defectors. Regimes also enhance trust, continuity and stability in a world of ungoverned anarchy.

Neo-realists and neo-liberals disagree about how states conceive of their own interests. Whereas neo-realists, such as Waltz, argue that states are concerned with 'relative gains' – meaning gains assessed in comparative terms (who will gain more?), neo-liberals claim that states are concerned with maximizing their 'absolute gains' – an assessment of their own welfare independent of their rivals (what will gain me the most?). Accordingly, neo-realists argue that states will baulk at cooperation if they expect to gain less than their rivals. Liberal institutionalists, on the other hand, believe international relations need not be a zero-sum game, as many states feel secure enough to maximize their own gains regardless of what accrues to others. Mutual benefits arising out of cooperation are possible because states are not always preoccupied with relative gains.

Liberal institutionalists acknowledge that cooperation between states is likely to be fragile, particularly where enforcement procedures are weak. However, in an environment of growing regional and global integration, states can often discover – with or without the encouragement of a hegemon – a coincidence of strategic and economic interests which can be turned into a formalized agreement determining the rules of conduct. In areas such as environmental degradation and the threat of terrorism, the argument for formalized cooperation between states is compelling.

According to Rosecrance (1986), the growth of economic interdependency has been matched by a corresponding decline in the value of territorial conquest for states. In the contemporary world the benefits of trade and cooperation among states greatly exceed that of military competition and territorial control. Nation-states have traditionally regarded the acquisition of territory as the principal means of increasing national wealth. In recent years, however, it has become apparent that additional territory does not necessarily help states to compete in an international system where the 'trading state' rather than the 'military state' is becoming dominant. In the 1970s state elites began to realize that wealth is determined by their share of the world market in value-added goods and services. This understanding has had two significant effects. First, the age of the independent, self-sufficient state is over. Complex layers of economic interdependency ensure that states cannot act aggressively without risking economic penalties imposed by other members of the international community, a fate even for great powers. It also makes little sense for a state to threaten its commercial partners, whose markets and capital investment are essential for its own economic growth. Secondly, territorial conquest in the nuclear age is both dangerous and costly for rogue states. The alternative – economic development through trade and foreign investment – is a much more attractive and potentially beneficial strategy (Rosecrance 1986; Strange 1991).

Neo-realists have two responses to the liberal claim that economic interdependency is pacifying international relations (Grieco 1988). First, they argue that in any struggle between competing disciplines, the anarchic environment and the insecurity it engenders will always take priority over the quest for economic prosperity. Economic interdependency will never take precedence over strategic security because states must be primarily concerned with their survival. Their capacity to explore avenues of economic cooperation will therefore be limited by how secure they feel, and the extent to which they are required to engage in military competition with others. Secondly, the idea of economic interdependence implies a misleading degree of equality and shared vulnerability to economic forces in the global economy. Interdependence does not eliminate hegemony and dependency in inter-state relations because power is very unevenly distributed throughout the world's trade and financial markets. Dominant players such as the United States have usually framed the rules under which interdependency has flourished. Conflict and cooperation is therefore unlikely to disappear, though it may be channelled into more peaceful forms.

Human rights

The advocacy of democracy and free trade foreshadows another idea which liberal internationalism introduced to international theory. Liberals have always believed that the legitimacy of domestic political orders was largely contingent upon upholding the rule of law and the state's respect for the human rights of its citizens. If it is wrong for an individual to engage in socially unacceptable or criminal behaviour, it is also wrong for states.

References to essential human needs are implicit in some of the earliest written legal codes from ancient Babylon, as well as early Buddhist,

Confucian and Hindu texts, though the first explicit mention of universal principles governing common standards of human behaviour can be found in the West.

The idea of universal human rights has its origins in the Natural Law tradition, debates in the West during the Enlightenment over the 'rights of man' and in the experience of individuals struggling against the arbitrary rule of the state. The Magna Carta in 1215, the development of English Common Law and the Bill of Rights in 1689 were significant, if evolutionary steps along the path to enshrining basic human rights in law, as were intellectual contributions from Grotius (the law of nations), Rousseau (the social contract) and Locke (popular consent, limits of sovereignty). An early legal articulation of human rights can be found in the American Declaration of Independence in 1776 ('we take these truths to be self-evident, that all men are created equal, and that they are endowed by their Creator with certain unalienable Rights, that amongst these are Life, Liberty and the pursuit of Happiness') and in France's Declaration of the Rights of Man and the Citizen in 1789 ('all men are born free and equal in their rights').

Human beings are said to be endowed – purely by reason of their humanity – with certain fundamental rights, benefits and protections. These rights are regarded as inherent in the sense they are the birthright of all, inalienable because they cannot be given up or taken away and universal since they apply to all regardless of nationality, status, gender or race.

The extension of these rights to all peoples has a particularly important place in liberal thinking about foreign policy and international relations, for two reasons. First, these rights give a legal foundation to emancipation, justice and human freedom. Their denial by state authorities is an affront to the dignity of all and a stain on the human condition. Secondly, states which treat their own citizens ethically and allow them meaningful participation in the political process are thought to be less likely to behave aggressively internationally. The task for liberals has been to develop and promote moral standards which would command universal consent, knowing that in doing so states may be required to jeopardize the pursuit of their own national interests. This has proven to be a difficult task, despite evident progress on labour rights, the abolition of slavery, the political emancipation of women in the West, the treatment of indigenous peoples and the end of white supremacism in South Africa.

The creation of important legal codes, instruments and institutions in the post-Second World War period is a measure of achievement in the area. The most important instruments are the Universal Declaration of Human Rights (1948), the International Covenant on Civil and Political Rights (1966) and the International Covenant on Economic, Social and

Cultural Rights (1966), while the International Labour Organisation (ILO) and the International Court of Justice (ICJ) play a significant institutional and symbolic role in the protection of human rights. A greater concern about genocidal crimes, the outlawing of cruel and inhuman punishment and the rights of detainees apprehended on the battlefield are a reflection of progress in the area.

In his seminal account, Vincent (1986) identified the right of the individual to be free from starvation as the only human right which is likely to receive the support of a global consensus. The world community, regardless of religious or ideological differences, agrees that a right to subsistence was essential to the dignity of humankind. Beyond this right, nation-states struggle to find agreement, not least because the developing world is suspicious that human rights advocacy from metropolitan centres is little more than a pretext for unwarranted interference in their domestic affairs. Most states are reluctant to give outsiders the power to compel them to improve their ethical performance, although there is a growing belief that the principle of territorial sovereignty should no longer be used by governments as a credible excuse for avoiding legitimate international scrutiny.

Marxists have dismissed liberal human rights as mere bourgeois freedoms which fail to address the class-based nature of exploitation contained within capitalist relations of production. Realists would add that 'conditions of profound insecurity for states do not permit ethical and humane considerations to override their primary national considerations' (Linklater 1992b: 27). After all, it is interests which determine political action and in the global arena, politics is the amoral struggle for power to advance these interests.

Liberals struggle to avoid the charge that their conceptions of democracy and human rights are culturally specific, ethnocentric and therefore irrelevant to societies which are not Western in cultural orientation. To many societies, appeals to universality may merely conceal the means by which one dominant society imposes its culture upon another, while infringing on its sovereign independence. The promotion of human rights from the core to the periphery assumes a degree of moral superiority – that the West not only possesses moral truths which others are bound to observe, but that it can sit in judgement on other societies.

The issue is further complicated by the argument that economic, social and cultural rights should precede civil and political rights – one made earlier by Communist states and more recently by a number of East Asian governments, and which is a direct challenge to the idea that human rights are indivisible and universal, a revolt against the West. It implies that the alleviation of poverty and economic development in these societies depends on the initial denial of political freedoms and human rights to the citizen. However, the claim that rights can be prioritized in this way or that procedural and substantive freedoms are incompatible is problematic and widely seen, with some justification, as a rationalization by governments for authoritarian rule.

An increasing number of conservative political leaders in East Asia have also argued that there is a superior Asian model of political and social organization comprising the principles of harmony, hierarchy and consensus (Confucianism) in contrast to what they regard as the confrontation, individualism and moral decay which characterizes Western liberalism. Regardless of how self-serving this argument is – and it is rarely offered by democratically elected rulers – it poses a fundamental challenge to Fukuyama's suggestion that in the post-Cold War period liberal democracy faces no serious universal challenges. It is clear that these states are not striving to imitate the Western route to political modernization. Some reject it outright.

Even if universal rules and instruments could be agreed upon, how could compliance with universal standards be enforced? Liberals are divided over this issue, between non-interventionists who defend state sovereignty, and those who feel that the promotion of ethical principles can justify intervention in the internal affairs of other states (see Bull 1984a).

Recent examples of so-called 'humanitarian intervention' in Cambodia, Rwanda, Serbia, Somalia and East Timor pose a growing challenge to the protection from outside interference traditionally afforded by sovereignty claims. This also applies to the prosecution of those suspected of committing war crimes and crimes against humanity by international tribunals such as the ICJ (Forbes and Hoffman 1993). The embryonic International Criminal Court (ICC) can be seen as a further expression of liberal sentiments which oppose the arbitrary cruelty of political leaders and the use of agencies of the state to inflict harm on minorities and opponents. However, its very structure and functions limit the sovereign right of a government to administer the internal affairs of their state free from outside interference. States like the United States, which refuse to ratify the ICC for reasons of sovereignty, will therefore come under increasing pressure in the years ahead to conform with what appears to be a growing global consensus.

Celebrated trials (Milošević, Saddam) and attention given to non-trials (Pinochet, Suharto) indicate a significant shift away from the traditional provision of sovereign immunity to heads of state and others guilty of war crimes and crimes against humanity. Whereas in the past justice, if dispensed at all, would come from within the state, the establishment of international legal fora and the further development of international law in this area are largely due to the influence of liberal internationalism and its emphasis on the importance of global benchmarks and the rule of law. It is true that cases like these never truly escape the political atmosphere of the day, in particular the domestic political climate in each country directly involved, however the fact that they arise at all within international legal jurisdictions indicates significant progress towards a system of global justice.

Modern forms of humanitarian intervention follow a pattern established in the middle of the eighteenth century when the British and Dutch successfully interceded on behalf of Prague's Jewish community, which was threatened with deportation by authorities in Bohemia. The protection of Christian minorities at risk in Europe and in the Orient in the eighteenth and nineteenth centuries by the Treaty of Kucuk-Kainardji (1774) and the Treaty of Berlin (1878) are also part of the same legal precedent, as is the advocacy of British Prime Minister Gladstone in the second half of the nineteenth century and US President Wilson early in the twentieth century. Vietnam's invasion of Cambodia in 1978, when refracted through the ideological prism of the Cold War, highlighted the politically contingent nature of humanitarian intervention in the modern period. Liberals who support both the sovereign rights of independent states and the right of external intervention in cases where there is an acute humanitarian crisis, find it difficult to reconcile both international norms (Chomsky 1999a).

Economy and terrorism

Fukuyama's post-Cold War optimism is on firmer ground if we consider the extent to which economic liberalism has become the dominant ideology of the contemporary period. The move towards a global political economy organized along neo-liberal lines is a trend as significant as the likely expansion of the zone of peace. As the new century opens, the world economy more closely resembles the prescriptions of Smith and Ricardo than at any previous time. And as MacPherson forecast, this development is also a measure of 'how deeply the market assumptions about the nature of man and society have penetrated liberal-democratic theory' (MacPherson 1977: 21). The dark cloud on the horizon, however, is as serious as it was unexpected. The recent wave of anti-Western Islamist terror represents a significant blockage on the path to globalization and confronts liberals with a range of intellectual dilemmas and policy reversals for which they were unprepared.

Before examining the extent to which liberalism has shaped the contours of the world economy today and the impact of Islamist terror, it is important to recognize that the experience of laissez faire capitalism in the nineteenth century challenged many liberal assumptions about human beings, the market and the role of the state. This is often forgotten or not well understood by contemporary economic liberals.

Critics such as Polanyi highlighted the extent to which material self-gain in a market society was necessary for survival in an unregulated market society, rather than a reflection of the human condition in its natural state. It is therefore unwise for liberals to generalize from the specific case of market capitalism – to believe that behaviour enforced as a result of a new and presumably transient form of political economy was a true reflection of a human being's inner self (Polanyi 1944; Block and Somers 1984).

State intervention in the economic life of a society was in fact an act of community self-defence against the destructive power of unfettered markets which, according to Polanyi, if left unregulated, threatened to annihilate society. However, state intervention in the economy was also necessary for markets to function – free trade, commercial exchanges and liberal markets have always been policies of the state and have not emerged organically or independently of it.

As List and many since have explained, the state plays a crucial role in the economic development of industrial societies, protecting embryonic industries from external competition until they are ready to win global market shares on an equal footing. There are few, if any examples of states emerging as industrial powerhouses by initially adopting a policy of free trade. Protectionism and state coordinated economic development have been key early ingredients of economic success in the modern world, as the post-war experience of East Asia suggests.

Liberalism and globalization

To a significant extent, the globalization of the world economy coincided with a renaissance of neo-liberal thinking in the Western world. The political triumph of the 'New Right' in Britain and the United States in particular during the late 1970s and 1980s was achieved at the expense of Keynesianism, the first coherent philosophy of state intervention in economic life. According to the Keynesian formula, the state intervened in the economy to smooth out the business cycle, provide a degree of social equity and security and maintain full employment. Neo-liberals, who had always favoured the free play of 'market forces' and a minimal role for the state in economic life, wanted to 'roll back' the welfare state, in the process challenging the social-democratic consensus established in most Western states during the post-war period.

Just as the ideological predilection of Western governments became more concerned with efficiency and productivity and less concerned with welfare and social justice, the power of the state to regulate the market was eroded by the forces of globalization, in particular the de-regulation of finance and currency markets. The means by which domestic societies could be managed to reduce inequalities produced by inherited social structures and accentuated by the natural workings of the market, declined significantly. In addition, the disappearance of many traditional industries in Western economies, the effects of technological change, increased competition for investment and production and the mobility of capital, undermined the bargaining power of labour. The sovereignty of capital began to reign over both the interventionary behaviour of the state and the collective power of organized working people.

There is a considerable debate over globalization, between liberals who believe it constitutes a fundamentally new phase of capitalism and statists who are sceptical of such claims (Held *et al.* 1999; Held and McGrew 2000). Liberals point to the increasing irrelevance of national borders to the conduct and organization of economic activity. They focus on the growth of free trade, the capacity of transnational corporations (TNCs) to escape political regulation and national legal jurisdictions, and the liberation of capital from national and territorial constraints (Ohmae 1995; Friedman 2000; Micklewait and Wooldridge 2000). Sceptics, on the other hand, claim that the world was less open and globalized at the end of the twentieth century than it was in the nineteenth. They suggest that the volume of world trade relative to the size of the world economy is much the same as it was in 1914, though they concede that the enormous explosion of short-term speculative capital transfers since the collapse of the Bretton Woods system in the early 1970s has restricted the planning options for national governments. Significantly, sceptics want to distinguish between the idea of an international economy with growing links between separate national economies, which they concede, and a single global political economy without meaningful national borders or divisions, which they deny (Weiss 1998; Chomsky 1999b; Hirst and Thompson 1996; Hobsbawm 2000).

The next section will examine the claims made by liberals and the extent to which their ideas have shaped the current economic order. It will focus on the contemporary nature of world trade, the questions of sovereignty and foreign investment and the challenges to liberal ideas recently posed by Islamic terrorism.

The nature of 'free trade'

For neo-liberals, the principles of free trade first enunciated by Smith and Ricardo continue to have contemporary relevance. Commercial traders should be allowed to exchange money and goods without concern for national barriers. There should be few legal constraints on international commerce, and no artificial protection or subsidies constraining the freedom to exchange. An open global market, where goods and services can pass freely across national boundaries, should be the objective of policy makers in all nation-states. Only free trade will maximize economic growth and generate the competition that will promote the most efficient use of resources, people and capital.

Conversely, 'protectionism' is seen as a pernicious influence on the body politic. Policies which protect uncompetitive industries from market principles corrupt international trade, distort market demand, artificially lower prices and encourage inefficiency, while penalizing fair traders. Protection is the cry of 'special' or 'vested' interests in society and should be resisted by government in 'the national interest'. It penalizes developing nations by excluding them from entry into the global marketplace where they can exploit their domestic advantage in cheap labour.

The cornerstone of the free trade argument is the theory of 'comparative advantage', which discourages national self-sufficiency by advising states to specialize in goods and services they can produce most cheaply – their 'factor endowments'. They can then exchange their goods for what is produced more cheaply elsewhere. As everything is then produced most efficiently according to the price mechanism, the production of wealth is maximized and everyone is better off. For Smith, the 'invisible hand' of market forces directs every member of society in every state to the most advantageous position in the global economy. The self-interest of one becomes the general interest of all.

The relevance of the theory of comparative advantage in the era of globalization has recently come under question (Strange 1985; Bairoch 1993; Daly and Cobb 1994; Clairmont 1996). The first difficulty is that it was devised at a time when there were national controls on capital movements. Ricardo and Smith assumed that capital was immobile and available only for national investment. They also assumed that the capitalist was first and foremost a member of a national political community, which was the context in which he established his commercial identity: Smith's 'invisible hand' presupposed the internal bondings of community, so that the capitalist felt a 'natural disinclination' to invest abroad. Smith and Ricardo could not have foreseen 'a world of cosmopolitan money managers and TNCs which, in addition to having limited liability and immorality conferred on them by national governments, have now transcended those very governments and no longer see the national community as their context' (Daly and Cobb 1994: 215). The emergence of capitalists who freed themselves from community obligations and loyalties, and who had no 'natural disinclination' to invest abroad, would have appeared absurd. Highly mobile and volatile capital markets are a major challenge for the theory of comparative advantage.

The second problem is that the forms of international trade have changed dramatically over recent decades. The idea of national, sovereign states trading with each other as discrete economic units is becoming an anachronism. Intra-industry or intra-firm trade dominates the manufacturing sector of the world economy. Over 40 per cent of all trade now comprises intra-firm transactions, which are centrally managed interchanges within TNCs (that cross international borders) guided by a highly 'visible hand'. Intra-firm trade runs counter to the theory of comparative advantage which advises nations to specialize in products where factor endowments provide a comparative cost advantage. The mobility of capital and technology, and the extent to which firms trade with each other, means that 'governments in virtually all industrial societies now take an active interest in trying to facilitate links between their own domestic firms – including offshoots of multinationals – and the global networks' in the strategic industries. They can no longer remain at arm's length from business as neo-liberal economic theory demands (Emy 1993: 173).

Similarly, the globalization of the world economy has seen the spread of manufacturing industries to many developing countries and the relocation of transnational manufacturing centres to what are often low-wage, high-repression areas – regions with low health and safety standards where organized labour is frequently suppressed or illegal. TNCs are becoming increasingly adept at circumventing national borders in their search for cheap labour and access to raw materials, and few states can refuse to play host to them. The creation of new centres of production occurs wherever profit opportunities can be maximized because investment decisions are governed by absolute profitability rather than comparative advantage. For liberals, this is nevertheless the best way of encouraging much-needed foreign investment in the developing world and establishing a trade profile for countries which might otherwise be excluded from world trade altogether.

Modern trading conditions have diverged significantly from the assumptions which underpin the neo-liberal analysis of how markets and trade actually work. The internationalization of production, the mobility of capital and the dominance of transnational corporations are just three developments which render theories of comparative advantage somewhat anachronistic. The idea of national sovereign states trading with each other as discrete economic units is steadily becoming the exception rather than the rule. Neo-mercantilist theory, which stresses the maximization of national wealth, also fails to explain contemporary trade realities. A more accurate description is 'corporate mercantilism', with 'managed commercial interactions within and among huge corporate groupings, and regular state intervention in the three major Northern blocs to subsidise and protect domestically-based international corporations and financial institutions' (Chomsky 1994: 95). If there is such a thing as a nation's comparative advantage it is clearly a human achievement and certainly not a gift of nature, though this view remains unorthodox within powerful economic circles.

The third challenge to the relevance of the theory of comparative advantage is the steady erosion of the rules which have underpinned multilateral trade in the post-war era. While there has been a reduction in barriers to trade *within* blocs such as the European Union and the North American Free Trade Agreement (NAFTA), they have been raised *between* blocs. Tariffs have come down but they have been replaced by a wide assortment of non-tariff barriers (NTBs), including import quotas and voluntary restraint agreements. This is a concern to small, 'fair' traders which are incapable of matching the subsidies provided by Europeans and North Americans. States which unilaterally adopt free market doctrines while leading industrial societies head in the opposite direction place themselves in a vulnerable position in the world economy. But regardless of whether tariff barriers and NTBs are dismantled, the world market would not be 'free' in any meaningful sense, because of the power of the TNCs to control and distort markets through transfer pricing and other devices.

The proliferation of free trade agreements and organizations such as NAFTA, Asia Pacific Economic Cooperation (APEC) and the WTO and the growing importance of international organizations such as the G8, the International Monetary Fund (IMF) and World Bank is indicative of the influence of neo-liberalism in the post-Cold War period. These are powerful transnational bodies which embody free trade as their governing ideology. To their supporters, they provide developing societies with the only opportunity to overcome financial hardship and modernize their economies. To their critics, however, they impose free market strictures on developing societies. They are primarily organizations which formalize and institutionalize market relationships between states. By locking the developing world into agreements which force them to lower their protective barriers, NAFTA and the WTO, for example, prevent the South from developing trade profiles which diverge from the model dictated by their supposed 'comparative advantage'. The IMF and the World Bank, on the other hand, make the provision of finance (or, more accurately, 'debt') to developing societies conditional on their unilateral acceptance of free market rules for their economies – the 'conditionality' of the so-called 'structural adjustment policies' or SAPs.

Critics attack these institutions for legitimizing only one kind of global order, based on unequal market relations. Specifically, the institutions are criticized for imposing identical prescriptions for economic development on all countries, regardless of what conditions prevail locally. Developing societies are expected to adopt the free market blueprint (sometimes called the 'Washington Consensus') – opening their economies up to foreign investment, financial de-regulation, reductions in government expenditure and budgetary deficits, the privatization of government-owned enterprises, the abolition of protection and subsidies, developing export orientated economies – or risk the withholding of much needed aid and finance. And because they are required to remove national controls on capital movements – which make it possible for states to reach their own conclusions about investment and spending priorities – the direction of their economic development is increasingly set by amorphous financial markets which act on profit opportunities rather than out of any consideration of national or community interest.

Arguments for free trade are still powerfully made on the grounds of economic efficiency and as the only way of integrating the developing world into the wider global economy. Protectionism within the North is said primarily to hurt the South by pricing their economies out of markets in the industrialized world, thus denying them the opportunity to modernize their economies.

For leading players, however, free trade is often non-reciprocal and an ideological weapon used to regulate the economic development of subordinate societies. Their rhetoric supporting the sanctity of market principles is rarely matched by their own economic behaviour. This tendency, together with fundamental changes to the structure of the world economy and the forms of international trade, casts some doubt on the extent to which liberals can explain the globalization of the world economy solely on their own terms.

Sovereignty and foreign investment

The enormous volumes of unregulated capital liberated by the collapse of the Bretton Woods system in the early 1970s, have transformed the relationships between states and markets. Credit (bonds and loans), investment (Foreign Direct Investment, or FDI) and money (foreign exchange) now flow more freely across the world than commodities. The resulting increase in the power of transnational capital and the diminution of national economic sovereignty is perhaps the most dramatic realization of liberal economic ideas (Strange 1996, 1998).

The relationship between a nation's economic prosperity and the world's money markets is decisive. Because most states are incapable of generating sufficient endogenous wealth to finance their economic development, governments need to provide domestic economic conditions which will attract foreign investment into their countries. In a world where capital markets are globally linked and money can be electronically transferred around the world in microseconds, states are judged in terms of their comparative 'hospitality' to foreign capital: that is, they must offer the most attractive investment climates to relatively scarce supplies of money. This gives the foreign investment community significant leverage over policy settings and the course of a nation's economic development generally, and constitutes a diminution in the country's economic sovereignty.

The power of transnational finance capital in the modern period can scarcely be overestimated. The volume of foreign exchange trading in the major financial centres of the world, estimated at over $US1.5 trillion per day, has come to dwarf international trade by at least sixty times. UN statistics suggest that the world's 100 largest TNCs, with assets of over $US5 trillion, account for a third of the total FDI of their home states, giving them increasing influence over the economies of host countries.

The brokers on Wall Street and in Tokyo, the clients of the 'screen jockeys' in the foreign exchange rooms, and the auditors from credit ratings agencies such as Moody's and Standard & Poor's, now pass daily judgements on the management of individual economies, and signal to the world's financial community the comparative profit opportunities to be found in a particular country. Inappropriate interventionary policies by government can be quickly deterred or penalized with a (threatened) reduction in the nation's credit rating, a 'run' (sell off) on its currency or an investment 'strike'. The requirements of the international markets can be ignored only at a nation's economic peril. Not only have nation-states lost direct control over the value of their currencies and the movements of capital around the world, they can no longer determine the institutional settings in which capital markets operate. Neo-liberal financial commentators regard this development as a positive change, believing that on the question of allocating resources, markets rather than the governments know what is in peoples' best interests.

Finance markets, dominated by large banks and financial institutions, insurance companies, brokers and speculators, exist only to maximize their own wealth. There is no compelling reason for them to act in the interests of the poor, the homeless, the infirm or those who are deprived of their basic human rights by their own governments. States which cede economic sovereignty to these global players in the name of free trade and commerce therefore run the risk of elevating private commercial gain to the primary foreign policy objective of the state.

When the foreign investment community is freed from state barriers and controls, and able to choose the most profitable location for its capital, it has the effect of homogenizing the economic development of nation-states across the globe. In what is effectively a 'bidding war' for much-needed infusions of capital, states are driven by the lowest common denominator effect to reduce their regulations, standards, wages and conditions, in order to appear attractive to the investor community. Priority is given to the drive for efficiency and profits. The threat of disinvestment becomes the stick for markets to wield over the heads of government. For liberals, this is a pleasing reversal of modern history which they see as a struggle for liberation from the clutches of arbitrary state power. Ironically, in many instances the key to attracting overseas investment is for the host government to provide the transnational investor with subsidies and protection from market forces. In some cases, this is the only way states can win and maintain the confidence of global markets.

The ill-fated Multilateral Agreement on Investments (MAI) was a vivid illustration of just how far governments in the developed world have been prepared to follow liberal advice and surrender their discretionary economic power to the markets. In this case Organization for Economic Cooperation and Development (OECD) members were offering voluntarily to restrict their own ability to discriminate against foreign capital. The MAI is a reminder that, as with the establishment of national markets in the nineteenth century, globalization is not the result of the gradual and spontaneous emancipation of the economic sphere from government control. On the contrary, it has been the outcome of conscious and sometimes violent state intervention by advanced capitalist states. Just as domestically the labour market can be 'freed' only by legislative restrictions placed on trades unions, the creation of the post-war liberal trading regime and the de-regulation of the world's capital markets in the 1970s required deliberate acts by interventionary states.

During the current phase of globalization, national economic sovereignty has not so much been lost but either enthusiastically given away or begrudgingly surrendered. The state's capacity to direct the national economy has been deliberately and significantly undercut by the globalization of relations of production and exchange. Significant sovereign power has been ceded to bond holders, funds managers, currency traders, speculators, transnational banks and insurance companies – groups that by definition are democratically unaccountable in any national jurisdiction. In effect, the world economy has come to resemble the global strategic environment. It has become anarchic in character and, as a consequence, the competition for economic security is as intense as the search for strategic security.

Unsurprisingly, concern about a growing 'democratic deficit' has arisen within liberal political philosophy. David Held's (1995) advocacy of cosmopolitan democracy is seen as somewhat utopian by hard-nosed realists, however it is a serious attempt to bring some of the forces of globalization under a degree of popular control. The proposals such as regional parliaments and the devolution of sovereign power to regional bodies, universal human rights benchmarks entrenched in domestic jurisdictions and monitored by international courts, radical reform of the United Nations and the promotion of a global civil society are serious suggestions for extending and modernizing democratic politics. The work of Held and his colleagues is an important reminder that as well as rendering significant economic change, globalization has important political challenges and implications which liberals cannot ignore (Held 1995; Archibugi and Held 1995; Archibugi 1998).

Non-state terrorism

Whether or not the current wave of Islamic militancy is the latest chapter in a long-standing revolt against the West, there can be little doubt that it represents a direct challenge to both the claim that liberal democracy is the universal destination for the species and the assumption that globalization is inexorable. However incoherent and unlikely it is as a political programme, Islamic terrorism is profoundly anti-secular and an opponent of liberal modernity (Gray 2004).

It therefore seems premature and misleading for liberals to claim that the emergence of Al-Qaeda and affiliated groups which perpetrate transnational terrorism constitutes a victory for the deterritorialization of world politics (Buzan 2003: 297, 303). Rather as David Harvey notes, 'the war on terror, swiftly followed by the prospect of war with Iraq ... [has] allowed the state to accumulate more power', a claim difficult to refute and one that poses an unexpected new challenge to liberals who believed that globalization was finally eroding the sovereign significance of the state (Harvey 2003: 17). The national security state has been revived.

The resuscitation of state power across the industrialized world after the 9/11 attacks has taken numerous forms, including new restrictions on civil liberties, greater powers of surveillance and detention, increased military spending and the expansion of intelligence services. The threats posed by Islamic terror and the dangers of Weapons of Mass Destruction (WMD) have also been met by an increase in state intervention around the world, in particular by US-led coalitions acting in Afghanistan and Iraq. With each subsequent terrorist assault, states which consider themselves innocent victims have been emboldened to interfere in each others' internal affairs – even pre-emptively.

Pre-emption, the disarmament of states alleged to possess WMD, regime change, humanitarianism and the spread of democracy have all been invoked as public justifications for these interventions, although critics have pointed to traditional geo-strategic rationales beneath the surface. Many states, such as China, Israel and Russia, have also used the cover provided by the 'war against terror' to settle domestic scores with secessionists, dissidents and those resisting their territorial occupations. Others seem to be victims of 'blowback', reaping disastrous and unintended consequences from earlier foreign policy actions. Regardless of what the true motives of these interventions are, the irony of socially conservative, economically neo-liberal governments expanding the reach and size of government should not be lost on anyone (Johnson 2002).

The return of the overarching state is perhaps an unsurprising response to community calls for protection from non-state terrorism. When citizens of a state require emergency medical relief, as many victims of the Bali bombings did in October 2002, there is little point appealing to market forces for help. Nor can those responsible for attacks such as the Beslan school atrocity in September 2004 be hunted down, disarmed and prosecuted by privately owned TNCs. Even if the state is no longer prepared to insulate its citizens from the vicissitudes of the world economy, it is still expected to secure them from the threat of terrorism. Only the state can meet these and many other challenges such as 'border protection' and transnational crime. There are no market-based solutions to the dangers posed by what seems to be the latest chapter in the revolt against the West.

Since the end of the Cold War, realists such as Kenneth Waltz have argued that in the absence of effective countervailing pressures, the United States is likely to become increasingly unilateral in seeking to secure its foreign policy interests, and in so doing rely on military power to realize its vision of a new world order. The 'war against terror' has seemingly changed little in this regard. If anything, these events have enhanced a trend which some liberals had either believed or hoped had passed into history.

The Marxist historian Eric Hobsbawm has observed that 'the basic element to understanding the present situation is that 9/11 did not threaten the US. It was a terrible human tragedy which humiliated the US, but in no sense was it any weaker after those attacks. Three, four or five attacks will not change the position of the US or its relative power in the world' (Hobsbawm 2002).

This view is similar to Waltz's claim that the problem of terrorism does not challenge the continuities of international politics. 'Although terrorists can be terribly bothersome', says Waltz, 'they hardly pose threats to the fabric of a society or the security of the state … Terrorism does not change the first basic fact of international politics – the gross imbalance of world power' in favour of the United States. 'Instead, the effect of September 11 has been to enhance American power and extend its military presence in the world' (Waltz 2002: 348–53). So much for the end of the nation-state.

Realists in the United States also led the intellectual opposition to Washington's attack on Iraq in March 2003, arguing that Saddam Hussein had been successfully contained, that he was prevented from using his WMD against the West because of the likely consequences to him and that for similar reasons he couldn't risk passing these weapons – if he in fact possessed them – to groups such as Al-Qaeda. As during the Second Cold War, realists found themselves in the unusual position of being at the limits of respectable dissent in debates over the Iraq war as a consequence of the influence of the misnamed neo-conservatives, whose muscular liberalism underwrote the administration of George W. Bush (Mearsheimer and Walt 2002).

Conclusion

At the beginning of this chapter, it was argued that liberalism was an 'inside-out' approach to international relations, because liberals favour a world in which the endogenous determines the exogenous. Their challenge is to extend the legitimacy of domestic political arrangements found within democratic states to the relationships between all nation-states. To put it another way, liberals believe that democratic society, in which civil liberties are protected and market relations prevail, can have an international analogue in the form of a peaceful global order. The domestic free market has its counterpart in the open, globalized world economy. Parliamentary debate and accountability is reproduced in international fora such as the United Nations. And the legal protection of civil rights within liberal democracies is extended to the promotion of human rights across the world. With the collapse of Communism as an alternative political and economic order, the potential for continuity between the domestic and the international became greater than in any previous period.

Fukuyama had reason to be optimistic. The spread of liberal democracies and the zone of peace was an encouraging development, as is the realization by states that trade and commerce is more closely correlated with economic success than territorial conquest. The number of governments enjoying civilian rather than military rule is increasing, and there are signs that ethical considerations and ideas of human justice have a permanent place on the diplomatic agenda. The collapse of Marxism as a legitimate alternative political order removes a substantial barrier to the spread of liberal democracies, and there can be little doubt that the great powers are now much less inclined to use force to resolve their political differences with each other. It appears that liberal democracies are in the process of constructing a separate peace.

The globalization of the world economy means that there are few obstacles to international trade. Liberals want to remove the influence of the state in commercial relations between businesses and individuals, and the decline of national economic sovereignty is an indication that the corrupting influence of the state is rapidly diminishing. TNCs and capital markets wield significant influence over the shape of the world economy, in the process homogenizing the political economies of every member state of the international community.

Globalization has undermined the nation-state in other ways that have pleased liberals. The capacity of each state to direct the political loyalties of its citizens has been weakened by an increasing popular awareness of the problems faced by the entire human species. The state cannot prevent its citizens turning to a range of sub-national and transnational agents to secure their political identities and promote their political objectives. Sovereignty is no longer an automatic protection against external interference called 'humanitarian intervention'. And decision making on a range of environmental, economic and security questions has become internationalized, rendering national administration often much less important than transnational political cooperation.

Despite these important changes, there are also counter-trends which can be identified. Realists would argue that liberals such as Ohmae are premature in announcing the demise of the nation-state. They would remind the enthusiasts for globalization that as a preferred form of political community, the nation-state still has no serious rival. There are currently over 200 nation-states in the world asserting their political independence.

Realists cite a number of important powers retained by the state despite globalization, including monopoly control of the weapons of war and their legitimate use, and the sole right to tax its citizens. They would argue that only the nation-state can still command the political allegiances of its citizens or adjudicate in disputes between them. And it is still only the nation-state which has the exclusive authority to bind the whole community to international law.

They would question the extent to which globalization today is an unprecedented phenomenon, citing the nineteenth century as period when similar levels of economic interdependence existed. They would also point to the growing number of states which reject the argument that Western modernity is universally valid or that political development always terminates at liberal-capitalist democracy. More recently realists have highlighted the expanding power and reach of the state as a result of the latest wave of anti-Western Islamic militancy – a significant reversal for liberals who anticipated the imminent decline of the nation-state in modern life. Islamism is a direct challenge to liberal assumptions about economics and politics terminating at a liberal capitalist consensus.

Unpredictable challenges of this kind have left liberalism on the back foot, questioning whether the linear path to improving the human condition is as straight and as inexorable as they thought only a few short years ago.

Chapter 4

The English School

ANDREW LINKLATER

'The English School' is a term coined in the 1970s to describe a group of predominantly British or British-inspired writers for whom international society is the primary object of analysis (Jones 1981; Linklater and Suganami 2006). Its most influential members include Hedley Bull, Martin Wight, John Vincent and Adam Watson whose main publications appeared in the period between the mid-1960s and late 1980s (see Bull 1977; Bull and Watson 1984; Wight 1977, 1991; Vincent 1986; Watson 1982). Robert Jackson, Tim Dunne and Nicholas Wheeler have been among the most influential members of the English School in more recent years (Jackson 2000; Dunne 1998; Wheeler 2000). Since the late 1990s, the English School has enjoyed a renaissance in large part because of the efforts of Barry Buzan, Richard Little and a number of other scholars (Buzan 2001, 2003; Little 2000). The English School remains one of the most important approaches to international politics although its influence is probably greater in Britain than in most other societies where International Relations is taught.

The foundational claim of the English School is that sovereign states form a society, albeit an anarchic one in that they do not have to submit to the will of a higher power. The fact that states have succeeded in creating a society of sovereign equals is for the English School one of the most fascinating dimensions of international relations. There is, they argue, a surprisingly high level of order and a surprisingly low level of violence between states given that their condition is one of anarchy (in the sense of the absence of a higher political authority). They invite their readers to reflect on the probable level of violence, fear, insecurity and distrust in even the most stable of domestic societies if sovereign authority collapsed. A condition of chaos would be the most likely result, and yet this is not the central characteristic of world politics.

This is not to suggest that the English School ignores the phenomenon of violence in relations between states. Its members regard violence as an endemic feature of the 'anarchical society' (the title of Hedley Bull's most famous work, 1977) but they also stress that it is controlled to an important extent by international law and morality. Even so, confusion about the central purpose of the School can result from the fact that its members seem distinctively realist at times. This is most obvious in Wight's influential essay, 'Why is there no International Theory?' (1966), where he maintained that domestic politics is the sphere of the good life whereas international politics is the realm of security and survival (Wight 1966a: 33). Realism is also evident in his argument that international relations is 'incompatible with progressivist theory'. In a statement that seems to place him squarely in the realist camp, Wight (1996: 26) maintained that Sir Thomas More would recognize the basic features of international politics in the 1960s since nothing fundamental had changed during the last few centuries. Some have argued that the English School is essentially a British variant on realism which exaggerates the importance of the veneer of society and pays too little attention to its role in safeguarding the privileges of the leading powers and other dominant interests (for a critique of this interpretation, see Wheeler and Dunne 1996).

Members of the English School are attracted by elements of realism and idealism, yet gravitate towards the middle ground, never wholly reconciling themselves to either point of view. This is precisely how Wight (1991) described 'rationalism' or the 'Grotian tradition', from which the English School is descended, in a famous series of lectures delivered at the London School of Economics in the 1950s. He argued in those lectures that 'rationalism' was the 'via media' between realism and what he called revolutionism – a group of perspectives which believed in the possibility of replacing international order with peace and justice (see also Wight 1966: 91). In this context, he refers to Grotius' comment in his great work, *De Jure Belli ac Pacis* which was published in 1625, that those who believe that anything goes in war are as wrong as those who believe the use of force can never be justified. Grotius envisaged an international society in which violence between Catholic and Protestant states would be replaced by a condition of relative peaceful coexistence. In his lectures, Wight lamented the fact that the debates between realism and utopionism in the inter-war years had led to the neglect of the *via media* with its concentration on international society.

In short, members of the English School maintain that the international political system is more civil and orderly than realists and neo-realists suggest. However, the fact that violence is ineradicable in their view puts them at odds with utopians who believe in the possibility of perpetual peace. There is no expectation among its members that the international political system will come to enjoy levels of close cooperation and the relatively high level of security found in the world's more stable national societies. There is, they argue, more to international politics than realists suggest but there will always be much less than the cosmopolitan desires. This is why it makes sense to argue that members of the English School belief there has been a limited degree of progress in international politics.

The nature of the '*via media*' can be explored further by noting the contrasts with realism and 'revolutionism' (as noted, a term Wight used to describe various perspectives including cosmopolitanism which aim to replace international order with a universal community of humankind) and by further clarifying the claim that members of the English School offer a limited progressivist account of world politics. As discussed in Chapter 3, realism emphasizes the unending competition for power and security in the world of states. Sovereignty, anarchy and the security dilemma are crucial terms in its lexicon; in the main, the idea of global progress is absent from its vocabulary. Moral principles and social progress are seen as relevant to domestic politics where trust prevails because security is provided by the state, but cosmopolitan projects are said to have little importance for international relations where states must provide for their own security and trust few of their neighbours. In the latter domain, moral principles serve to legitimate national interests and to stigmatize principal competitors: they are not the basis for a new form of world political organization which will supersede the nation-state.

The existence of a more or less unbridgeable gulf between domestic and international politics is a central theme in realist and especially in neo-realist thought. By contrast, cosmopolitan thinkers envisage a world order – but not necessarily a world government – in which universal moral principles are taken seriously and the gulf between domestic and international politics is reduced or eliminated. Global political reform is not only possible but of vital importance to end the struggle for power and security. The tension between these two approaches has been crucial to the history of international thought and was clearly evident in the early twentieth-century debate between realists and idealists.

The characteristics of that debate need not detain us. Suffice it to note that it was largely about whether the development of a strong sense of moral obligation to human beings everywhere was the key to building peaceful International Relations. Liberal internationalists believed that realism was unjustifiably pessimistic about the feasibility of radical change and revealed a lack of political imagination. Realists thought that liberal internationalists were naively optimistic about the prospects for a new world order based on the rule of law, open diplomacy and collective security, and they thought their ideas were dangerous because they distracted attention from the main task of foreign policy which is to ensure the security and survival of the state. The violence of 'the inter-war years' and the tensions peculiar to the bipolar era secured the victory of realism.

Bull argued that realists focus on the struggle for power and security in an international system while their liberal or utopian opponents focus on the possibility of a world community. The English School recognizes that each approach contains insights about the condition of international politics. The realist's claim that states, unlike individuals in civil society, are forced to provide for their own security in the condition of anarchy is valuable, as is its emphasis on how adversaries seek to outmanoeuvre, control and overpower one another. However, this perspective captures only part of the substance of world politics. The international system is not a state of war despite the fact that each state has a monopoly of control of the instruments of violence within its territory. Because of a common interest in placing restraints on the use of force, states have developed the art of accommodation and compromise which makes an international society possible.

Watson (1987) later argued that a 'strong case can be made out, on the evidence of past systems as well as the present one, that the regulatory rules and institutions of a system usually, and perhaps inexorably, develop to the point where the members become conscious of common values and the system becomes an international society'. This might seem to give the utopian thinker hope that further progress is achievable, but this is not a position that the English School generally endorses. They argue that the utopian vision of a universal human community draws on the fact that concerns about human rights, peace and justice have long influenced the development of world politics. Like realists, members of the English School begin with the condition of anarchy but they are more inclined to take arguments for global reform seriously rather than to regard them as either peripheral issues in world politics or as simply one of the ways in which states compete for influence and power. But they stress that the visionaries are wrong in thinking that the current international order is merely a stepping stone to a universal community. The crucial point is not that states are obsessed simply with the struggle for power but that many have different conceptions of human rights and global justice and conflicting views about how such ideals can be implemented. The contemporary debate about whether the time has come to introduce a principle of humanitarian intervention where a state is guilty of the gross violation of human rights is a classic example of the kind of moral disagreement which the English School regards as typical of the society of states (Jackson 2000; Wheeler 2000). Indeed, members of the English School stress that efforts to improve international politics can produce major moral disagreements which sour relations between states and damage international order. Most have been sceptical of proposals for large-scale global reform and most have doubted that any of them will ever appeal to the majority of nation-states or to their most powerful members.

The crucial point is that neither realism nor revolutionism recognizes the extent to which states have succeeded in creating an international society. The English School insists, however, that the survival of international order can never be taken for granted because it can be undermined by revolutionary or aggressive powers. There is no guarantee that any international society will survive indefinitely or succeed in keeping crude self-interest at bay, but for as long as international society exists it is important to ask whether it can be improved. Noting that demands for morality and justice have always formed an important part of the history of international relations, Wight (1977: 192) argued that 'the fundamental political task at all times [is] to provide order, or security, from which law, justice and prosperity may afterwards develop'. Members of the English School were understandably inclined to stress the importance of order rather than justice or prosperity during the Cold War years, but since the mid-1980s many have taken a more explicitly normative stance on questions of poverty and human rights. In the more optimistic world of the 1990s, members of the 'critical international society' approach became particularly interested in the possibility that states could be 'good international citizens' promoting a more cosmopolitan world order (Dunne 1998; Wheeler and Dunne 1998).

Members of the English School have long argued that the great powers can be 'great responsibles' which do not place their own interests before the task of strengthening international order. However, it is usually the great powers that pose the greatest threat to the survival of international society (Wight 1991: 130). In the age of American hegemony, members of the English School have returned to one of its central concerns – whether international society can survive in the absence of a balance of power. Dunne (2003) highlights this question in his account of the contemporary phase of US hegemony with the stress on preventive war to deal with regimes which are believed to be prepared to share weapons of mass destruction with terrorist organizations. The threat to international society is stressed in this account. Other members of the English School continue to examine the ways in which international society can be improved. This is especially evident in Wheeler's writings on the need to introduce a limited principle of humanitarian intervention and in Keal's argument for changes which will improve the position of indigenous peoples (Wheeler 2000; Keal 2003). Indeed, one would expect proponents of a perspective which is located between the poles of realism and utopianism to explore the prospects for improving international society and the constraints that stand in the way. No member of the

English School is naïve about the possibilities for radical change; but increasing divisions between more 'radical' and more 'conservative' proponents have appeared in recent years, not least over the question of whether the society of states should introduce a principle of humanitarian intervention.

We will return to these themes later in this chapter which is organized under four main headings. The first focuses on the idea of order and society in core English School texts. The second considers the English School's analysis of the relative importance of order and justice in the traditional European society of states. This is followed by an assessment of the 'revolt against the West' and the emergence of the universal society of states in which various demands for justice are frequently heard. The fourth section returns to the question of whether the English School remains committed to the notion that only limited progress is possible in international relations and whether its claim to be the *via media* between realism and revolutionism is convincing in the light of current debates and developments in the field.

From power to order: international society

We have seen that the English School is principally concerned with explaining the surprisingly high level of order which exists between independent political communities in the condition of anarchy. Some such as Wight (1977: 43) were fascinated by the small number of international societies which have existed in human history and by their relatively short life-spans, all previous examples having been destroyed by empire after a few centuries. Wight (1977: 35–9) also noted the propensity for internal schism in the form of international revolutions which bring transnational political forces and ideologies rather than separate states into conflict. He posed the interesting question of whether commerce first brought different societies into contact and provided the context within which a society of states would later develop (1977: 33). In his remarks about the three international societies about which a great deal is known (the Ancient Chinese, the Graeco-Roman and the modern society of states) Wight (1977: 33–5) maintained each had emerged in a region with a high level of linguistic and cultural unity. Crucially, independent political communities felt they belonged to the civilized world and were superior to their neighbours. Their sense of their 'cultural differentiation' from allegedly semi-civilized and barbaric peoples facilitated communication between them and made it easier to agree on the rights and duties which bound them together as members of an exclusive society of states.

Writing on the evolution of the modern society of states Wight's protégé, Hedley Bull (1977: 82) observed that in 'the form of the doctrine of natural law, ideas of human justice historically preceded the development of ideas of interstate or international justice and provided perhaps the principal intellectual foundations upon which these latter ideas at first rested'. This seems to echo Wight's position that some sense of cultural unity is needed before an international society can develop but, in the end, this was not Bull's position. He believed that international societies can exist in the absence of linguistic, cultural or religious agreement. To clarify the point, Bull introduced a distinction between an international system and an international society which does not exist in Wight's own work. A 'system of states (or international system)', he argued, 'is formed when two or more states have sufficient contact between them, and have sufficient impact on one another's decisions to cause them to behave – at least in some measure – as parts of a whole' (1977: 9–10). A 'society of states', on the other hand, comes into being 'when a group of states, conscious of certain common interests and common values, form a society in the sense that they conceive themselves to be bound by a common set of rules in their relations with one another, and share in the working of common institutions' (1977: 13). This is an important distinction which highlights the need to give a more precise account of how international societies have evolved.

As we have seen, Bull maintained that order can exist between states which do not feel they belong to a common civilization. John Vincent (1984b: 213) made the same point when he argued that international society is 'functional' or utilitarian rather than 'cultural' or moral in character. A pragmatic need to coexist is enough to produce what Bull (1977: 316) called a 'diplomatic culture' – that is, a system of conventions and institutions which preserves order between states with radically different cultures, ideologies and aspirations. He added that the diplomatic culture will be stronger if anchored in an 'international political culture' – that is, if states have a similar way of life. Illustrating the point, Bull and Watson argued that the modern society of states which is the first truly global one does not rest on an international political culture in the way that the European society of states did in the nineteenth century. However, the basic rules of the international society which originated in Europe have been accepted by a large majority of its former colonies, now equal sovereign members of the first global society of states. No international political culture underpins and supports the diplomatic culture, yet Bull (1977: 316–17) thought that this might change if different elites across the world came to share a 'cosmopolitan culture' of modernity.

Bull's *The Anarchical Society* (1977) provides the most detailed analysis of the foundations of international order. He argues that all societies – domestic and international – have arrangements for protecting the three 'primary goals' of placing constraints on violence, upholding property rights and ensuring agreements are kept (Bull 1977: 53–5). The fact that these primary goals are common to domestic and international society explains Bull's rejection of 'the domestic analogy' which is the idea that order will come into being only if states surrender their sovereign powers to centralized institutions of the kind that provide order within nation-states (Suganami 1989). As we have seen, English School writers break with realism because they believe that states can enjoy the benefits of society without surrendering their sovereign powers to a higher authority. Bull's approach argues that states are usually committed to limiting the use of force, ensuring respect for property and preserving trust not only in relations between citizens but in their dealings with one another as independent political communities. This shared ground rather than any common culture or way of life is the real foundation of international society.

Domestic societies and international society are both concerned with the satisfaction of primary goals but the latter is distinctive because it is an 'anarchical society'. Citizens of the modern state are governed by the 'primary rules' of society which set out how they should behave, and also by 'secondary rules' which determine how these basic rules concerning conduct should be created, interpreted and enforced (Bull 1977: 133). In the modern state, central institutions have the right to make primary and secondary rules whereas, in international society, states create primary rules as well as secondary rules pertaining to their creation, interpretation and enforcement. A related point is that international society has a set of primary goals which are uniquely its own (1977: 16–20). The idea that entities must be sovereign to be members of international society is one of its distinctive features, as is the conviction that the society of states is the only legitimate form of global political organization and the belief that states have a duty to respect the sovereignty of all others. These goals may conflict with one another, as Bull observed in his writings on order and justice which will be considered later in this chapter.

Societies of states exist because most political communities want to place constraints on the use of force and bring civility to their external relations. An interesting question is whether some national societies are more likely than others to attach special value to international society and to take care of its institutions which include diplomacy, international law and the practice of balancing the military power of states that may aspire to lay down the law to others. English School writers argue that international society can be multidenominational and include states with different cultures and philosophies of government. A central task of diplomacy in their view is to find some common ground between radically different and often mutually suspicious states. They are unconvinced by those who believe that the members of the society of states should have identical political ideologies, a point Wight (1991: 41–2) made against liberals such as Kant. However, writers such as Wight have also argued that societies with a strong commitment to constitutional politics and a history of resistance to political absolutism played a vital role in the formation of the European society of states and in the development of international law (Linklater 1993). It is worth considering this theme in the light of neo-realist and liberal discussions of the relationship between the states-system and its constituent parts.

The neo-realist argument of Kenneth Waltz (1979) maintains that the international system compels all states to take part in the struggle for power and security irrespective of regime type and ideological commitment. In opposition to neo-realism, Michael Doyle (1986) has argued that liberal states have a strong predisposition towards peace with each other, though not with non-liberal states to the same extent. The crucial question here is how far the 'inside' affects the 'outside', or how far domestic national preferences are overridden by the need to promote power and security in the condition of anarchy. For members of the English School it is essential to understand how the 'inside' influences the 'outside' and vice versa. Wight's work (1977) on international legitimacy illustrates the point. One part of this essay deals with the move from the dynastic principle of government to the conviction that the state should represent the nation as a whole, and with how the rules governing membership of international society changed in the process. In this context Wight (1977: 153) noted that 'these principles of legitimacy mark the region of approximation *between* international and domestic politics. They are principles that prevail (or are at least proclaimed) *within* a majority of the states that form international society, as well as in the relations between them' (emphases in the original). Exactly the same point can be made about contemporary claims that the legitimate members of international society should respect human rights or be committed to democracy. This is one of the respects in which the English School differs from neo-realism. From the latter standpoint, the relations between states are rather like the relations between firms in a marketplace – all actors are caught up in a world of quasi-physical forces. The English School rejects this systemic approach to international politics which ignores the way in which domestic and international principles of right conduct or reasonable behaviour interact to shape the society of states. This focus on the 'normative' and 'institutional' factors which give international society its own 'logic' ultimately distinguishes the English School from neo-realism (Bull and Watson 1984: 9). This focus makes the English School a natural ally of constructivism, which is discussed in Chapter 8.

Order and justice in international relations

The English School is interested in the processes which transform systems of states into societies of states and in the norms and institutions which prevent the collapse of civility and the re-emergence of unbridled power. It is also concerned with the question of whether societies of states can develop means of promoting justice for individuals and their immediate associations. Bull in particular distinguished between international societies and international systems, but he also identified different types of international society in order to cast light on the relationship between order and justice in world affairs.

In an early essay (1966a), Bull distinguished between the 'solidarist' or 'Grotian' and 'pluralist' conceptions of international society. He maintained that the 'central Grotian assumption is that of the solidarity, or potential solidarity, of the states comprising international society, with respect to the enforcement of the law' (Bull 1966a: 52). Solidarism is apparent in the Grotian conviction that there is a clear distinction between just and unjust wars, and in the assumption 'from which [the] right of humanitarian intervention is derived ... that individual human beings are subjects of international law and members of international society in their own right' (1966a: 64). Pluralism, as expounded by the eighteenth-century international lawyer, Vattel, rejects this approach, arguing that 'states do not exhibit solidarity of this kind, but are capable of agreeing only for certain minimum purposes which fall short of that of the enforcement of the law' (1966a: 52). A related argument is that states rather than individuals are the basic members of international society (1966a: 68). Having made this distinction, Bull asked whether there was any evidence that the pluralist international society of the post-Second World War era was becoming more solidarist. His answer in *The Anarchical Society* was that expectations of greater solidarity were seriously 'premature' (Bull 1977: 73).

To understand the reasons for this conclusion it is necessary to turn to Bull's discussion of the conflict between the primary goals of international society (1977: 16–18, Chapter 4). Bull argued that the goal of preserving the sovereignty of each state has often clashed with the goal of preserving the balance of power and maintaining peace. Polish independence was sacrificed on three occasions in the eighteenth century for the sake of international equilibrium. The League of Nations chose not to defend Abyssinia from Italian aggression because Britain and France needed Italy to balance the power of Nazi Germany. In such cases, order took priority over justice which requires that each sovereign state should be treated equally. Contemporary international society contains other examples of the tension between order and justice. Order requires efforts to prevent further additions to the nuclear club, but justice suggests all states have an equal right to acquire weapons of mass destruction (1977: 227–8).

A related point is that states have different and often conflicting ideas about justice, and that there is a danger they will undermine international society if states try to impose their views on others. Efforts to apply principles of justice to international relations are often highly selective in any event, as was the case with the war crimes tribunals at the end of the Second World War (1977: 89). What some thought was the reasonable response of the civilized world was 'victor's justice' to others. The same point has been made by Milošević and Saddam Hussein in recent times. The different responses to NATO's action against Serbia in 1999 also illustrate the point. What leaders such as Blair regard as essential if the world is to be rid of murderous regimes is for others nothing other than the promotion of Western norms and interests which results in a new imperialism. Significantly, Bull was keen to stress that Western liberal conceptions of human rights had to recognize their values did not appeal to many non-Western groups. His argument was that the advocates of universal human rights had to appreciate that tensions over the meaning of such rights were unavoidable in a multicultural society of states; they had to try to understand these deep moral and cultural differences rather than conclude that other peoples were less rational and enlightened (1977: 126; see also Bull 1979a).

States may not agree on the meaning of justice but, Bull argued, they can concur about how to maintain order among themselves. Most agree that each state should respect the sovereignty of the others and observe the principle of non-intervention. Each society can then promote its notion of the good life within its own territory, recognized as an equal by all others. But although Bull drew attention to the tension between order and justice, he also argued that international order has moral value since 'it is instrumental to the goal of order in human society as a whole'. 'Order among all mankind', he argued, '[is] of primary value, not order within the society of states' (1977: 22), and 'a world society or community' is a goal which all 'intelligent and sensitive persons' should take seriously (1977: 289). This apparent cosmopolitanism stands uneasily alongside his conviction that there is little evidence that different societies are about to agree on what it would mean to build a world community. But the implication seems to be that states should try to improve international society whenever circumstances allow (see Buzan 2004 for a recent discussion of the relationship between international society and world society in the English School).

Wight's claim that 'rationalism' is the *via media* between realism and revolutionism is worth recalling at this point. Read alongside Bull's writings on order and justice, this can be taken to mean that the English School believes that the existence of a society of states is evidence that progress has been made in agreeing on some basic principles of coexistence and rudimentary forms of cooperation. The tension between order and justice is a reminder that progress has not advanced very far. Revolutionists or Kantians are accused of failing to recognize the difficulty that states face in progressing together in the same normative direction. It follows that the English School must always be interested in how naked power or a lack of prudent diplomacy can undo the limited progress that has occurred; and it must also be interested in whether there are any signs that states are making progress in creating a more just international society.

The development of English School thinking about human rights is fascinating in this regard. Bull (1977: 83) argued that in the recent history of international society pluralism has triumphed over solidarism. In recent centuries, the solidarist belief in the primacy of individual human rights had survived albeit 'underground'. It might even appear that states had entered into 'a conspiracy of silence ... about the rights and duties of their respective citizens' (1977: 83). In addition, most states – and Europe's former colonies since the end of the Second World War – have feared that human rights law might be used as a pretext for interfering in their domestic affairs. Bull was concerned that Western arrogance and complacency about human rights might damage the delicate framework of international society. He also noted that relative silence on the importance of human rights had produced a strong counter-reaction, and that states in the twentieth century had come under increasing pressure to ensure their protection (Bull 1984a).

This is the starting-point of John Vincent's book, *Human Rights and International Relations* (1986), which argued that the right of the individual to be free from starvation is one human right on which all states can agree despite their ideological differences. Vincent argued that global action to end starvation is essential since the absence of the basic means of subsistence should always shock the conscience of humankind. Consensus on this matter would be a significant advance in relations between the Western world, which has traditionally been concerned with order rather than justice, and the non-Western world, which has stressed the need for greater justice. In one of his last essays Vincent returned to the theme of his first book which defended the principle of non-intervention. He observed that states are increasingly open to external scrutiny and under pressure to comply with the international law of human rights (Vincent and Wilson 1994). Some violations of human rights might be so shocking that states have to set aside the convention that they should not intervene in each other's internal affairs.

Whether and how they should do so are questions that became central to international relations with the destruction of Yugoslavia and genocide in Rwanda (Dunne and Wheeler 1999). International action to try persons suspected of war crimes and gross human rights violations has progressed but, as the debate over NATO's military action against Serbia demonstrated, there is no global consensus about when sovereignty can be overridden for the sake of human rights.

In fact, two very different tendencies have appeared in the English School in recent years. Dunne and Wheeler (1999) argued in the late 1990s that the end of bipolarity made it possible that states could agree on how to introduce new principles of humanitarian intervention into the society of states. They added that the aspiring 'good international citizen' should be prepared to intervene in societies where there was a 'supreme humanitarian emergency' even though their action was in breach of international law. This argument has been rejected by Jackson (2000: 291ff.) who stresses, citing the example of Russia's long-standing affinity with Serbia, the danger that humanitarian intervention might disturb order between the great powers. Jackson (2000) argues that the greatest violations of human rights take place in times of war, and so preserving constraints on violence between states should have priority over the use of force to safeguard human rights, whenever it is necessary to choose between them.

The 'revolt against the West' is a subject for the next section, but one of its dimensions, namely the demand for racial equality, is pertinent to the present discussion. Bull (in Bull and Watson 1984) and Vincent (1984b) argued that the rejection of white supremacism has been a central theme in the transition from a European to the first universal society of states. The demand for racial equality demonstrated that international order may not endure unless Third World peoples realize their basic aspirations for justice. Although order was also an issue – disorder in Southern Africa was possible while white supremacist regimes endured – the deeper matter was the immorality of apartheid. This dimension of the revolt against racial equality adds force to Wight's point that the modern society of states differs from its predecessors in making the legitimacy or illegitimacy of particular forms of government a matter of importance for the entire international community (Wight 1977: 41). Disgust with apartheid was a matter on which the whole of international society was agreed. Mindful of the ideological competition between the United States and the Soviet Union, Bull added, however, that agreement on apartheid was about as far as the global moral consensus extended in the 1970s and 1980s (Bull 1982: 266).

The revolt against white supremacism reveals how progress towards greater solidarism can be made. As Bull (1977: 95) put it, if 'there is overwhelming evidence of a consensus in international society as a whole in favour of change held to be just, especially if the consensus embraces all the great powers [then] change may take place without causing other than a local and temporary disorder, after which the international order as a whole may emerge unscathed or even appear in a stronger position than before'. Whether Bull thought that a global moral consensus could emerge in other areas is unclear although Watson (1987: 152) maintains that Bull and he 'inclined [towards the] optimistic view' that states in the contemporary system are 'consciously working out, for the first time, a set of transcultural values and ethical standards'. Perhaps a growing consensus about the need for democratic government – or at the very least for constitutional safeguards for human rights – reveals that further progress has been made. As noted earlier, exactly how far this consensus can extend is disputed in recent writings by members of the English School. It is worth adding that Bull (1983: 127–31) wrote in the 1980s that neither superpower seemed to have the requisite 'moral vision' for dealing with the central problems between 'North' and 'South'. At the present time one crucial question is whether the United States and the United Kingdom have displayed a similar lack of vision which threatens to deepen the divisions in international society by combining the defence of liberal-democratic values with a 'war against terror' which included regime change in Iraq without UN approval.

It is hard to tell whether Bull and Watson believed the expansion of international society to include the West's former colonies would lead to greater solidarism or demonstrate that aspirations in that direction were still 'premature' – and few contemporary members of the School have built on their comments (Wheeler 2000; see also Mayall 1996). An exception is Jackson (2000: 181), who believes that the diverse nature of international society in the postcolonial era makes it all the more important to defend the pluralist conception of international society which Jackson regards as the best arrangement yet devised for promoting peaceful relations between societies which value their differences and independence. For his part, Bull (1977: 317) did think that a elite cosmopolitanism was emerging – and observers might now add that he was touching on the impact of globalization on the society of states – but he was quick to add that this 'nascent cosmopolitan culture ... is weighted in favour of the dominant cultures of the West'. Incorporating non-Western ideas in international law would help to overcome this problem but, Bull (1984a: 6) argued, there was clear evidence that the West and the Third World were drifting further apart:

we have to remember that when these demands for justice were first put forward, the leaders of Third World peoples spoke as supplicants in a world in which the Western powers were still in a dominant position. The demands that were put forward had necessarily to be justified in terms of ... conventions of which the Western powers were the principal authors; the moral appeal had to be cast in terms that would have most resonance in Western societies. But as ... non-Western peoples have become stronger ... and as the Westernised leaders of the early years of independence have been replaced in many countries by new leaders more representative of local or indigenous forces, Third World spokesmen have become freer to adopt a rhetoric that sets Western values aside, or ... places different interpretations upon them. Today there is legitimate doubt as to how far the demands emanating from the Third World coalition are compatible with the moral ideas of the West.

Intriguing questions about the future of solidarism are raised by these comments, which foreshadowed the more recent analysis of the coming 'clash of civilizations' and discussions about whether the rise of 'indigenous' values and the development of radical or militant Islamic groups will deepen rivalries with the West (Huntington 1993). Yet nothing in Bull's writings suggests that the breakdown of international society is imminent. As we shall see in the next section, Bull believed that the majority of new states accepted the basic principles of international society including the ideas of sovereignty and non-intervention. Despite cultural and other differences which seemed to be increasing, new states and old could agree on some universal principles of coexistence and on some moral universals such as the principle of racial equality. How different societies come to agree on the universal principles pertinent to either a pluralist or solidarist conception of international society is the central theme in a form of analysis which steers clear of the fatalism of neo-realism and a naïve belief in the inevitability of global progress which occasionally surfaces in triumphalist forms of liberalism. In the end, diplomatic practice decides how far states can agree on moral and political universals which transcend cultural and other differences. On such foundations does the claim to be the *via media* between realism and revolutionism finally rest.

The revolt against the West and the expansion of international society

The impact of the revolt against the West upon the modern society of states was central to Bull and Watson's writings in the 1980s. Their key question was whether the diverse civilizations which had been brought together by the expansion of Europe have similar views about how to maintain order and belong to an international society rather than an international system. To answer this question it was necessary to recall the world of the late eighteenth century. In that era, there were four dominant regional international orders (the Chinese, European, Indian and Islamic). Moreover, 'most of the governments in each group had a sense of being part of a common civilization superior to that of the others' (Bull and Watson 1984: 87). Although European states were committed to the principle of sovereign equality within their own continent, they rejected the view that other societies had the same sovereign rights. Exactly how Europe should behave towards its colonies was always a matter of dispute. Some claimed the right to enslave or annihilate conquered peoples while others argued that they were equally members of the universal society of humankind and entitled to be treated humanely. The dominant theories of empire in the twentieth century, as expressed in the League of Nations' mandates system and the trusteeship system of the United Nations, maintained that colonial powers had a duty to prepare non-European peoples for their eventual admission into the society of states on equal terms with Western members (Bain 2003).

The Europeans believed that this transition would take many decades if not centuries, in part because other civilizations had to divest themselves of a hegemonial conception of international society in which they were believed to be at the centre of the world. China, for example, saw itself as the Middle Kingdom which deserved tribute from other societies which were thought to be at a lower stage of development. Traditional Islamic views of International Relations distinguished between the House of Islam (Dar al Islam) and the House of War (Dar al Harb) – between believers and infidels – though the possibility of a temporary truce (Dar al Suhl) with non-Islamic powers was allowed. No less committed to a hegemonial view of international order, the European powers believed that membership of the society of states was impossible for those that had yet to reach their 'standard of civilization' (Gong 1984).

What this meant was that different civilizations belonged to an international system in the eighteenth century. With the expansion of Europe, other peoples were forced to comply with its conception of the world and, gradually, most of those societies came to accept European principles of international society. But they came to enjoy equal membership of the international society of states only after a long struggle to dismantle Europe's sense of its own moral superiority and political invincibility.

Bull (in Bull and Watson 1984: 220–4) called this struggle 'the revolt against the West' and argued that it had five main components. The first was 'the struggle for equal sovereignty' undertaken by societies such as China and Japan which had 'retained their formal independence' but were considered 'inferior' to the Western powers. These societies were governed by unequal treaties 'concluded under duress'; because of the principle of 'extra-territoriality', they were denied the right to settle disputes involving foreigners according to domestic law. As a consequence of the legal revolt against the West, Japan joined the society of states in 1900, Turkey in 1923, Egypt in 1936 and China in 1943. The political revolt against the West was a second phase in this process. In this case, the former colonies which had lost their former independence demanded freedom from colonial domination. The racial revolt against the West which included the struggle to abolish slavery and the slave trade as well as all forms of white supremacism was the third part of the quest for freedom and dignity; a fourth dimension was the economic revolt against the forms of inequality and exploitation associated with a Western-dominated global commercial and financial system. The fifth revolt, the cultural revolt, was a protest against all forms of Western cultural imperialism, including the West's assumption that it was entitled to decide how other peoples should live, not least by universalizing liberal-individualistic conceptions of human rights.

Bull maintained that the first four dimensions of the revolt of the Third World appealed to Western conceptions of freedom and equality and tried to make the colonial powers take their own principles seriously in their relations with the non-European parts of the world. This seemed to signify a desire to emulate the West's path of social and political development. But as already noted the cultural revolt was different because it was often 'a revolt against Western values as such' (Bull and Watson 1984: 223). The inevitable question was whether the expansion of international society which occurred because of the revolt against the West would lead to new forms of conflict and disharmony. The importance of this question has been underlined by the religious revolt, and specifically by certain Islamic forms of revolt against the West, embodied in Al-Qaeda, which are opposed to American support for Israel, to its policy of supporting what are held to be corrupt pro-Western elites in the Middle East and to the spread of Western secular values. Significantly, the 'September 11' terrorist attacks on the United States were not followed by diplomatic demands which are usually compromised as part of the usual 'give and take' of politics. This was a new form of revolt against the West, one in which the use of force did not conform with Clausewitz's famous dictum that war is the continuation of politics by other means.

Where this new revolt against the West will lead, and what it means for the future of international society, will be central questions in the field for years to come. For some, there is no sharper reminder of the value of Samuel Huntington's controversial thesis that, contrary to Francis Fukuyama's belief in the triumph of liberal democracy, new fault-lines are emerging around ancient divisions between civilizations (Fukuyama 1992; Huntington 1993). Some who find Huntington's view of civilizations too simplistic stress that it is important not to lose sight of what the larger cultural revolt against the West means for international society. Chris Brown (1988) has argued that the revolt against the West has challenged 'the modern requirement', which is the belief that the West can assume that it has the right to make other societies live in accordance with its values. This raises the interesting question of whether an agreement about pluralist principles of world political organization is all that very different societies can achieve, and perhaps all they should aim for.

Bull and Watson's view in the 1980s was that growing cultural conflict and an emerging cosmopolitan culture of modernity were developing in tandem. This is to suggest, contrary to the views summarized in the preceding paragraph, that tensions between the 'pluralist' and 'solidarist' conceptions of international society might well deepen in future. If this was their prediction, then it has turned out to be broadly correct, as we can see from the widening gulf between those who believe in promoting universal human rights (by force if necessary) and those who believe it is necessary to strengthen respect for national sovereignty in the face of the new imperialism. Bull and Watson believed that an international order which reflected the interests of non-Western states had been largely constructed by the 1980s. They were also clear that international society would not command the support of the majority of non-Western peoples unless more radical change took place (Bull and Watson 1984: 429). In particular, there would need to be a radical redistribution of power and wealth from North to South (Bull 1977: 316–17). This is important, given Bull's earlier thinking about the tension between order and justice. Although Bull continued to argue that 'justice is best realised in the context of order', he was much more inclined in his last writings to argue that greater justice is needed to ensure the survival of international order. We see this in his claim that the 'measures that are necessary to achieve justice for peoples of the Third World are the same measures that will maximise the prospects of international order or stability, at least in the long run' (Bull 1984a: 18).

Bull did not live to witness the further expansion of international society through the fragmentation of the Soviet bloc and the disintegration of several Third World societies. New challenges for international society have been posed by national–secessionist movements which argue that sometimes justice can be realized only 'at the price of order' (Keal 1983: 210). New problems have been created by the appearance of 'failed states' (Helman and Ratner 1992–3), by gross violations of human rights in civil conflicts, by regimes which are in a state of war with sections of their own population, by governments such as the Taliban in Afghanistan which provided a safe haven for terrorist organisations such as Al-Qaeda and by authoritarian regimes such as Iraq under Saddam Hussein where the United States and the United Kingdom feared that WMD might end up in the hands of terrorist organizations dedicated to causing as much suffering as possible to civilian populations. But, as we shall see, such developments reinforce Bull and Watson's claim that modern international society is increasingly divided between pluralist and solidarist principles of world political organization (Hurrell 2002).

Robert Jackson's *Quasi-States* (1990) offered a new approach to the expansion of international society by focusing on what has become a core issue of world politics, namely the problem of the 'failed state'. Jackson's starting-point was that Third World states were admitted into the society of states as sovereign equals without any assurance that they could govern themselves effectively. Indeed, in 1960 the UN General Assembly consciously departed from the long-standing principle that a people had to demonstrate a capacity for good government before its claim for self-government could hope to succeed. Many new states acquired 'negative sovereignty' – the right to be free from external interference – when they clearly lacked 'positive sovereignty' – the ability to satisfy the basic needs of their populations. One consequence of the acquisition of sovereignty was that ruling elites were legally free to do as they pleased within their respective territories. Violators of human rights were then in a position to appeal to Article 2, para.7 of the UN Charter, which asserts that the international community does not have the right 'to intervene in matters which are essentially within the domestic jurisdiction of any state'.

Jackson (1990) raised the question of whether a more effective system of global trusteeship could have prepared the colonies for political independence, and some have argued that the international community has to take responsibility for governing states which are no longer economically or politically viable (see also Helman and Ratner 1992–3). A related question in this context was whether the consent of the government of the target state is absolutely necessary before the international community can take action of this kind (1992–3).

Genocide in Rwanda, violence against the people of East Timor, the humanitarian crisis in Sudan in 2004–5 and ethnic cleansing in the Balkans have reopened the debate about the rights and wrongs of humanitarian intervention. The debate over NATO's involvement in Kosovo in 1999 revealed there is no consensus on whether the right of sovereignty can be overridden by an allegedly higher moral principle of protecting human rights. Some observers supported NATO's actions on the grounds that states have duties to the whole of humanity and not just to co-nationals (Havel 1999: 6). Others criticized NATO for what they saw as a breach of the UN Charter, for its highly selective approach to dealing with human rights violations and for acts of violence which compounded the misery of the local population (Chomsky 1999a). The debate over the war against Iraq has deepened these divisions, with some such as Blair arguing that the war was justified not only because the regime was a danger to other societies but because it was guilty of gross violations of human rights. Others argue that the American and British governments are guilty of placing themselves above international society by acting outside the UN system where each state has legal equality (although Bush and Blair have maintained that they are defending that society by developing new principles such as the doctrine of preventive war in the face of previously unimagined threats). The echoes of an older tension between the 'pluralist' and 'solidarist' conceptions of international society can be heard in these different reactions to how to deal with human rights violators and with regimes that are deemed to be 'outlaws' in international society. It remains to be seen whether the society of states can agree on the need for intervention in the case of supreme humanitarian emergences while at the same time resisting any more general attempt to weaken respect for the principle of non-intervention' (Roberts 1993; see also Vincent and Wilson 1994). In examining the diplomacy which surrounds such debates, the English School comes into its own.

Progress in international relations

Quite how far progress in international relations is possible is one of the most intriguing questions in the field. In one essay, Wight (1966: 26) maintained that the international system is 'the realm of recurrence and repetition', a formulation which is repeated in Waltz's classic statement of neo-realism (Waltz 1979: 66). The argument of this chapter is that the English School is principally about progress in the form of agreements about how to maintain order and, to a lesser degree, about how to promote support for principles of justice. Bull's writings on this subject often suggested that order is prior to justice, the point being that international order is a fragile achievement and that states have been unable to agree on the meaning of global justice. At times, Bull seems to be aligned with what Wight described as the 'realist' wing of rationalism but, on other occasions, he is much closer to its 'idealist' wing (Wight 1991: 59). Towards the end of his life, it has been argued, Bull moved significantly towards a more 'solidarist' point of view (see Dunne 1998: Chapter 7).

This apparent change of heart is most pronounced in the Hagey Lectures delivered at the University of Waterloo in Canada in 1983 (Bull 1984b). It is illustrated by the comment that 'the idea of sovereign rights existing apart from the rules laid down by international society itself and enjoyed without qualification has to be rejected in principle', not least because 'the idea of the rights and duties of the individual person has come to have a place, albeit an insecure one' within the society of states 'and it is our responsibility to seek to extend it' (Bull 1984b: 11–12). The 'moral concern with welfare on a world scale' was evidence of a 'growth of ... cosmopolitan moral awareness' which amounted to 'a major change in our sensibilities' (1984b: 13). The changing global agenda made it necessary for states to become the 'local agents of a world common good' (1984b: 14).

It would be a mistake to suggest that Bull had come to think that solutions to global problems would be any easier to find and that 'terrible choices' would no longer have to be made (1984b: 14). Scepticism invariably blunted the visionary impulse. This is clear from his observation that new, post-sovereign political communities might yet develop in Western Europe. An intriguing passage in *The Anarchical Society* (1977) states that the time may be ripe for new principles of regional political organization which recognize the need for sub-national, national and supranational tiers of government but reject the notion that any of them should enjoy exclusive sovereignty (Bull 1977: 267). A 'neo-medievalist' Western Europe could 'avoid the classic dangers of the system of sovereign states' by encouraging 'overlapping structures and criss-crossing loyalties' (1977: 255). But such a world would not be free from dangers. Medieval international society, with its complex structure of overlapping jurisdictions and multiple loyalties, had been even more violent than the modern system of states (1977: 255). Bull (1979b) set out a qualified defence of the society of states which argued, against the revolutionists, that most states still play a 'positive role in world affairs'. Despite its many faults, the society of states was unlikely to be bettered by any other form of world political organization in the foreseeable future.

We have considered how the English School differs from realism and neo-realism; it is now necessary to turn to its assessment of 'revolutionism' and the various critiques of the international society of states which have been developed by advocates of that perspective. Bull (1977: 22) argued that the essence of revolutionism can be found in the Kantian belief in 'a horizontal conflict of ideology that cuts across the boundaries of states and divides human society into two camps – the trustees of the immanent community of mankind and those who stand in its way, those who are of the true faith and the heretics, the liberators and the oppressed'. The Kantian interpretation of international society believed that diplomatic conventions should be set aside in the quest for the unification of humankind. 'Good faith with heretics' had no intrinsic value; it had no more than 'tactical convenience' because 'between the elect and the damned, the liberators and the oppressed, the question of mutual acceptance of rights to sovereignty or independence does not arise' (1977: 24).

Many writers, including Stanley Hoffmann (1990: 23–4), have argued that Kant was 'less cosmopolitan and universalist in his writings on international affairs than Bull suggests'. Indeed, for all his cosmopolitanism Kant defended a society of sovereign states which respected the principle of non-intervention. For this reason, 'Kantianism' seems an inappropriate term for describing a group of visionary perspectives which Bull and Wight ultimately rejected. The idea of revolutionism is also troubling because it groups together thinkers as diverse as Kant, Lenin (who defended the violent overthrow of the bourgeois international order) and Gandhi (who believed in non-violent resistance). However, what most troubled English School thinkers such as Bull and Wight was the 'revolutionist' belief that peace will not come about in international relations until all societies share the same universal ideology. Wight thought that Kant believed that peace would exist only when the whole world consisted of republican states (Wight 1991: 421–2), although recent scholars have challenged this interpretation (MacMillan 1995). The important point to comprehend, however, was that the English School has defended international society from those who are intolerant of its deficiencies, impatient to see change and keen to use force and chicanery to bring other societies round to their preferred ideology. There is a parallel here with those classical realists who were opposed to the crusading mentality in international relations (see Chapter 3 in this volume).

Wight always stressed that 'rationalism' overlapped with realism and revolutionism. We have seen one point of convergence between realism and the English School. One point of overlap between the English School and revolutionism can be found in Wight's lectures where he described Kant as like the rationalist who is first and foremost 'a reformist, the practitioner of piecemeal social engineering' (Wight 1991: 29). The classic works of the English School tended to shy away from visions of how the world could or should be organized. In Bull's case, this was because there was no reason to suppose that political philosophers would succeed where diplomats had repeatedly failed, namely in identifying moral principles which all or most societies could regard as the foundations of an improved international order. On the other hand, Bull's argument that international order must ultimately be judged by what it contributes to world order, and Wight's claim that the main political task is to promote order and security 'from which law, justice and prosperity may afterwards develop', both suggest that something can be said about the direction which international society should ideally take. Interestingly, this might have taken Bull and Wight closer to Kant, who thought the challenge was to build law and civility not only within or between separate states but across the whole of world society. Some thinkers such as Habermas (1997), who see their task as building on Kant's thought, believe this goal is best achieved by developing international criminal law and by creating cosmopolitan democratic institutions which will work to ensure that all global actors (states, multinational corporations (MNCs) and so forth) are accountable to those they affect.

What is principally at stake here is the question of how states and other actors can create a world community without jeopardising the existence of the society of states. Interestingly, Bull (1969/1995) thought that Karl Deutsch's writings on 'security communities' (communities whose members have renounced the use of force in their relations with one another in accordance with a heightened sense of 'we-feeling') were 'pregnant with implications for a general theory of international relations'. Deutsch, Bull argued, was unusual in reflecting on different types of political community, on their 'distinguishing features', on the 'elements' that provide for their 'cohesion' and, crucially, on the extent of their 'responsiveness' to the interests and well-being of other peoples (Bull 1966b). This interest in Deutsch's thinking is unsurprising because a society of states can exist only if independent political communities are sensitive to one another's legitimate economic and political interests and tolerant of diverse moral and cultural standpoints (Wight 1991: 120, 248). Similarly, the development of the elements of a world community, however rudimentary, depends on the extent to which states are moved by 'purposes beyond themselves' – not only by maintaining order between separate, sovereign states but by promoting a world order which is concerned with security and justice for individuals (Bull 1973: 137). These are themes which became more important to the English School with Bull's later solidarism, Vincent's defence of the universal human right to be free from starvation, in Dunne and Wheeler's essays on human rights and good international citizenship and in Wheeler's argument for intervention in the case of 'supreme humanitarian emergencies' and for stronger protection for civilians in times of war. The common theme here is the need for greater international cooperation, not to impose a set of moral principles on reluctant states but to do as much as possible to help what Dunne and Wheeler (1999) have called 'suffering humanity'.

Before drawing this chapter to a close it is useful to note how the English School stands in relation to some other current branches of International Relations theory. There is a parallel between the English School's study of international society and neo-liberal institutionalist arguments about how cooperation is possible even in the context of anarchy. Members of the English School have not followed neo-liberal institutionalists by using game theory to explain how cooperation can evolve between rational egotists (Keohane 1989a). Indeed, the notion that international theory can start with rational egotists is anathema to members of the English School, who believe that the interests of states are always defined in relation to, and shaped, by the moral and legal principles of international society. There is a parallel with constructivism (see Chapter 8 in this volume) which claims that state interests are socially constructed and influenced by global norms. Similarly, members of the English School agree with constructivism that anarchy is to use Wendt's famous phrase, 'what states make of it' (Wendt 1992). Likewise, both schools see sovereignty not as an unchanging reality of world politics but as a phenomenon whose meaning alters in accordance with shifting ideas about, for example, the place that human rights should have in international society. As Bull points out, states can make an international system or an international society out of the condition of anarchy, and there are times when they may be able to make their society conform with some basic principles of human justice (see also Wight 1977 and Reus-Smit 1999). Nothing is pre-ordained here; everything depends on how states think of themselves as separate political communities and what they take to be their rights against, and duties to, the rest of humankind. This is why members of the English School have been especially interested in the legal and moral dimensions of world politics, in the relationship between order and justice in international affairs, in how much progress states have made in creating society and whether or not they are likely to succeed in building a world community.

Reference was made earlier to the extent to which critical approaches have influenced the English School (see p. 88). It is also the case that different branches of critical theory (whether derived from the Frankfurt School or from postmodern approaches – see Chapters 6 and 7 in this volume) have also drawn on English School writing (Der Derian 1987; Linklater 1998). Members of the English School have long had an interest in cultural diversity in international politics and in some ways predate postmodern inquiries into 'otherness'. The fourth chapter of Wight's *International Theory: The Three Traditions* (1991) reveals a close interest in approaches to the 'colonized other'. As noted, Bull and Watson's analysis of the expansion of international society displays a special concern with the revolt against the West and poses a question which has drawn the attention of various critical approaches to international relations, specifically whether culturally diverse societies can agree on any universal legal and moral principles or are destined to be divided over how far these express sectional interests and parochial preferences.

Understandably, the English School has devoted much attention to the 'diplomatic dialogue' between states (Watson 1982), while recognizing that states are often tempted to use force to realize their objectives or to resolve major differences. It is important to stress that Bull's analysis of the revolt against the West brought out moral differences between 'North' and 'South' which cannot be resolved by force but require the search for agreement through a process of dialogue. It has been argued that Bull's claim that the modern society of states should come to rest on the consent of all peoples, the majority of whom live in the poorest regions of the world, has been developed further in notions of 'cosmopolitan conversations' which hold that all human beings have the moral right to participate in making decisions that may adversely affect them (Linklater 1998: Chapter 6; Shapcott 1994). But it is important not to press these points too far. It is essential to remember that Bull had little time for visions of alternative forms of world political organization which stray too far from the practicalities of foreign policy; that Jackson gives expression to a powerful element in the English School approach when he argues that the role of the analyst is to understand the actual world of international politics rather than give vent to moral preferences; and that most members of the School doubt whether states – even the best-intentioned – have the political will, vision and competence to create a better form of world political organisation (Mayall 2000). It is perfectly possible that had they lived, Wight, Bull and Vincent would have applauded recent attempts to promote human rights, to weaken the principle of sovereign immunity and to prosecute those accused of committing war crimes; but they might not have been wholly surprised that the new humanitarian discourse has resulted in forms of violence such as the war against Iraq which have created new divisions in international society.

Conclusion

In *The Twenty Years' Crisis 1919–1939*, E. H. Carr (1939/1945/1946: 12) argued that international theory should avoid the 'sterility' of realism and the 'naivety' of idealism. The English School can claim to have passed this test of a good international theory. They have analysed elements of society and civility which have been of little interest to realists. Although they have been principally concerned with understanding international order, they have also considered the prospects for global justice and some have made the moral case for creating a more just world order. Members of the English School are not convinced by utopian or revolutionist arguments which maintain that states can settle their most basic differences about morality and justice. The idea that the English School is the *via media* between realism and revolutionism rests on such considerations.

The English School argues that international society is a precarious achievement but the only context within which more radical developments can take place. Advances in the global protection of human rights, they argue, will not occur in the absence of international order. It is to be expected that there will always be two sides to the English School: the side that is quick to detect threats to international society and the side that identifies ways in which that society might become more responsive to the needs of individuals and their various associations. The relationship between these different orientations changes and will continue to change in response to historical circumstances. The Cold War years did little to encourage the search for alternative principles of world order; the 'solidarist' conception of international society was deemed to be 'premature'. In many respects the passing of bipolarity was more conducive to the development of solidarism although discussions about whether states should intervene to prevent human rights violations have brought the 'solidarist' concern with individual rights into conflict with the 'pluralist' stress on the dangers involved in breaching national sovereignty. The age of American hegemony inevitably raises the question of whether the 'solidarist' theme has been hijacked by the dominant political interests in the United States and the United Kingdom, and whether the society of states now confronts new challenges to its survival. In contemporary debates about such matters, one can see echoes of the English School's long discussion about the relative importance of 'system', 'society' and 'community' in international affairs. Its reflections on these matters look certain to remain important for future efforts to understand the shifting sands of world politics.

Chapter 5

Marxism

ANDREW LINKLATER

In the mid-1840s Marx and Engels wrote that capitalist globalization was seriously eroding the foundations of the international system of states. Conflict and competition between nation-states had not yet ended in their view but the main fault-lines in future looked certain to revolve around the two principal social classes: the national bourgeoisie, which controlled different systems of government, and an increasingly cosmopolitan proletariat. The outline of a radically new social experiment was already contained within the most advanced political movements of the industrial working class. Through revolutionary action, the international proletariat would embed the Enlightenment ideals of liberty, equality and fraternity in an entirely new world order which would free all human beings from exploitation and domination (Marx and Engels 1977).

Many traditional theorists of international relations have pointed to the failures of Marxism or 'historical materialism' as an account of world history. Marxism has been the foil for their argument that international politics have long revolved around competition and conflict between independent political communities, and will do so well into the future. Realists such as Kenneth Waltz claimed that Marxism was a 'second-image' account of international relations which believed that the rise of socialist as opposed to capitalist *regimes* would eliminate conflict between states. Its utopian aspirations were bound to be dashed because the struggle for power and security is an inescapable consequence of international anarchy which only 'third-image' analysis can explain (Waltz 1979). English School thinkers such as Martin Wight maintained that Lenin's *Imperialism: The Highest Stage of Capitalism* (1916) might seem to be a study of international politics but it was far too preoccupied with the economic aspects of human affairs to be taken seriously as a contribution to the field (Wight 1966). Marxists had underestimated the crucial importance of nationalism, the state and war, and the significance of the balance of power, international law and diplomacy for the structure of world politics.

New interpretations of Marxism have appeared since the 1980s: the perspective has been an important weapon in the critique of realism and there have been many innovative attempts to use its ideas to develop a more historically aware conception of the development of modern international relations (Cox 1981, 1983; Gill 1993a; Halliday 1994; Rosenberg 1994; Teschke 2003). Its impact on the critical theory of international relations has been immense. It has also been an important resource in the area of international political economy, where scholars have analysed the interplay between states and markets, the states-system and the capitalist world economy, the spheres of power and production. For some, the collapse of the Soviet Union and the triumph of capitalism over socialism marked the death of Marxism as social theory and political practice. In the 1990s, some argued that the relevance of Marxism had increased with the passing of the age of bipolarity and the rapid emergence of a new phase of economic globalization (Gamble 1999). A biography of Marx which appeared in the late 1990s argued that, following the collapse of the Soviet Union, his analysis of how capitalism breaks down Chinese Walls and unifies the human race had finally come of age (Wheen 1999). For others, the resurgence of national security politics since the terrorist attacks of '9/11' is a simple reminder that Marxism has little grip on the most fundamental realities of international politics. Assessing these different evaluations of Marx's writings and the contributions of Marxism is the central purpose of this chapter.

It was unwise to claim too much for Marxism in the 1990s, notwithstanding considerable prescience about how capitalism was becoming the dominant form of production across the world. This was not only because Marxism took the view that the triumph of capitalism would be short-lived and that its inexorable laws would lead to its destruction and eventual replacement by Communism. Nor is it just because Marxism had a poor grasp of the importance of the nation-state and violence in the modern world, a point that Marxists conceded in the 1970s and 1980s (see Giddens 1985). It is also because modern forms of globalization have been accompanied by renewed ethnic violence and national fragmentation which Marx and Engels, insightful though they were about the march of capitalist globalization and growing economic inequalities, could not have foreseen. Other Marxist writers saw things differently. Lenin, for example, believed that capitalism caused national fragmentation as well as unprecedented advances in globalization, but that does not necessarily mean that Marxism offers the best explanation of how globalization and fragmentation have unfolded in tandem in modern times and especially since the collapse of the Soviet Union.

An evaluation of Marxism can scarcely avoid the conclusion that its exponents were too preoccupied with production and class conflict to grasp the peculiarities of the modern age or to develop an adequate critical theory of the modern world. But it might nevertheless be found that Marxist analyses of capitalist globalization and fragmentation invite reconsideration of Waltz and Wight's argument that Marxism may not be regarded as a serious contribution to the study of international politics or is clearly inferior to conventional approaches in the field. It might also be argued that its project of developing a critical theory of world society is one respect in which Marxism supersedes the dominant approaches in the Anglo-American study of international politics. If so, the question is how to build on its foundations, how to preserve its strengths and how to move beyond its errors and weaknesses. This was the task that the early members of the Frankfurt School set themselves. Frankfurt School thinkers such as Horkheimer maintained in the 1930s that the challenge was to preserve the 'spirit' while departing from the 'letter' of classical Marxism (Friedman 1981: 35–6). Working within the same tradition, Habermas argued in the 1970s that the key task was to bring about the 'reconstruction of historical materialism' (Linklater 1990b; see also Chapter 6 in this volume).

The first section of this chapter describes the main features of historical materialism and explains how international relations fitted within that framework and the second summarizes key themes in the Marxist analysis of nationalism and imperialism. A brief overview of the orthodox critique of Marxism within International Relations comes next and of its rehabilitation in the 1980s when political economy and critical theory came to the fore. The final section evaluates the Marxist tradition in the light of recent developments in the theory of international relations.

Class, production and international relations in Marx's writings

For Marx, human history has been a laborious struggle to satisfy basic material needs, to understand and tame the physical world, to resist class domination and exploitation and to overcome fear and distrust of the rest of the human race. The main achievements of human history have included the gradual conquest of hostile natural forces which were once beyond human control and understanding, the steady elimination of ignorance and superstition, the growing capacity to abolish crippling material scarcity and exploitation and the potential for remaking society so that all human beings can develop a range of creative powers which are unique to their species. But modern history shaped by capitalism had unfolded tragically in Marx's view. The power of society over nature had expanded to an unprecedented degree but individuals had become trapped within an international social division of labour, exposed to unfettered market forces and exploited by new forms of factory production which turned workers into appendages to the machine (Marx 1977a: 477). Marx thought that capitalism had made massive advances in reducing feelings of estrangement between societies. Nationalism, he believed, had no place in the hearts and minds of the most advanced sections of the proletariat which were committed to a cosmopolitan political project. But capitalism was a system of largely unchecked exploitation in which the bourgeoisie controlled the labour-power of members of the proletariat and profited from their work. It was the root cause of an alienating condition in which the human race – the bourgeoisie as well as the proletariat – was at the mercy of structures and forces which it had created. Marx wrote that philosophers had only interpreted the world whereas the real point was to change it (Marx 1977b: 158). An end to alienation, exploitation and estrangement was Marx's main political aspiration and the point of his efforts to understand the laws of capitalism and the broad movement of human history. This was his chief legacy to thinkers in the Marxist tradition.

Marx believed that the historical import of the forces of production (technology) and the relations of production (and especially the division between those who own the means of production and those who must work for them to survive) had been neglected by the Hegelian movement with which he was closely associated in his formative intellectual years. Hegel had focused on the many forms of religious, philosophical, artistic, historical and political thinking – the diverse types of self-consciousness – which the human race had passed through in its long journey of coming to know itself. After his death, and as part of the struggle over Hegel's legacy, the Left Hegelians attacked religion, believing it was a form of 'false consciousness' which prevented human beings from acquiring a deep understanding of what they are and what they can become. But, for Marx, religious belief was not an intellectual error which had to be corrected by philosophical analysis but an expression of the frustrations and aspirations of people struggling with the material conditions of everyday life. Religion was 'the opium of the masses' and the 'sigh of an oppressed creature' (Marx 1977c: 64) and revolutionaries had to understand and challenge the social conditions which gave rise to the solace of religious beliefs. 'The critique of heaven', as Marx put it, had to become 'the critique of earth' (1977c).

The pivotal theme in Marx's materialist conception of history is that individuals must first satisfy their most basic physical or material needs before they can do anything else. In practice, this has meant the mass of humanity, in order to survive, has had to surrender control of its labour power to those that own the instruments of production. Given the basic reality of property relations, the dominant classes throughout history have been able to exploit the subordinate classes but this had always led to class conflict. Indeed, Marx believed that class struggle had been the principal form of conflict in the whole of human history. Political revolution had been the main agent of historical development while technological innovation had been the driving-force behind social change.

Marx wrote that history was the continuous transformation of human nature (Marx 1977d: 105). Put differently, human beings do not only modify nature by working on it; they also change themselves and develop new hopes and needs. The history of the development of the human species could be understood only by tracing the development of the dominant modes of production which, in the West, included primitive communism, slave societies, feudalism and capitalism which would soon be replaced by socialism on an international scale. The fact that Marx thought socialism would be a global rather than a European phenomenon deserves further comment. Whereas war, imperialism and commerce had simply destroyed the isolation of earlier human societies, capitalism directed all sections of the human race into a single historical stream. Few mainstream students of International Relations recognized the importance of this preoccupation with the economic and technological unification of the human species, with the widening of the boundaries of social cooperation and with the forces that blocked advances in human solidarity (Gill 1993a). Few traditional scholars commented on his fascination with the relationship between internationalization and internationalism, but these are crucial themes in his writings which contain much that should interest the student of contemporary international affairs (Halliday 1988a).

In his reflections on capitalism, Marx argued that universal history came into being when the social relations of production and exchange became global and when more cosmopolitan tastes emerged, as illustrated by the desire to consume the products of distant societies and to enjoy an increasingly 'world literature'. But the forces which unified humanity also checked the growth of universal solidarity by pitting members of the bourgeoisie against the proletariat (and against each other), and by forcing members of the working class to compete for scarce employment. Yet the very tension between the wealth generated by capitalism and the poverty of many individual lives generated new forms of solidarity among the exploited classes. International working class solidarity was also triggered by the remarkable way in which capitalist societies used the language of freedom and equality to justify existing social relations, while systematically denying real freedom and equality to the poorer classes.

Large normative claims are raised by the question of what it means to be truly free and equal. In general, Marx and his collaborator, Engels, were dismissive of the study of ethics, but they were hardly engaged in the dispassionate analysis of nineteenth-century industrial capitalism (even though they did believe it was possible to develop a science of the laws of capitalist development modelled on the physical sciences). There is no doubt their inquiry into capitalism was normative through and through (Lukes 1985; Brown 1992). Indeed, Marx's own purpose was made clear in the introductory remarks to *The Eighteenth Brumaire of Louis Bonaparte*, where he wrote that human beings make their own history but not under conditions of their own choosing (Marx 1977e: 300). His point was that humans make their own history because they possess the power of self-determination which other species either do not have or cannot exercise to the same degree. And yet humans cannot make history as they please because class structures stand over them and greatly constrain their freedom of action. A distinctive political project is already contained within this observation, namely how human beings can come to make more of their history under conditions freely chosen by themselves.

Although Marx rejected Hegel's study of history and politics, he kept faith with one of Hegel's most central themes which is that in the course of their history human beings acquire a deeper appreciation of what it means to be free and a better understanding of why society will have to be changed before freedom can be realized more completely. In line with his belief that history revolves around the labour process, Marx observed that freedom and equality under capitalism mean that bourgeois and proletarian enter into a labour contract as legal equals, but massive social inequalities place workers at the mercy of the bourgeoisie and reduce their freedom and equality. He took the view that proletarian organizations were developing an understanding of how socialism could make good the claims to freedom and equality which were already present in capitalist societies. Marx's passionate condemnation of capitalism has to be seen in this light. It is a critique from inside the capitalist order rather than a challenge from outside which appeals to some notion of a higher morality.

Marx rejected the ethical standpoint, which one finds in Kant's writings, that human beings can agree on universal truths by using reason, but he shared Kant's conviction that all political efforts to realize freedom within the sovereign state were ultimately futile because they could be rapidly destroyed by the sudden shock of external events. For Kant, war was the dominant threat to the creation of the perfect society; hence his belief in the priority of working for perpetual peace. For Marx, global capitalist crisis was the recurrent danger. Consequently, the idea of 'socialism in one country' was irrelevant in his view in the context of capitalist globalization. Human freedom could be achieved only through universal solidarity and cooperation to remake world society as a whole. This is one reason why Marx had little to say about relations between states, but focused instead on the significance of capitalist globalization for the struggle to realize equality and freedom. Marx and Engels (whose nickname was 'The General', given his keen interest in strategy and war) were aware of the importance of geopolitics in human history; they knew that conquest in which economic motives were usually predominant had led to the development of ever-larger political associations. They were aware that the struggle for power between the European states led to imperial expansion, although they believed that economic motives were the main reason for the development of world trade and a global market. In short, their analysis was far less concerned with what warring states had contributed to the process of globalization than with explaining how the internal dynamics of capitalism led inexorably to this condition. Although states may have contributed to the globalization of social and political life, they did this largely and increasingly, in Marx's view, because of the internal laws of motion of the capitalist system of production.

Some of the most striking passages in Marx and Engels' writings emphasize the logic of expansionism which is peculiar to modern capitalism. The essence of capitalism is to 'strive to tear down every barrier to intercourse', to 'conquer the whole earth for its market' and to annihilate the tyranny of distance by reducing 'to a minimum the time spent in motion from one place to another' (Marx 1973: 539). In a famous passage in *The Communist Manifesto* (Marx and Engels 1977), which reveals that Marx and Engels were among the first theorists of globalization, they argued that:

> The bourgeoisie has through its exploitation of the world-market given a cosmopolitan character to production and consumption in every country ... All old-fashioned national industries have been destroyed or are daily being destroyed ... In place of the old wants, satisfied by the productions of the country, we find new wants, requiring for their satisfaction the products of different lands and climes. In place of the old local and national seclusion and self-sufficiency, we have intercourse in every direction, universal interdependence of nations ... The bourgeoisie, by the rapid improvement of all instruments of production, by the immensely facilitated means of communication, draws all, even the most barbarian nations, into civilisation. The cheap prices of its commodities are the heavy artillery with which it batters down all Chinese walls, with which it forces the barbarians' intensely obstinate hatred of foreigners to capitulate. It compels all nations, on pain of extinction, to adopt the bourgeois mode of production ... i.e. to become

bourgeois themselves. In one word, it creates a world after its own image. (Marx and Engels 1977: 224–5)

This remarkable statement had clear implications for revolutionary strategy. The sense of 'nationality' might already be 'dead' among the most enlightened members of the proletariat, but humanity was still divided into nation-states and national bourgeoisies remained in control of state structures which they used to promote allegedly national interests. Marx and Engels believed that each proletariat would first have to settle scores with its own national bourgeoisie, but revolutionary struggle would be national only in form. It would not end with the capture of state power because the proletariat's political objectives and aspirations were international (1977: 230, 235).

Realists such as Waltz have argued that members of the proletariat concluded during the First World War that they had more in common with their own national bourgeoisie than with the working classes of other countries. The argument was that no-one with a good under-standing of nationalism, the state and war should have been even mildly surprised by this turn of events, yet many socialists were dismayed by the actions of the European proletariat. For realists, the failure to anticipate this outcome demonstrates the central flaw in Marxism – its economic reductionism, as manifested in the belief that understanding capitalism would explain the mysteries of the modern world and its unprecedented political opportunities (Waltz 1959: Chapter 5). This is one of the most famous criticisms of Marxism within the study of inter-national relations. There are three points to make about it.

First, although Marx and Engels were clearly aware of the globalization of economic and social life, they believed that class conflict within separate, but not autonomous, societies would trigger the great political revolutions of the time (Giddens 1981). Their assumption was that revolution would quickly spread from the society in which it first erupted to all other leading capitalist societies. According to this view of the world, burgeoning transnational capitalist activity shattered the illusion of apparently separate societies – an illusion created by geographical boundaries separating peoples governed by different political systems. It has been argued that the relatively peaceful nature of the international system in the middle of the nineteenth century encouraged such beliefs; the theory of the state gave way to theories of society and the economy (Gallie 1978). Reflecting one of the dominant tendencies of the age, Marx (1973: 109) argued that relations between states were important but 'secondary' or 'tertiary' forces in human affairs when compared with modes of production and their laws of development. In a letter to Annenkov, Marx (1966: 159) asked whether 'the whole organisation of nations, and all their international relations [is] anything else than the expression of a particular division of labour. And must not these change when the division of labour changes?'. This is a question rather than an answer yet many have argued – Waltz is an example – that Marxism largely ignored geopolitics, nationalism and war. Even the most sympathetic reader of Marx's work has to concede the point. There can be absolutely no doubt that Marx believed that capitalist globalization and class conflict would determine the fate of the modern world.

Second, Marx and Engels were forced to reconsider their ideas about the nation because of the importance of nationalism in the 1848 revolutions and its growing political influence later in the century. They wrote that the Irish and the Poles were the victims of national domination rather than class exploitation, and added that freedom from national dominance was essential if subordinated peoples were to become allies of the international proletariat (Marx and Engels 1971; see also Benner 1995). These remarks indicate that while Marx and Engels were primarily concerned with the class structure of capitalist societies, they were well aware of the persistence of ancient animosities between national groups – but they almost certainly continued to believe that national differences would eventually decline in importance and might even disappear altogether (Halliday 1999: 79). The growing threat of inter-state violence in the last part of the nineteenth century led to other adjustments to their thinking. Engels' writings, which stressed the role of war in human history, envisaged unprecedented levels of violence and suffering in the next major European conflict. He thought that military competition rather than capitalist crisis might be the spark that ignited the proletarian revolution. Interestingly, Engels argued that the increased possibility of major war meant that the socialist movement had to take matters of national security and the defence of the homeland very seriously (Gallie 1978; see also Carr 1953).

Third, as Gallie (1978) has noted, those intriguing comments about nationalism, the state and war did not lead Marx and Engels to rework their early statements about the explanatory power of historical materialism. An unhelpful distinction between the economic base and the legal, political and ideological superstructure of society remained central to most summaries of the perspective. Too often, the state was regarded as an instrument of the ruling class, although it was thought capable of acquiring some degree of autonomy from the ruling class in unusual political circumstances. Marx and Engels' political writings revealed growing subtlety but the main statements of their theoretical position continued to privilege class and production, to regard economic power as dominant form of power and to regard the revolutionary project as fundamentally about promoting the transition from capitalism to socialism (Cummins 1980).

Marx developed an analysis of capitalism which must remain a key reference point for anyone interested in a critical theory of world politics concerned with the promotion of human emancipation. An account of the alienating and exploitative character of industrial capitalism was linked with a political vision which looked forward to the democratization of the labour process (regarded as being as important as democratizing the institutions of the state, and possibly of greater significance). Brilliant though the analysis was of the expansion of capitalism to all sectors of modern societies and to all parts of the globe, it is clear the pre-occupation with class domination and material inequalities obscured other forms of social exclusion and human suffering which must also feature in a comprehensive critical theory of world politics. These include the forms of domination and discrimination anchored in notions of racial and gender superiority as well as in ideas about nation and class.

Marx and Engels created some of the foundations of a critical theory, and it was up to later radical theorists to build on their achievements. Something of this kind is evident in the writings of the Austro-Marxists, who developed a more subtle and complex analysis of capitalist global-ization and national fragmentation in a manner that remained true to the spirit but not to the letter of foundational texts. Writing in the early part of the twentieth century, Austro-Marxists such as Karl Renner and Otto Bauer argued that Marx and Engels had underestimated the impact of cultural differences on human history, the continuing strength of national loyalty and the need to satisfy demands for cultural autonomy in the future socialist world (Bottomore and Goode 1978). Whereas, Marx and Engels had been vague about whether or not national differ-ences would survive in the socialist world order, the Austro-Marxists envisaged a future in which increasing cultural diversity would be celebrated while cosmopolitanism, understood as 'friendship towards the whole human race' rather than 'the want of national attachment', would develop. This was to combine a sociology of class and national identity with a broader vision of universal human emancipation.

The Austro-Marxist response to the twin forces of globalization and fragmentation imagined a world in which human beings would enjoy levels of solidarity and cultural diversity which had no parallel in earlier times. These were controversial ideas which clashed with the socialist idea which developed in Soviet Russia under Lenin and Stalin but they indi-cated one way of building on the Marxian legacy and of reconstructing historical materialism. However, the rise of Soviet Marxism–Leninism meant that what Gouldner (1980) described as the anomalies, contradic-tions and latent possibilities within the Marxist tradition were sup-pressed in a closed, quasi-scientific system of supposed truths that destroyed the potential for further growth and development. Numerous encrustations formed around Marxism in this period, as Anderson (1983) noted, but the Marxist literature on nationalism and imperialism early in the twentieth century did move the discussion of capitalist globalization and national fragmentation forward in intriguing ways.

Nationalism and imperialism

We have seen that Marx and Engels were mainly interested in modes of production, class conflict, social and political revolution and the economic and technological unification of the human race. Their writings raised key questions about the tension between centrifugal and centripetal forces in capitalist societies. They focused on the national ties which bound the members of modern societies together and separated them from the rest of the human race; they analysed what they saw as the weakening of national bonds because of capitalist globalization while recognizing the resilience of national loyalties in many of Europe's nation-states; they discussed what they regarded as the development of new forms of human solidarity and the slow emergence of a global community which would eventually include the whole human race. So, in their account of modern Europe, they analysed how early capitalism brought scattered, local groups together in increasingly homogeneous nation-states. In this period, ruling classes created national bonds which checked the formation of divisive class identities. Later, capitalism burst out of its national bounds. Increased exploitation in the era of capitalist globalization produced internationalist sentiments and alliances amongst the industrial proletariat. Somewhat simplistic assumptions about how capitalist internationalization would be followed by socialist internationalism had to be rethought in the late nineteenth and early twentieth centuries because of the revival of nationalism and the increased danger of major war. The theory of capitalist imperialism should be viewed in this context.

Lenin (1968) and Bukharin (1972) developed the theory of imperialism to explain the causes of the First World War. They argued that war was the product of a desperate need for new outlets for the surplus capital accumulated by dominant capitalist states. The theory of capitalist imperialism has been discredited on account of its economic reductionism but, despite its flaws, it was concerned with the central question of how political communities closed in on themselves in the period in question – an inescapable preoccupation given the earlier Marxian assumption that the dominant trend was towards greater cooperation between the proletariat of different nations (Linklater 1990b: Chapter 4). The theory of imperialism developed Marx and Engels' analysis of the relationship between nationalism and internationalism, and globalization and fragmentation. In so doing, it highlighted the tension between forces promoting the expansion and forces promoting the contraction of the sense of community.

Above else, however, the study of imperialism criticized the liberal proposition that late capitalism was committed to free trade internationalism which would lead to peace between nations; it was a restatement of Marx's claim that capitalism was destined to experience frequent crises. Lenin and Bukharin claimed the dominant tendency of the age was the emergence of new mercantilist states ever more willing to use force to achieve their economic and political objectives. National accumulations of surplus capital were regarded as the chief reason for the demise of a relatively peaceful international system (although Lenin thought the decline of British hegemony and the changing balance of power had contributed in a secondary way to the relaxation of constraints on force in relations between the major capitalist states).

Lenin and Bukharin maintained that nationalist and militarist ideologies had blurred class loyalties and stymied class conflict in this changing international environment. In *Imperialism: The Highest Stage of Capitalism*, Lenin (1968: 102) claimed that no 'Chinese wall separates the [working class] from the other classes'. Indeed, a labour aristocracy bribed by colonial profits and closely aligned with the bourgeoisie had developed in monopoly capitalist societies. With the outbreak of the First World War, the working classes which had become 'chained to the chariot of ... bourgeois state power' rallied around pleas to defend the homeland (Bukharin 1972: 166). But it was thought that the shift of the 'centre of gravity' from class conflict to inter-state rivalry would not last indefinitely. The horrors of war would show the working classes that their 'share in the imperialist policy [was] nothing compared with the wounds inflicted by the war' (1972: 167). Instead of 'clinging to the narrowness of the national state' and succumbing to the patriotic ideal of 'defending or extending the boundaries of the bourgeois state' the proletariat would return to the main project of 'abolishing state boundaries and merging all the peoples into one Socialist family' (1972: 167).

As noted earlier, Marx and Engels believed that capitalism created the preconditions for extending human loyalty from the nation to the species – and Lenin and Bukharin thought the destruction of national community and the return to cosmopolitanism would resume after a brief detour down the disastrous path of militarism and war. Their idea that the superabundance of finance capital was the reason for the First World War was mistaken, but that does not mean their analysis lacks all merit. Like Marx and Engels before them they were dealing with a fundamentally important theme which has received too little attention in mainstream International Relations. This is how political communities are shaped by the struggle between nationalism and internationalism in a world political system; it is what unusually high levels of globalization and fragmentation mean for the future of political community and for the level of human solidarity; and it is how national and global economic and political structures affect the lives of the marginal and most vulnerable groups in society.

Marxist writings on nationalism dealt with the boundaries of loyalty and community in greater detail. Recent claims about how the contemporary world is shaped by globalization and fragmentation have an interesting parallel in Lenin's thought:

> Developing capitalism knows two historical tendencies in the national question. The first is the awakening of national life and national movements, the struggle against all national oppression, and the creation of national states. The second is the development and growing frequency of international intercourse in every form, the breakdown of national barriers, the creation of the international unity of capital, of economic life in general, of politics, science etc. (Lenin 1964: 27)

Globalization and fragmentation were inter-related in Lenin's account of how capitalism spreads unevenly across the world. This theme was central to Trotsky's analysis of the 'combined and uneven development' of capitalism and to the later phenomenon of Third World Marxism (Knei-Paz 1978). According to the latter perspective, the metropolitan core capitalist societies, including the proletariat, exploited the peripheral societies which had been brought under their control. Their understandable response was not to seek to develop alliances with the working classes in affluent societies but to strive for national independence.

Lenin knew that particular groups such as the Jews were oppressed because of their religion and ethnicity, and that the demand for national self-determination was their unsurprising riposte. Socialists had to recognize that estrangement between religious and national groups was a huge barrier to universal cooperation. Although Lenin argued that socialists should support progressive national movements and try to harness them to their cause, he rejected the Austro-Marxists' approach to the 'national question'. They had advocated a federal approach which would give national cultures significant autonomy within existing national communities. Lenin's view was that national movements should be made to choose between complete secession from the state or continued membership on the basis of equal and identical rights with all other groups. His judgement was that most national movements would decide against secession for the simple reason that small-scale societies would not enjoy the levels of economic growth found in larger and more populous societies. Those movements that chose secession would gain freedom from the forms of domination and discrimination which bred national enmity or distrust. In the longer term, national secession would permit the development of solidarity between different national proletariats. This approach to nationalism was designed to prevent the proletariat from fragmenting into 'separate national rivulets' (Stalin 1953: 343, 354). Lenin and many other Marxists believed that national fragmentation was an inevitable consequence of the global spread of capitalism, but with the exception of Austro-Marxism they believed it was essential to avoid a socialist compromise with nationalism. Proletarian internationalism was more important than creating multicultural political communities.

Theories of imperialism shared Marx's belief that capitalism was a progressive force because it would bring industrial development and the basis for material prosperity to all peoples. The assumption was that Western models of capitalist and then socialist development would be imitated by other regions of the world. Trotsky's notion of the combined and uneven development of capitalism contemplated different possibilities: the encounter between the capitalist and pre-capitalist regions of the world would lead to entirely new types of society (Knei-Paz 1978). Post-Second World War theories of development and underdevelopment built on this theme. Dependency theorists argued that exploitative alliances between the dominant class interests in core and peripheral societies prevented the latter from industrializing (Frank 1967). They believed that secession from the capitalist world economy was crucial for peripheral industrial development. World-systems theory, as developed by Wallerstein in the 1970s and 1980s, also challenged the classical Marxist view that capitalism brings industrial development to the whole world, although he argued that development was possible in at least some 'semi-peripheral' societies (Wallerstein 1979). Dependency theory and the world-systems approach have been described as 'neo-Marxist' because they do not believe that the spread of capitalism will bring industrial development to poorer regions, and because they shifted the analysis from relations of production to such phenomena as 'unequal exchange' in world markets (Emmanuel 1972). Marxist and neo-Marxist theories of the world economy enjoyed their greatest prominence in the 1970s and 1980s, but they remain significant in the contemporary era of increasing global inequalities (Thomas 1999: 428).

It was noted earlier that several Third World Marxists argued that the proletariat in the industrial world is one of the beneficiaries of neo-imperialism; they supported the national revolt of the periphery rather than the Western socialist ideal of proletarian internationalism (Emmanuel 1972). Western Marxists disagreed profoundly about whether or not to support national liberation movements in non-Western societies, and many displayed considerable unease with forms of nationalist politics which would dilute the internationalist commitments of classical Marxism (Warren 1980; Nairn 1981). The fact that Marxism is a Western doctrine with its roots in the European Enlightenment is the crucial point here. Marxist cosmopolitanism was developed in the era of European dominance – in the colonial era which Marx greatly admired – and at a time when it was reasonable to assume that the non-European world would become more similar to the West in most ways. The rise of Third World Marxism in the 1960s and 1970s was a powerful reminder that the modern world was gradually entering the post-European age. Its emergence might be regarded as an illustration of 'the cultural revolt against the West' or as an attempt to adapt European ideas to very different circumstances (Bull 1984a; Brown 1988). In more recent years, many non-Western governments and movements have openly rejected Western models of economic and political development, and many oppose what they see as alien and decadent Western values. In this context, all forms of cosmopolitanism – whether Marxist or not – meet with suspicion. The main problem is not that classical Marxism underestimated the importance of nationalism, the state and geopolitics but, many would argue, that it expressed a culture-bound view of the world which was inherited from the European Enlightenment. Classical Marxism may have defended the ideal of universal human emancipation, but its vision of the future assumed the non-European would and should become the same as the modern West. The issue then is whether its project of emancipation was always at heart a project of domination or assimilation.

The changing fortunes of Marxism in International Relations

To recapitulate: Marxist approaches to international relations reflected on the processes which had led to the economic and social unification of the human race and stressed the role that modern capitalism played in accelerating this development. Replacing alienation, exploitation and estrangement with a form of universal cooperation which would promote freedom for all was its ethical aspiration. The international proletariat was deemed to be the historical subject which would realize these objectives, but rising nationalism and the growing danger risk of war in Europe led Marx and Engels to reconsider the nature of the path to universal emancipation. From the beginning through to more recent analyses of global inequality, Marxists have faced the question of whether capitalist globalization is destined to prepare the way for internationalism or whether powerful national loyalties would thwart this process. The discussion below and in Chapters 6 and 7 explains how the main strands of critical theory came to abandon 'the paradigm of production', jettisoned the belief that the working class is the privileged instrument of radical change and broke with the Marxian vision of universal emancipation. But, as previously noted, this does not mean that students of International Relations have nothing to learn from Marxism.

Until quite recently, the broad consensus in the study of International Relations was that Marxism had little if anything to offer the serious analyst. Realists argued that Marxism was concerned with how societies have interacted with nature rather than with how they have interacted with each other in ways that often led to major war. The paradigm of production analysed class structure and class conflict rather than persistent national loyalties, state power and geopolitical rivalry. A failure to understand these phenomena meant that Marxists were wrong in thinking that capitalist globalization was the prelude to a more peaceful, cosmopolitan world. Illustrating the point, Waltz argued that Marxists failed to appreciate the implications of the belief that socialism would first be established within one or more nation-states. The upshot of this expectation was that governments would have to ensure their national survival before they could hope to export socialism to other parts of the world (Waltz 1959). Trotsky's remark that he would issue a few revolutionary proclamations as Russia's Commissar for Foreign Affairs before closing shop has often been cited as evidence of the naïvety of Marxists regarding the persistent realities of international affairs.

The speed with which the Soviet regime resorted to traditional methods of diplomacy to promote its survival and security appears to confirm the realist point of view. Lenin stressed in 1919 that 'we are living not merely in a state, but in a system of states' (quoted in Halliday 1999: 312) – yet far from transforming the international system Marxism was transformed by it and contributed to its reproduction. The Soviet domination of Eastern Europe provoked nationalist demands for self-determination which realized their goals in many cases. Vietnam's invasion of Cambodia, and the war between China and Vietnam, were also cited as evidence of the validity of the realist claim that traditional power politics would survive the transition from capitalism to state socialism (Kubalkova and Cruickshank 1980; Giddens 1981: 250). The failure of Marxists to anticipate this outcome was for realists the inevitable outcome of their flawed theory of the state.

This is a point which many Marxists conceded in the 1970s and 1980s. The essence of Marx's position is often thought to be contained in his remark that the state in capitalist societies is simply 'the executive committee of the bourgeoisie'. His assumption was that power in the sphere of production is the key to power over society as a whole (Marx and Engels 1977: 223). In the 1960s and 1970s, Marxists moved away from this crude reductionism. Many argued that the state had to have some autonomy from the ruling class to ensure the survival of capitalism and to pacify subordinate class forces – whether by ensuring the labour force has access to a basic education and health care or by preventing capitalists from driving down wages to the point where the very survival of the system might be threatened. Some Marxists took a more radical path, by recognizing the importance of Max Weber's claim that the state derives immense power from its monopoly control of the instruments of violence and legitimacy from its responsibility for protecting 'society' from internal and external threats. A large literature in the 1970s and 1980s sought to reorient Marxism so that it took full account of the realm of geopolitical competition and war in which the state often has considerable autonomy from the dominant class forces (Anderson 1974; Skocpol 1979; Block 1980).

At the very time when Marxism was absorbing ideas which are associated with classical realism, International Relations began to take account of many of the concerns of Marxists and neo-Marxists. Dependency theory was crucial for two reasons: it forced students of International Relations to analyse material inequalities which are at least partly the result of the organization of the capitalist world economy, and it argued for a moral engagement with the problem of global inequality. It argued for a critical engagement with the world – for not only interpreting the world but with trying to understand how to change it – in a period when the newly independent states were forcing the issue of global economic and social justice onto the diplomatic agenda.

The study of global inequality was the vehicle which brought the Marxist tradition more directly into contact with the study of international relations. Robert Cox's analysis of social forces, states and world order remains one of the most ambitious attempts to use historical materialism to escape the limitations of statecentric international relations theory. His materialist conception of global economic and political structures focused on the interaction between modes of production – specifically the capitalist mode – states and world order but in such as way as to avoid economic reductionism. Cox claimed that production shapes other realms such as the nature of state power and strategic interaction to a far greater extent than traditional international relations theory has realized but it is also shaped by them. The relative importance of each domain in any era was an empirical question rather than a matter that could be settled *a priori*. However, Cox was especially interested in first analysing the dominant forms of production and then moving to a discussion of the other constituent parts of the global order. He placed special emphasis on the internationalization of relations of production in the modern capitalist era and on forms of global governance which perpetuate inequalities of power and wealth. Developing a theme which was introduced by the Italian Marxist, Antonio Gramsci in the 1920s and 1930s, Cox focused on the hegemonic nature of world order – that is, on how the political architecture of global capitalism helps to maintain material inequalities through a combination of coercion and efforts to win consent (Cox 1993).

The neo-Gramscian school approach to international political economy has been particularly interested in developing the study of the origins, development and possible transformation of global hegemony (Gill 1993b). Its members have analysed how hegemony is maintained through forms of close cooperation between powerful elites inside and outside the core regions of the world system and through the growing network of international economic and political institutions which are responsible for global governance (Gill 1993b; see also Cox 1983). The idea of 'disciplinary neo-liberalism' takes this form of investigation further by analysing the 'new constitutionalism' in which global institutions press national governments to accept the dictates of neo-liberal conceptions of the state, society and economy (Gill 1995). Crucial here are forms of global governance exercised through political 'conditionality' and international pressures to deregulate various sectors of the domestic economy and to permit the expansion of global capitalism. The analysis focuses on how transnational capitalist development, state structures and international economic institutions interact to generate a particular form of global hegemony and associated inequalities of power, resources and opportunities. It also focuses on 'the resistances these engender' (Rupert 2003: 181).

These approaches lend support to Halliday's comment that 'the modern inter-state system emerged in the context of the spread of capitalism across the globe, and the subjugation of pre-capitalist societies. This socio-economic system has underpinned both the character of individual states and of their relations with each other: no analysis of international relations is possible without reference to capitalism, the social formations it generated and the world system they comprise' (Halliday 1994: 61; see also Rosenberg 1994). This is perfectly compatible with the realist argument that states often pursue their own agenda and act independently of dominant class forces, although it is a clear invitation not to exaggerate the autonomy of most states, especially under modern conditions of capitalist globalization which compel most of them to respect the power of global financial markets and institutions. Various analyses of the development of the modern form of international relations over the last few centuries stress how little will be understood by relying on a realist explanation. The writings of Rosenberg (1994) and Teschke (2003) are powerful examples of how historical materialism is being used to show that geopolitical systems are anchored in particular productive relations and to analyse the ways in which the modern states-system and capitalist forms of production have developed together.

The upshot of these developments is that Marxism is no longer guilty of ignoring state power and the classical world of international relations, as realists understand it. Not that Marxists will concede for one moment that international relations can be reduced to rivalry between the great powers along the lines of Waltz's argument (see Chapter 3 earlier). During the Cold War, Marxists and their sympathisers were critical of realist arguments that strategic competition could be considered apart from the struggle between two radically different social systems and ideological perspectives, although this view had few adherents in the mainstream study of international relations (Halliday 1983). The collapse of bipolarity and the accelerated rise of the 'global business civilization' encouraged a reconsideration of Marx's writings on capitalist globaliza-tion. Marxism may appear less relevant given the revival of national security politics since 9/11, but its analysis of the relationship between capitalism and the state can still contribute to the study of global gover-nance in a period when the subordination of many states to the dictates of global capitalism is so evident (Bromley 1999; Hay 1999). Marxism comes into its own when analysing the relationship between the states-system and global capitalism and when considering the structure of global hegemony. These are two respects in which it is best placed to contribute to the study of international relations (Gamble 1999).

Marxism has been influential in the development of approaches to international political economy which have a critical or emancipatory intent. Marx wrote about the origins and development of modern capi-talism, but not as an end in itself: he was especially interested in the social forces that would bring about its downfall with the result that the mass of humanity would be free from domination and exploitation. Neo-Gramscian approaches work in the same spirit by focusing on the role of counter-hegemonic political forces in the global order – that is, on the various groups which are opposed to a world system which produces among other things massive global inequalities and damage to the natural environment. Mainstream International Relations theory has long been opposed to what it sees as manifestly 'political' scholarship, although its claims to neutrality and objectivity have been challenged in the critical lit-erature (see Chapters 6 and 7 in this volume). Realism and neo-realism have been criticized on the grounds that they have a 'problem-solving' rather than a 'critical' purpose. The importance of this distinction will be considered in more detail in Chapter 6 in this volume. It is necessary to introduce it at this stage, however, in order to make some observations about the idea of the reconstruction of historical materialism.

The distinction between problem-solving and critical theory was made by Cox (1981: 128) in conjunction with his much-quoted remark that 'knowledge is always for someone and for some purpose'. Put another way, political inquiry is never objective and value-free but supports, however unintentionally, particular conceptions of society which favour identifiable sectional interests. Cox argued that neo-realism is a version of problem-solving theory which takes the existing international order for granted and asks how it can be made to 'function more smoothly'. In the main, this means concentrating on the problems resulting from relations between the great powers. By contrast, critical theory asks how the existing global political and economic order came into being, and whether it might be changing. Following the example of Marx's study of capitalism, and mindful of his observation that 'all that is solid eventually melts into air' (Marx and Engels 1977: 224) critical theory focuses on challenges to an international order which will probably disappear one day to join the other dead civilizations; it concentrates on what may be the first stirrings of a more humane form of world political organization. The upshot of this argument is that mainstream international theorists were too quick to dismiss Marxism simply because of its economic reductionism and utopianism. What was missing from their account was any recognition of the fact that Marxism is not just a sociology of what is 'out there'; it is a consciously political account of forms of domination and the forces which are working against them. One of the main outcomes of the belated engagement with Marxism is that such considerations are now more central to the theory of international relations.

But Marxist-inspired political inquiry is only one strand of contemporary critical theory. Approaches such as feminism, postmodernism and postcolonialism have been concerned with patriarchy and with constructions of identity and otherness in national and global politics which have not been central dimensions of Marxist studies of world politics. However, Cox's version of historical materialism has taken account of the recent upsurge of identity politics associated with minority nations and indigenous peoples; he has also attached particular importance to analysing the political consequences of civilisational identities in the post-European world order. The normative vision which runs through Cox's writings on this subject moves beyond the Left's classical focus on reducing material inequalities. He states that 'a post-hegemonic order would be one in which different traditions of civilization could coexist, each based on a different intersubjectivity defining a distinct set of values and a distinct path towards development'. 'Mutual recognition and mutual understanding' are seen as the necessary foundations of a just world order in which different cultural identities have their rightful place (Cox 1992b, 1993: 265).

The focus on culture and civilization overlaps with the project of reconstructing historical materialism associated with the writings of the Frankfurt School critical theorist, Jürgen Habermas. He maintained in the 1970s that Marxism was guilty of overestimating the importance of 'labour' for social structure and historical change and of underestimating the role of 'interaction' – that is, the forms of communication which enable human being to live together. The achievement of Marxism was to be found in the 'paradigm of production', which made the ways in which human beings work on nature central to modern social and political inquiry; its main shortcoming was to fail to deal with the equally important question of how human beings use language to create orderly societies and how they have developed the principle that good societies should express the will of their members. For Habermas, the 'paradigm of production', which focuses on how human beings learn to control nature, has to be complemented by the 'paradigm of communication', which focuses on how human beings have developed the moral expectation that all individuals have the right to be involved in any decision making processes which can affect them. What was absent from its normative vision was the recognition that universal emancipation requires not only the reduction of class inequalities but the democratization of all dimensions of social, economic and political life (Habermas 1979; Roderick 1986). On this formulation, one can hear the echo of Marx's claim that the purpose of political theory and action is to understand and help create a world in which human beings can make more of their history under conditions of their own choosing.

The reconstruction of historical materialism led to a complex argument about the universal features of communication, and on this basis Habermas has built 'discourse ethics' or 'the discourse theory of morality'. The most straightforward way of explaining the discourse approach is that many human beings in the modern world have lost the belief that certain moral principles are right because they are anchored in deeper religious truths or because they rest on the authority of tradition. They see themselves as living in a morally diverse world where there is little or no prospect of reaching a consensus that there is a single moral code which is true for all. The philosophical question is whether human beings can agree on the importance of following certain neutral procedures which will make it possible for the exponents of very different world-views to live together. Habermas argues that the discourse theory of morality provides the best answer to this question. Its key requirement is that all individuals must be prepared to bring their different ethical positions before the tribunal of open discussion. They should be prepared to listen to all persons and to respect all standpoints, recognizing that prior to dialogue itself there can be no certainty about 'who will learn from whom' or about the 'better argument'. The point is that through open dialogue human beings with different religious and cultural backgrounds and conflicting moral and political standpoints can explore the possibility of a consensus about the best lines of moral argument. If no consensus emerges – and consensus must never be forced – they are left with the task of finding a fair compromise between competing positions (Habermas 1990).

Two points need to be made about the outcome of Habermas' reconstruction of historical materialism. First, Habermas has long rejected classical Marxist claims about the primacy of production and the centrality of class conflict in any form of life. The idea of universal emancipation as the reduction and eradication of class inequality is superseded by a vision of the good society in which there is greater human understanding and in which no-one deprives 'the other of otherness' (Habermas 1994: 119–20). The logic of his argument owes much to the 'spirit' of Marx and Marxism but its 'letter' rejects what many Marxists regard as the essence of their position, namely the primacy of the paradigm of production. This raises the question of how those who are broadly sympathetic with Marxist critical theory should build on its legacy. We return to this matter in the next section. Second, notwithstanding his critique of Marxism, Habermas is still broadly committed to the Enlightenment project of creating a cosmopolitan world in which human beings enjoy greater freedom. Admittedly, this vision does not include a defence of classical Marxist ideals such as the abolition of private property, the end of the commodification of labour, the joint ownership of the means of production and so forth. It is a vision which takes account of growing cultural diversity and moral conflict in the post-European age, but it is a thin vision because Habermas says even less than Marx about the nature of the good society. What is offered is a vision of a world in which human beings rely on specific procedures to work out political principles which will enable them to live together.

It is a reasonable argument that one does not have to be a Marxist to support this vision of a 'universal communication community'. It is sufficient to be a liberal or to have a broadly liberal-democratic persuasion. For some writers, herein lies one of the main problems in this attempt to build on the Marxist tradition of critical theory. Like Marx and classical Marxists, Habermas is already committed to an essentially Western conception of society, in this case to a vision of radical democracy at both the national and international levels which is rejected in many non-Western regions of the world (and, indeed, by many political movements within the West). The Eurocentrism of his discourse position is even more pronounced when it is recognized that the development of a universal communication community requires the removal of all 'asymmetries' in society – not just the elimination of gross material inequalities and an end to notions of racial or ethnic superiority but the dismantling of patriarchal structures which perpetuate the subjection of women (Apel 1980; see also Cohen 1990). All that need be added at this point is that many outside the West regard feminism as a Western ideology which is alien to their ways (for further discussion, see Chapter 9 in this volume). Complex debates surround these issues, as the later chapters in this volume will explain. But, it should be added, the questions which lie at the heart of these debates mostly concern those who are interested in the fate of Marxism and Marxist-influenced critical theory. They are less central to scholars who believe that historical materialism provides essential tools for explaining the relationship between the international states-system and the capitalist world economy or the structure and dynamics of global hegemony.

Marxism and international relations theory today

Until quite recently, Marxism was the dominant powerful form of critical social theory: it combined a powerful analysis of the development of human history with a detailed study of the evolution of capitalism and with reflections on how universal emancipation could be achieved through class struggle. Its attachment to the paradigm of production made Marxists vulnerable to the charge of neglecting racial, ethnic, religious and gender inequalities. Feminist and postmodern writers have developed new forms of critical social theory which owe very little to Marxism, and many reject the idea of universal emancipation on the grounds that all cosmopolitan projects contain the seeds of new forms of domination. They have the evidence of Marxism in power to support them. Efforts to reconstruct historical materialism and to import ideas from other traditions have taken place, as the development of Habermas' thought reveals. One question which arises out of these challenges to, and revisions, of Marxism is whether the perspective now has a special contribution to make to the future of critical international theory. The question is whether the initiative now lies clearly with approaches which are post-Marxist or outside the Marxist tradition.

One answer is that classical Marxism has been superseded by new forms of critical theory which have abandoned the idea that human history can be reduced to one grand historical narrative moving towards a condition of universal emancipation. This argument can be traced back to the writings of Horkheimer and Adorno (1972) – the founders of Frankfurt School critical theory – who argued in the 1940s that the problems of Marxism were a product of the failures of European Enlightenment. They maintained that Marx and Marxism shared the Enlightenment view that the growth of scientific knowledge and technological know-how would lead to greater human freedom; in fact, they led to new forms of bureaucratic domination. In the 1970s, the French postmodern writer Jean-François Lyotard (1984) also argued that the belief that human history was a journey from domination and superstition to freedom and enlightenment overlooked the dark side of Western rationality and scientific progress. To a significant extent, these arguments were a response to Soviet totalitarianism and to Stalinism.

An additional point – although this is more controversial – is that Enlightenment thinkers were largely disparaging about non-Western societies (Vogel 2003). Leaving the debate to one side, there is no doubt that Marx and Engels were often condescending towards and contemptuous of non-Western societies. They were convinced that Western imperialism and the spread of capitalism were necessary to liberate the 'historyless peoples' from religious myth and the tyranny of tradition. It is important at this point to recall the way in which classical Marxists agonised over the role of national liberation movements in the struggle for socialism and the place of the nation in the future socialist world order. More recent strands of critical theory have been bolder to celebrate human diversity and cultural difference. In Lyotard's case, the defence of the rights of the other is connected with the ideal of a 'global speech community' which has some parallels with Habermas' position on discourse ethics and cosmopolitan democracy – which some see as an extension of the radical democratic ethos which exists in Marx's writings (Carver 1998). Lyotard (1993) argues that all human beings have an equal right to 'establish their community by contract' using 'reason and debate'. But, against Habermas, Lyotard stresses the dangers inherent in privileging some idealized notion of dialogue, specifically that radical diversity will be sacrificed in the course of striving for consensus.

Marxists will ask if these visions of a world moving towards greater dialogue and diversity deal with the issue of how material inequalities prevent the establishment of communities of contract and consent. The writings of Jacques Derrida, the founder of deconstructionism, deserve attention at this point (for further discussion, see Chapter 7 in this volume). In his analysis of the contemporary relevance of Marx and Engels' *The Communist Manifesto*, Derrida (1994a, 1994b) defends a 'new International' on the grounds that 'violence, inequality, exclusion, famine, and thus economic oppression [have never] affected as many human beings in the history of the Earth and of humanity'. Defending the 'spirit of Marxism', Derrida (1994a: 56) argues for revising Marx's ideal of the 'withering away of the state'. This should be freed from earlier claims about socialist internationalism and the dictatorship of the proletariat. The 'new International' should protest against 'the state of international law, the concepts of state and nation' and break with inherited assumptions about exclusionary sovereign states and national conceptions of citizenship. Derrida (1994a: 58) envisages new forms of political community in which the state no longer possesses 'a space which it ... dominates' and which 'it never dominated without division'. The emphasis here is on new political arrangements which are in some ways more cosmopolitan than their predecessors (because they are con-cerned with the right of all human beings to a decent life), more sensitive to cultural and other differences (thereby realizing one of the main aspira-tions of the Austro-Marxists) and more committed to the reduction of global economic inequalities, so keeping faith with the central tenets of classical Marxism (Linklater 1998). Derrida stresses, however, that those who work in 'spirit of Marxism' should devote more attention to analysing the state, citizenship, political community and international law.

We return at this point to the central criticism of Marxism in the mainstream literature on international relations, which is its failure to deal with the state, nationalism and war, or its neglect of diplomacy, the balance of power and international law. Realists and neo-realists have argued that geo-politics is more important than economic globalization, and that is why human beings continue to rely on nation-states for their security rather than strive to create new forms of political community. They stress that Marxist internationalism was broken on the wheel of power politics during the First World War; it has no real relevance to a world of states.

The argument raises fundamental questions about the purpose of studying international relations. Here, there can be no doubt that two world wars in the twentieth century, and the bipolar struggle which dominated the second half of the century, made it easier for realism and neo-realism to define the discipline. The recent revival of national security politics and the wars against the Taliban and against Saddam Hussein have encouraged the realists to argue that recent events have demonstrated once again that international politics is 'the realm of recurrence and repetition', the realm of politics that does not change in its most fundamental respects (Waltz 2002). They claim that in the 1990s some analysts of international relations were dazzled by apparent novelties – increasing levels of economic globalization, 'the obsolescence of force' and so on. These criticisms are mainly directed at liberals although the neo-realist will maintain that they apply to Marxism as well. The fact that Marxism is not even mentioned in this context is a function of its virtual absence from the American study of international relations.

Those who make the case for taking Marxism seriously will not necessarily dispute these observations about the importance of national security politics, but they will invariably argue that a more comprehensive understanding of how the modern international system has developed over the last few centuries and at the present time cannot ignore the evolution of modern capitalism, its dominance across the world and its impact on international institutions and international law; nor can it ignore the structure and dynamics of global hegemony, the growth of economic inequalities and the changing fortunes of counter-hegemonic movements which defend visions of a more just world order. In part, this is an argument about how to understand the structure of world politics; in part it is a debate about how that structure producers 'winners' and 'losers'. In the 1960s and 1970s, some Marxist approaches replaced the humanism of the early Marx with dry structural analysis which lost sight of the ethical issues which are at stake in politics. However Marxism has always come into its own when combining the empirical analysis of global structures and processes with a morally infused commitment to understanding and challenging deep inequalities of power, resources and opportunities. Indeed, its belief that the concern with asymmetries and inequalities should drive the analysis remains a major achievement with lasting significance for the study of international relations.

Conclusion

Despite its weaknesses, Marxism contributes to the theory of international relations in at least four respects. First, historical materialism with its emphasis on production, property relations and class is an important counter-weight to realist theories which assume that the struggle for power and security determines the structure of world politics. This leads to two further points which are that Marxism has long been centrally concerned with capitalist globalization and international inequalities and that, for Marxism, the global spread of capitalism is the backdrop to the development of modern societies and the organization of their international relations. A fourth theme, which first appeared in Marx's critique of liberal political economy, is that explanations of the social world are never as objective and innocent as they may seem. Applied to international politics, the argument is that the analysis of basic and unchanging realities can all too easily ignore relations of power and inequality not between states but between *individuals*. Dominant strands of Marxist thought have taken the view that one of the main functions of scholarship is to understand the principal forms of domination and to imagine a world order which is committed to reducing material inequalities. This critical orientation to world politics can no longer be simply 'Marxist' in the largely superseded sense of using the paradigm of production to analyse class inequalities. But it can nevertheless remain true to the 'spirit of Marxism' by combining the empirical analysis of the dominant forms of power and inequality with a moral vision of a more just world order. This critical approach can extend beyond the analysis of capitalist globalization and rising international inequalities to the ways in which states conduct national security politics. One of the failings of Marxism as a source of critical international theory is its ingrained tendency to focus on the former at the expense of the latter field of inquiry. Later chapters discuss whether other strands of critical international theory have succeeded in overcoming this limitation.

Chapter 6

Critical Theory

RICHARD DEVETAK

If there is anything that holds together the disparate group of scholars who subscribe to 'critical theory' it is the idea that the study of international relations should be oriented by an emancipatory politics. The terrorist attacks of September 11, 2001 and the subsequent 'war on terrorism' showed, among other things, that unnecessary human suffering remains a central fact of international life. It would be easy, and perhaps understandable, to overestimate the novelty or significance of September 11 for world order. After all, the world's greatest power was dealt a devastating blow in its national capital, Washington, and its greatest city, New York. In attacking the Pentagon and the World Trade Centre, the perpetrators were attacking two icons of America's global power projection: its military and financial centres. For critical theory, any assessment of the degree to which September 11 changed world order will depend on the extent to which various forms of domination are removed and peace, freedom, justice and equality are promoted. The unfinished 'war on terrorism' fought by Washington and London has so far done little to satisfy the critical theorist's concerns. Indeed, it has been argued by many critical theorists that it is more likely to introduce 'de-civilizing' forces into international relations.

This chapter is divided into three main parts: firstly, a sketch of the origins of critical theory; secondly, an examination of the political nature of knowledge claims in international relations; and, thirdly, a detailed account of critical international theory's attempt to place questions of community at the centre of the study of international relations. This will provide an opportunity to discuss how critical theory reflects on the events of September 11 and the subsequent 'war on terrorism'.

Origins of critical theory

Critical theory has its roots in a strand of thought which is often traced back to the Enlightenment and connected to the writings of Kant, Hegel and Marx. While this is an important lineage in the birth of critical theory it is not the only possible one that can be traced, as there is also the imprint of classical Greek thought on autonomy and democracy to be considered, as well as the thinking of Nietzsche and Weber. However, in the twentieth century critical theory became most closely associated with a distinct body of thought known as the Frankfurt School (Jay 1973; Wyn Jones 2001). It is in the work of Max Horkheimer, Theodor Adorno, Walter Benjamin, Herbert Marcuse, Erich Fromm, Leo Lowenthal and, more recently, Jürgen Habermas that critical theory acquired a renewed potency and in which the term *critical theory* came to be used as the emblem of a philosophy which questions modern social and political life through a method of immanent critique. It was largely an attempt to recover a critical and emancipatory potential that had been overrun by recent intellectual, social, cultural, political, economic and technological trends.

Essential to the Frankfurt School's critical theory was a concern to comprehend the central features of contemporary society by understanding its historical and social development, and tracing contradictions in the present which may open up the possibility of transcending contemporary society and its built-in pathologies and forms of domination. Critical theory intended 'not simply to eliminate one or other abuse', but to analyse the underlying social structures which result in these abuses with the intention of overcoming them (Horkheimer 1972: 206). It is not difficult to notice the presence here of the theme advanced by Marx in his eleventh thesis on Feuerbach: 'philosophers have only interpreted the world in various ways; the point is to change it' (Marx 1977a: 158). This normative interest in identifying immanent possibilities for social transformation is a defining characteristic of a line of thought which extends, at least, from Kant, through Marx, to contemporary critical theorists such as Habermas. This intention to analyse the possibilities of realizing emancipation in the modern world entailed critical analyses of both obstructions to, and immanent tendencies towards, 'the rational organization of human activity' (Horkheimer 1972: 223). Indeed, this concern extends the line of thought back beyond Kant to the classical Greek conviction that the rational constitution of the *polis* finds its expression in individual autonomy and the establishment of justice and democracy. Politics, on this understanding, is the realm concerned with realizing the just life.

There is, however, an important difference between critical theory and the Greeks which relates to the conditions under which knowledge claims can be made regarding social and political life. There are two points worth recalling in this regard: firstly, the Kantian point that reflection on the limits of what we can know is a fundamental part of theorizing and, secondly, a Hegelian and Marxian point that knowledge is always, and irreducibly, conditioned by historical and material contexts; in Mark Rupert's words (2003: 186), it is always 'situated knowledge'. Since critical theory takes society itself as its object of analysis, and since theories and acts of theorizing are never independent of society, critical theory's scope of analysis must necessarily include reflection on theory. In short, critical theory must be *self-reflective*; it must include an account of its own genesis and application in society. By drawing attention to the relationship between knowledge and society, which is so frequently excluded from mainstream theoretical analysis, critical theory recognizes the political nature of knowledge claims.

It was on the basis of this recognition that Horkheimer distinguished between two conceptions of theory, which he referred to as 'traditional' and 'critical' theories. Traditional conceptions of theory picture the theorist at a remove from the object of analysis. By analogy with the natural sciences, they claim that subject and object must be strictly separated in order to theorize properly. Traditional conceptions of theory assume there is an external world 'out there' to study, and that an inquiring subject can study this world in a balanced and objective manner by withdrawing from the world it investigates, and leaving behind any ideological beliefs, values, or opinions which would invalidate the inquiry. To qualify as theory it must at least be value-free. On this view, theory is possible only on condition that an inquiring subject can withdraw from the world it studies (and in which it exists) and rid itself of all biases. This contrasts with critical conceptions that deny the possibility of value-free social analysis.

By recognizing that theories are always embedded in social and political life, critical conceptions of theory allow for an examination of the purposes and functions served by particular theories. However, while such conceptions of theory recognize the unavoidability of taking their orientation from the social context in which they are situated, their guiding interest is one of emancipation from, rather than legitimation and consolidation of, existing social forms. The purpose underlying critical, as opposed to traditional, conceptions of theory is to improve human existence by abolishing injustice (Horkheimer 1972). As articulated by Horkheimer (1972: 215), this conception of theory does not simply present an expression of the 'concrete historical situation', it also acts as 'a force within [that situation] to stimulate change'. It allows for the intervention of humans in the making of their history.

It should be noted that while critical theory has not directly addressed the international level, this in no way implies that international relations is beyond the limits of its concern. The writings of Kant and Marx, in particular, have demonstrated that what happens at the international

level is of immense significance to the achievement of universal emancipation. It is the continuation of this project in which critical international
theory is engaged. The Frankfurt School, however, never addressed
international relations in its critiques of the modern world, and Habermas
has made only scant reference to it until recently (see Habermas 1998,
2003; Habermas and Derrida 2003). The main tendency of critical
theory is to take individual society as the focus and to neglect the dimension of relations between and across societies. For critical international
theory, however, the task is to extend the trajectory of Frankfurt School –
critical theory beyond the domestic realm to the international – or, more
accurately, global – realm. It makes a case for a theory of world politics
which is 'committed to the emancipation of the species' (Linklater
1990a: 8). Such a theory would no longer be confined to an individual
state or society, but would examine relations between and across them,
and reflect on the possibility of extending the rational, just and democratic organization of political society across the globe (Neufeld 1995:
Chapter 1; Shapcott 2001).

To summarize, critical theory draws upon various strands of Western
social, political and philosophical thought in order to erect a theoretical
framework capable of reflecting on the nature and purposes of theory
and revealing both obvious and subtle forms of injustice and domination
in society. Critical theory not only challenges and dismantles traditional
forms of theorizing, it also problematizes and seeks to dismantle entrenched
forms of social life that constrain human freedom. Critical international
theory is an extension of this critique to the international domain. The
next part of the chapter focuses on the attempt by critical international
theorists to dismantle traditional forms of theorizing by promoting more
self-reflective theory.

The politics of knowledge in International Relations theory

It was not until the 1980s, and the onset of the so-called 'third debate',
that questions relating to the politics of knowledge would be taken
seriously in the study of international relations. Epistemological questions
regarding the justification and verification of knowledge claims, the
methodology applied and the scope and purpose of inquiry, and ontological questions regarding the nature of the social actors and other
historical formations and structures in international relations, all carry
normative implications that had been inadequately addressed. One of
the important contributions of critical international theory has been to
widen the object domain of International Relations, not just to include

epistemological and ontological assumptions, but to explicate their connection to prior political commitments.

This section outlines the way in which critical theory brings knowledge claims in International Relations under critical scrutiny. Firstly, it considers the question of epistemology by describing how Horkheimer's distinction between traditional and critical conceptions of theory has been taken up in International Relations; and secondly, it elaborates the connection between critical theory and emancipatory theory. The result of this scrutinizing is to reveal the role of political interests in knowledge formation. As Robert Cox (1981) succinctly and famously said, 'theory is always for someone and for some purpose'. As a consequence, critical international theorists reject the idea that theoretical knowledge is neutral or non-political. Whereas traditional theories would tend to see power and interests as *a posteriori* factors affecting outcomes in interactions between political actors in the sphere of international relations, critical international theorists insist that they are by no means absent in the formation and verification of knowledge claims. Indeed, they are *a priori* factors affecting the production of knowledge, hence Kimberly Hutchings' (1999: 69) assertion that 'International Relations theory is not only about politics, it also is itself political'.

Problem-solving and critical theories

In his pioneering 1981 article, Robert Cox followed Horkheimer by distinguishing critical theory from traditional theory – or, as Cox prefers to call it, problem-solving theory. Problem-solving or traditional theories are marked by two main characteristics: first by a positivist methodology; second, by a tendency to legitimize prevailing social and political structures.

Heavily influenced by the methodologies of the natural sciences, problem-solving theories suppose that positivism provides the only legitimate basis of knowledge. Positivism is seen, as Steve Smith (1996: 13) remarks, as the 'gold standard' against which other theories are evaluated. There are many different characteristics that can be identified with positivism, but two are particularly relevant to our discussion. First, positivists assume that facts and values can be separated; secondly, that it is possible to separate subject and object. This results in the view not only that an objective world exists independently of human consciousness, but that objective knowledge of social reality is possible insofar as values are expunged from analysis.

Problem-solving theory, as Cox (1981: 128) defines it, 'takes the world as it finds it, with the prevailing social and power relationships and the institutions into which they are organised, as the given framework for action. It does not question the present order, but has the effect of legitimising and reifying it'. Its general aim, says Cox (1981: 129), is to make the existing order 'work smoothly by dealing effectively with particular sources of trouble'. Neo-realism, *qua* problem-solving theory, takes seriously the realist dictum to work with, rather than against, prevailing international forces. By working within the given system it has a stabilizing effect, tending to preserve the existing global structure of social and political relations. Cox points out that neo-liberal institutionalism also partakes of problem-solving. Its objective, as explained by its foremost exponent, is to 'facilitate the smooth operation of decentralized international political systems' (Keohane 1984: 63). Situating itself between the states-system and the liberal capitalist global economy, neo-liberalism's main concern is to ensure that the two systems function smoothly in their coexistence. It seeks to render the two global systems compatible and stable by diffusing any conflicts, tensions, or crises that might arise between them (Cox 1992b: 173). As James Bohman (2002: 506) says, such an approach 'models the social scientist on the engineer, who masterfully chooses the optimal solution to a problem of design'. In summary, traditional conceptions of theory tend to work in favour of stabilizing prevailing structures of world order and their accompanying inequalities of power and wealth.

The main point that Cox wishes to make about problem-solving theory is that its failure to reflect on the prior framework within which it theorizes means that it tends to operate in favour of prevailing ideological priorities. Its claims to value-neutrality notwithstanding, problem-solving theory is plainly 'value-bound by virtue of the fact that it implicitly accepts the prevailing order as its own framework' (Cox 1981: 130). As a consequence, it remains oblivious to the way power and interests precede and shape knowledge claims.

By contrast, critical international theory starts from the conviction that because cognitive processes themselves are contextually situated and therefore subject to political interests, they ought to be critically evaluated. Theories of international relations, like any knowledge, necessarily are conditioned by social, cultural and ideological influence, and one of the main tasks of critical theory is to reveal the effect of this conditioning. As Richard Ashley (1981: 207) asserts, 'knowledge is always constituted in reflection of interests', so critical theory must bring to consciousness latent interests, commitments, or values that give rise to, and orient, any theory. We must concede therefore that the study of international relations 'is, and always has been, unavoidably normative' (Neufeld 1995: 108), despite claims to the contrary. Because critical international theory sees an intimate connection between social life and cognitive processes, it rejects the positivist distinctions between fact and value, object and subject. By ruling out the possibility of objective knowledge critical international theory seeks to promote greater 'theoretical reflexivity' (1995: Chapter 3). Cox (1992a: 59) expresses this reflexivity in terms of a double process: the first is 'self-consciousness of one's own historical time and place which determines the questions that claim attention', the second is 'the effort to understand the historical dynamics that brought about the conditions in which these questions arose'. Similarly, Bohman (2002: 503) advocates a form of theoretical reflexivity based on the 'perspective of a critical-reflective participant'. By adopting these reflexive attitudes critical theory is more like a meta-theoretical attempt to examine how theories are situated in prevailing social and political orders, how this situatedness impacts on theorizing, and, most importantly, the possibilities for theorizing in a manner that challenges the injustices and inequalities built into the prevailing world order.

Critical theory's relation to the prevailing order needs to be explained with some care. For although it refuses to take the prevailing order as it finds it, critical theory does not simply ignore it. It accepts that humans do not make history under conditions of their own choosing, as Marx observed in *The Eighteenth Brumaire of Louis Bonaparte* (1977e), and so a detailed examination of present conditions must necessarily be undertaken. Nevertheless, the order which has been 'given' to us is by no means natural, necessary or historically invariable. Critical international theory takes the global configuration of power relations as its object and asks how that configuration came about, what costs it brings with it and what alternative possibilities remain immanent in history.

Critical theory is essentially a critique of the dogmatism it finds in traditional modes of theorizing. This critique reveals the unexamined assumptions that guide traditional modes of thought, and exposes the complicity of traditional modes of thought in prevailing political and social conditions. To break with dogmatic modes of thought is to 'denaturalize' the present, as Karin Fierke (1998: 13) puts it, to make us 'look again, in a fresh way, at that which we assume about the world because it has become overly familiar'. Denaturalizing '[allegedly] objective realities opens the door to alternative forms of social and political life'. Implicitly therefore critical theory *qua* denaturalizing critique serves 'as an instrument for the delegitimisation of established power and privilege' (Neufeld 1995: 14). The knowledge critical international theory generates is not neutral; it is politically and ethically charged by an interest in social and political transformation. It criticizes and debunks theories that legitimize the prevailing order and affirms progressive alternatives that promote emancipation.

This immediately raises the question of how ethical judgements about the prevailing world order can be formed. Since there are no objective theoretical frameworks there can be no Archimedean standpoint outside history or society from which to engage in ethical criticism or judgement. It is not a matter of drafting a set of moral ideals and using them as a transcendent benchmark to judge forms of political organization. There is no utopia to compare to facts. This means that critical international theory must employ the method of immanent critique rather than abstract ethics to criticize the present order of things (Linklater 1990b: 22–3).

The task, therefore, is to 'start from where we are', in Rorty's words (quoted in Linklater 1998: 77), and excavate the principles and values that structure our political society, exposing the contradictions or inconsistencies in the way our society is organized to pursue its espoused values. This point is endorsed by several other critical international theorists, especially Kimberly Hutchings, whose version of critical international theory is heavily influenced by Hegel's phenomenological version of immanent critique. Immanent critique is undertaken 'without reference to an independently articulated method or to transcendent criteria' (Hutchings 1999: 99). Following Hegel's advice, critical international theory must acknowledge that the resources for criticizing and judging can be found only 'immanently', that is, in the already existing political societies from where the critique is launched. The critical resources brought to bear do not fall from the sky, they issue from the historical development of concrete legal and political institutions. The task of the political theorist is therefore to explain and criticize the present political order in terms of the principles presupposed by and embedded in its own legal, political and cultural practices and institutions (Fierke 1998: 114; Hutchings 1999: 102).

Fiona Robinson (1999) similarly argues that ethics should not be conceived as separate from the theories and practices of international relations, but should instead be seen as embedded in them. In agreement with Hutchings she argues for a 'phenomenology of ethical life' rather than an 'abstract ethics about the application of rules' (Robinson 1999: 31). On her account of a 'global ethics of care', however, it is necessary also to submit the background assumptions of already existing moral and political discourses to critical scrutiny. Hutchings and Robinson agree with Linklater that any critical international theory must employ a mode of immanent critique. This means that the theorist must engage critically with the background normative assumptions that structure our ethical judgements in an effort to generate a more coherent fit between modes of thought and forms of political organization, and without relying on a set of abstract ethical principles.

Critical theory's task as an emancipatory theory

If problem-solving theories adopt a positivist methodology and end up reaffirming the prevailing system, critical theories are informed by the traditions of hermeneutics and *Ideologiekritik*. Critical international theory is not concerned only with understanding and explaining the existing realities of world politics, it also intends to criticize in order to transform them. It is an attempt to comprehend essential social processes for the purpose of inaugurating change, or at least knowing whether change is possible. In Hoffman's words (1987: 233), it is 'not merely an expression of the concrete realities of the historical situation, but also a force for change within those conditions'. Neufeld (1995: Chapter 5) also affirms this view of critical theory. It offers, he says, a form of social criticism that supports practical political activity aimed at societal transformation.

Critical theory's emancipatory interest is concerned with 'securing freedom from unacknowledged constraints, relations of domination, and conditions of distorted communication and understanding that deny humans the capacity to make their future through full will and consciousness' (Ashley 1981: 227). This plainly contrasts with problem-solving theories which tend to accept what Linklater (1997) calls the 'immutability thesis'. Critical theory is committed to extending the rational, just and democratic organization of political life beyond the level of the state to the whole of humanity.

The conception of emancipation promoted by critical international theory is largely derived from a strand of thought which finds its origin in the Enlightenment project. This project was generally concerned with breaking with past forms of injustice to foster the conditions necessary for universal freedom (Devetak 1995b). To begin with, emancipation, as understood by Enlightenment thinkers and critical international theorists, generally expresses a negative conception of freedom which consists in the removal of unnecessary, socially created constraints. This understanding is manifest in Booth's (1991b: 539) definition of emancipation as 'freeing people from those constraints that stop them carrying out what freely they would choose to do'. The emphasis in this understanding is on dislodging those impediments or impositions which unnecessarily curtail individual or collective freedom. More substantively, Ashley (1981: 227) defines emancipation as the securing of 'freedom from unacknowledged constraints, relations of domination, and conditions of distorted communication and understanding that deny humans the capacity to make their own future through full will and consciousness'. The common thrust of these understandings is that emancipation implies a quest for autonomy. 'To be free', says Linklater

(1990a: 135), is 'to be self-determining or to have the capacity to initiate action. The objective of critical international theory therefore is to extend the human capacity for self-determination' (Linklater 1990b: 10).

In Linklater's account of critical international theory two thinkers are integral: Immanuel Kant and Karl Marx. Kant's approach is instructive because it seeks to incorporate the themes of power, order *and* emancipation (Linklater 1990b: 21–2). As expressed by Linklater (1992b: 36), Kant 'considered the possibility that state power would be tamed by principles of international order and that, in time, international order would be modified until it conformed with principles of cosmopolitan justice'. Kant's theory of international relations is an early attempt to map out a critical international theory by absorbing the insights and criticizing the weaknesses in realist and rationalist thought under an interest in universal freedom and justice. While Linklater believes Marx's approach to be too narrow in its focus on class-based exclusion, he thinks it nevertheless provides the basis of a social theory on which critical international theory must build. As Linklater observed (1990a: 159), both Marx and Kant share 'the desire for a universal society of free individuals, a universal kingdom of ends'. Both held strong attachments to the Enlightenment themes of freedom and universalism, and both launched strong critiques of particularistic life-forms with the intention of expanding moral and political community.

To conclude this part of the chapter, critical international theory makes a strong case for paying closer attention to the relations between knowledge and interests. One of critical international theory's main contributions in this regard is to expose the political nature of knowledge-formation. Underlying all this is an explicit interest in challenging and removing socially produced constraints on human freedom, thereby contributing to the possible transformation of international relations (Linklater 1990b: 1, 1998).

Rethinking political community

Informing critical international theory is the spirit, if not the letter, of Marx's critique of capitalism. Like Marx, critical international theorists seek to expose and critically analyse the sources of inequality and domination that shape global power relations with the intention of eliminating them. Since the mid-1990s one of the core themes that has grown out of critical international theory is the need to develop more sophisticated understandings of community as a means of identifying and eliminating global constraints on humanity's potential for freedom, equality and self-determination (Linklater 1990b: 7). Linklater's approach to this task, which has set the agenda, is first to analyse the way in which inequality and domination flow from modes of political community tied to the sovereign state, and secondly to consider alternative forms of political community which promote human emancipation.

This section elaborates three dimensions on which critical international theory rethinks political community (see Linklater 1992a: 92–7). The first dimension is normative, and pertains to the philosophical critique of the state as an exclusionary form of political organization. The second is sociological, and relates to the need to develop an account of the origins and evolution of the modern state and states-system. The third is the praxeological dimension concerning practical possibilities for reconstructing International Relations along more emancipatory and cosmopolitan lines. The overall effect of critical international theory, and its major contribution to the study of International Relations, is to focus on the normative foundations of political life.

The normative dimension: the critique of ethical particularism and social exclusion

One of the key philosophical assumptions that has structured political and ethical thought and practice about international relations is the idea that the modern state is the natural form of political community. The sovereign state has been 'fetishized', to use Marx's term, as the normal mode of organizing political life. Critical international theorists, however, wish to problematize this fetishization and draw attention to the 'moral deficits' that are created by the state's interaction with the capitalist world economy. In this section, I outline critical international theory's philosophical inquiry into the normative bases of political life and its critique of ethical particularism and the social exclusion it generates.

The philosophical critique of particularism was first, and most systematically, set out in Andrew Linklater's *Men and Citizens* (1990a). His main concern there was to trace how modern political thought had constantly differentiated ethical obligations due to co-citizens from those due to the rest of humanity. In practice, this tension between 'men' and 'citizens' has always been resolved in favour of citizens – or, more accurately, members of a particular sovereign state. Even if it was acknowledged, as it was by most early modern thinkers, that certain universal rights were thought to extend to all members of the human community, they were always residual and secondary to particularistic ones.

Men and Citizens is, among other things, a work of recovery. It seeks to recover a political philosophy based on universal ethical reasoning which has been progressively marginalized in the twentieth century, especially with the onset of the Cold War and the hegemony of realism.

That is, it seeks to recover and reformulate the Stoic–Christian ideal of human community. While elements of this ideal can be found in the natural law tradition, it is to the Enlightenment tradition that Linklater turns to find a fuller expression of this ideal. Linklater here is strongly influenced by the thought of Kant, for whom war was undeniably related to the separation of humankind into separate, self-regarding political units, Rousseau, who caustically remarked that in joining a particular community individual citizens necessarily made themselves enemies of the rest of humanity, and Marx who saw in the modern state a contradiction between general and private interests.

The point being made here is that particularistic political associations lead to inter-societal estrangement, the perpetual possibility of war and social exclusion. This type of argument underlies the thought of several Enlightenment thinkers of the eighteenth century, including Montesquieu, Rousseau, Paine and Kant among others, for whom war was simply an expression of *ancien régime* politics and a tool of state. Marx extended the critique of the modern state by arguing that, in upholding the rule of law, private property and money, it masks capitalism's alienation and exploitation behind bourgeois ideals of freedom and equality. Marx, of course, viewed the separation of politics and economics as a liberal illusion created to mask capitalism's power relations. In Rupert's words (2003: 182), one of Marx's enduring insights is 'that the seemingly apolitical economic spaces generated by capitalism – within and across juridical states – are permeated by structured relations of social power deeply consequential for political life'. From this Marxian perspective, modern international relations, insofar as it combines the political system of sovereign states and the economic system of market capitalism, is a form of exclusion where particular class interests parade themselves as universal. The problem with the sovereign state therefore is that as a 'limited moral community' it promotes exclusion, generating estrangement, injustice, insecurity and violent conflict between self-regarding states by imposing rigid boundaries between 'us' and 'them' (Cox 1981: 137, Linklater 1990a: 28).

Such arguments have led in recent times, and especially in a century which saw unprecedented flows of stateless peoples and refugees, to more general and profound questions about the foundations on which humanity is politically divided and organized. In particular, as Kimberly Hutchings (1999: 125) notes, it has led critical international theory to a 'questioning of the nation-state as a normatively desirable mode of political organisation'. Consistent with other critical international theorists Hutchings (1999: 122, 135) problematizes the 'idealised fixed ontologies' of nation and state as subjects of self-determination.

Hutchings goes further than Linklater, however, by also problematizing the individual 'self' of liberalism. Her intention is to examine the status of all normative claims to self-determination, whether the 'self' is understood as the individual, nation, or state. But insofar as her critique is aimed at placing the 'self' in question as a self-contained entity, Hutchings' analysis complements and extends the philosophical critique of particularism undertaken by Linklater.

Richard Shapcott (2000b, 2001) also continues this critique by inquiring into the way different conceptions of the 'self' shape relations to 'others' in international relations. Shapcott's main concern is with the possibility of achieving justice in a culturally diverse world. Although the main influences on his argument are Tzvetan Todorov and Hans-Georg Gadamer rather than Habermas, Shapcott's critique of the self is consistent with Linklater's and Hutchings'. He rejects both liberal and communitarian conceptions of the self for foreclosing genuine communication and justice in the relationship between self and other. Liberal conceptions of the self, he says, involve a 'significant moment of assimilation' because they are incapable of properly recognizing difference (2000b: 216). Communitarians, on the other hand, tend to take the limits of political community as given and, as a consequence, refuse to grant outsiders or non-citizens an equal voice in moral conversations. In other words, 'liberals underestimate the moral significance of national differences, while communitarians overestimate them. Both, in short, fail to do justice to difference' (Shapcott 2001: Chapter 1).

The common project of Hutchings, Linklater and Shapcott here is to question the boundedness of identity. A less dogmatic attitude towards national boundaries is called for by these critical international theorists, as national boundaries are recognized as 'neither morally decisive nor morally insignificant' (Linklater 1998: 61). They are perhaps unavoidable in some form. The point, however, is to ensure that national boundaries do not obstruct principles of openness, recognition and justice in relations with the 'other' (Linklater 1998: Chapter 2; Hutchings 1999: 138; Shapcott 2000a: 111).

Critical international theory has highlighted the dangers of unchecked particularism which can too readily deprive 'outsiders' of certain rights. This philosophical critique of particularism has led critical international theory to criticize the sovereign state as one of the foremost modern forms of social exclusion and therefore as a considerable barrier to universal justice and emancipation. In the following section we outline critical international theory's sociological account of how the modern state came to structure political community.

The sociological dimension: states, social forces and changing world orders

Rejecting realist claims that the condition of anarchy and the self-regarding actions of states are either natural or immutable, critical international theory has always been a form of small-'c' constructivism. One of its essential tasks is therefore to account for the social and historical production of both the agents and structures taken for granted by traditional theories.

Against the positivism and empiricism of various forms of realism, critical international theory adopts a more hermeneutic approach, which conceives of social structures as having an intersubjective existence. 'Structures are socially constructed' – that is, says Cox (1992a: 138), 'they become a part of the objective world by virtue of their existence in the intersubjectivity of relevant groups of people'. Allowing for the active role of human minds in the constitution of the social world does not lead to a denial of material reality, it simply gives it a different ontological status. Although structures, as intersubjective products, do not have a physical existence like tables or chairs, they nevertheless have real, concrete effects (1992b: 133). Structures produce concrete effects because humans act *as if* they were real (Cox 1986: 242). It is this view of ontology which underlies Cox's and critical international theory's attempts to comprehend the present order.

In contrast to individualist ontologies which conceive of states as atomistic, rational and possessive, and as if their identities existed prior to or independently of social interaction (Reus-Smit 1996: 100), critical international theory is more interested in explaining how both individual actors and social structures emerge in, and are conditioned by, history. For example, against the Westphalian dogma that the state is a state is a state (Cox 1981: 127), critical international theory views the modern state as a distinctive form of political community, bringing with it particular functions, roles, and responsibilities that are socially and historically determined. Whereas the state is taken for granted by realism, critical international theory seeks to provide a social theory of the state.

Crucial to critical international theory's argument is that we must account for the development of the modern state as the dominant form of political community in modernity. What is therefore required is an account of how states construct their moral and legal duties and how these reflect certain assumptions about the structure and logic of international relations. Using the work of Michael Mann and Anthony Giddens in particular, Linklater (1998: Chapters 4–5) undertakes what he calls an historical sociology of 'bounded communities'.

Linklater's *Beyond Realism and Marxism* (1990b) had already begun to analyse the interplay of different logics or rationalization processes in the making of modern world politics. But in *Transformation of Political Community* (1998), he carries this analysis further by providing a more detailed account of these processes and by linking them more closely to systems of inclusion and exclusion in the development of the modern state. His argument is that the boundaries of political community are shaped by the interplay of four rationalization processes: state-building, geopolitical rivalry, capitalist industrialization and moral–practical learning (Linklater 1998: 147–57). Five monopoly powers are acquired by the modern state through these rationalization processes. These powers, which are claimed by the sovereign state as indivisible, inalienable and exclusive rights, are: the right to monopolize the legitimate means of violence over the claimed territory, the exclusive right to tax within this territorial jurisdiction, the right to demand undivided political allegiance, the sole authority to adjudicate disputes between citizens and the sole subject of rights and representation in international law (1998: 28–9).

The combining of these monopoly powers initiated what Linklater refers to as the 'totalizing project' of the modern, Westphalian state. The upshot was to produce a conception of politics governed by the assumption that the boundaries of sovereignty, territory, nationality and citizenship must be co-terminous (1998: 29, 44). The modern state concentrated these social, economic, legal and political functions around a single, sovereign site of governance that became the primary subject of international relations by gradually removing alternatives. Of crucial concern to Linklater is how this totalizing project of the modern state modifies the social bond and consequently changes the boundaries of moral and political community. Though the state has been a central theme in the study of international relations there has been little attempt to account for the changing ways that states determine principles which, by binding citizens into a community, separate them from the rest of the world.

Linklater's focus on the changing nature of social bonds has much in common with Cox's (1999) focus on the changing relationship between state and civil society. The key to rethinking International Relations, according to Cox, lies in examining the relationship between state and civil society, and thereby recognizing that the state takes different forms, not only in different historical periods, but also within the same period.

Lest it be thought that critical international theory is simply interested in producing a theory of the state alone, it should be remembered that the state is but one force which shapes the present world order. Cox (1981: 137–8) argues that a comprehensive understanding of the present order and its structural characteristics must account for the interaction between social forces, states and world orders. Within Cox's approach the state plays an 'intermediate though autonomous role' between, on the one hand, social forces shaped by production, and on the other, a world order which embodies a particular configuration of power determined by the states-system and the world economy (1981: 141).

There are two fundamental and intertwined presuppositions upon which Cox founds his theory of the state. The first reflects the Marxist–Gramscian axiom that 'World orders ... are grounded in social relations' (Cox 1983: 173). This means that observable changes in military and geo-political balances can be traced to fundamental changes in the relationship between capital and labour. The second presupposition stems from Vico's argument that institutions such as the state are historical products. The state cannot be abstracted from history as if its essence could be defined or understood as *prior to* history (Cox 1981: 133). The end result is that the definition of the state is enlarged to encompass 'the underpinnings of the political structure in civil society' (Cox 1983: 164). The influence of the church, press, education system, culture and so on, has to be incorporated into an analysis of the state, as these 'institutions' help to produce the attitudes, dispositions and behaviours consistent with, and conducive to, the state's arrangement of power relations in society. Thus the state, which comprises the machinery of government, plus civil society, constitute and reflect the 'hegemonic social order' (1983).

This hegemonic social order must also be understood as a dominant configuration of 'material power, ideology and institutions' that shapes and bears forms of world order (Cox 1981: 141). The key issue for Cox therefore is how to account for the transition from one world order to another. He devotes much of his attention to explaining 'how structural transformations have come about in the past' (Cox 1986: 244). For example, he has analysed in some detail the structural transformation that took place in the late nineteenth century from a period characterized by craft manufacture, the liberal state and *pax britannica*, to a period characterized by mass production, the emerging welfare–nationalist state and imperial rivalry (Cox 1987). In much of his recent writing, Cox has been preoccupied with the restructuring of world order brought about by globalization. In brief Cox, and his colleague Stephen Gill, have offered extensive examinations of how the growing global organization of production and finance is transforming Westphalian conceptions of society and polity. At the heart of this current transformation is what Cox calls the 'internationalization of the state', whereby the state becomes little more than an instrument for restructuring national economies so that they are more responsive to the demands and disciplines of the capitalist global economy. This has allowed the power of capital to grow – 'relative to labour and in the way it reconstitutes certain ideas, interests, and forms of state' – and given rise to a neo-liberal 'business civilization' (Gill 1996: 210, see also Cox 1993, 1994; Gill 1995).

Drawing upon Karl Polanyi, and in a similar vein to John Ruggie, Cox and Gill see the social purposes of the state being subordinated to the market logics of capitalism, disembedding the economy from society, and producing a complex world order of increasing tension between principles of territoriality and interdependence (Cox 1993: 260–3; Gill 1996). Some of the consequences of this economic globalization are, as Cox (1999) and Gill (1996) note, the polarization of rich and poor, increasing social anomie, a stunted civil society and, as a result, the rise of exclusionary populism (extreme right, xenophobic and racist groups).

The point of reflecting on changing world orders, as Cox (1999: 4) notes, is to 'serve as a guide to action designed to change the world so as to improve the lot of humanity in social equity'. After all, as both Cox (1989) and Maclean (1981) argue, an understanding of change should be a central feature of any theory of international relations. So it is with the express purpose of analysing the potential for structural transformations in world order that critical international theory identifies and examines 'emancipatory counter-hegemonic' forces. Counter-hegemonic forces could be states, such as a coalition of 'Third World' states which struggles to undo the dominance of 'core' countries, or the 'counter-hegemonic alliance of forces on the world scale', such as trade unions, non-governmental organizations (NGOs) and new social movements, which grow from the 'bottom-up' in civil society (Cox 1999; Maiguaschca 2003; Eschle and Maiguaschca 2005).

The point of critical international theory's various sociological analyses is to illuminate how already existing social struggles might lead to decisive transformations in the normative bases of global political life. This has prompted Linklater (2002a) to undertake what he calls a 'sociology of states-systems'. More specifically, Linklater wishes to compare states-systems across time on the basis of how they deal with harm. What kinds of harm are generated in particular states-systems, and to what extent are rules and norms against harm built into these states-systems? Linklater's initial research suggests that the modern states-system may be unique in its development of 'cosmopolitan harm conventions' that have the effect of eroding the domestic jurisdiction of states and promoting moral duties (Linklater 2001).

However, the civilizing gains made by the modern states-system may be under threat by developments since September 11. Though there are different responses to the terrorist attacks perpetrated by al-Qaeda, Linklater is concerned that the dominant rhetoric of a civilizational war against evil would unleash 'de-civilizing' potentials. The US-led 'war on terrorism', by privileging military means, putting more innocent lives at risk and suspending the rule of international law, raised the question of 'whether the vision of a world in which fewer human beings are burdened with preventable suffering has been dealt a blow from which it will not easily recover' (Linklater 2002b: 304). As he succinctly expresses the problem: 'Compassion seems set to lose out in the struggle to deal with threats to security' (2002b: 309). Implicit in Linklater, and explicit in the writings of others, is the argument that the greatest threat to world order may not be the terrorists who perpetrated such inexcusable harm, but the reaction by the United States. By placing itself outside the rules, norms and institutions of international society in its prosecution of the war on terrorism, the United States is not only diminishing the prospects of a peaceful and just world order, but undermining the very principles on which it was founded (Habermas 2003; Dunne 2003; Devetak 2005).

The praxeological dimension: cosmopolitanism and discourse ethics

One of the main intentions behind a sociology of the state is to assess the possibility of undoing the monopoly powers and totalizing project and moving towards more open, inclusive forms of community. This reflects critical international theory's belief that while totalizing projects have been tremendously successful, they have not been complete in colonizing modern political life. They have not been able to 'erode the sense of moral anxiety when duties to fellow-citizens clash with duties to the rest of humankind' (Linklater 1998: 150–1). In this section, I outline critical international theory's attempt to rethink the meaning of community in the light of this residual moral anxiety and an accumulating 'moral capital' which deepens and extends cosmopolitan citizenship. This involves not simply identifying the forces working to dismantle practices of social exclusion, but also identifying those working to replace the system of sovereign states with cosmopolitan structures of global governance.

Linklater's three volumes, *Men and Citizens* (1990a), *Beyond Realism and Marxism* (1990b) and *The Transformation of Political Community* (1998), form the most sustained and extensive interrogation of political community in International Relations. In (1998), Linklater elaborates his argument in terms of a 'triple transformation' affecting political community. The three transformational tendencies Linklater identifies are: a progressive recognition that moral, political and legal principles ought to be universalized, an insistence that material inequality ought to be reduced and greater demands for deeper respect for cultural, ethnic and gender differences. The triple transformation identifies processes that open the possibility of dismantling the nexus between sovereignty, territory, citizenship and nationalism and moving towards more cosmopolitan forms of governance. In this respect, the praxeological dimension closes the circle with the normative dimension by furthering the critique of the modern state's particularism. However, we should note a slight revision of this critique. Modern states are not just too particularistic for Linklater's liking, they are also too universalistic (Linklater 1998: 27). He here finesses his earlier critique of particularism by acknowledging the feminist and postmodern arguments that universalism runs the risk of ignoring or repressing certain marginalized or vulnerable groups unless it respects legitimate differences. Nonetheless, it remains consistent with the Enlightenment critique of the system of sovereign states, and the project to universalize the sphere in which human beings treat each other as free and equal.

If critical international theory's overall objective is to promote the reconfiguration of political community, not just by expanding political community beyond the frontiers of the sovereign state, but also by deepening it within those frontiers, then it must offer a more complex, multitiered structure of governance. Ultimately, it depends on reconstituting the state within alternative frameworks of political action that reduce the impact of social exclusion and enlarge democratic participation.

The key to realizing this vision is to sever the link between sovereignty and political association which is integral to the Westphalian system (Devetak 1995a: 43). A post-exclusionary form of political community would according to Linklater be post-sovereign or post-Westphalian. It would abandon the idea that power, authority, territory and loyalty must be focused around a single community or monopolized by a single site of governance. The state can no longer mediate effectively or exclusively among the many loyalties, identities and interests that exist in a globalizing world (see Devetak 2003; Waller and Linklater 2003). Fairer and more complex mediations can be developed, argues Linklater (1998: 60, 74), only by transcending the 'destructive fusion' achieved by the modern state and promoting wider communities of dialogue. The overall effect would thus be to 'de-centre' the state in the context of a more cosmopolitan form of political organization.

This requires states to establish and locate themselves in overlapping forms of international society. Linklater (1998: 166–7) lists three forms. First, a pluralist society of states in which the principles of coexistence work 'to preserve respect for the freedom and equality of independent political communities'. Second, a 'solidarist' society of states that have agreed to substantive moral purposes. Third, a post-Westphalian framework where states relinquish some of their sovereign powers so as to institutionalize shared political and moral norms. These alternative frameworks of international society would widen the boundaries of political community by increasing the impact which duties to 'outsiders' have on decision making processes and contribute to what Linklater (1998) and Shapcott (2001) call 'dialogical cosmopolitanism'.

Linklater and Shapcott make the case for what they refer to as 'thin cosmopolitanism'. A 'thin cosmopolitanism' would need to promote universal claims yet do justice to difference (Shapcott 2000b, 2001). Within such a setup, loyalties to the sovereign state or any other political association cannot be absolute (Linklater 1998: 56; Devetak 2003). In recognizing the diversity of social bonds and moral ties, a 'thin cosmopolitan' ethos seeks to multiply the types and levels of political community. It should be noted, however, that this does not mean that duties to humanity override all others. There is no fixed 'moral hierarchy' within a 'thin cosmopolitan' framework (Linklater 1998: 161–8, 193–8). It is important to note here that this version of a 'thin cosmopolitanism' places the ideals of dialogue and consent at the centre of its project.

Another version of cosmopolitanism has been advanced, individually and collectively, by David Held and Daniele Archibugi (Archibugi and Held 1995; Archibugi 2002, 2004a). Their work stems from an appreciation of the dangers and opportunities globalization poses to democracy. It seeks to globalize democracy even as it democratizes globalization (Archibugi 2004a: 438). The thrust of *cosmopolitan* democracy is captured by the question Archibugi asks (2002: 28): 'why must the principles and rules of democracy stop at the borders of a political community?' As he explains, it is not simply a matter of 'replicating, *sic et simpliciter*, the model we are acquainted with across a broader sphere' (2002: 29). It is a matter of strengthening the rule of law and citizens' participation in political life through differentiated forms of democratic engagement. Archibugi (2004b) has gone so far as to outline cosmopolitan principles governing humanitarian intervention. This controversial proposal stems from post-Cold War developments and a growing willingness on the part of international society to suspend sovereignty when extreme, large-scale cases of human suffering occur. Though difficult practical questions remain about 'who is authorized to decide when a humanitarian intervention is needed', Archibugi (2004b) strongly rejects the idea that states can unilaterally intervene under the humanitarian cause (see also Devetak 2002).

In this final section I outline briefly how the emphasis on dialogue is utilized in critical international theory. Linklater resorts to Habermas' notion of discourse ethics as a model for his dialogical approach. Discourse ethics is essentially a deliberative, consent oriented approach to resolving political issues within a moral framework. As elaborated by Habermas (1984: 99), discourse ethics builds upon the need for communicating subjects to account for their beliefs and actions in terms which are intelligible to others and which they can then accept or contest. It is committed to the Kantian principle that political decisions or norms must be generalizable and consistent with the normative demands of public scrutiny if they are to attain legitmacy. At such moments when an international principle, social norm, or institution loses legitimacy, or when consensus breaks down, then discourse ethics enters the fray as a means of consensually deciding upon new principles or institutional arrangements. According to discourse ethics newly arrived at political principles, norms, or institutional arrangements can be said to be valid only if they can meet with the approval of all those who would be affected by them (Habermas 1993: 151).

There are three features worthy of note for our purposes. Firstly, discourse ethics is *inclusionary*. It is oriented to the establishment and maintenance of the conditions necessary for open and non-exclusionary dialogue. No individual or group which will be affected by the principle, norm, or institution under deliberation should be excluded from partic- ipation in dialogue. Secondly, discourse ethics is *democratic*. It builds on a model of the public sphere which is bound to democratic deliberation and consent, where participants employ an 'argumentative rationality' for the purpose of 'reaching a mutual understanding based on a reasoned consensus, challenging the validity claims involved in any communication' (Risse 2000: 1–2). Combining the inclusionary and democratic impulses, discourse ethics provides a method that can test which principles, norms, or institutional arrangements would be 'equally good for all' (Habermas 1993: 151). Thirdly, discourse ethics is a form of *moral–practical reasoning*. As such, it is not simply guided by utilitarian calculations or expediency, nor is it guided by an imposed concept of the 'good life'; rather, it is guided by *procedural fairness*. It is more concerned with the method of justifying moral principles than with the substantive content of those principles.

It is possible to identify three general implications of discourse ethics for the reconstruction of world politics which can only be briefly out- lined here. Firstly, by virtue of its consent oriented, deliberative approach, discourse ethics offers procedural guidance for democratic decision making processes. In light of social and material changes brought about by the globalization of production and finance, the move- ment of peoples, the rise of indigenous peoples and sub-national groups, environmental degradation and so on, the 'viability and accountability of national decision-making entities' is being brought into question (Held 1993: 26). Held (1993: 26–7) highlights the democratically deficient nature of the sovereign state when he asks: 'Whose consent is necessary and whose participation is justified in decisions concerning, for instance, AIDS, or acid rain, or the use of non-renewable resources?

What is the relevant constituency: national, regional or international?' Under globalizing conditions it is apt that discourse ethics raises questions not only about 'who' is to be involved in decision making processes, but also 'how' and 'where' these decisions are to be made. The key here is 'to develop institutional arrangements that concretise the dialogic ideal' at all levels of social and political life (Linklater 1999). This directs attention to an emerging global or international public sphere where 'social movements, non-state actors and "global citizens" join with states and international organizations in a dialogue over the exercise of power and authority across the globe' (Devetak and Higgott 1999: 491). As Marc Lynch (1999, 2000) has shown, this network of overlapping, transnational publics not only seeks to influence the foreign policy of individual states, it seeks to change international relations by modifying the structural context of strategic interaction. The existence of a global public sphere ensures that, as Risse (2000: 21) points out, 'actors have to regularly and routinely explain and justify their behaviour'. More than that, according to Risse (2004), arguing and communicative action enable global governance institutions to attain greater legitimacy by providing 'voice opportunities to various stakeholders' and improved 'problem-solving capacity' through deliberation.

Secondly, discourse ethics offers a procedure for regulating violent conflict and arriving at resolutions which are acceptable to all affected parties. The cosmopolitan democratic procedures devised by Archibugi, Held and Linklater as much as Habermas and Kant are all geared towards removing harm from international relations as far as possible. The invasion of Iraq by the United States and United Kingdom in March 2003 led Habermas (2003: 369) to pronounce that 'multilateral will-formation in interstate relations is not simply one option among others'. By giving up its role as guarantor of international rights and violating international law and the United Nations, Habermas (2003: 365) says, 'the normative authority of the United States of America lies in ruins'. Even though the fall of a brutal regime is a great political good, Habermas condemned the war and rejected comparisons with the Kosovo war which, though controversial, he and other critical theorists had supported as a humanitarian intervention. Habermas' reasons for condemning the war are that it failed to satisfy any of the criteria of discourse ethics. Not only did the United States and United Kingdom base their arguments on questionable intelligence, they also contravened established norms of dispute resolution and showed a less than convincing commitment to 'truth-seeking' aimed at mutual understanding and reasoned consensus.

Mark Hoffman and others have argued that the practice of third-party facilitation offers a discourse–ethical approach to conflict resolution.

Third-party facilitation aims at achieving a non-hierarchical, non-coercive resolution of conflict by including both or all affected parties as participants in the dialogue (Hoffman 1992: 265). As Fierke (1998: 136–7) explains, dialogue differs from negotiation. Whereas negotiation belongs to an 'adversarial model' constructed around an 'us' versus 'them' mentality, dialogue can have a transformative effect on identities. The dialogue fostered by third-party facilitation involves the conflicting parties in the reversing of perspectives and encourages them to reason from the other's point of view. As Hoffman (1993: 206) observes, third-party facilitation seeks 'to promote a self-generated and self-sustaining resolution to the conflict'. Because the outcome must be acceptable to all concerned it is more likely to promote compliance. In plainly Habermasian language Hoffman (1992: 273) says that 'third-party facilitation could be characterised as the promotion of consensual decision-making towards the resolution of conflict via a process of undistorted communication'. Deiniol Jones (1999, 2001), though more sceptical of this approach than Hoffman, also endorses third-party mediation in critical-theoretical terms, arguing that it should aim 'to enhance the strength and quality of the cosmopolitan communicative ethic'.

Thirdly, discourse ethics offers a means of criticizing and justifying the principles by which humanity organizes itself politically. By reflecting on the principles of inclusion and exclusion, discourse ethics can reflect on the normative foundations of political life. From the moral point of view contained within discourse ethics, the sovereign state as a form of community is unjust because the principles of inclusion and exclusion are not the outcome of open dialogue and deliberation where all who stand to be affected by the arrangement have been able to participate in discussion. Against the exclusionary nature of the social bond underlying the sovereign state, discourse ethics has the inclusionary aim 'to secure the social bond of all with all' (Habermas 1987: 346). In a sense, it is an attempt to put into practice Kant's ideal of a community of co-legislators embracing the whole of humanity (Linklater 1998: 84–9). As Linklater (1998: 10) argues, 'all humans have *a prima facie* equal right to take part in universal communities of discourse which decide the legitimacy of global arrangements'. In sum, discourse ethics promotes a cosmopolitan ideal where the political organization of humanity is decided by a process of unconstrained and unrestricted dialogue.

Conclusion

There can be little doubt that critical international theory has made a major contribution to the study of international relations. One of these contributions has been to heighten our awareness of the link between knowledge and politics. Critical international theory rejects the idea of the theorist as objective bystander. Instead, the theorist is enmeshed in social and political life, and theories of international relations, like all theories, are informed by prior interests and convictions, whether they are acknowledged or not. A second contribution critical international theory makes is to rethink accounts of the modern state and political community. Traditional theories tend to take the state for granted, but critical international theory analyses the changing ways in which the boundaries of community are formed, maintained and transformed. It not only provides a sociological account, it provides a sustained ethical analysis of the practices of inclusion and exclusion. Critical international theory's aim of achieving an alternative theory and practice of international relations rests on the possibility of overcoming the exclusionary dynamics associated with modern system of sovereign states and establishing a cosmopolitan set of arrangements that will better promote freedom, justice and equality across the globe. It is thus an attempt radically to rethink the normative foundations of global politics.

Chapter 7

Postmodernism

RICHARD DEVETAK

Postmodernism remains among the most controversial of theories in the humanities and social sciences. It has regularly been accused of moral and political delinquency. Indeed, after the terrorist attacks of September 11, some commentators went so far as to blame postmodernism. In a time when moral certitude appeared to be necessary, postmodernism was charged with a dangerous tendency towards moral equivocation or even sympathy towards terrorism. If nothing else, these absurd allegations served to prove a central claim of postmodernism, that knowledge claims are intimately connected to politics and power. Moreover, as James Der Derian (2002: 15) has provocatively argued, despite everything that differentiates America's president, George W. Bush, from the terrorist leader behind the attacks, Osama bin Laden, they are united in their moral and epistemological certitude. It is precisely this conviction that their moral and epistemological claims are beyond question that postmodernism challenges.

Before continuing, we should point out that a great deal of disagreement exists as to what exactly 'postmodernism' means. The meaning of postmodernism is in dispute not just between proponents and critics, but also among proponents. Indeed, many theorists associated with postmodernism never use the term, sometimes preferring the term 'post-structuralism', sometimes 'deconstruction', sometimes rejecting any attempt at labelling altogether. In lieu of a clear or agreed definition of postmodernism this chapter adopts a pragmatic and nominalistic approach. Theorists who are referred to, or who regard their own writing, as postmodern, post-structuralist or deconstructive will be considered here as postmodern theorists.

The chapter is divided into four main sections. The first deals with the relationship between power and knowledge in the study of international relations. The second outlines the textual strategies employed by postmodern approaches. The third is concerned with how postmodernism deals with the state. The final part of the chapter outlines postmodernism's attempt to rethink the concept of the political.

Power and knowledge in International Relations

Within orthodox social scientific accounts, knowledge ought to be immune from the influence of power. The study of international relations, or any scholarly study for that matter, is thought to require the suspension of values, interests and power relations in the pursuit of objective knowledge – knowledge uncontaminated by external influences and based on pure reason. Kant's (1970: 115) caution that 'the possession of power inevitably corrupts the free judgement of reason', stands as a classic example of this view. It is this view that Michel Foucault, and postmodernism generally, have begun to problematize.

Rather than treat the production of knowledge as simply a cognitive matter, postmodernism treats it as a normative and political matter (Shapiro 1999: 1). Foucault wanted to see if there was not some common matrix which hooked together the fields of knowledge and power. According to Foucault, there is a general consistency, which cannot be reduced to an identity, between modes of interpretation and operations of power. Power and knowledge are mutually supportive; they directly imply one another (Foucault 1977: 27). The task therefore is to see how operations of power fit with the wider social and political matrices of the modern world. For example, in *Discipline and Punish* (1977), Foucault investigates the possibility that the evolution of the penal system is intimately connected to the human sciences. His argument is that a 'single process of "epistemologico-juridical" formation' underlies the history of the prison on the one hand, and the human sciences on the other (1997: 23). In other words, the prison is consistent with modern society and modern modes of apprehending 'man's' world.

This type of analysis has been attempted in International Relations by various thinkers. Richard Ashley has exposed one dimension of the power–knowledge nexus by highlighting what Foucault calls the 'rule of immanence' between knowledge of the state and knowledge of 'man'. Ashley's (1989a) argument, stated simply, is that, '[m]odern statecraft is modern mancraft'. He seeks to demonstrate how the 'paradigm of sovereignty' simultaneously gives rise to a certain epistemological disposition and a certain account of modern political life. On the one hand, knowledge is thought to depend on the sovereignty of 'the heroic figure of reasoning man who knows that the order of the world is not God-given, that man is the origin of all knowledge, that responsibility for supplying meaning to history resides with man himself, and that, through reason, man may achieve total knowledge, total autonomy, and total power' (1989a: 264–5). On the other hand, modern political life finds in sovereignty its constitutive principle. The state is conceived by analogy with sovereign man as a pre-given, bounded entity which enters into relations with other sovereign presences. Sovereignty acts as the 'master signifier' as Jenny Edkins and Véronique Pin-Fat (1999: 6) put it. Both 'Man' and the state are marked by the presence of sovereignty, which contrasts with international relations which is marked, and violently so, by the absence of sovereignty (or alternatively stated, the presence of multiple sovereignties). In short, both the theory and practice of international relations are conditioned by the constitutive principle of sovereignty.

Genealogy

It is important to grasp the notion of genealogy, as it has become crucial to many postmodern perspectives in International Relations. Genealogy is, put simply, a style of historical thought which exposes and registers the significance of power–knowledge relations. It is perhaps best known through Nietzsche's radical assault on the concept of origins. As Roland Bleiker (2000: 25) explains, genealogies 'focus on the process by which we have constructed origins and given meaning to particular representations of the past, representations that continuously guide our daily lives and set clear limits to political and social options'. It is a form of history which historicizes those things which are thought to be beyond history, including those things or thoughts which have been buried, covered, or excluded from view in the writing and making of history.

In a sense genealogy is concerned with writing counter-histories which expose the processes of exclusion and covering which make possible the teleological idea of history as a unified story unfolding with a clear beginning, middle and end. History, from a genealogical perspective, does not evidence a gradual disclosure of truth and meaning. Rather, it stages 'the endlessly repeated play of dominations' (Foucault 1987: 228). History proceeds as a series of dominations and impositions in knowledge and power, and the task of the genealogist is to unravel history to reveal the multifarious trajectories that have been fostered or closed off in the constitution of subjects, objects, fields of action and domains of knowledge. Moreover, from a genealogical perspective there is not one single, grand history, but many interwoven histories varied in their rhythm, tempo, and power–knowledge effects.

Genealogy affirms a perspectivism which denies the capacity to identify origins and meanings in history objectively. A genealogical approach is anti-essentialist in orientation, affirming the idea that all knowledge is situated in a particular time and place and issues from a particular perspective. The subject of knowledge is situated in, and conditioned by, a political and historical context, and constrained to function with particular concepts and categories of knowledge. Knowledge is never unconditioned. As a consequence of the heterogeneity of possible contexts and positions, there can be no single, Archimedean perspective which trumps all others. There is no 'truth', only competing perspectives. David Campbell's analysis of the Bosnian War in *National Deconstruction* (1998a) affirms this perspectivism. As he rightly reminds us, 'the same events can be represented in markedly different ways with significantly different effects' (1998a: 33). Indeed, the upshot of his analysis is that the Bosnian War can be known only through perspective.

In the absence of a universal frame of reference or overarching perspective, we are left with a plurality of perspectives. As Nietzsche (1969: III, 12) put it: 'There is *only* a perspective seeing, *only* a perspective "knowing".' The modern idea, or ideal, of an objective or all-encompassing perspective is displaced in postmodernism by the Nietzschean recognition that there is always more than one perspective and that each perspective embodies a particular set of values. Moreover, these perspectives do not simply offer different views of the same 'real world'. The very *idea* of the 'real world' has been 'abolished' in Nietzsche's thought (1990: 50–1), leaving *only* perspectives, *only* interpretations of interpretations, or in Derrida's (1974: 158) terms, *only* 'textuality'.

Perspectives are thus not to be thought of as simply optical devices for apprehending the 'real world', such as a telescope or microscope, but also as the very fabric of that 'real world'. For postmodernism, following Nietzsche, perspectives are integral to the constitution of the 'real world', not just because they are our only access to it, but because they are basic and essential elements of it. The warp and woof of the 'real world' is woven out of perspectives and interpretations, none of which can claim to correspond to reality-in-itself, to be a 'view from nowhere', or to be exhaustive. Perspectives are thus component objects and events that go towards making up the 'real world'. In fact, we should say that there is no object or event outside or prior to perspective or narrative. As Campbell explains, after Hayden White, narrative is central, not just to understanding an event, but in constituting that event. This is what Campbell (1998a: 34) means by the 'narrativizing of reality'. According to such a conception events acquire the status of 'real' not because they occurred but because they are remembered and because they assume a place in a narrative (1998a: 36). Narrative is thus not simply a re-presentation of some prior event, it is the means by which the status of reality is conferred on events. But historical narratives also perform vital political functions in the present; they can be used as resources in contemporary political struggles (1998a: 84, 1999: 31).

The event designated by the name 'September 11' is a case in point. Is it best conceived as an act of terrorism, a criminal act, an act of evil, an act of war, or an act of revenge? Perhaps it is best thought of as an instance of 'Islamo-fascism' or the clash of civilization? Or perhaps as 'blowback'? Furthermore, which specific acts of commission and omission constitute this event? Did 'September 11' begin at 8.45a.m. when American Airlines flight 11 crashed into the north tower of the World Trade Centre, or at 7.59a.m. when the plane departed from Boston? Did it commence when the perpetrators began planning and training for the attack? Or did it begin even earlier, as a reaction (however unjustified) to US Middle East policy? These questions show that the event of 'September 11' is only constituted in a narrative that integrates it into a sequence of other events and thereby confers significance upon it.

It may be that, as Jenny Edkins (2002: 245–6) says, events like 'September 11' cannot be experienced in any normal sense. Rather, they exceed experience and our normal social and linguistic frameworks. Nevertheless, there will be, as Campbell (2002a: 1) notes, struggles over the meaning of 'September 11'. He, like Edkins, cautions against a hasty attempt to fix the meaning of 'September 11'. In particular he shows that, despite the White House asserting the unprecedented nature of the September 11 attacks, the 'war on terrorism' has returned to past foreign policy practices; in his words, it has morphed into the Cold War (1999: 17). 'This return of the past means that we have different objects of enmity, different allies, but the same structure for relating to the world through foreign policy' (2002a: 18). Cynthia Weber (2002) makes a similar argument, suggesting instead that the Pearl Harbor attacks of 7 December 1941 provide an interpretive framework for the US military response today. 'September 11' is thus read as if it had the same meaning as '7 December'. For postmodernism, the representation of any political event will always be susceptible to competing interpretations.

Genealogy is a reminder of the essential agonism in the historical constitution of identities, unities, disciplines, subjects and objects. From this perspective, 'all history, including the production of order, [is comprehended] in terms of the endless power political clash of multiple wills' (Ashley 1987: 409). Metaphors of war and battle are central to genealogy. In a series of lectures given at the Collège de France in 1975–6 under the title 'Society Must be Defended', Foucault employs genealogy to analyze power relations in the state. He explores a historico-political discourse dating from the end of the civil and religious wars of the sixteenth century, that understood war to be 'a permanent social relationship, the ineradicable basis of all relations and institutions of power' (Foucault 2003: 49). This discourse, found in Sir Edward Coke, John Lilburne and Henri Comte de Boulainvilliers among others, challenged the prevailing assumption of the day that society is at peace. Instead, beneath the calm, peaceful order of law-governed society posited by philosophico-juridical discourses, this discourse perceives 'a sort of primitive and permanent war', according to Foucault (2003: 47).

Foucault (2003: 15) characterizes this discourse through an inversion of Clausewitz's famous proposition: 'politics is the continuation of war by other means'. Foucault means to analyse how war became viewed as an apt way of describing politics. He wants to know when political thought began to imagine, perhaps counter-intuitively, that war serves as a principle for the analysis of power relations within political order. This conflictual understanding of society is equally at odds with Kantian liberalism and Hobbesian realism. If anything, it seems to pre-empt Nietzsche's emphasis on struggle. Political power, instituted and legitimized in the sovereign state, does not bring war to an end; rather, 'In the smallest of its cogs, peace is waging a secret war' (2003: 50). This 'war discourse' posits a binary structure that pervades civil society, wherein one group is pitted against another in continuing struggle.

Foucault (1987: 236) claims as one of genealogy's express purposes the 'systematic dissociation of identity'. There are two dimensions to this purpose. First, it has a purpose at the ontological level: to avoid substituting causes for effects (metalepsis). It does not take identity or agency as given but seeks to account for the forces which underwrite this apparent agency. Identity or agency is an *effect* to be explained, not assumed. This means resisting the temptation to attribute essences to agents, things or events in history, and requires a transformation of the question 'what is?' into 'how is?' For Nietzsche, Foucault and thus postmodernism, it is more important to determine the forces that give shape to an event or a thing than to attempt to identify its hidden, fixed essence. Secondly, it has an ethico-political purpose in problematizing prevailing identity formations which appear normal or natural. It refuses to use history for the purpose of affirming present identities, preferring to use it instead to disturb identities that have become dogmatized, conventionalized or normalized.

A good example of this genealogical method is to be found in Maja Zehfuss's (2003) analysis of 'September 11' and the war on terrorism. She challenges assumptions about unified agency and about the relationship between causes and effects. As she points out, to imply that the events of 'September 11' were an attack on 'the West', as the US and UK governments do, is to ignore the ambiguous character of Western identity. At a minimum, it is to ignore the fact that Western nations are complicit with the technologies and perpetrators, but it also ignores political dissent from those who do not wish the memory of the dead to be used to perpetuate further violence (2003: 524–5). Following Nietzsche, Zehfuss (2003: 522) also questions cause-and-effect thinking; 'cause and effect are … never as easily separated' as they appear to be. For example, governments leading the so-called war on terrorism imply that 'September 11' *caused* the war on terrorism. It is as if 'September 11' were 'an "uncaused" cause' (Zehfuss 2003: 521), or as if, in Judith Butler's (2004: 6) words, 'There is no relevant prehistory to the events of September 11'. But this ignores a good deal of prior political history which is essential to any adequate understanding.

It would be a mistake, however, to think that genealogy focuses only on what is forgotten. Zehfuss draws our attention to the politics of memory also. She points out that both Osama bin Laden and President George W. Bush want the world to remember the events of September 11. Bin Laden wants the world to remember the humbling of a hyperpower, Bush wants the world to remember the loss of innocent life. Both, Zehfuss's says (2003: 514), 'have an interest in our memory of the events'. Zehfuss's (2003: 525) argument is that a 'certain way of using memory has become politically powerful', especially in the United States, where the White House has exploited the memory of 'September 11' to justify the curtailment of civil liberties at home, and an aggressive military response abroad. Her point is that we need to forget the dominant narratives before we can understand what makes 'September 11' a distinctive event.

It is in view of such genealogical analyses as these that we can understand Foucault's (1977: 31) attempt at 'writing the history of the present'. A history of the present asks: How have we made the present seem like a normal or natural condition? What has been forgotten and what has been remembered in history in order to legitimize the present and present courses of action?

One of the important insights of postmodernism, with its focus on the power–knowledge nexus and its genealogical approach, is that many of the problems and issues studied in International Relations are not just matters of epistemology and ontology, but of *power* and *authority*; they are struggles to impose authoritative interpretations of international relations. As Derrida (2003: 105) himself says in an interview conducted after September 11: 'We must also recognize here the strategies and relations of power. The dominant power is the one that manages to impose and, thus, to legitimate, indeed to legalize ... on a national or world stage, the terminology and thus the interpretation that best suits it in a given situation'. The following section outlines a strategy which is concerned with destabilizing dominant interpretations by showing how every interpretation systematically depends on that for which it cannot account.

Textual strategies of postmodernism

Der Derian (1989: 6) contends that postmodernism is concerned with exposing the 'textual interplay behind power politics'. It might be better to say it is concerned with exposing the textual interplay *within* power politics, for the effects of textuality do not remain behind politics, but are intrinsic to them. The 'reality' of power politics (like any social reality) is always already constituted through textuality and inscribed modes of representation. It is in this sense that David Campbell (1992) refers to 'writing' security, Gearóid Ó Tuathail (1996) refers to 'writing' global space, and Cynthia Weber (1995) refers to 'writing' the state. Two questions arise: (1) what is meant by textual interplay? and (2) how, by using what methods and strategies, does postmodernism seek to disclose this textual interplay?

Textuality is a common postmodern theme. It stems mainly from Derrida's redefinition of 'text' in *Of Grammatology* (1974). It is important to clarify what Derrida means by 'text'. He is not restricting its meaning to literature and the realm of ideas, as some have mistakenly thought, rather, he is implying that the world is *also* a text–or, better, the 'real' world is constituted like a text, and 'one cannot refer to this "real" except in an interpretive experience' (Derrida 1988: 148). Postmodernism firmly regards interpretation as necessary and fundamental to the constitution of the social world, and it is for this reason that Derrida (1978: 278) quotes Montaigne: 'We need to interpret interpretations more than to interpret things.' 'Textual interplay' refers to the supplementary and mutually constitutive relationship between different interpretations in the representation and constitution of the world. In order to tease out the textual interplay, postmodernism deploys the strategies of *deconstruction* and *double reading*.

Deconstruction

Deconstruction is a general mode of radically unsettling what are taken to be stable concepts and conceptual oppositions. Its main point is to demonstrate the effects and costs produced by the settled concepts and oppositions, to disclose the parasitical relationship between opposed terms and to attempt a displacement of them. According to Derrida conceptual oppositions are never simply neutral but are inevitably hierarchical. One of the two terms in the opposition is privileged over the other. This privileged term supposedly connotes a presence, propriety, fullness, purity, or identity which the other lacks (for example, sovereignty as opposed to anarchy). Deconstruction attempts to show that such oppositions are untenable, as each term *always already* depends on the other. Indeed, the prized term gains its privilege only by disavowing its dependence on the subordinate term.

From a postmodern perspective, the apparently clear opposition between two terms is neither clear nor oppositional. Derrida often speaks of this relationship in terms of a structural parasitism and contamination, as each term is structurally related to, and already harbours, the other. Difference *between* the two opposed concepts or terms is always accompanied by a veiled difference *within* each term. Neither term is pure, self-same, complete in itself, or completely closed off from the other, though as much is feigned. This implies that totalities, whether conceptual or social, are never fully present and properly established. Moreover, there is no pure stability, only more or less successful stabilizations as there is a certain amount of 'play', or 'give', in the structure of the opposition.

As a general mode of unsettling, deconstruction is particularly concerned with locating those elements of instability or 'give' which ineradicably threaten any totality. Nevertheless, it must still account for stabilizations (or stability-effects). It is this equal concern with undoing or deconstitution (or at least their ever-present possibility) which marks off deconstruction from other more familiar modes of interpretation. To summarize, deconstruction is concerned with both the constitution and deconstitution of any totality, whether a text, theory, discourse, structure, edifice, assemblage, or institution.

Double reading

Derrida seeks to expose this relationship between stability-effects and destabilizations by passing through two readings in any analysis. As expressed by Derrida (1981: 6), double reading is essentially a duplicitous strategy which is 'simultaneously faithful and violent'. The first reading is a commentary or repetition of the dominant interpretation – that is, a reading which demonstrates how a text, discourse or institution achieves the stability-effect. It faithfully recounts the dominant story by building on the same foundational assumptions, and repeating conventional steps in the argument. The point here is to demonstrate how the text, discourse, or institution appears coherent and consistent with itself. It is concerned, in short, to elaborate how the identity of a text, discourse, or institution is put together or constituted. Rather than yield to the monologic first reading, the second, counter-memorializing reading unsettles it by applying pressure to those points of instability within a text, discourse, or institution. It exposes the internal tensions and how they are (incompletely) covered over or expelled. The text, discourse, or institution is never completely at one with itself, but always carries within it elements of tension and crisis which render the whole thing less than stable.

The task of double reading as a mode of deconstruction is to understand how a discourse or social institution is assembled or put together, but at the same time to show how it is always already threatened with its undoing. It is important to note that there is no attempt in deconstruction to arrive at a single, conclusive reading. The two mutually inconsistent readings, which are in a performative (rather than logical) contradiction, remain permanently in tension. The point is not to demonstrate the truthfulness or otherwise of a story, but to expose how any story depends on the repression of internal tensions in order to produce a stable effect of homogeneity and continuity.

Ashley's double reading of the *anarchy problematique*

Richard Ashley's double reading of the *anarchy problematique* is one of the earliest and most important deconstructions in the study of international relations. His main target is the conception of anarchy and the theoretical and practical effects. The *anarchy problematique* is the name Ashley gives to the defining moment of most inquiries in International Relations. It is exemplified by Oye's (1985: 1) assertion that: 'Nations dwell in perpetual anarchy, for no central authority imposes limits on the pursuit of sovereign interests.' Most importantly, the *anarchy problematique* deduces from the absence of central, global authority, not just an empty concept of anarchy, but a description of international relations as power politics, characterised by self-interest, *raison d'état*, the routine resort to force, and so on.

The main brunt of Ashley's analysis is to problematize this deduction of power politics from the lack of central rule. Ashley's many analyses of the *anarchy problematique* can be understood in terms of double reading. The first reading assembles the constitutive features, or 'hard core' of the *anarchy problematique*, while the second reading disassembles the constitutive elements of the *anarchy problematique*, showing how it rests on a series of questionable theoretical suppositions or exclusions.

In the first reading, Ashley outlines the *anarchy problematique* in conventional terms. He describes not just the absence of any overarching authority, but the presence of a multiplicity of states in the international system, none of which can lay down the law to the individual states. Further, the states which comprise this system have their own identifiable interests, capabilities, resources and territory. The second reading questions the self-evidence of international relations as an anarchical realm of power politics. The initial target in this double reading is the opposition between sovereignty and anarchy, where sovereignty is valorized as a regulative ideal, and anarchy is regarded as the absence or negation of sovereignty. Anarchy takes on meaning only as the antithesis of sovereignty. Moreover, sovereignty and anarchy are taken to be mutually exclusive and mutually exhaustive. Ashley demonstrates, however, that the *anarchy problematique* works only by making certain assumptions regarding sovereign states. If the dichotomy between sovereignty and anarchy is to be tenable at all, then inside the sovereign state must be found a domestic realm of identity, homogeneity, order and progress guaranteed by legitimate force; and outside must lie an anarchical realm of difference, heterogeneity, disorder and threat, recurrence and repetition. But to represent sovereignty and anarchy in this way (that is, as mutually exclusive and exhaustive), depends on converting differences *within* sovereign states into differences *between* sovereign states (Ashley 1988: 257). Sovereign states must expunge any traces of anarchy that reside within them in order to make good the distinction between sovereignty and anarchy. Internal dissent and what Ashley (1987, 1989b) calls 'transversal struggles' which cast doubt over the idea of a clearly identifiable and demarcated sovereign identity must be repressed or denied to make the *anarchy problematique* meaningful. In particular, the opposition between sovereignty and anarchy rests on the possibility of determining a 'well-bounded sovereign entity possessing its own "internal" hegemonic centre of decision-making capable of reconciling "internal" conflicts and capable, therefore, of projecting a singular presence' (Ashley 1988: 245).

The general effect of the *anarchy problematique* is to confirm the opposition between sovereignty and anarchy as mutually exclusive and exhaustive. This has two particular effects: (1) to represent a domestic domain of sovereignty as a stable, legitimate foundation of modern political community, and (2) to represent the domain beyond sovereignty as dangerous and anarchical. These effects depend on what Ashley (1988: 256) calls a 'double exclusion'. They are possible only if, on the one hand, a single representation of sovereign identity can be imposed and, on the other hand, if this representation can be made to appear natural and indisputable. The double reading problematizes the *anarchy problematique* by posing two questions: first, what happens to the *anarchy problematique* if it is not so clear that fully present and completed sovereign states are ontologically primary or unitary? And, secondly, what happens to the *anarchy problematique* if the lack of central global rule is not overwritten with assumptions about power politics?

Problematizing sovereign states

States, sovereignty and violence are long-standing themes in the established traditions of International Relations that have gained renewed importance after the September 11 terrorist attacks. They are also central themes in postmodern approaches to international relations. However, rather than adopt them uncritically from traditional approaches, postmodernism revises them in view of insights gained from genealogy and deconstruction.

Postmodernism seeks to address a crucial issue regarding interpretations and explanations of the sovereign state that state-centric approaches have obscured – namely, its historical constitution and reconstitution as the primary mode of subjectivity in world politics. This returns us to the type of question posed by Foucault's genealogy: how, by virtue of what political practices and representations, is the sovereign state instituted as the normal mode of international subjectivity? Posing the question in this manner directs attention, in Nietzschean fashion, less to what is the essence of the sovereign state than to how the sovereign state is made possible, how it is naturalized and how it is made to appear as if it had an essence.

To the extent that postmodernism seeks to account for the conditions which make possible the phenomenon of the state as something which concretely affects the experience of everyday life, it is phenomenological. Yet this is no ordinary phenomenology. It might best be called a 'quasi-phenomenology' for, as already noted, it is equally concerned with accounting for those conditions which destabilize the phenomenon or defer its complete actualization. In this section, postmodernism's quasi-phenomenology of the state will be explained. This comprises four main elements: (1) a genealogical analysis of the modern state's 'origins' in violence, (2) an account of boundary inscription, (3) a deconstruction of identity as it is defined in security and foreign policy discourses and (4) a revised interpretation of statecraft. The overall result is to rethink the ontological structure of the sovereign state in order to respond properly to the question of how the sovereign state is (re)constituted as the normal mode of subjectivity in international relations.

Violence

Modern political thought has attempted to transcend illegitimate forms of rule (such as tyranny and despotism) where power is unconstrained, unchecked, arbitrary and violent, by founding legitimate, democratic forms of government where authority is subject to law. In modern politics, it is *reason* rather than power or violence which has become the measure of legitimacy. However, as Campbell and Dillon (1993: 161) point out, the relationship between politics and violence in modernity is deeply ambivalent for, on the one hand, violence 'constructs the refuge of the sovereign community' and, on the other hand, it is 'the condition from which the citizens of that community must be protected'. The paradox here is that violence is both poison and cure.

The link between violence and the state is revealed in Bradley Klein's genealogy of the state as strategic subject. Klein's (1994: 139) broad purpose in *Strategic Studies and World Order* is to analyse 'the violent making and remaking of the modern world'. His more particular purpose is to explain the historical emergence of war making states. Rather than assume their existence, as realists and neo-realists tend to do, Klein examines how political units emerge in history which are capable of relying upon force to distinguish a domestic political space from an exterior one. Consistent with other postmoderns, he argues that 'states rely upon violence to constitute themselves as states', and in the process, 'impose differentiations between the internal and external' (1994: 38). Strategic violence is constitutive of states; it does not merely 'patrol the frontiers' of the state, it 'helps constitute them as well' (1994: 3).

The point made by postmodernism regarding violence in modern politics needs to be clearly differentiated from traditional approaches. In general, traditional accounts take violent confrontation to be a normal and regular occurrence in international relations. The condition of anarchy is thought to incline states to war as there is nothing to stop wars from occurring. Violence is not constitutive in such accounts as these, but is 'configurative', or 'positional' (Ruggie 1993: 162–3). The ontological structure of the states is taken to be set up already before violence is undertaken. The violence merely modifies the territorial configuration, or is an instrument for power–political, strategic manoeuvres in the distribution or hierarchy of power. Postmodernism, however, exposes the constitutive role of violence in modern political life. Violence is fundamental to the ontological structuring of states, and is not merely something to which fully formed states resort for power–political reasons. Violence is, according to postmodernism, inaugural as well as augmentative.

This argument about the intimate and paradoxical relationship between violence and political order is taken even further by Jenny Edkins, who places the Nazis, concentration camps, NATO and refugee camps on the same continuum. All, she claims, are determined by a sovereign power that seeks to extend control over life. She argues that even humanitarianism can be placed on the spectrum of violence since it, too, is complicit with the modern state's order of sovereign power and violence, notwithstanding claims to the contrary. Indeed, she says that famine-relief camps are like concentration camps since they are both sites of 'arbitrary decisions between life and death, where aid workers are forced to choose which of the starving they are unable to help' (Edkins 2000: 13). Famine victims appear only as 'bare life' to be 'saved'; stripped of their social and cultural being, they are depoliticized, their political voices ignored (2000: 13–14). In different language, Campbell

(1998b: 506) affirms this view by arguing that prevailing forms of humanitarianism construct people as victims, 'incapable of acting without intervention'. This insufficiently political or humane form of humanitarianism, therefore, 'is deeply implicated in the production of a sovereign political power that claims the monopoly of the legitimate use of violence' (Edkins 2000: 18). Mick Dillon and Julian Reid offer a similar reading of humanitarian responses to 'complex emergencies', but rather than assume an equivalence between humanitarianism and sovereign power, they see a susceptibility of the former to the operations of the latter. Global governance, they say, 'quite literally threatens nongovernmental and humanitarian agencies with recruitment into the very structures and practices of power against which they previously defined themselves' (Dillon and Reid 2000: 121).

Edkins and Dillon and Reid draw upon an influential and richly textured argument advanced by the Italian philosopher Giorgio Agamben in *Homo Sacer: Sovereign Power and Bare Life* (1998). Following Carl Schmitt, Agamben posits sovereignty as the essence of the political. The sovereign claims the right to decide the exception. This leads, among other things, to the sovereign's right to decide who is in and who is out of a political community. If one of the main concerns of critical theory (as outlined in Chapter 6) is examination of possibilities for more inclusive forms of community, Agamben focuses on exclusion as a condition of possibility of political community. He argues that 'In Western politics, bare life has the peculiar privilege of being that whose exclusion founds the city of men' (Agamben 1998: 7). 'Bare life', most basically, is the simple biological fact of not being dead. But Agamben assigns a further meaning to bare life, a meaning captured in the term *homo sacer* (sacred man), which refers to a life that can be taken but not sacrificed, a holy but damned life. Banished from society, *homo sacer* acts as the 'constitutive outside' to political life. But, in truth, *homo sacer* is neither inside nor outside political community in any straightforward sense. Instead, he occupies a 'zone of indistinction' or 'no-man's land'. Indeed, as Agamben (1998: 74, 80) points out, the Roman concept of *homo sacer* precedes the distinction between sacred and profane, which is why, paradoxically, a so-called '*sacred* man' can be killed. The clearest expression of this was the system of camps established under the Nazis before and during the Second World War. But similar systems were established during the Bosnian War. As David Campbell (2002b: 157) spells out, the Bosnian Serb camps at Omarska and Trnopolje were 'extra-legal spaces' integrated into an 'ethnic-cleansing strategy based on an exclusive and homogeneous' political community.

Judith Butler, in a brilliant essay titled 'Indefinite Detention' (in Butler 2004), applies Agamben's arguments in her reflections on America's 'war on terrorism'. Drawing from Agamben's writing on sovereign power, she notes how states suspend the rule of law by invoking a 'state of emergency'. There can be no more significant act demonstrating the state's sovereignty than withdrawing or suspending the law. Referring to the controversial detainment of terrorism suspects at Guantánamo Bay, Butler says: 'It is not just that constitutional protections are indefinitely suspended, but that the state (in its augmented executive function) arrogates to itself the right to suspend the Constitution or to manipulate the geography of detentions and trials so that constitutional and international rights are effectively suspended' (Butler 2004: 63–4). The detainees are thus reduced to bare life in a no-man's land beyond the law. Butler (2004: 68) observes that 'to be detained indefinitely ... is precisely to have no definitive prospect for a reentry into the political fabric of life, even as one's situation is highly, if not fatally, politicized'. By employing Agamben, these postmodern works seek to show how sovereign states, even liberal democratic ones, constitute themselves through exclusion and violence.

Boundaries

To inquire into the state's (re)constitution, as postmodernism does, is partly to inquire into the ways in which global political space is partitioned. The world is not naturally divided into differentiated political spaces, and nor is there a single authority to carve up the world. This necessarily leads to a focus on the 'boundary question', as Dillon and Everard (1992: 282) call it, because any political subject is constituted by the marking of physical, symbolic and ideological boundaries.

Postmodernism is less concerned with *what* sovereignty is, than *how* it is spatially and temporally produced and how it is circulated. How is a certain configuration of space and power instituted? And with what consequences? The obvious implication of these questions is that the prevailing mode of political subjectivity in international relations (the sovereign state) is neither natural nor necessary. There is no necessary reason why global political space has to be divided as it is, and with the same bearing. Of crucial importance in this differentiation of political space is the inscription of *boundaries*. Marking boundaries is not an innocent, pre-political act. It is a political act with profound political implications as it is fundamental to the production and delimitation of political space. As Gearóid Ó Tuathail (1996: 1) affirms, '[g]eography is about power. Although often assumed to be innocent, the geography of the world is not a product of nature but a product of histories of struggle between competing authorities over the power to organize, occupy, and administer space'.

There is no political space in advance of boundary inscription. Boundaries function in the modern world to divide an interior, sovereign space from an exterior, pluralistic, anarchical space. The opposition between sovereignty and anarchy rests on the possibility of clearly dividing a domesticated political space from an undomesticated outside. It is in this sense that boundary inscription is a defining moment of the sovereign state. Indeed, neither sovereignty nor anarchy would be possible without the inscription of a boundary to divide political space. This 'social inscription of global space', to use Ó Tuathail's (1996: 61) phrase, produces the effect of completed, bounded states, usually built around what Campbell (1998a: 11) calls the 'nationalist imaginary'.

However, as Connolly (1994: 19) points out, boundaries are highly ambiguous since they 'form an indispensable protection against violation and violence; but divisions they sustain in doing so also carry cruelty and violence'. At stake here is a series of questions regarding boundaries: how boundaries are constituted, what moral and political status they are accorded, how they operate simultaneously to include and exclude and how they simultaneously produce order and violence. Clearly, these questions are not just concerned with the location of cartographic boundaries, but with how these cartographic boundaries serve to represent, limit, and legitimate a political identity. But how, through which political practices and representations, are boundaries inscribed? And what implications does this hold for the mode of subjectivity produced?

Identity

There is, as Rob Walker (1995a: 35–6) notes, a privileging of spatiality in modern political thought and practice. By differentiating political spaces, boundaries are fundamental to the modern world's preference for the 'entrapment of politics' within discrete state boundaries (Magnusson 1996: 36). Postmodernism asks: how has political identity been imposed by spatial practices and representations of domestication and distancing? And how has the concept of a territorially-defined self been constructed in opposition to a threatening other?

Of utmost importance here are issues of how security is conceived in spatial terms and how threats and dangers are defined and articulated, giving rise to particular conceptions of the state as a secure political subject. Debbie Lisle (2000) has shown how even modern tourism participates in the reproduction of this spatialized conception of security. By continuously reaffirming the distinction between 'safety here and now' and 'danger there and then' tourist practices help sustain the geopolitical security discourse. Her reading suggests that war and tourism, rather than being two distinct and opposed social practices, are actually intimately connected by virtue of being governed by the same global security discourse.

A detailed account of the relationship between the state, violence and identity is to be found in David Campbell's post-structuralist account of the Bosnian war, in *National Deconstruction* (1998a). His central argument there is that a particular norm of community has governed the intense violence of the war. This norm, which he calls 'ontopology', borrowing from Derrida, refers to the assumption that political community requires the perfect alignment of territory and identity, state and nation (Derrida 1994a: 82; Campbell 1998a: 80). It functions to disseminate and reinforce the supposition that political community must be understood and organized as a single identity perfectly aligned with and possessing its allocated territory. The logic of this norm, suggests Campbell (1998a: 168–9), leads to a desire for a coherent, bounded, monocultural community. These 'ontopological' assumptions form 'the governing codes of subjectivity in international relations' (1998a: 170). What is interesting about Campbell's (1999a: 23) argument is the implication that the outpouring of violence in Bosnia was not simply an aberration or racist distortion of the ontopological norm, but was in fact an exacerbation of this same norm. The violence of 'ethnic cleansing' in pursuit of a pure, homogeneous political identity is simply a continuation, albeit extreme, of the same political project inherent in any modern nation-state. The upshot is that all forms of political community, insofar as they require boundaries, will be given to some degree of violence (Campbell 1998a: 13).

Postmodernism focuses on the discourses and practices which substitute threat for difference in the constitution of political identity. Simon Dalby, for instance (1993), explains how cold wars result from the application of a geo-political reasoning which defines security in terms of spatial exclusion and the specification of a threatening other. 'Geopolitical discourse constructs worlds in terms of Self and Others, in terms of cartographically specifiable sections of political space, and in terms of military threats' (1993: 29). The geo-political creation of the external other is integral to the constitution of a political identity (self) which is to be made secure. But to constitute a coherent, singular political identity often demands the silencing of internal dissent. There can be internal others that endanger a certain conception of the self, and must be necessarily expelled, disciplined, or contained. Identity, it can be surmised, is an effect forged, on the one hand, by disciplinary practices which attempt to normalize a population, giving it a sense of unity and, on the other, by exclusionary practices which attempt to secure the domestic identity through processes of spatial differentiation, and various diplomatic, military and defence practices. There is a supplementary relationship between containment of domestic and foreign others, which helps to constitute political identity by expelling 'from the resultant "domestic" space ... all that comes to be regarded as alien, foreign and dangerous' (Campbell 1992: Chapters 5,6, 1998a: 13).

If it is plain that identity is defined through difference, and that a self requires an other, it is not so plain that difference or otherness necessarily equates with threat or danger. Nevertheless, as Campbell (1992) points out the sovereign state is predicated on discourses of danger. 'The constant articulation of danger through foreign policy is thus not a threat to a state's identity or existence', says Campbell (1992: 12), 'it is its condition of possibility'. The possibility of identifying the United States as a political subject, for example, rested, during the Cold War, on the ability to impose an interpretation of the Soviet Union as an external threat, and the capacity of the US government to contain internal threats (1992: Chapter 6). Indeed, the pivotal concept of containment takes on a Janus-faced quality as it is simultaneously turned inwards and outwards to deal with threatening others, as Campbell (1992: 175) suggests. The end result of the strategies of containment was to ground identity in a territorial state.

It is important to recognize that political identities do not exist prior to the differentiation of self and other. The main issue is how something which is different becomes conceptualized as a threat or danger to be contained, disciplined, negated, or excluded. There may be an irreducible possibility that difference will slide into opposition, danger, or threat, but there is no necessity. Political identity need not be constituted against, and at the expense of, others, but the prevailing discourses and practices of security and foreign policy tend to reproduce this reasoning. Moreover, this relation to others must be recognized as a morally and politically loaded relation. The effect is to allocate the other to an inferior moral space, and to arrogate the self to a superior one. As Campbell (1992: 85) puts it, 'the social space of inside/outside is both made possible by and helps constitute a moral space of superior/inferior'. By coding the spatial exclusion in moral terms it becomes easier to legitimize certain politico-military practices and interventions which advance national security interests at the same time that they reconstitute political identities. As Shapiro (1988a: 102) puts it, 'to the extent that the Other is regarded as something not occupying the same moral space as the self, conduct toward the Other becomes more exploitive'. This is especially so in an international system where political identity is so frequently defined in terms of territorial exclusion.

Statecraft

The above section has sketched how violence, boundaries and identity function to make possible the sovereign state. This only partly deals with the main genealogical issue of how the sovereign state is (re)constituted as a normal mode of subjectivity. Two questions remain if the genealogical approach is to be pursued: how is the sovereign state naturalized and disseminated? And how is it made to appear as if it had an essence?

Postmodernism is interested in how prevailing modes of subjectivity neutralize or conceal their arbitrariness by projecting an image of normalcy, naturalness, or necessity. Ashley has explored the very difficult question of how the dominant mode of subjectivity is normalized by utilizing the concept of hegemony. By 'hegemony' Ashley (1989b: 269) means not an 'overarching ideology or cultural matrix', but 'an ensemble of normalized knowledgeable practices, identified with a particular state and domestic society … that is regarded as a practical paradigm of sovereign political subjectivity and conduct'. 'Hegemony' refers to the projection and circulation of an 'exemplary' model, which functions as a regulative ideal. Of course the distinguishing characteristics of the exemplary model are not fixed but are historically and politically conditioned. The sovereign state, as the currently dominant mode of subjectivity, is by no means natural. As Ashley (1989b: 267) remarks, sovereignty is fused to certain 'historically normalized interpretations of the state, its competencies, and the conditions and limits of its recognition and empowerment'. The fusion of the state to sovereignty is, therefore, conditioned by changing historical and cultural representations and practices which serve to produce a political identity.

A primary function of the exemplary model is to negate alternative conceptions of subjectivity or to devalue them as underdeveloped, inadequate, or incomplete. Anomalies are contrasted with the 'proper', 'normal', or 'exemplary' model. For instance, 'quasi-states' or 'failed states' represent empirical cases of states which deviate from the model by failing to display the recognizable signs of sovereign statehood. In this failure, they help to reinforce the hegemonic mode of subjectivity as the norm, and to reconfirm the sovereignty/anarchy opposition which underwrites it.

In order for the model to have any power at all, though, it must be replicable; it must be seen as a universally effective mode of subjectivity which can be invoked and instituted at any site. The pressures applied on states to conform to normalized modes of subjectivity are complex and various, and emanate both internally and externally. Some pressures are quite explicit, such as military intervention, others less so, such as conditions attached to foreign aid, diplomatic recognition and general processes of socialization. The point is that modes of subjectivity achieve dominance in space and time through the projection and imposition of power.

How has the state been made to appear as if it had an essence? The short answer to this question is that the state is made to appear as if it had an essence by performative enactment of various domestic and foreign policies, or what might more simply be called 'statecraft', with the emphasis on 'craft'. Traditionally, 'statecraft' refers to the various policies and practices undertaken by states to pursue their objectives in the international arena. The assumption underlying this definition is that the state is already a fully formed, or bounded, entity before it negotiates its way in this arena. The revised notion of statecraft advanced by postmodernism stresses the ongoing political practices which found and maintain the state, having the effect of keeping the state in perpetual motion.

As Richard Ashley (1987: 410) stressed in his path-breaking article, subjects have no existence prior to political practice. Sovereign states emerge on the plane of historical and political practices. This suggests it is better to understand the state as performatively constituted, having no identity apart from the ceaseless enactment of the ensemble of foreign and domestic policies, security and defence strategies, protocols of treaty making and representational practices at the United Nations, among other things. The state's 'being' is thus an effect of performativity. By 'performativity' we must understand the continued iteration of a norm or set of norms, not simply a singular act, which produces the very thing it names. As Weber (1998: 90) explains, 'the identity of the state is performatively constituted by the very expressions that are said to be its result'.

It is in this sense that David Campbell (1998a: ix–x), in his account of the war in Bosnia, focuses on what he calls 'metaBosnia', by which he means 'the array of practices through which Bosnia ... comes to be'. To help come to terms with the ceaseless production of Bosnia as a state or subject Campbell recommends that we recognize that we are never dealing with a given, *a priori* state of Bosnia, but with metaBosnia–that is, the performative constitution of 'Bosnia' through a range of enframing and differentiating practices. 'Bosnia', like any other state, is always under a process of construction.

To summarize then, the sovereign state, as Weber (1998: 78) says, is the 'ontological effect of practices which are performatively enacted'. As she explains, 'sovereign nation-states are not pre-given subjects but subjects in process' (1998), where the phrase 'subjects in process' should also be understood to mean 'subjects on trial' (as the French '*en procès*' implies). This leads to an interpretation of the state (as subject) as always in the process of being constituted, but never quite achieving that final moment of completion (Edkins and Pin-Fat 1999: 1). The state thus should not be understood as if it were a prior presence, but instead should be seen as the simulated presence produced by the processes of statecraft. It is never fully complete but is in a constant process of 'becoming-state'. Though 'never fully realised, [the state] is in a continual process of concretization' (Doty 1999: 593). The upshot is that, for postmodernism, there is statecraft, but there is no completed state (Devetak 1995a).

Lest it be thought that that postmodern theories of international relations mark a return to realist state-centrism, some clarification will be needed to explain its concern with the sovereign state. Postmodernism does not seek to explain world politics by focusing on the state alone, nor does it take the state as given. Instead, as Ashley's double reading of the anarchy problematique testifies, it seeks to explain the conditions which make possible such an explanation and the costs consequent on such an approach. What is lost by taking a state-centric perspective? And most importantly, to what aspects of world politics does state-centrism remain blind?

Beyond the paradigm of sovereignty: rethinking the political

One of the central implications of postmodernism is that the paradigm of sovereignty has impoverished our political imagination and restricted our comprehension of the dynamics of world politics. In this section, we review postmodern attempts to develop a new conceptual language to represent world politics beyond the terms of state-centrism in order to rethink the concept of the political.

Campbell (1996: 19) asks the question: 'can we represent world politics in a manner less indebted to the sovereignty problematic?' The challenge is to create a conceptual language that can better convey the novel processes and actors in modern (or postmodern) world politics. Campbell (1996: 20) recommends 'thinking in terms of a *political prosaics* that understands the *transversal* nature' of world politics. To conceptualize world politics in terms of 'political prosaics' is to draw attention to the multitude of flows and interactions produced by globalization that cut across nation-state boundaries. It is to focus on the many political, economic and cultural activities that produce a 'deterritorialization' of modern political life; activities that destabilize the paradigm of sovereignty.

The argument here draws heavily upon the philosophical work of Gilles Deleuze and Felix Guattari (1977, 1987). They have developed a novel conceptual language which has been deployed by postmodern theorists of international relations to make sense of the operation and impact of various non-state actors, flows and movements on the political institution of state sovereignty. The central terms here are reterritorialization and deterritorialization (see Patton 2000; Reid 2003). The former is associated with the totalizing logic of the paradigm of sovereignty, or 'State-form' as Deleuze and Guattari say, whose function is defined by processes of capture and boundary-marking. The latter, deterritorialization, is associated with the highly mobile logic of nomadism whose function is defined by its ability to transgress boundaries and avoid capture by the State-form. The one finds expression in the desire for identity, order and unity, the other in the desire for difference, flows and lines of flight.

The 'political prosaics' advocated by Campbell and others utilize this Deleuzian language to shed light on the new political dynamics and demands created by refugees, immigrants, and new social movements as they encounter and outflank the State-form. These 'transversal' groups and movements not only transgress national boundaries, they call into question the territorial organization of modern political life. As Roland Bleiker (2000: 2) notes, they 'question the spatial logic through which these boundaries have come to constitute and frame the conduct of international relations'. In his study of popular dissent in international relations, Bleiker argues that globalization is subjecting social life to changing political dynamics. In an age of mass media and telecommunications, images of local acts of resistance can be flashed across the world in an instant, turning them into events of global significance. Globalization, Bleixer suggests, has transformed the nature of dissent, making possible global and transversal practices of popular dissent (2000: 31). No longer taking place in a purely local context, acts of resistance 'have taken on increasingly transversal dimensions. They ooze into often unrecognised, but nevertheless significant grey zones between domestic and international spheres', blurring the boundaries between inside and outside, local and global (2000: 185). By outflanking sovereign controls and crossing state boundaries, the actions of transversal dissident groups can be read as 'hidden transcripts' that occur 'off-stage', as it were, behind and alongside the 'public transcript' of the sovereign state. The 'hidden transcripts' of transversal movements are therefore deterritorializing in their function, escaping the spatial codes and practices of the dominant actors and making possible a critique of the sovereign state's modes of reterritorialization and exclusion (2000: Chapter 7).

This is also the case with refugees and migrants. They hold a different relationship to space than citizens. Being nomadic rather than sedentary, they are defined by movement across and between political spaces. They problematize and defy the 'territorial imperative' of the sovereign state (Soguk and Whitehall 1999: 682). Indeed, their wandering movement dislocates the ontopological norm which seeks to fix people's identities within the spatial boundaries of the nation-state (1999: 697).

As a consequence they disrupt our state-centric conceptualizations, problematizing received understandings of the character and location of the political.

Similar arguments are advanced by Peter Nyers and Mick Dillon regarding the figure of the refugee. As Nyers (1999) argues, the figure of the refugee, as one who cannot claim to be a member of a 'proper' political community, acts as a 'limit-concept', occupying the ambiguous zone between citizen and human. Dillon (1999) argues that the refugee/ stranger remains outside conventional modes of political subjectivity which are tied to the sovereign state. The very existence of the refugee/ stranger calls into question the settled, sovereign life of the political community by disclosing the estrangement that is shared by both citizens and refugees. As Soguk and Whitehall (1999: 675) point out, refugees and migrants, by moving across state boundaries and avoiding capture, have the effect of rupturing traditional constitutive narratives of international relations.

Sovereignty and the ethics of exclusion

Postmodernism's ethical critique of state sovereignty needs to be understood in relation to the deconstructive critique of totalization and the deterritorializing effect of transversal struggles. Deconstruction has already been explained as a strategy of interpretation and criticism that targets theoretical concepts and social institutions which attempt totalization or total stability. It is important to note that the postmodern critique of state sovereignty focuses on *sovereignty*.

The sovereign state may well be the dominant mode of subjectivity in international relations today, but it is questionable whether its claim to be the primary and exclusive political subject is justified. The most thoroughgoing account of state sovereignty's ethico-political costs is offered by Rob Walker in *Inside/Outside* (1993). Walker sets out there the context in which state sovereignty has been mobilized as an analytical category with which to understand international relations, and as the primary expression of moral and political community. Walker's critique suggests that state sovereignty is best understood as a constitutive political practice which emerged historically to resolve three ontological contradictions. The relationship between time and space was resolved by containing time within domesticated territorial space. The relationship between universal and particular was resolved through the system of sovereign states which gave expression to the plurality and particularity of states on the one hand, and the universality of one system on the other. This resolution also allowed for the pursuit of universal values to be pursued within particular states. Finally, the relationship between self and other is also resolved in terms of 'insiders' and 'outsiders', friends and enemies (Walker 1995a: 320–1, 1995b: 28). In deconstructive fashion, Walker's (1993: 23) concern is to 'destabilise [these] seemingly opposed categories by showing how they are at once mutually constitutive and yet always in the process of dissolving into each other'. The overall effect of Walker's inquiry into state sovereignty, consistent with the 'political prosaics' outlined above, is to question whether it is any longer a useful descriptive category and an effective response to the problems that confront humanity in modern political life.

The analysis offered by Walker suggests that it is becoming increasingly difficult to organize modern political life in terms of sovereign states and sovereign boundaries. He argues that there are 'spatiotemporal processes that are radically at odds with the resolution expressed by the principle of state sovereignty' (1993: 155). For both material and normative reasons, Walker refuses to accept state sovereignty as the only, or best, possible means of organizing modern political life. Modern political life need not be caught between mutually exclusive and exhaustive oppositions such as inside and outside. Identity need not be exclusionary, difference need not be interpreted as antithetical to identity (1993: 123), and the trade-off between men and citizens built into the modern state need not always privilege claims of citizens above claims of humanity (Walker 2000: 231–2).

To rethink questions of political identity and community without succumbing to binary oppositions is to contemplate a political life beyond the paradigm of sovereign states. It is to take seriously the possibility that new forms of political identity and community can emerge which are not predicated on absolute exclusion and spatial distinctions between here and there, self and other (Walker 1995a: 307).

Connolly delivers a postmodern critique which brings the question of democracy to bear directly on sovereignty. His argument is that the notion of state sovereignty is incompatible with democracy, especially in a globalized late modernity. The point of his critique is to challenge the sovereign state's 'monopoly over the allegiances, identifications and energies of its members' (Connolly 1991: 479). The multiple modes of belonging and interdependence, and the multiplication of global risks that exist in late modernity, complicate the neat simplicity of binary divisions between inside and outside. His point is that obligations and duties constantly overrun the boundaries of sovereign states. Sovereignty, Connolly says, 'poses too stringent a limitation to identifications and loyalties extending beyond it', and so it is necessary to promote an ethos of democracy which exceeds territorialization by cutting across the state at all levels (1991: 480). He calls this a 'disaggregation of democracy', or what might better be called a 'deterritorialization of democracy'.

'What is needed politically', he says, 'is a series of cross-national, nonstatist movements organized across state lines, mobilized around specific issues of global significance, pressing states from inside and outside simultaneously to reconfigure established convictions, priorities, and policies' (Connolly 1995: 23).

A similar argument is advanced by Campbell. According to Campbell (1998a: 208), the norm of ontopology produces a 'moral cartography' that territorializes democracy and responsibility, confining it to the limits of the sovereign state. But Campbell, like Connolly, is interested in fostering an ethos of democratic pluralization that would promote tolerance and multiculturalism within and across state boundaries. By promoting an active affirmation of alterity it would resist the sovereign state's logics of territorialization and capture.

Postmodern ethics

Postmodernism asks, what might ethics come to mean outside a paradigm of sovereign subjectivity? There are two strands of ethics which develop out of postmodernism's reflections on international relations. One strand challenges the ontological description on which traditional ethical arguments are grounded. It advances a notion of ethics which is not predicated on a rigid, fixed boundary between inside and outside. The other strand focuses on the relation between ontological grounds and ethical arguments. It questions whether ontology must precede ethics.

The first strand is put forward most fully by Ashley and Walker (1990) and Connolly (1995). Fundamental to their writing is a critique of the faith invested in boundaries. Again, the main target of postmodernism here is the sovereign state's defence of rigid boundaries. Territorial boundaries, which are thought to mark the limits of political identity or community, are taken by postmodernism to be historically contingent and highly ambiguous products (Ashley and Walker 1990). As such, they hold no transcendental status. As a challenge to the ethical delimitations imposed by state sovereignty, postmodern ethics, or the 'diplomatic ethos', as Ashley and Walker call it, is not confined by any spatial or territorial limits. It seeks to 'enable the rigorous practice of this ethics in the widest possible compass' (1990: 395). No demarcatory boundaries should obstruct the universalization of this ethic which flows across boundaries (both imagined and territorial):

Where such an ethics is rigorously practised, no voice can effectively claim to stand heroically upon some exclusionary ground, offering this ground as a source of a necessary truth that human beings must violently project in the name of a citizenry, people, nation, class, gender, race, golden age, or historical cause of any sort. Where this ethics is rigorously practised, no totalitarian order could ever be. (1990: 395)

In breaking with the ethics of sovereign exclusion, postmodernism offers an understanding of ethics which is detached from territorial limitations. The diplomatic ethos is a 'deterritorialized' ethics which unfolds by transgressing sovereign limits. This transgressive ethics complements the deterritorialized notion of democracy advanced by Connolly. Underlying both ideas is a critique of state sovereignty as a basis for conducting, organizing and limiting political life.

The other ethical strand is advanced by Campbell. He follows Derrida and Levinas by questioning traditional approaches which deduce ethics from ontology, specifically an ontology or metaphysics of presence (Campbell 1998a: 171–92; and see Levinas 1969: Section 1A). It does not begin with an empirical account of the world as a necessary prelude to ethical consideration. Rather, it gives primacy to ethics as, in a sense, 'first philosophy'. The key thinker in this ethical approach is Emmanuel Levinas who has been more influenced by Jewish theology than Greek philosophy. Indeed, the differences between these two styles of thought are constantly worked through in Levinas' thought as a difference between a philosophy of alterity and a philosophy of identity or totality.

Levinas overturns the hierarchy between ontology and ethics, giving primacy to ethics as the starting point. Ethics seems to function as a condition which makes possible the world of beings. Levinas offers a redescription of ontology such that it is inextricably tied up with, and indebted to, ethics, and is free of totalizing impulses. His thought is antagonistic to all forms of ontological and political imperialism or totalitarianism (Levinas 1969: 44; Campbell 1998a: 192). In Levinas' schema, subjectivity is constituted through, and as, an ethical relation. The effect of the Levinasian approach is to recast notions of subjectivity and responsibility in light of an ethics of otherness or alterity. 'Ethics redefines subjectivity as ... heteronomous responsibility' (Levinas, quoted in Campbell 1994: 463, 1998a: 176).

This gives rise to a notion of ethics which diverges from the Kantian principle of generalizability and symmetry that we find in critical theory. Rather than begin with the Self and then generalize the imperative universally to a community of equals, Levinas begins with the Other. The Other places certain demands on the Self, hence there is an asymmetrical relationship between Self and Other. The end result is to advance a 'different figuration of politics, one in which its purpose is the struggle *for* – or *on behalf of* – alterity, and not a struggle to efface, erase, or eradicate alterity' (Campbell 1994: 477, 1998a: 191). But as Michael Shapiro (1998b: 698–9) has shown, this ethos may not be so different from a Kantian ethic of hospitality that encourages universal tolerance of difference as a means of diminishing global violence.

The consequence of taking postmodernism's critique of totality and sovereignty seriously is that central political concepts such as community, identity, ethics and democracy are rethought to avoid being persistently reterritorialized by the sovereign state. Indeed, de-linking these concepts from territory and sovereignty underlies the practical task of a postmodern politics or ethics. As Anthony Burke (2004: 353) explains in a forceful critique of Just War theory after September 11, postmodernism's conception of an 'ethical peace' would refuse 'to channel its ethical obligations solely through the state, or rely on it to protect us violently'. It should be noted, however, that postmodernism, as a critique of totalization, opposes concepts of identity and community only to the extent that they are tied dogmatically to notions of territoriality, boundedness and exclusion. The thrust of postmodernism has always been to challenge both epistemological and political claims to totality and sovereignty and thereby open up questions about the location and character of the political.

Conclusion

Postmodernism makes several contributions to the study of international relations. First, through its genealogical method it seeks to expose the intimate connection between claims to knowledge and claims to political power and authority. Secondly, through the textual strategy of deconstruction it seeks to problematize all claims to epistemological and political totalization. This holds especially significant implications for the sovereign state. Most notably, it means that the sovereign state, as the primary mode of subjectivity in international relations, must be examined closely to expose its practices of capture and exclusion. Moreover, a more comprehensive account of contemporary world politics must also include an analysis of those transversal actors and movements that operate outside and across state boundaries. Thirdly, postmodernism seeks to rethink the concept of the political without invoking assumptions of sovereignty and reterritorialization. By challenging the idea that the character and location of the political must be determined by the sovereign state, postmodernism seeks to broaden the political imagination and the range of political possibilities for transforming international relations. These contributions seems more important than ever after the events of September 11.

Chapter 8

Constructivism

CHRISTIAN REUS-SMIT

During the 1980s two debates structured International Relations scholarship, particularly within the American mainstream. The first was between neo-realists and neo-liberals, both of which sought to apply the logic of rationalist economic theory to international relations, but reached radically different conclusions about the potential for international cooperation. The second was between rationalists and critical theorists, the latter challenging the epistemological, methodological, ontological and normative assumptions of neo-realism and neo-liberalism, and the former accusing critical theorists of having little of any substance to say about 'real-world' international relations. Since the end of the Cold War, these axes of debate have been displaced by two new debates: between rationalists and constructivists, and between constructivists and critical theorists. The catalyst for this shift was the rise of a new constructivist approach to international theory, an approach that challenged the rationalism and positivism of neo-realism and neoliberalism while simultaneously pushing critical theorists away from metatheoretical critique to the empirical analysis of world politics.

This chapter explains the nature and rise of constructivism in international theory, situating it in relation to both rationalist and critical theories. Constructivism is characterized by an emphasis on the importance of normative as well as material structures, on the role of identity in shaping political action and on the mutually constitutive relationship between agents and structures. When using the terms rationalism or rationalist theory, I refer not to the 'Grotian' or 'English' School of international theory, discussed by Andrew Linklater in Chapter 4 in this volume, but to theories that are explicitly informed by the assumptions of rational choice theory, principally neo-realism and neo-liberalism. I use the term 'critical theory' broadly to include all post-positivist theory of the Third Debate and after, encompassing both the narrowly defined critical theory of the Frankfurt School and postmodern international theory, discussed by Richard Devetak in Chapters 6 and 7, respectively. After revisiting the rationalist premises of neo-realism and neo-liberalism, and reviewing the broad-based critique of those premises mounted by critical theorists during the 1980s, I examine the origins of constructivism and its principal theoretical premises. I then distinguish between three different forms of constructivist scholarship in International Relations: systemic, unit-level and holistic. This is followed by some reflections on the emergent discontents that characterize constructivism as a theoretical approach, by a discussion of the contribution of constructivism to international relations theory, and by a brief consideration of developments in constructivism in the last five years, particularly since the terrorist attacks of 11 September 2001.

Rationalist theory

After the Second World War, realism became the dominant theory of international relations. Yet this dominance did not go unchallenged, with new theoretical perspectives emerging, forcing revisions in realist theory. In the 1970s, the classical realism of Claude, Carr, Morgenthau, Niebuhr and others was challenged by liberals, such as Robert Keohane and Joseph Nye, who emphasized interdependence between states, transnational relations and non-state actors, particularly multinational corporations (MNCs). International relations was not to be conceived as a system of 'colliding billiard balls', but as a cobweb of political, economic and social relations binding sub-national, national, transnational, international and supranational actors (Keohane and Nye 1972). This view was subsequently modified to pay greater attention to the role and importance of sovereign states, with Keohane and Nye reconceiving state power in the light of 'complex interdependence' (Keohane and Nye 1977). States were acknowledged to be the principal actors in world politics, but pervasive interdependence was thought to alter the nature and effectiveness of state power, with the balance of military power, so long emphasized by realists, no longer determining political outcomes, as sensitivity and vulnerability to interdependence produced new relations of power between states.

This challenge to realism did not go unanswered. As Jack Donnelly explains in Chapter 2 in this volume, in 1979 Kenneth Waltz published the *Theory of International Politics* (1979), in which he advanced a radically revised realist theory, subsequently labelled 'neo-realism' or 'structural realism'. Waltz drew on two sources of intellectual inspiration: the philosopher of science Imre Lakatos' model of theory construction, and microeconomic theory. The first led him to devise a theory with minimal assumptions, a parsimonious set of heuristically powerful propositions that could generate empirically verifiable hypotheses about international relations; the second encouraged him to emphasize the structural determinants of state behaviour. The resulting neo-realist theory built on two assumptions: that the international system is anarchical, in the sense that it lacks a central authority to impose order; and that in such a system states are primarily interested in their own survival. Waltz went on to argue that to ensure their survival states must maximize their power, particularly their military power. Because such power is zero-sum – with an increase in the military power of one state necessarily producing a decrease in the relative power of another – Waltz argued that states are 'defensive positionalists'. They are conscious of their position within the power hierarchy of states, and at a minimum seek to maintain that position, at a maximum to increase it to the point of domination. For this reason, Waltz claimed that the struggle for power is an enduring characteristic of international relations and conflict is endemic. In such a world, he argued, cooperation between states is at best precarious, at worst non-existent.

Theory of International Politics reinvigorated realism, giving realists a new identity – as neo- or structural realists – and a new confidence to the point of arrogance. Not all were convinced, though, and criticisms mounted on several fronts. The most moderate of these came from a new school of neo-liberal institutionalists, led by the repositioned Robert Keohane. Moving away from his previous concern with transnational relations and interdependence, Keohane took up the task of explaining cooperation under anarchy. Realists had long argued that if international cooperation was possible at all, it was only under conditions of hegemony, when a dominant state was able to use its power to create and enforce the institutional rules necessary to sustain cooperation between states. By the end of the 1970s, however, America's relative power was clearly on the wane, yet the framework of institutions it had sponsored after the Second World War to facilitate international economic cooperation was not collapsing. How could this be explained? In his 1984 book, *After Hegemony*, Keohane proposed a neo-liberal theory of international cooperation, a theory that embraced three elements of neo-realism: the importance of international anarchy in shaping state behaviour, the state as the most important actor in world politics and the assumption of states as essentially self-interested. He also endorsed the Lakatosian model of theory construction that informed neo-realism (Keohane 1984, 1989a).

Despite this common ground with neo-realism, neo-liberalism draws very different conclusions about the potential for sustained international cooperation. As noted above, neo-liberals accept that states have to pursue their interests under conditions of anarchy. In Axelrod and Keohane's words, anarchy 'remains a constant' (1993: 86). Nevertheless, anarchy alone does not determine the extent or nature of international cooperation. Neo-realists are closest to the mark, neo-liberals argue, when there is low interdependence between states. When economic and political interactions between states are minimal, there are few common interests to spur international cooperation. When interdependence is high, however, as since the Second World War, states come to share a wide range of interests, from the management of international trade to global environmental protection. The existence of mutual interests is a prerequisite for international cooperation, but neo-liberals insist that the existence of such interests does not itself explain the extent and nature of cooperative relations between states – international cooperation remains difficult to achieve. Even when states have interests in common, the lack of a central world authority often deters them from incurring the reciprocal obligations that cooperation demands. Without a central authority, states fear that others will cheat on agreements; they can see cooperation as too costly, given the effort they would have to expend; and often they lack sufficient information to know that they even have common interests with other states. This not only explains why states fail to cooperate even when they have common interests, it explains how they cooperate when they do. According to neo-liberals, states construct international institutions, or regimes, to overcome these obstacles to cooperation. Defined as 'sets of implicit or explicit principles, norms, rules and decision-making procedures around which actors' expectations converge in a given area of international relations', international regimes are said to raise the cost of cheating, lower transaction costs and increase information, thus facilitating cooperation under anarchy (Keohane 1984: 57, 85–109).

The debate between neo-realists and neo-liberals is often characterized as a debate between those who think that states are preoccupied with *relative* gains versus those who think that states are more interested in *absolute* gains. Because anarchy makes states fear for their survival, and because power is the ultimate guarantor of survival, neo-realists believe that states constantly measure their power against that of other states. They constantly monitor whether their position in the international power hierarchy is stable, declining, or on the rise, fearing decline above all else. This is why neo-realists are sceptical about international cooperation: if states are worried about relative gains, they will forgo cooperation if they fear that their gains will be less than those that accrue to others. Even if a trading agreement promises to net State *A* $100 million in profit, if that same agreement will net State *B* $200 million, State *A* may refuse to cooperate. In other words, the promise of absolute gains may not be sufficient to encourage states to cooperate, as they are primarily interested in relative gains. Neo-liberals deny that relative gains calculations pose such an obstacle to international cooperation.

The world imagined by neo-realists is too simplistic, they argue. States that are confident in their survival, which amounts to a significant proportion of states, are not as preoccupied with relative gains as neo-realists think; states tend to evaluate the intentions of other states as well as their relative capabilities; and when states have multiple relationships with multiple states the constant calculation of relative gains is simply impractical. Neo-liberals thus characterize states not as defensive positionalists, as neo-realists do, but as utility-maximizers, as actors that will entertain cooperation so long as it promises absolute gains in their interests.

In spite of these differences, neo-realism and neo-liberalism are both rationalist theories; they are both constructed upon the choice-theoretic assumptions of microeconomic theory. Three such assumptions stand out. First, political actors–be they individuals or states–are assumed to be atomistic, self-interested and rational. Actors are treated as *pre-social*, in the sense that their identities and interests are autogenous. In the language of classical liberalism, individuals are the source of their own conceptions of the good. Actors are also *self-interested*, concerned primarily with the pursuit of their own interests. And they are *rational*, capable of establishing the most effective and efficient way to realize their interests within the environmental constraints they encounter. Second, and following from the above, actors' interests are assumed to be exogenous to social interaction. Individuals and states are thought to enter social relations with their interests already formed. Social interaction is not considered an important determinant of interests. Third, and following yet again from the above, society is understood as a strategic realm, a realm in which individuals or states come together to pursue their pre-defined interests. Actors are not, therefore, inherently social; they are not products of their social environment, merely atomistic rational beings that form social relations to maximize their interests.

These assumptions are most starkly expressed in neo-realism. As we have seen, states are defined as 'defensive positionalists', jealous guardians of their positions in the international power hierarchy. The formation of state interests is of no interest to neo-realists. Beyond maintaining that international anarchy gives states a survival motive, and that over time the incentives and constraints of the international system socialize states into certain forms of behaviour, they have no theory of interest formation, nor do they think they should have (Waltz 1979: 91–2, 127–8). Furthermore, international relations are considered so thoroughly strategic that neo-realists deny the existence of a society of states altogether, speaking of an 'international system' not an international society. How does neo-liberalism compare? The assumption of self-interest is expressed in the neo-liberal idea of states as rational egoists: actors who are concerned primarily with their own narrowly defined interests, and who pursue those interests in the most efficacious manner possible. Like neo-realists, neo-liberals treat state interests as exogenous to inter-state interaction, and see no need for a theory of interest formation. In fact, explaining the origins of state interests is explicitly excluded from the province of neo-liberal theory. Finally, neo-liberals move beyond the stark systemic imagery of neo-realism to acknowledge the existence of an international society, but their conception of that society remains strategic. States certainly come together in the cooperative construction and maintenance of functional institutions, but their identities and interests are not shaped or constituted in any way by their social interactions.

The challenge of critical theory

While neo-realists and neo-liberals engaged in a rationalist family feud, critical theorists challenged the very foundations of the rationalist project. Ontologically, they criticized the image of social actors as atomistic egoists, whose interests are formed prior to social interaction, and who enter social relations solely for strategic purposes. They argued, in contrast, that actors are inherently *social*, that their identities and interests are socially constructed, the products of inter-subjective social structures. Epistemologically and methodologically, they questioned the neo-positivism of Lakatosian forms of social science, calling for interpretive modes of understanding, attuned to the unquantifiable nature of many social phenomena and the inherent subjectivity of all observation. And normatively, they condemned the notion of value-neutral theorizing, arguing that all knowledge is wedded to interests, and that theories should be explicitly committed to exposing and dismantling structures of domination and oppression (Hoffman 1987; George and Campbell 1990).

Beneath the umbrella of this broad critique, modern and postmodern critical theorists stood united against the dominant rationalist theories. Just as the rationalists were internally divided, though, so too were the critics. The postmodernists, drawing on the French social theorists, particularly Jacques Derrida and Michel Foucault, adopted a stance of 'radical interpretivism'. They opposed all attempts to assess empirical and ethical claims by any single criterion of validity, claiming that such moves always marginalize alternative viewpoints and moral positions, creating hierarchies of power and domination. The modernists, inspired by the writings of Frankfurt School theorists such as Jürgen Habermas, assumed a position of 'critical interpretivism'. They recognized the contingent nature of all knowledge – the inherent subjectivity of all claims and the connection between knowledge and power – but they insisted that some criteria were needed to distinguish plausible from implausible knowledge claims, and that without minimal, consensually grounded ethical principles, emancipatory political action would be impossible. Mark Hoffman has characterized this difference between modernists and postmodernists in terms of a distinction between 'anti-foundationalism' and 'minimal foundationalism' (1991: 169–85).

Despite these important differences, the first wave of critical theory had a distinctive meta-theoretical or quasi-philosophical character. Critical international theorists roamed broadly over epistemological, normative, ontological and methodological concerns, and their energies were devoted primarily to demolishing the philosophical foundations of the rationalist project. Noteworthy empirical studies of world politics were certainly published by critical theorists, but the general tenor of critical writings was more abstractly theoretical, and their principal impact lay in the critique of prevailing assumptions about legitimate knowledge, about the nature of the social world, and about the purpose of theory (Cox 1987; Der Derian 1987). This general orientation was encouraged by a widely shared assumption among critical theorists about the relationship between theory and practice. This assumption was evident in the common refrain that realism constituted a 'hegemonic discourse', by which they meant two things. First, that realist assumptions, particularly dressed up in the garb of rationalism and neo-positivism, as was neo-realism, defined what counts as legitimate knowledge in the field of International Relations. And, second, that the influence of these assumptions extended far beyond the academy to structure policy making, particularly in the United States. Rationalist theories were thus doubly insidious. Not only did they dominate the discourse of International Relations, to the exclusion of alternative perspectives and forms of knowledge, they informed Washington's Cold War politics, with all the excesses of power these engendered. From this standpoint, theory was seen as having a symbiotic relationship with practice, and critiquing the discourse of International Relations was considered the essence of substantive analysis (Price and Reus-Smit 1998).

Constructivism

The end of the Cold War produced a major reconfiguration of debates within the dominant American discourse of international relations theory, prompted by the rise of a new 'constructivist' school of thought. While constructivism owes much to intellectual developments in sociology– particularly sociological institutionalism (see Finnemore 1996) – Richard

Price and Chris Reus-Smit have argued that constructivism should be seen primarily as an outgrowth of critical international theory, as many of its pioneers explicitly sought to employ the insights of that theory to illuminate diverse aspects of world politics. Constructivism differs from first-wave critical theory, however, in its emphasis on *empirical analysis*. Some constructivists have continued to work at the meta-theoretical level (Onuf 1989; Wendt 1999), but most have sought conceptual and theoretical illumination through the systematic analysis of empirical puzzles in world politics. The balance of critical scholarship has thus shifted away from the previous mode of abstract philosophical argument toward the study of human discourse and practice beyond the narrow confines of international relations theory. Where first-wave critical theorists had rejected the rationalist depiction of humans as atomistic egoists and society as a strategic domain – proffering an alternative image of humans as socially embedded, communicatively constituted and culturally empowered – constructivists have used this alternative ontology to explain and interpret aspects of world politics that were anomalous to neo-realism and neo-liberalism. And where earlier theorists had condemned the neo-positivist methodology of those perspectives, calling for more interpretive, discursive and historical modes of analysis, constructivists have employed these techniques to further their empirical explorations.

The rise of constructivism was prompted by four factors. First, motivated by an attempt to reassert the pre-eminence of their own conceptions of theory and world politics, leading rationalists challenged critical theorists to move beyond theoretical critique to the substantive analysis of international relations. While prominent critical theorists condemned the motives behind this challenge, constructivists saw it as an opportunity to demonstrate the heuristic power of non-rationalist perspectives (Walker 1989). Second, the end of the Cold War undermined the explanatory pretensions of neo-realists and neo-liberals, neither of which had predicted, nor could adequately comprehend, the systemic transformations reshaping the global order. It also undermined the critical theorists' assumption that theory drove practice in any narrow or direct fashion, as global politics increasingly demonstrated dynamics that contradicted realist expectations and prescriptions. The end of the Cold War thus opened a space for alternative explanatory perspectives and prompted critically inclined scholars to move away from a narrowly defined meta-theoretical critique. Third, by the beginning of the 1990s a new generation of young scholars had emerged who embraced many of the propositions of critical international theory, but who saw potential for innovation in conceptual elaboration and empirically informed theoretical development (Klotz 1995: 20;

Kier 1997; Price 1997; Hall 1999; Lynch 1999; Reus-Smit 1999; Tannenwald 1999; Rae 2002). Not only had the end of the Cold War thrown up new and interesting questions about world politics (such as the dynamics of international change, the nature of basic institutional practices, the role of non-state agency and the problem of human rights), the rationalist failure to explain recent systemic transformations encouraged this new generation of scholars to revisit old questions and issues so long viewed through neo-realist and neo-liberal lenses (including the control of WMD, the role and nature of strategic culture and the implications of anarchy). Finally, the advance of the new constructivist perspective was aided by the enthusiasm that mainstream scholars, frustrated by the analytical failings of the dominant rationalist theories, showed in embracing the new perspective, moving it from the margins to the mainstream of theoretical debate.

Echoing the divisions within critical international theory, constructivists are divided between modernists and postmodernists. They have all, however, sought to articulate and explore three core ontological propositions about social life, propositions which they claim illuminate more about world politics than rival rationalist assumptions. First, to the extent that structures can be said to shape the behaviour of social and political actors, be they individuals or states, constructivists hold that *normative* or *ideational* structures are just as important as material structures. Where neo-realists emphasize the material structure of the balance of military power, and Marxists stress the material structure of the capitalist world economy, constructivists argue that systems of shared ideas, beliefs and values also have structural characteristics, and that they exert a powerful influence on social and political action. There are two reasons why they attach such importance to these structures. Constructivists argue that 'material resources only acquire meaning for human action through the structure of shared knowledge in which they are embedded' (Wendt 1995: 73). For example, Canada and Cuba both exist alongside the United States, yet the simple balance of military power cannot explain the fact that the former is a close American ally, the latter a sworn enemy. Ideas about identity, the logics of ideology and established structures of friendship and enmity lend the material balance of power between Canada and the United States and Cuba and the United States radically different meanings. Constructivists also stress the importance of normative and ideational structures because these are thought to shape the social identities of political actors. Just as the institutionalized norms of the academy shape the identity of a professor, the norms of the international system condition the social identity of the sovereign state. For instance, in the age of Absolutism (1555–1848) the norms of European international society held that Christian monarchies were the only legitimate form of sovereign state, and these norms, backed by the coercive practices of the community of states, conspired to undermine Muslim, liberal or nationalist polities.

Second, constructivists argue that understanding how non-material structures condition actors' identities is important because identities inform interests and, in turn, actions. As we saw above, rationalists believe that actors' interests are exogenously determined, meaning that actors, be they individuals or states, encounter one another with a pre-existing set of preferences. Neo-realists and neo-liberals are not interested in where such preferences come from, only in how actors pursue them strategically. Society – both domestic and international – is thus considered a *strategic domain*, a place in which previously consti- tuted actors pursue their goals, a place that does not alter the nature or interests of those actors in any deep sense. Constructivists, in contrast, argue that understanding how actors develop their interests is crucial to explaining a wide range of international political phenomenon that rationalists ignore or misunderstand. To explain interest formation, constructivists focus on the social identities of individuals or states. In Alexander Wendt's words, 'Identities are the basis of interests' (Wendt 1992: 398). To return to the previous examples, being an 'academic' gives a person certain interests, such as research and publication, and being a Christian monarch in the age of Absolutism brought with it a range of interests, such as controlling religion within your territory pursuing rights of succession beyond that territory and crushing nationalist movements. Likewise, being a liberal democracy today encourages an intolerance of authoritarian regimes and a preference for free-market capitalism.

Third, constructivists contend that agents and structures are *mutually constituted*. Normative and ideational structures may well condition the identities and interests of actors, but those structures would not exist if it were not for the knowledgeable practices of those actors. Wendt's emphasis on the 'supervening' power of structures, and the predilection of many constructivists to study how norms shape behaviour, suggest that constructivists are structuralists, just like their neo-realist and Marxist counterparts. On closer reflection, however, one sees that con- structivists are better classed as structurationists, as emphasizing the impact of non-material structures on identities and interests but, just as importantly, the role of practices in maintaining and transforming those structures. Institutionalized norms and ideas 'define the meaning and identity of the individual actor and the patterns of appropriate eco- nomic, political, and cultural activity engaged in by those individuals' (Boli, Meyer and Thomas 1989: 12), and it 'is through reciprocal interaction that we create and instantiate the relatively enduring social structures in terms of which we define our identities and interests' (Wendt 1992: 406). The norms of the academy give certain individuals an academic identity which brings with it an interest in research and publication, but it is only through the routinized practices of academics that such norms exist and are sustained. Similarly, the international norms that uphold liberal democracy as the dominant model of legitimate statehood, and which license intervention in the name of human rights and the promotion of free trade, exist and persist only because of the continued practices of liberal democratic states (and powerful non-state actors).

Normative and ideational structures are seen as shaping actors' identities and interests through three mechanisms: imagination, communication and constraint. With regard to the first of these, constructivists argue that non-material structures affect what actors see as the realm of possibility: how they think they should act, what the perceived limitations on their actions are and what strategies they can imagine, let alone entertain, to achieve their objectives. Institutionalized norms and ideas thus condition what actors consider necessary and possible, in both practical and ethical terms. A president or prime minister in an established liberal democracy will only imagine and seriously entertain certain strategies to enhance his or her power, and the norms of the liberal democratic polity will condition his or her expectations. Normative and ideational structures also work their influence through communication. When an individual or a state seeks to justify their behaviour, they will usually appeal to established norms of legitimate conduct. A president or prime minister may appeal to the conventions of executive government, and a state may justify its behaviour with reference to the norms of sovereignty–or, in the case of intervention in the affairs of another state, according to international human rights norms. As the latter case suggests, norms may conflict with one another in their prescriptions, which makes moral argument about the relative importance of international normative precepts a particularly salient aspect of world politics (Risse 2000). Finally, even if normative and ideational structures do not affect an actor's behaviour by framing their imagination or by providing a linguistic or moral court of appeal, constructivists argue that they can place significant constraints on that actor's conduct. Realists have long argued that ideas simply function as rationalizations, as ways of masking actions really motivated by the crude desire for power. Constructivists point out, though, that institutionalized norms and ideas work as rationalizations only because they already have moral force in a given social context. Furthermore, appealing to established norms and ideas to justify behaviour is a viable strategy only if the behaviour is in some measure consistent with the proclaimed principles.

The very language of justification thus provides constraints on action, though the effectiveness of such constraints will vary with the actor and the context (Reus-Smit 1999: 35–6).

Given the preceding discussion, constructivism contrasts with rationalism in three important respects. First, where rationalists assume that actors are atomistic egoists, constructivists treat them as deeply *social*: not in the sense that they are 'party animals', but in the sense that their identities are constituted by the institutionalized norms, values and ideas of the social environment in which they act. Second, instead of treating actors' interests as exogenously determined, as given prior to social interaction, constructivists treat interests as *endogenous* to such interaction, as a consequence of identity acquisition, as learned through processes of communication, reflection on experience and role enactment. Third, while rationalists view society as a strategic realm, a place where actors rationally pursue their interests, constructivists see it as a *constitutive realm*, the site that generates actors as knowledgeable social and political agents, the realm that makes them who they are. From these ontological commitments, it is clear why constructivists are called 'constructivists', for they emphasize the social determinants of social and political agency and action.

In the 1990s, three different forms of constructivism evolved: systemic, unit-level and holistic constructivism. The first of these follows neo-realists in adopting a 'third-image' perspective, focusing solely on interactions between unitary state actors. Everything that exists or occurs within the domestic political realm is ignored, and an account of world politics is derived simply by theorizing how states relate to one another in the external, international domain. Wendt's influential writings provide the best example of systemic constructivism. In fact, one could reasonably argue that Wendt's writings represent the only true example of this rarified form of constructivism (Wendt 1992, 1994, 1995, 1999). Like other constructivists, Wendt believes that the identity of the state informs its interests and, in turn, its actions. He draws a distinction, though, between the social and corporate identities of the state: the former referring to the status, role or personality that international society ascribes to a state; the latter referring to the internal human, material, ideological, or cultural factors that make a state what it is. Because of his commitment to systemic theorizing, Wendt brackets corporate sources of state identity, concentrating on how structural contexts, systemic processes, and strategic practices produce and reproduce different sorts of state identity. Though theoretically elegant, this form of constructivism suffers from one major deficiency: it confines the processes that shape international societies within an unnecessarily and unproductively narrow realm. The social identities of states are thought to be constituted by the normative and ideational structures of international society, and those structures are seen as the product of state practices. From this perspective, it is impossible to explain how fundamental changes occur, either in the nature of international society or in the nature of state identity. By bracketing everything domestic, Wendt excludes by theoretical fiat most of the normative and ideational forces that might prompt such change.

Unit-level constructivism is the inverse of systemic constructivism. Instead of focusing on the external, international domain, unit-level constructivists concentrate on the relationship between domestic social and legal norms and the identities and interests of states, the very factors bracketed by Wendt. Here Peter Katzenstein's writings on the national security policies of Germany and Japan (1996, 1999) are emblematic. Setting out to explain why two states, with common experiences of military defeat, foreign occupation, economic development, transition from authoritarianism to democracy and nascent great-power status, have adopted very different internal and external national security policies, Katzenstein stresses the importance of institutionalized regulatory and constitutive national social and legal norms. He concludes that:

> In Germany the strengthening of state power through changes in legal norms betrays a deep-seated fear that terrorism challenges the core of the state. In effect, eradicating terrorism and minimizing violent protest overcome the specter of a 'Hobbesian' state of nature ... In Japan, on the other hand, the close interaction of social and legal norms reveals a state living symbiotically within its society and not easily shaken to its foundation. Eliminating terrorism and containing violent protest were the tasks of a 'Grotian' community ... Conversely, Germany's active involvement in the evolution of international legal norms conveys a conception of belonging to an international 'Grotian' community. Japan's lack of concern for the consequences of pushing terrorists abroad and its generally passive international stance is based on a 'Hobbesian' view of the society of states. (Katzenstein 1996: 153–4)

While not entirely disregarding the role of international norms in conditioning the identities and interests of states, Katzenstein draws attention to the internal, domestic determinants of national policies. Unit-level constructivism of this sort has the virtue of enabling the explanation of variations of identity, interest and action across states, something that systemic constructivism obscures. It follows, though, that this form of constructivism has difficulty accounting for similarities between states, for patterns of convergence in state identity and interest.

Where systemic and unit-level constructivists reproduce the traditional dichotomy between the international and the domestic, holistic constructivists seek to bridge the two domains. To accommodate the entire range of factors conditioning the identities and interests of states, they bring the corporate and the social together into a unified analytical perspective that treats the domestic and the international as two faces of a single social and political order. Concerned primarily with the dynamics of global change – particularly the rise and possible demise of the sovereign state – holistic constructivists focus on the mutually constitutive relationship between this order and the state. This general perspective has spawned two distinctive, yet complementary, analyses of international change: one focusing on grand shifts between international systems, the other on recent changes within the modern system. The former is typified by John Ruggie's path-breaking work on the rise of sovereign states out of the wreck of European feudalism, work that emphasizes the importance of changing social epistemes, or frameworks of knowledge (1986, 1993). The latter is exemplified by Friedrich Kratochwil's writings on the end of the Cold War, which stress the role of changing ideas of international order and security (Kratochwil 1993; Koslowski and Kratochwil 1995). Though less parsimonious and elegant than systemic constructivism, holistic scholarship has the merit of being able to explain the development of the normative and ideational structures of the present international system, as well as the social identities they have engendered. The more concerned this form of constructivism becomes with grand tectonic transformations, however, the more structuralist it tends to become, and human agency tends to drop out of the story. Ideas change, norms evolve, and culture transforms, but these seem to move independently of human will, choice, or action.

Constructivism and its discontents

The articulation of a constructivist theoretical framework for the study of international relations has significantly altered the axes of debate within the field. The internecine debate between neo-realists and neo-liberals, which, until the middle of the 1990s was still being hailed as *the* contemporary debate, has been displaced as rationalists have haphazardly joined forces to confront a common constructivist foe. The rise of constructivism has also displaced the debate between rationalists and critical international theorists. The veracity of the epistemological, methodological and normative challenges that critical theorists levelled at rationalism has not diminished, but the rise of constructivism has focused debate on ontological and empirical issues, pushing the metatheoretical debate of the 1980s off centre stage. The core debate now animating the field revolves around the nature of social agency, the relative importance of normative versus material forces, the balance between continuity and transformation in world politics and a range of other empirical–theoretical questions. This does not mean, though, that rationalism and constructivism constitute unified, unproblematic or fully coherent theoretical positions, standing pristine in opposition to one another. We have already seen the significant differences within the rationalist fold, and the remainder of this chapter considers the discontents that characterize contemporary constructivism. Four of these warrant particular attention: the disagreements among constructivists over the nature of theory, the relationship with rationalism, the appropriate methodology and the contribution of constructivism to a critical theory of international relations.

It has long been the ambition of rationalists, especially neo-realists, to formulate a general theory of international relations, the core assumptions of which would be so robust that they could explain its fundamental characteristics, regardless of historical epoch or differences in the internal complexions of states. For most constructivists, such ambitions have little allure. The constitutive forces they emphasize, such as ideas, norms and culture, and the elements of human agency they stress, such as corporate and social identity, are all inherently variable. There is simply no such thing as a universal, transhistorical, disembedded, culturally autonomous idea or identity. Most constructivists thus find the pursuit of a general theory of international relations an absurdity, and confine their ambitions to providing compelling interpretations and explanations of discrete aspects of world politics, going no further than to offer heavily qualified 'contingent generalizations'. In fact, constructivists repeatedly insist that constructivism is not a theory, but rather an analytical framework. The one notable exception to this tendency is Wendt, who has embarked on the ambitious project of formulating a comprehensive social theory of international relations, placing himself in direct competition with Waltz. In pursuit of this goal, however, Wendt makes a number of moves that put him at odds with almost all other constructivists: namely, he focuses solely on the systemic level, he treats the state as a unitary actor and he embraces an epistemological position called 'scientific realism' (Wendt and Shapiro 1997). While these represent the theoretical proclivities of but one scholar, Wendt's prominence in the development of constructivism makes them important sources of division and disagreement within the new school. His *Social Theory of International Politics* (1999) is the most sustained elaboration of constructivist theory yet, and for many in the field it will define the very nature of constructivism. However, the vision of theory it presents has been vigorously contested by other constructivists, thus forming one of the principal axes of tension within constructivism over the coming years.

The second discontent within constructivism concerns the relationship with rationalism. Some constructivists believe that productive engagement is possible between the two approaches, engagement based on a scholarly division of labour. We have seen that constructivists emphasize how institutionalized norms shape the identities and interests of actors, and that rationalists, treating interests as unexplained givens, stress how actors go about pursuing their interests strategically. The first focuses on interest-formation, the second on interest satisfaction. Seeking to build bridges instead of fences between the two approaches, some constructivists see in this difference a possible division of labour, with constructivists doing the work of explaining how actors gain their preferences and rationalists exploring how they realize those preferences. Constructivism is thus not a rival theoretical perspective to rationalism at all, but rather a complementary one. 'The result', Audie Klotz argues, 'is a reformulated, complementary research agenda that illuminates the independent role of norms in determining actors' identities and interests. Combined with theories of institutions and interest-based behaviour, this approach offers us a conceptually consistent and more complete understanding of international relations' (1995: 20). As attractive as this exercise in bridge-building appears, not all constructivists are convinced. Reus-Smit has demonstrated that the institutionalized norms that shape actors' identities help define not only their interests but also their strategic rationality (1999). Attempts to confine constructivist scholarship to the realm of interest-formation, and to concede rationalists the terrain of strategic interaction, have thus been criticized for propagating an unnecessarily 'thin form of constructivism' (Laffey and Weldes 1997).

Another discontent within constructivism involves the question of methodology. Critical theorists have long argued that the neo-positivist methodology championed by neo-realists and neo-liberals is poorly suited to the study of human action, as the individuals and groups under analysis attach meanings to their actions, these meanings are shaped by a pre-existing 'field' of shared meanings embedded in language and other symbols, and the effect of such meanings on human action cannot be understood by treating them as measurable variables that cause behaviour in any direct or quantifiable manner (Taylor 1997: 111). This led early constructivists to insist that the study of ideas, norms and other meanings requires an interpretive methodology, one that seeks to grasp 'the relationship between "intersubjective meanings" which derive from self-interpretation and self-definition, and the social practices in which they are embedded and which they constitute' (Kratochwil and

Ruggie 1986; Kratochwil 1988/9; Neufeld 1993: 49). Curiously, these arguments have been forgotten by a number of constructivists, who defend a position of 'methodological conventionalism', claiming that their explanations 'do not depend exceptionally upon any specialized separate "interpretive methodology" ' (Jepperson, Wendt and Katzenstein 1996: 67). They justify this position on the grounds that the field has been bogged down for too long in methodological disputes and, at any rate, the empirical work of more doctrinaire constructivists such as Kratochwil and Ruggie does not look all that different from that of conventional scholars. Neither of these grounds addresses the substance of the original constructivist argument about methodology, nor do the advocates of methodological conventionalism recognize that the similarity between mainstream empirical work and that of interpretive constructivists may have more to do with the failure of rationalists ever to meet their own neo-positivist standards. The gap between these rival methodological standpoints within constructivism is most clearly apparent in the contrast between those studies that employ quantitative methodological techniques and those that adopt genealogical approaches (Johnston 1995; Price 1997).

The final discontent concerns the relationship between constructivism and critical international theory. It is reasonable, we have seen, to view constructivism as an outgrowth of critical theory, and Price and Reus-Smit (1998) have argued that its development has great potential to further the critical project. Andrew Linklater (1992a) has identified three dimensions of that project: the normative task of critically assessing and revising how political organization, particularly the sovereign state, has been morally justified; the sociological task of understanding how moral community – locally, nationally and globally – expands and contracts; and the praxeological task of grasping the constraints and opportunities that bear on emancipatory political action (1992a: 92–4). Nowhere is the second of these tasks being undertaken with greater energy and rigour than within constructivism. Exploring the development and the impact of the normative and ideational foundations of international society is the constructivist stock in trade, and dialogue between constructivists and those engaged in the more philosophical project of normative critique and elaboration is the most likely path toward true praxeological knowledge. Constructivism is divided, however, between those who remain cognizant of the critical origins and potentiality of their sociological explorations, and those who have embraced constructivism simply as an explanatory or interpretive tool. Both standpoints are justifiable, and the work of scholars on both sides of this divide can be harnessed to the critical project, regardless of their individual commitments. It is imperative, though, that the former group of scholars work to bring constructivist research into dialogue with moral and philosophical argument, otherwise constructivism will lose its ethical veracity and critical international theory one of its potential pillars.

It is tempting to explain these discontents in terms of differences between modern and postmodern constructivists, differences outlined earlier. Yet disagreements over the nature of theory, the relationship to rationalism, the appropriate method and the contribution to critical international theory do not map neatly onto the divide between minimal and anti-foundationalism. While postmodern constructivists would never advocate the development of a general theory of international relations, task-sharing with rationalists, methodological conventionalism, or pure explanation, neither would many modern constructivists. Here Ted Hopf's (1998) distinction between 'conventional' and 'critical' constructivisms may be more fruitful: 'To the degree that constructivism creates theoretical and epistemological distance between itself and its origins in critical theory, it becomes "conventional" constructivism (1998: 181). The discontents outlined above reflect the differences between those who have consciously or unconsciously created such distance and those who wish to stay in touch with constructivism's roots. Among the latter group, important differences remain between modernists and postmodernists. The most important of these differences concerns the questions they address, with the former focusing on *why* questions, the latter on *how* questions. For instance, Reus-Smit (1995) takes up the question of why different international societies have evolved different institutional practices to solve cooperation problems and facilitate coexistence among states, while Cynthia Weber asks 'How is the meaning of sovereignty fixed or stabilized historically via practices of international relations theorists and practices of political intervention' (1995: 3).

The contribution of constructivism

In spite of these discontents, which are as much a sign of dynamism as division, the rise of constructivism has had several important impacts on the development of international relations theory and analysis. Thanks largely to the work of constructivists, the social, historical and normative have returned to the centre stage of debate, especially within the American core of the discipline.

Until the late 1980s, two factors conspired to marginalize societal analysis in International Relations scholarship. The first was the overwhelming materialism of the major theoretical perspectives. For neorealists, the principal determinant of state behaviour is the underlying distribution of material capabilities across states in the international system, a determinant that gives states their animating survival motive, which in turn drives balance of power competition. To the extent that they discussed it, neo-liberals also saw state interests as essentially material, even if they did posit the importance of international institutions as intervening variables. The second factor was the prevailing rationalist conception of human action. As we have seen, both neo-realists and neo-liberals imagined humans – and, by extension, states – as atomistic, self-interested, strategic actors, thus positing a standard form of instrumental rationality across all political actors. When combined, the materialism and rationalism of the prevailing theories left little room for the social dimensions of international life, unless of course the social is reduced to power-motivated strategic competition. Materialism denied the causal significance of shared ideas, norms and values, and rationalism reduced the social to the strategic and ignored the particularities of community, identity and interest. By re-imagining the social as a constitutive realm of values and practices, and by situating individual identities and interests within such a field, constructivists have placed sociological inquiry back at the centre of the discipline. Because of the prominence of the 'international society' school, such inquiry had never disappeared from British International Relations scholarship. Constructivists, however, have brought a new level of conceptual clarity and theoretical sophistication to the analysis of both international and world society, thus complementing and augmenting the work of the English School.

By resuscitating societal analysis, the rise of constructivism has also sparked a renewed interest in international history. So long as International Relations theorists were wedded to the idea that states are driven by context-transcendent survival motives or universal modes of rationality, the lessons of history were reduced to the proposition that nothing of substance ever changes. Such assumptions denied the rich diversity of human experience and the possibilities of meaningful change and difference, thus flattening out international history into a monotone tale of 'recurrence and repetition'. Historical analysis became little more than the ritualistic recitation of lines from the celebrated works of Thucydides, Machiavelli and Hobbes, all with aim of 'proving' the unchanging nature of international relations, licensing the formulation of increasingly abstract theories. Such history had the paradoxical effect of largely suffocating the study of international history in the American core of the discipline. Aided by the momentous changes that attended the end of the Cold War, and also by the ongoing processes of globalization, the constructivist interest in the particularities of culture, identity, interest and experience created space for a renaissance in the study of history and world politics. If ideas, norms, and practices matter, and if they differ from one social context to another, then history in turn matters. Not surprisingly, in their efforts to demonstrate the contingency of such factors and their impact on the conduct of world politics, constructivists have sought to re-read the historical record, to re-think what has long been treated as given in the study of international relations. While a similar impulse came from International Relations scholars inspired by the re-birth of historical sociology, constructivists have dominated the new literature on international history (Hall 1999; Kier 1997; Philpott 2001; Rae 2002; Reus-Smit 1999; Ruggie 1986, 1993; Thomson 1994; Welch 1993).

Finally, constructivism may be credited with helping to re-invigorate normative theorizing in International Relations. Not because constructivists have been engaged in philosophical reflection about the nature of the good or the right, a project that has itself been re-energized by the multitude of ethical dilemmas thrown up by the end of the Cold War and the march of globalization, but because they have done much to demonstrate the power of ideas, norms and values in shaping world politics. While talk of the 'power of ideas' has at times carried considerable rhetorical force outside of academic International Relations, such talk within the field has long been dismissed as naïve and even dangerous idealism. Material calculations, such as military power and wealth, have been upheld as the motive forces behind international political action, and ideational factors have been dismissed as mere rationalizations or instrumental guides to strategic action. Through sustained empirical research, constructivists have exposed the explanatory poverty of such materialist scepticism. They have shown how international norms evolve, how ideas and values come to shape political action, how argument and discourse condition outcomes and how identity constitutes agents and agency, all in ways that contradict the expectations of materialist and rationalist theories. While this 'empirical idealism' provides no answers to questions probed by international ethicists, it contributes to more philosophically oriented normative theorizing in two ways: it legitimizes such theorizing by demonstrating the possibility of ideas driven international change; and it assists by clarifying the dynamics and mechanisms of such change, thus furthering the development E. H. Carr's proposed 'realistic utopianism'.

Constructivism after 9/11

Since the turn of the new millennium, debates within constructivism have continued apace, even if their general trajectory has remained largely the same. As noted above, four discontents have characterized constructivism's evolution: differences over whether constructivists should aspire to a general theory of international relations, over the relationship with rationalism, over questions of method and over the relationship between constructivism and critical theory.

Since 2000, the first of these discontents has dissipated. Neo-realists and rationalists still call for constructivism's codification as a theoretical paradigm, capable of generating testable hypotheses and law-like propositions. But among constructivists, the centre of gravity has moved away from Wendtian-style theorizing, even if Wendt himself has continued to produce innovative and challenging theory (see Wendt 2003). The centre of gravity has move toward, on the one hand, a more eclectic, problem-driven kind of research and, on the other, the critical strand of constructivism that has been there from the outset. This has not, however, produced a strong consensus among constructivists. As the centre of gravity has moved away from general theorizing, the other discontents concerning the relationship with rationalism, questions of method and the critical nature of constructivism have become more pronounced. The tendencies for constructivists in the American mainstream to advocate an analytical division of labour with rationalists, and to deny that constructivism's focus on inter-subjective meanings demands an interpretive methodology, have persisted. But they have also transmuted into a new style of scholarship, one barely recognizable as constructivism. Katzenstein has called for an 'eclectic' form of theorizing, one that starts from concrete empirical puzzles and draws on diverse theories to construct compelling explanations (Katzenstein and Okawara 2001/2; Suh, Katzenstein and Carlsen 2004). Constructivism thus becomes one tool among many in the scholar's toolkit, and methodological conventionalism is taken as the norm. Parallel to these developments, other scholars have sought to retain constructivism's critical edge, largely by pushing its engagement with normative and ethical theory (Kratochwil 2000; Reus-Smit 2000, 2002a; Shapcott 2000a). Constructivism, in their view, should not only be about the politics of ethics, but also the ethics of politics.

A curious feature of these developments has been their relative autonomy from the events of 11 September 2001 and their aftermath. Theoretical developments in International Relations have generally – though not always – responded to catalytic historical events: liberalism got a boost after the First World War, realism emerged ascendant after the crises of the inter-war period and the Second World War and, as we have seen, constructivism's rise had much to do with the end of the Cold War. Yet the terrorist attacks of September 11, which were just as momentous as fall of the Berlin Wall, have not sparked a tectonic shift in the nature of constructivism, or in the general terrain of

International Relations theorizing. There is a general sense that history has drawn the field back to questions of power, hegemony and the state, and some have concluded that this advantages realist forms of thinking. We are yet to see, however, significant theoretical innovations from realists, constructivists, or others.

In many respects, the paucity of an innovative constructivist response to the post-9/11 world is surprising, as many of the big and important questions now facing the international community (and which pose ample scholarly challenges) play to constructivism's strengths. Three of these deserve particular attention: the nature of power, the relationship between international and world society and the role of culture in world politics.

Discussions of power in international relations have traditionally been seen as the preserve of realists. 'Absolute power', 'relative power', 'structural power' and 'the balance of power' are all realist conceptions, as are notions of 'the struggle for power' and 'hegemonic stability'. Yet, as Wendt persuasively argues, the 'proposition that the nature of international politics is shaped by power relations ... cannot be a *uniquely* Realist claim.' (1999: 96–7). What is uniquely realist is the 'hypothesis that the effects of power are constituted primarily by brute material forces' (1999: 97). Recent events, however, cast doubt over this hypothesis. The United States presently enjoys a greater degree of material preponderance than perhaps any other state in history, yet across a wide spectrum of issue areas it is struggling to translate that material advantage into sustained political influence or intended (as opposed to unintended) political outcomes. Power, it seems, is also constituted by non-material factors, most notably legitimacy and legitimacy is in turn conditioned by established or emergent norms of rightful agency and action. The debate in the Security Council over war with Iraq highlighted this complex interplay between institutional norms and processes, the politics of international legitimacy and the power of the United States. Washington commanded the material resources to oust Saddam Hussein from power, but without Security Council endorsement it has struggled to shake off an aura of illegitimacy and illegality, seriously undermining its capacity to socialize the costs of the occupation and reconstruction. The unilateralist turn in American foreign policy, the 'war against terrorism' and the advent of 'preventive' war against rogue states has prompted a number of constructivists to articulate a social conception of power that accommodates the complex relationship between norms, legitimacy and hegemonic power, yet this remains lightly ploughed terrain (Ikenberry 2000; Cronin 2001; Barnett and Duvall 2004; Reus-Smit 2004a). Relevant here is the growing body of constructivist work on international law, an institution intimately related to the politics of norms, legitimacy and power (Brunnee and Toope 2000; Finnemore and Toope 2001; Reus-Smit 2004b).

It is common to distinguish conceptually between an 'international society' and a 'world society', the former being the 'club of states', with its norms and institutions of coexistence and cooperation, the latter being the broader web of social relations that enmesh states, NGOs, international organizations and other global social actors (Bull 1977). Without denying the continued relevance of the system of sovereign states, constructivists have done much to show how international society and its institutions have been shaped by actors within the wider world society. Margaret Keck and Kathryn Sikkink (1998) have demonstrated the ways in which NGOs operating within states, in association with international NGOs, have mobilized human rights norms to constrain the domestic exercise of state power. More recently, Michael Barnett and Martha Finnemore (2004) have shown how international organizations – created by states for state purposes – can gain degrees of autonomy that enable them to condition the terrain of international state action. Important as these insights are, constructivists have yet to see their relevance for understanding the normative politics of transnational terrorism. Like many humanitarian NGOs, transnational terrorist organizations operate in the social space transcending state borders and, like these NGOs, groups such as Al-Qaeda use forms of moral suasion and symbolic politics to redefine the terms of political discourse affecting state interests and actions. The novelty and magnitude of the violence they unleash often blinds us to the fact that they are ultimately seeking to transform ideas and values, both those of the 'West' and those of politically disaffected and economically alienated Moslems. Constructivists have taken two steps in the right direction by considering the way in which world society forces constitute the political fabric of international society, and by highlighting the politics of values that attends this process of constitution. Their task now is to confront three questions: What is the relationship between the exercise of violence and the erosion and propagation of social and political values, both by states and non-state actors? How has this constituted international society historically? And what are the implications of this nexus between violence and normative changes for international and global order?

The study of culture and international relations is closely identified with constructivism, an association reinforced by book titles such as 'Cultural Realism' and 'The Culture of National Security'. By 'culture', however, constructivists generally mean social and legal norms and the ways in which these are deployed, though argument and communication, to constitute actors' identities and interests. Methodologically, this generally involves the identification of a particular norm, or set of norms, and the tracing of its effect on political action. Culture, understood more holistically as the broader framework of inter-subjective meanings and practices that give a society a distinctive character, has been largely neglected. The events of September 11 have, however, thrust culture, in this more expansive sense, on to the international agenda, creating an opening and an obligation for constructivists. Samuel Huntington's 'clash of civilizations' thesis has gained a new lease of life, with commentators, from diverse quarters, no longer inhibited in attributing essentialist characteristics to 'The West' and 'Islam'. Few now deny that culture is important in world politics, but the overwhelming tendency is to naturalize and reify culture, carving ethically and racially defined lines across the globe. The need for a constructivist voice here is crucial, as constructivists think culture matters but that it is inherently socially constructed, not rooted in blood and soil. Research is needed into how ideas of 'The West' and 'Islam', as radically different transnational communities, have been constituted, on how these ideas are related to the constitution, or erosion, of state power and on how these ideas can be mobilized to sustain system-transforming political projects, either on the part of liberal democracies, seeking to redefine the norms of sovereignty and global governance, or terrorist organizations seeking an end to the liberal capitalist world order.

Conclusion

The rise of constructivism has heralded a return to a more sociological, historical and practice oriented form of International Relations scholarship. Where rationalists had reduced the social to strategic interaction, denied the historical by positing disembedded, universal forms of rationality and reduced the practical art of politics to utility maximizing calculation, constructivists have re-imagined the social as a constitutive domain, reintroduced history as realm of empirical inquiry and emphasized the variability of political practice. In many respects, constructivism embodies characteristics normally associated with the 'English School', discussed by Linklater in Chapter 4 in this volume. Constructivists have taken up the idea that states form more than a system, that they form a society and they have pushed this idea to new levels of theoretical and conceptual sophistication. Their interest in international history also represents an important point of convergence with the English School, as does their stress on the cultural distinctiveness of different societies of states. Finally, their initial emphasis on interpretive methods of analysis echoes Hedley Bull's call for a classical approach, 'characterized above all by explicit reliance upon the exercise of judgement' rather than neo-positivist standards of 'verification and proof' (1969, 1995: 20–38).

These similarities, as well as constructivism's roots in critical international theory, appeared to pose a challenge to conventional understandings of the field. An 'Atlantic divide' has long structured understandings of the sociology of International Relations as a discipline, with the field seen as divided between North American 'scientists' and European (mainly British) 'classicists'. Two of the defining 'great debates' of the discipline – between realists and idealists and positivists and traditionalists – have been mapped onto this divide, lending intellectual divisions a cultural overtone. At first glance, constructivism appears to confuse this way of ordering the discipline. Despite having taken up many of the intellectual commitments normally associated with the English School, constructivism has its origins in the United States. Its principal exponents were either educated in or currently teach in the leading American universities, and their pioneering work has been published in the premier journals and by the leading university presses. The United States also spawned much of the earlier wave of critical international theory, especially of a postmodern variety, but that work never achieved the same centrality within the American sector of the discipline. One of the reasons for constructivism's success in the United States has been its emphasis on empirically informed theorizing over meta-theoretical critique, an orientation much less confronting to the mainstream. With success, however, has come normalization, and this has seen the neglectful forgetting, or active jettisoning, of theoretical commitments that were central to constructivism in the early years. Disappearing, in the American discipline, are the foundational ideas that constructivism rests on a social ontology radically different from rationalism's, that studying norms, as social facts, demands an interpretive methodology, and that constructivism was linked, in important ways, to the emancipatory project of critical theory. The continued importance of these commitments to non-American constructivism suggests that a new manifestation of the 'Atlantic divide' may now be emerging.

Chapter 9

Feminism

JACQUI TRUE

Breaking with the powerful bond among manly men, states and war, feminist theories of international relations have proliferated since the early 1990s. These theories have introduced *gender* as a relevant empirical category and analytical tool for understanding global power relations as well as a normative position from which to construct alternative world orders. Together with a range of new perspectives on world politics, including postmodernism, constructivism, critical theory and green politics, feminist theories have contested the power and knowledge of mainstream realist and liberal International Relations. Like these other contemporary theories, feminism shifts the study of international relations away from a singular focus on inter-state relations toward a comprehensive analysis of transnational actors and structures and their transformations in global politics. Arguably, the political rupture created by the magnitude and significance of the events of September 11, 2001 has given new impetus to feminist perspectives on international relations. With their focus on non-state actors, marginalized peoples and alternative conceptualizations of power, feminist perspectives bring fresh thinking and action in the post-9/11 decentred and uncertain world.

Until relatively recently, the field of International Relations studied the causes of war and conflict and the global expansion of trade and commerce with no particular reference to people. Indeed the use of abstract categories such as 'the state', 'the system', strategic security discourses such as nuclear deterrence and positivist research approaches effectively removed people as agents embedded in social and historical contexts from theories of international relations. This is ironic since the scholarly field emerged, following the end of the First World War, to democratize foreign policy making and empower people as citizen-subjects rather than mere objects of elite statecraft (Hill 1999). So where does the study of people called 'women' and 'men' or the social construction of masculine and feminine genders fit within International Relations? How is the international system and the International Relations field gendered? To what extent do feminist perspectives help us to explain, understand

213

and improve international relations? This chapter explores these questions as they have been addressed by a diverse range of feminist scholars in and outside the IR field.

The chapter starts with a brief overview of the development of feminist International Relations. It differentiates three overlapping forms of feminist International Relations that represent a useful heuristic for discussing the varied contributions to the field. These are: (1) *empirical feminism*, that focuses on women and/or explores gender as an empirical dimension of international relations; (2) *analytical feminism*, that uses gender as a theoretical category to reveal the gender bias of International Relations concepts and explain constitutive aspects of international relations; and (3) *normative feminism*, that reflects on the process of theorizing as part of a normative agenda for social and political change. These forms do not prefigure or suggest any particular feminist epistemology. For example, Berman's (2003) analysis of the way in which European states secure their borders through anti-sex trafficking policies is an example of an empirical feminist approach using a poststructuralist epistemology. Empirical, analytical and normative feminist approaches that challenge the assumptions of mainstream International Relations and help to construct new theories of global politics are discussed in the second, third and fourth sections of the chapter.

Since the 1980s, feminist International Relations scholars have offered fresh and intriguing insights on global politics. International relations have had great significance for patterns of gender relations, just as gender dynamics have influenced global processes of militarization and economic globalization, for instance. Following on the wave of the worldwide feminist revolution, Cynthia Enloe dared to suggest that 'the personal which is political' is also, quite likely, 'international'. In *Bananas, Beaches and Bases* (1989), she exposed how international politics frequently involves intimate relationships, personal identities and private lives. These informal politics are altogether less transparent than the stuff of official politics and they are typically ignored by International Relations scholars. Taking the view from below, feminists have sought to demonstrate that gender relations are integral to international relations. Diplomatic wives smooth over the workings of power among states and statesmen; opaque but trustworthy marital contracts facilitate transnational money laundering and sex trafficking; global icons such as *Cosmopolitan* conquer foreign cultures and prepare them for the onslaught of Western capitalism; and women and men organize in kitchens, churches and kin-communities to overthrow authoritarian regimes and make peace in the face of brutal conflict (Cockburn 1998; True 2003).

Focusing on politics at the margins dispels the assumption that power is what comes out of the barrel of a gun or ensues from the declarations of world leaders. Indeed, feminist efforts to reinterpret power suggest that International Relations scholars have underestimated the pervasiveness of power and precisely what it takes, at every level and every day, to reproduce a grossly uneven and hierarchical world order (Enloe 1997). Feminist reconceptualizations of power and attention to the margins of global politics could seriously help International Relations scholars to recognize and comprehend new political phenomena such as the antisystemic acts of the 9/11 martyrs and transnational terrorism in general.

A first generation of feminist International Relations in the late 1980s sought to challenge the conventional ontological and epistemological focus of the field by engaging in what was called the 'third debate' among positivist and post-positivist International Relations scholars discussed in the previous chapters. In this debate, feminist scholars contested the exclusionary, state-centric and positivist nature of the discipline primarily at a meta-theoretical level. Many of these feminist contributions sought to deconstruct and subvert *realism*, the dominant 'power politics' explanation of post-war International Relations. Often implicit in their concern with gender relations was the assumption of a feminist standpoint epistemology. Such a standpoint maintains that women's lives on the margins of world politics afford us a more critical and comprehensive understanding of international relations than the objectivist view of the realist theorist or foreign policy lens of the statesman since they are less complicit with and/or blinded by existing institutions and elite power (Keohane 1989a: 245; Sylvester 1994a: 13; see also Harding 1986; Tickner 1992; Zalewski 1993).

The first-generation preoccupation with meta-theory obviously had its limits given feminism's normative claim to provide a radical alternative to realism (Runyan and Peterson 1991). As Richard Price and Christian Reus-Smit (1998: 263) argued 'the third debate was inward looking, concerned primarily with undermining the foundations of dominant discourses in International Relations'. While feminist challenges to International Relations opened the space for critical scholarship, they begged the question of what a feminist perspective on world politics would look like substantively, and how distinctive it would be (Zalewski 1995). Seventeen years after the first journal in the field devoted a special issue to 'women and international relations' (Millennium 1988) much has also been accomplished by feminist International Relations scholars, short of transforming the often gender-blind study of international relations. Most courses on International Relations theory worldwide now consider gender issues or feminist perspectives due to the publication of several exemplary texts and monographs by feminist International Relations scholars (Tickner 1992, 2001; Sylvester 1994a; Pettman 1996; Steans 1998; Peterson and Runyan 1999). Several key disciplinary journals have published whole issues on the subjects of women, gender and feminism in international relations, and in 1999 the *International Feminist Journal of Politics* was established to promote dialogue among scholars of feminism, politics and International Relations.

A second generation of feminist research promises a new phase in the development of feminist International Relations. This emerging body of scholarship seeks to make gender a central analytic category in studies of foreign policy, security, global political economy through an exploration of particular historical and geographic contexts (Moon 1997; Chin 1998; Hooper 2000; Prugl 2000; True 2003; Whitworth 2004; Stern 2005). More cautious and precise in its analytic use of the concept of gender, and more closely tied to developments in critical international theory, constructivism, post-Marxist political economy, feminist historical and anthropological methods, the newest feminist scholarship provides empirical support for first-generation challenges, while also generating new theoretical insight on the gendering of global politics, as the rest of the chapter illustrates.

Empirical feminism

Empirical feminism turns our attention to women and gender relations as empirical aspects of international relations. Feminist challenges to International Relations contend that women's lives and experiences have been, and still are, often excluded from the study of international relations. This sexist exclusion has resulted in research which presents only a partial, masculine view in a field in which the dominant theories claim to explain the reality of world politics (Halliday 1988b). Empirical feminism corrects the denial or misrepresentation of women in world politics due to false assumptions that male experiences can count for both men and women, and that women are either absent from international political activities or not relevant to global processes. It is not that women have not been present or their experiences relevant to international relations. Rather, as Cynthia Enloe's (1989, 1994, 2000) scholarship demonstrates, women are and have always been part of international relations – if we choose to see them there. Moreover, it is in part because women's lives and experiences have not been empirically researched in the context of world politics, as Grant and Newland (1991: 5) argue, that International Relations has been 'excessively focused on conflict and anarchy and a way of practising statecraft and formulating strategy that is excessively focused on competition and fear'. Studies of the norms and ideas that make the reproduction of the state-system possible and of the structural violence (poverty, environmental injustice, socio-political inequality) that underpins direct state-sanctioned violence are seen as secondary to the manly study of war and conflict in International Relations due to their association with domestic 'soft' (read: feminine) politics. As a result, neo-realist and neo-liberal International Relations scholars theorize politics and the international realm 'in a way that guarantees that women will be absent from their inquiry, and that their research agendas remain unaltered' (Steurnagel 1990: 79–80).

Feminist research is not a form of empiricism since feminist scholars often need greater conceptual clarity than is necessary for theoretical critique in order to conduct empirical research. For instance, to make abstract concepts and relationships amenable to empirical exploration the feminist researcher must identify those which can be seen to exist and are the most important for closer study, while also developing a research methodology for translating and analysing them empirically (see Caprioli 2004; Ackerly, Stern and True forthcoming).

Since the 1990s, empirical feminist research has taken a variety of methodological and substantive forms in International Relations. Studies under the rubric of 'women in international development' (WID), and more recently gender and development (GAD), have documented how male bias in the development process has led to poor implementation of projects and unsatisfactory policy outcomes in terms of eradicating poverty and empowering communities (Newland 1988; Goetz 1991; Kardam 1991; Kabeer 1994; Rathergeber 1995). This scholarship makes visible the central role of women as subsistence producers and providers of basic needs in developing countries (Beneria 1982; Charlton, Everett and Staudt 1989). Empirical studies reveal that the most efficient allocation of development assistance is often to provide women with appropriate agricultural technology, credit financing, education and health resources. For example, the United Nations (2000) estimates that while women's farming accounts for one-half of the food production in the developing world, it provides three-quarters of domestic food supply for family households. Gender sensitive researchers have found that investing in girls' education is one of the most cost-effective development policies, resulting in positive gains for a whole community by raising incomes and lowering population rates (see Sen 2001).

Economic globalization has intensified social and economic polarization, both within and across states. Feminist scholars document how this globalization process has increased the world-wide inequality between men and women, with disproportionate numbers of women in poverty – frequently referred to as the 'feminisation of poverty' – due to Third World debt crises, structural adjustment policies (SAPs) in the South and state restructuring in the North (Afshar and Dennis 1992; Sparr 1994;

Porter and Judd 2000). As economic policy has become increasingly governed by the global imperatives of export earnings, financial markets and comparative labour costs, states have struggled to meet their commitments to full employment and citizen well-being. Empirical feminist research shows how this shift from a largely domestic state to global market provision of services has imposed a disproportionate burden on women to pick up the slack of the state (Bakker 1994; United Nations Development Programme 1999; Marchand and Runyan 2000).

In the global context also, a gendered international division of labour has emerged as migrant Third World women become a cheap and flexible source of labour for MNCs in free trade zones (Mitter 1986; Standing 1992; Ong 1997). Saskia Sassen's (1991, 1998) research shows how global cities, the nodal points for global financial markets and economic transactions, are dependent on a class of women workers. Like 'intimate others' of economic globalization, domestic workers, typically immigrant women of colour, service the masculinized corporate elite in these urban centres (Boris and Prugl 1996; Stasilius and Bakan 1997; Chin 1998; Chang and Ling 2000). Empirical feminist research reveals an even darker 'underside' of globalization, however, in the phenomenal growth of sex-tourism, 'male-order' brides and transnational trafficking of women and girls for prostitution (Pettman 1996; Prugl and Meyer 1999; Berman 2003). For subordinate states in the world system, these economic activities are key sources of foreign exchange and national income (Jeffrey 2002; Hanochi 2003). For example, Chin (1998) shows how Malaysian political elites maintained the legitimacy of their export oriented development strategy in the 1980s and 1990s by importing female domestic servants from the Philippines and Indonesia.

But women are not only victimized by the global process of structural change; in many cases, they are empowered by it. Feminist researchers explore how global capitalism shapes women's subjectivities and transforms local gender relations. These researchers highlight how new credit and employment opportunities have brought cultural changes in the lives of poor women in rural, developing areas (Gibson, Law and McKay 2001). Naila Kabeer (1994), for example, has investigated how changing material incentives provided by the re-siting of TNCs' garment production, opened up possibilities for young Bangladeshi women to make a better living and at the same time to challenge patriarchal gender arrangements. Jacqui True (2003) shows how the spread of global consumption, culture and information after the end of communism has enabled Czech women to create new feminist identities.

Feminist empirical studies reveal the gendered construction of international organizations (IOs) which to an even greater extent than national institutions are dominated by elite men (Prugl and Meyer 1999). Gender mainstreaming initiatives have allowed more women to join their policy making ranks (True and Mintrom 2001). For instance, women now head many of the United Nations' agencies, including the World Health Organisation (WHO), the United Nations Children's Fund, the Office of the High Commissioner for Refugees, the World Food Programme and the World Population Fund. The Deputy Secretary General and the High Commissioner for Human Rights are also both women. Yet, as feminist studies point out, in institutions like the United Nations, women continue to be ghettoized in less powerful agencies and as secretarial helpmates, and are only gradually coming to have influence over the global security and development agenda (Pietila and Vickers 1996; Reanda 1999; Whitworth 2004).

IOs also institutionalize gender-based policies and priorities. In her study of the International Labour Organization (ILO) Sandra Whitworth (1994) shows how assumptions about gender relations shaped ILO policies that have had discriminatory effects in national and international labour markets, reinforcing women's inequality. Catherine Hoskyns (1996) shows how women's movements in member states have successfully used the European Union's supranational body of equal opportunities law and policy to address gender disparities at the national level. Hoskyns' gender-sensitive analysis shows how the process of European integration has had the effect of extending women's social citizenship rights in member states.

In the realm of foreign policy, feminist analyses have revealed the dominant masculine gender of policy makers and the gendered assumption that these policy makers are strategically rational actors who make life and death decisions in the name of an abstract conception of the 'national interest'. As Nancy McGlen and Meredith Sarkees (1993) have assessed in their study of the foreign policy and defence establishment, women are rarely 'insiders' of the actual institutions that make and implement foreign policy and conduct war. In 2004, the fact that twelve women were foreign ministers suggests that this male dominance is undergoing some change. In addition, feminists analyse the persistent 'gender gap' in the foreign policy beliefs of men and women foreign policy making elites and citizens; women leaders and citizens in Western states are consistently more likely to oppose the use of force in international actions and are typically more supportive of humanitarian interventions (Rosenau and Holsti 1982; Tessler, Nachtwey and Grant 1999). Attitudes toward gender equality and sexual liberty shape attitudes toward tolerance, human rights and democracy and are good predictors of more pacific attitudes to international conflict (Tessler and Warriner 1997).

Feminist research shows that those states with greater gender inequality are also more likely to go to war or to engage in state-sanctioned violence

(Goldstein 2001). Domestic gender equality also reduces the likelihood that a state will use force first in inter-state disputes, limits the escalation of violence and decreases the severity of violence during international crises (Caprioli 2000; Caprioli and Boyer 2001). By the same token, those states that come closest to gender parity tend also to be more pacific in their relations, more generous aid donors and generally good citizens in the international realm (Regan and Paskeviciute 2003). However, our pre-occupation with states prevents us from seeing the multiple non-state actors who also play significant roles in foreign-policy making. Feminist researchers such as Enloe (1989, 2000) make visible the women who provide support services for military activities (domestic, psychological, medical and sexual). If we see militarization as a social process consisting of many gendered assignments that make possible those ultimate acts of state violence then, she argues, the official provision of sexual services on military bases for instance can be seen as a central factor in a foreign intervention. In *Sex Among Allies*, Katherine Moon (1997) argues that the exploitative sexual alliances between Korean prostitutes (*kijich'on* women) and US soldiers defined and supported the similarly unequal military alliance between the United States and South Korea in the post-war era. Among other things, under the Nixon Doctrine *kijich'on* women as personal ambassadors became the main indicator of Seoul's willingness to accommodate US military interests.

Women are more likely to be among the group of non-state actors in global politics. Feminist empiricists highlight the activism of women, who are often marginalized, poor and vulnerable: whether in networks of sex-workers, home-workers, mothers or civil activists, in counter-cultural campaigns and performances. As well as highlighting local activism, however, feminist researchers have observed new forms of cross-border solidarity and identity formation. In recent years, women have played key roles in the global movement to ban landmines, the Campaign for Nuclear Disarmament (CND), the feminist network protesting violence against women globally and in anti-Western terrorist groups (Stienstra 1994; Friedman 1995; Rupp 1997; Clark, Friedman and Hochstetler, 1998; Williams and Goose 1998; True and Mintrom 2001). For example, in two troubled conflict zones of the world, Israel/Palestine and the former Yugoslavia, groups known as 'Women in Black' have protested against the escalation of militarism, weaponry and war, and men's violence against women and children (Sharoni 1993; Cockburn 1998; Korac 1998; Jacoby 1999). Feminist researchers high-light peace activists and mothers protesting against their sons being conscripted in international conflicts but also female suicide bombers who transgress gendered social norms to take their own lives and others with them as a global political statement.

Noting how new female subjectivities create the momentum for new forms of collective action, feminist researchers trace the growth of transnational women's networks, the alliances forged between women's organizations, governments and inter-governmental actors, and the development of international legal and policy mechanisms promoting gender justice. For example, due to these alliances human rights instruments and global declarations increasingly acknowledge the gender-specificity of human rights (Peters and Wolper 1995; Philapose 1996; Ackerly and Okin 1999; Ackerly 2000). In 1990, Amnesty International, the global human rights NGO recognized women's human rights by adding gender persecution to its list of forms of political persecution. Governments and international organizations have followed suit. For example, until the 1990s Yugoslav conflict, states and international agencies interpreted the persecution of women as a matter of personal privacy and cultural tradition (Rao 1995). However, as a result of the lobbying of transnational feminist networks and the widespread media coverage of rape as a specific war strategy in Yugoslavia, rape is now considered a war crime under the Geneva Convention Against War Crimes to be prosecuted by the new ICC (Niarchos 1995; Philapose 1996).

Bringing women's lives and gender relations into view through empirical research has policy-relevant and material effects. Indeed, feminists argue that only when women are recognized as fundamental players in economic and political processes will they share an equal role in societal decision making. By redressing the empirical neglect of women and gender relations, feminist scholars both improve our understanding of global politics and help to put women's voices and concerns on the global agenda. But in order to make gender an important dimension of the study of international relations, it is necessary to challenge the conceptual framework which has excluded women from this study in the first place. Empirical feminism is thus complemented by analytical feminism that reveals the theoretical exclusions of the International Relations field and seeks to revision International Relations from a gender-sensitive perspective.

Analytical feminism

Analytical feminism deconstructs the theoretical framework of International Relations, revealing the gender bias that pervades key concepts and inhibits an accurate and comprehensive understanding of international relations. The feminist concept of gender refers to the asymmetrical social constructs of masculinity and femininity as opposed to ostensibly 'biological' male–female differences (although feminist postmodernists contend that both sex and gender are socially constructed categories, see Butler 1990; Gatens 1991). The hegemonic Western brand of masculinity is associated with autonomy, sovereignty, the capacity for reason and objectivity and universalism, whereas the dominant notion of femininity is associated with the absence or lack of these characteristics. For example, the routine practices of militaries replicate these hegemonic gender identities by training soldiers both to protect 'womenchildren' through killing and to suppress (feminine) emotions associated with bodily pain and caring. Military training, in Barbara Roberts' (1984) words is 'socialization into masculinity carried to the extremes'. A common assumption is that gender identities are natural or 'human nature' and not subject to social constitution or human agency. When this assumption about gender is applied to other social and political phenomena, however, it has political effects in terms of reproducing the status quo or existing power relations. As Joan Scott (1988: 48) has stated, 'the binary opposition and the social process of gender relationships [have] both become part of the meaning of power itself' and, 'to question or alter any aspect of it, threatens the entire system'.

International Relations' key concepts are neither natural nor gender-neutral: they are derived from a social and political context where masculine hegemony has been institutionalized. Feminist scholars argue that notions of power, sovereignty, autonomy, anarchy, security and the levels of analysis typology in International Relations are inseparable from the gender division of public and private spheres institutionalized within and across states. These concepts are identified specifically with masculinity and men's experiences and knowledge derived from an exclusive, male-dominated public sphere. Theorizing, as Burchill and Linklater state in the Introduction to this volume, (Chapter 1) is 'the process by which we give meaning to an allegedly objectified world "out there" '. A feminist analysis reveals International Relations' conceptual framework as but one, partial attempt to make sense of world politics.

The discursive separation of domestic and international politics, together with the neo-realist aversion to domestic explanations for interstate relations, obscures the prior gendered public–private division within states and masculine aversion to the latter's association with emotion, subjectivity, reproduction, the body, femininity and women. Both mainstream and critical theories of world politics overlook this private sphere because it is submerged within domestic politics and state forms (Walker 1992; Sylvester 1994a). The ontology of mainstream International Relations theory conceives the private sphere like the international sphere as natural realms of disorder. The lower being, represented by women, the body and the anarchical system, must be subordinated to the higher being, represented by men, the rational mind and state authority. Jean Elshtain (1992) insists that the realist narrative of International Relations, in particular, pivots on this public–private division and its essentialist construction of femininity and masculinity as the respective cause of disorder and bringer of order.

For feminist analysts, the independence of domestic politics from international politics and the separation of public from private spheres cannot be the basis for a disciplinary boundary, since anarchy outside typically supports gender hierarchy at home and vice versa. Throughout modern history, for example, women have been told that they will receive equality with men, after the war, after liberation, after the national economy has been rebuilt and so on: but after all of these 'outside' forces have been conquered, the commonplace demand is for things to go back to normal, and women to a subordinate place. As Cynthia Enloe (1989: 131) has observed 'states depend upon particular constructions of the domestic and private spheres in order to foster smooth[er] relationships at the public/international level'.

In spite of feminist efforts to theorize the relationships between gender, domestic and international politics, International Relations' conventional levels of analysis mystifies them by treating the individual, the state and the international system as distinct analytic units. This theoretical schema has become 'the most influential way of classifying explanations of war, and indeed of organising our understanding of inter-state relations in general' (Walker 1987: 67). Toward the end of a relational, gender-sensitive theory of world politics feminist scholars deconstruct each level of analysis (Tickner 1992; Sylvester 1994a; Peterson and True 1998). Gender analysis undermines the divisions between the individual, state and international system by showing how each level is preconditioned by an image of rational man that excludes women and femininity.

Despite his advocacy of a systemic theory of international relations, Kenneth Waltz (1959: 188) frequently applies the analogy between man and the state as proof of the hostile reality that he observes in the anarchical system as a whole: '[a]mong men as among states there is no automatic adjustment of interests. In the absence of a supreme authority there is then the constant possibility that conflicts will be solved by force'. Reductionist arguments explaining international conflict through conceptions of 'evil' human nature are frequently used in realist International Relations. Hans Morgenthau argued that the objective 'national interest' is rooted deeply in human nature and thus, in the actions of statesmen (Tickner 1988). Even the neo-realist Waltz (1959: 238), who prefers systemic explanations, embraces Alexander Hamilton's polemic set forth in the *Federalist Papers*: 'to presume a lack of hostile motives among states is to forget that men are ambitious, vindictive and rapacious.' The upshot of this man/state analogy for feminist analysis,

Christine Sylvester (1990) argues, is that rationality is equated with men's behaviour and the state as a rational actor bears a male–masculine identity.

Feminist theorists interpret the state as the centralized, main organizer of gendered power, working in part through the manipulation of public and private spheres (Connell 1990). It is not a 'coherent identity subordinate to the gaze of a single interpretative centre' as in neo-realist theories (Ashley 1988: 230). This notion reflects, rather, an idealized model of hegemonic masculinity and the patriarchal foundations of the state form. International Relations feminists argue that the state manipulates gender identities for its own internal unity and external legitimacy. Men are socialized to identify with constructions of masculinity which emphasize autonomy, male superiority, fraternity, strength, public protector roles and ultimately the bearing of arms. Women, on the other hand, are taught to defer, as wives and daughters, to the protection and stronger will of men, while providing the private emotional, economic and social support systems for men's war activities. Moreover, feminist analysts view states as implicated in a range of forms of violence against women. For instance, the liberal state supports violence against women through its stance of non-intervention in the private sphere, and its legal definition of rape from a male standpoint, which assumes that the absence of overt coercion implies female consent despite the context of gendered power relations (Pateman 1989; Peterson 1992: 46–7).

In conventional International Relations theories, the rational, self-interested actor is a metaphor for state behaviour in an anarchical international system. Abstracted from a place in time and space, from particular prejudices, interests and needs, feminist theorists claim that the model of rational man cannot be generalized: he is a masculine agent derived from a context of unequal gender relations, where women's primary care work supports the development of autonomous male selves, making cooperation for them a daily reality and relieving men of these necessities. Consequently, the vast majority of people, social relationships, and institutions that cannot be interpreted as coherent rational selves are thus denied agency in international politics. International Relations theory, feminist analysts Grant and Newland (1991: 1) argue is 'constructed overwhelmingly by men working with mental models of human activity seen through a[n elite] male eye and apprehended through a[n elite] male sensibility'.

Some feminists posit an alternative *female* model of agency as connected, interdependent and interrelated (Gilligan 1982; Tronto 1989). However, most feminist International Relations scholars are sceptical of positing a nurturing account of feminine nature to correct the gender bias of Waltzian man/state (cf. Elshtain 1985: 41). International

Relations feminists search for richer, alternative models of agency that take account of both production and reproduction, redefine rationality to be less exclusive and instrumental and respect human relationships (across all levels) as well as the interdependence of human beings with nature (Tickner 1991: 204–6). For example, some scholars look for emancipatory models of agency at the margins – among Third World women and human rights activists for instance (Ackerly 2000). Feminist alternatives to International Relations' levels of analysis do not resort to more universal abstractions, they demand greater historical and cultural contextualization in order more adequately to reflect the complexity and indeterminacy of human agency and social structure.

Feminist scholars use gender analysis to uncover the bias of core International Relations concepts such as power and security. Such bias not only limits their theoretical application, it has detrimental consequences for international relations practice. *Power* in International Relations theory has been almost exclusively conceived of as 'power-over': the power to force or influence someone to do something that they otherwise would not (Jaquette 1984). An individual's power rests on his or her autonomy from the power of others. In this view, power cannot be shared nor can power be readily increased by relationships with others in the context of interdependent or common interests. The accumulation of power capabilities and resources, according to Morgenthau, is both an end and a means to security. In the context of an anarchical state system which is interpreted as necessarily hostile and self-helping, states that act 'rationally' instinctively deduce their national interests as their maximization of power-over other states. The Waltzian notion of power is only mildly different. Waltz conceptualizes power as a means for the survival of a state but not as an end-goal in itself, to the extent that a stable, bipolar, balance of power configuration exists between states. Consequently, in the Waltzian world-view, the only power that really matters is the power-capability of 'Great Powers', whose bipolar or multipolar arrangement brings limited order to an anarchic international realm.

How are International Relations' concepts of power gendered? In Tickner's (1988) critique of Morgenthau's six principles of power politics, the realist understanding of power is androcentric. It reflects male self-development and objectivist ways of knowing in patriarchal societies where men's citizenship and personal authority has traditionally relied on their head-of-household power-over women's sexuality and labour. This concept of power also rests on a particularly gender-specific notion of autonomous agency that makes human relationships and affective connections invisible. If the human world is exhaustively defined by such gendered constructions of 'power-over', as in realist accounts, feminists ask, how do children get reared, collective movements mobilize and everyday life reproduced? Christine Sylvester (1992: 32–8) argues that it is incoherent to posit self-help as the essential feature of world politics when many 'relations international' go on within households and other institutions. These relations include diplomatic negotiations, trade regimes and the socialization of future citizens, which are not based on self-help alone, but which take interdependent relations between self and other as the norm. The conventional International Relations' assumption that men and states are like units presents power politics as a self-fulfilling prophecy. Power politics, however, is a gendered and, therefore, biased account of world politics because its conceptualization of power depends upon the particular not the universal agency of rational man.

When Cynthia Enloe (1997) writes that paying attention to women can expose how much power it takes to maintain the international political system in its present form she is not referring to the sheer coercive force of men and states. Rather, she is intimating that power is a complex phenomenon of creative social forces which shape our personal and sexual identities as men, women and national citizens. To understand the nature of power at the international or global levels, feminist and other critical theorists urge that we study the domestic and transnational social relations, which not only support the foreign policies of states but actually constitute the state as the territorial authority with a monopoly over the use of legitimate force.

Security, as conceived by mainstream International Relations theorists, is also a biased concept when seen from a feminist perspective and as such may not bring much actual security to women and men. Rather, security, as conventionally defined by conventional International Relations, amounts to a situation of stability provided by militaristic states whose nuclear proliferation, ironically, is seen to prevent total war, if not the many limited wars fought on proxy territory. Security is examined only in the context of the presence and absence of war, because the threat of war is considered endemic to the sovereign state-system. Logically, then, this reactive notion of security is zero-sum and by definition 'national'. It presupposes what Peterson (1992a: 47–8) terms a 'sovereignty contract' established between states. According to this imaginary contract the use of military force is a necessary evil to prevent the outside – difference, irrationality, anarchy and potential conflict – from conquering the inside of homogeneous, rational and orderly states. States, in this feminist analysis, are a kind of 'protection racket' that by their very existence as bully 'protectors' create threats outside and charge for the insecurity that they bring to their 'protected' population 'inside'. In the name of protection, states demand the sacrifice of gendered citizens, including that of soldiers – in most cases men – through military conscription and mothers who devote their lives to socializing these dutiful citizens for the sovereign state (Elshtain 1992; Goldstein 2001).

Spike Peterson (1992a: 53) asks 'through which gendered identities do we seek security'? Like the state which has a monopoly on legitimate force, she points out that the institution of marriage has a monopoly on legitimate reproduction and property inheritance and acts as a protection racket, specifically for women. Women seek security in marriage or marriage-like relationships and the protection of a husband from the violence of other men or males in general, and from the economic insecurity of an international division of labour which devalues work associated with women and locates females in the poorest-paid and least secure sectors of the labour force. In the post-9/11 environment, citizens in the United States in particular looked for manly men – firemen, policemen, soldiers – to protect them from the unknown threats of angry, non-Westerners. American neoconservative discourse blamed feminism and homosexuality for pacifying the United States and weakening the resolve of the West to stamp out Islamic fundamentalism and other 'threats' (Bar On 2003: 456). Thus, gender analysis reveals men and states, domestic and international violence, to be inextricably related. The limited security they provide allows them to consolidate their authority over other men and states, but importantly also over women and territory, on whom they depend for a source of exploitable resources, and for the socio-cultural and biological reproduction of power relations.

Through their careful attention to women's as well as men's experiences, feminist analysts urge that security must be redefined. In particular, what is called 'national security' is profoundly endangering to human survival and sustainable communities (Tickner 1992). State military apparatuses create their own security dilemmas by purporting androcentric control and power-over to be the name of the game; a game we are persuaded to play in order to achieve the absolute and relative gains of state security.

A feminist analysis of security is particularly relevant in light of the events of 9/11 and their aftermath. Beliefs about gender and sexual difference are behind contemporary terrorist acts of violence against the West. The World Values Survey reveals that differences in values/ attitudes about gender and sexuality divide Western from the non-Western world (Norris and Ingelhart 2003). The statements of Osama Bin Laden and the diary account left behind by the 9/11 terrorists suggest that their actions were directed not merely against the West but against the Western gender identities perceived to be so threatening to their vision of an Islamic and/or pan Arabic culture (Tickner 2002). When Islamic fundamentalists deride the depraved morals of the West they are almost exclusively referring to gender norms. Their explicit rejection of Western gender relations, specifically relations of gender equality and women's individual rights, affects the relations between non-Western and Western states, heightening the possibility of conflict between them (True 2004). Gender, therefore, is not only a useful but a *necessary* analytical category for understanding post-9/11 international relations.

Tickner (1991) argues that ideas and key concepts such as 'rationality', 'security' and 'power' might be building blocks of explanation for a feminist theory of international politics. There is nothing inherent in the terms which suggests that they must be discarded, rather it is their narrow, gendered meanings in mainstream International Relations theory and practice which is problematic for feminist analysts. Runyan and Peterson (1991: 70) claim that dichotomous thinking – inside–outside, sovereignty–anarchy, domestic–international – prevents International Relations theory from being able to 'conceptualise, explain, or deliver the very things it says it is all about – security, power and sovereignty'. For International Relations feminists, these conceptual opposites repro-duce the self-fulfilling security dilemma and reinforce masculine power politics, thus limiting the possibilities for feminist alternatives.

Normative feminism

Normative feminism reflects on the process of International Relations theorizing as part of a normative agenda for global change. 'All forms of feminist theorising are normative, in the sense that they help us to question certain meanings and interpretations in IR theory' (Sylvester 2002: 248). Feminists are self-consciously explicit about the position from which they are theorizing, how they enter the International Relations field and go about their research. They view their social and political context and subjectivity as part of theoretical explanation. Empirical feminism and gender analysis are important contributions, but they are only starting points for feminist goals of transforming global social hierarchies (Persram 1994; Ship 1994; Hutchings 2000; Robinson forthcoming). Feminist theorists bring the insights of feminist *praxis* – for instance, care ethics and Third World women's social activism – to bear on debates about international ethics, humanitarian aid and intervention and human rights instruments (Cochran 1999; Robinson 1999; Hutchings 2000; Ackerly 2000). Gender is a *transformative* category, not because once we understand it at work we can deconstruct or do away with it, but because once we understand it we can transform how it works at all levels of social and political life.

Linklater (Chapter 4 in this volume) argues that the status of universalism is the key to the current debate between different modes of normative theory. Seen in this context, the different feminist epistemologies most commonly identified in International Relations' writings as feminist empiricism, feminist standpoint and feminist postmodernism are not autonomous or necessarily contradictory approaches to gender-sensitive knowledge in International Relations (see Keohane 1989b; Weber 1994). On the contrary, these epistemologies are inter-related feminist challenges to the masculine authority and dominance of science itself (McClure 1992: 359). They share a *normative* struggle to sustain connections to practical feminist politics and the concrete workings of gendered power. For example, the authors of *The 'Man' Question in International Relations* (1998) contend that international politics and institutions are themselves vital sites for the construction of masculinities and masculine identity (Zalewski and Parpart 1998; see also Hooper 2000).

Feminist scholars problematize the defining dichotomies of the International Relations field that are reinforced through their association with the masculine–feminine gender dichotomy: for example, the association of women with peace, cooperation, subjectivism and 'soft' domestic politics and men with war, competition, objectivity and 'high' international politics (Sylvester 1987, 1994a, 2002; Elshtain 1987). They question how these gender hierarchies are reproduced in International Relations theories and how they serve to naturalize other forms of power in world politics. From this normative perspective, gender difference is not merely about the relations between masculine and feminine, it is about the politics of knowledge: how and from what position in the hierarchy we can know.

For example, Cynthia Enloe's research radically subverts conventional ways of knowing and doing International Relations. To make sense of international politics, Enloe analyses the (extra)ordinary lives of women from below – which the history of the discipline would tell us is the least likely place for 'high politics'. Enloe reveals constructions of masculinity and femininity at the heart of international processes. She considers the withdrawal of Russian mothers' support for the Soviet army, due to the gross and unaccountable sacrifice of their sons in the USSR–Afghanistan war, as one of many personal expressions of gendered power that led to the delegitimization of the Soviet regime and the end of the Cold War (Enloe 1994). Her method encourages us to broaden conventional ways of knowing 'the truth' of international politics, and to question from whose perspective inter-state 'legitimate' force is the most significant expression of violence and potent explanation for war.

However, if asking questions about women's location in world politics, addressed by empirical feminism in International Relations, is dependent upon bringing gender in as an analytical construct in order to account for women's marginalization in International Relations, then normative feminist theory questions the binary concept of gender. The mutually exclusive opposition of masculinity and femininity is not 'the essence from which social organization can be explained' (Scott 1988: 2) rather it is a social construction which must be transformed. While analytical feminist theories created the category of gender to explain the social construction of women's oppression, normative feminist theories contextualize gender as an analytical device that harbours its own exclusions and, like International Relations theories, must also be deconstructed (Sylvester 2002).

Since the 1990s there has been some controversy over the application of gender in International Relations, and in feminist studies generally. In International Relations, two main criticisms of gender as a concept have arisen. The first criticism is that the analytic use of gender masks other forms of oppression prevalent in global politics. Speaking to a Western women's studies' audience in the 1980s from a Third World feminist standpoint, Chandra Mohanty (1991) criticized Western feminism for constructing the victimized 'Third World woman' based on universal, Western assumptions of gender, emptied of all historical, cultural and geographical specificity, including realities of race and class oppression. As in the adage, 'the master tools won't bring down the master's house', Mohanty made the point that Western categories cannot be used to challenge the imposition of Western categories and imperialist structures in non-Western societies.

The implications of this Third World feminist challenge for feminist International Relations is that gender-like International Relations concepts are a biased construct which cannot be easily applied globally. Indeed, if, as feminist scholars argue, gender relations are culturally and historically constructed, then it also follows that they cannot be the same everywhere. Nonetheless, there is a tendency in feminist International Relations to focus on gender constructions at the global level (Miller 1998; Baines 1999: 251; Prugl 2000). To be sure, the social and cultural practices which construct gender are now increasingly global, but they are altered at local levels and in specific historical and discursive contexts. Thus, even while feminist International Relations scholars are concerned primarily with world politics, their applications of gender must be grounded in local analysis.

Recognizing the Western imperialism behind universal categories of 'woman' or 'man', the newest feminist scholarship explores a dynamic intersectional relationship between the global political economy, the state and culturally, geographically, race- and class-specific gender relations rather than seeking to explain international and global processes through universal concepts of a *patriarchy* or *gender* hierarchy (Chan-Tierbergien 2004). For example, feminist scholars analysing the global sex trade address the complexity of global power relations (Berman 2003; Agathangelou 2004; Mackie 2001; Whitworth 2001). They explore the specific cultural and historical constructions of gender and sexuality in the sending and receiving countries, which in turn depend upon particular constructions of class, ethnicity, nationality, race and so on. Feminist scholars begin their research on the sex trade with the observation that women are the core labourers in this multibillion dollar business. However, as they engage in further research, drawing on non-elite knowledge and practice (such as that of the sex workers themselves) they are led to an understanding of the multiple and interlocking nature of oppressions, and of women's agency even in situations of physical coercion and other, more structural, forms of violence.

Normative feminism recognizes that there is no feminist 'high ground' from which to theorize about international relations. For instance, Christine Sylvester (1994a: 12) argues that 'all places to speak and act as women are problematic', because they are socially and historically constructed and exclude other identities. Effectively, Sylvester relinquishes the feminist standpoint position that women's experience can constitute the ground(s) for a more critical and universal theory of international relations, in favour of multiple feminist standpoints that question the discipline's hegemonic knowledge. Feminism, 'is the research posture of standing in many locations, illuminating important relations and practices darkened by the long shadows of official IR, of painting International Relations differently ... Feminism has many types and shifting forms. It is non-uniform and non-consensual; it is a complex matter with many internal debates' (Sylvester 2002: 269). International Relations feminism demonstrates that it is possible to do research and make normative claims, despite there being no given ontological starting points for theories of international relations (Sylvester 1994b: 317).

Feminist identity and solidarity are problematic insofar as achieving feminism's normative goal of ungendering social and political relations depends on politically organizing on the basis of gender 'as women'. Contrary to the tenets of 1970s radical feminisms, there is no easily realized, readily mobilized, global sisterhood. Rather, 'feminist internationality', as Christina Gabriel and Laura Macdonald (1994) show in their analysis of women's transnational organizing in the context of NAFTA, must be created by acknowledging and confronting, not ignoring, the differences among women. The very tension between positivist and post-positivist epistemologies that has divided contemporary theorists, including International Relations theorists, is the source of contemporary feminism's theoretical dynamism and political relevancy. International Relations feminism acknowledges the lack of a foundational collective subject 'woman', and a relatively bounded realm of the political, as well as the need to make a difference to women's daily lives, with the realization that gendered categories of 'woman/women and man/men' have historically served to marginalize women and some men.

Empirical and analytical feminist approaches challenge given ways of thinking about and doing International Relations, especially the dominant rationalist approaches. Asking why we have typically only seen statesmen and soldiers in International Relations theories, however, leads us to question the normative status of International Relations, including the identity of the knowers and the particular ways of knowing institutionalized in the International Relations field. Introducing the world-views of women who are differently situated in the present world order exemplifies the normative feminist perspective that there are multiple standpoints from which to view global politics, and that each may reveal diverse realities and relationships.

Conclusion

The three forms of feminism discussed in this chapter – empirical feminism, analytical feminism and normative feminism – all suggest that the theory and practice of international relations has suffered from its neglect of feminist perspectives. Feminists argue that conventional International Relations theories distort our knowledge of both 'relations' and the ongoing transformations of the 'international'. These International Relations theories overlook the political significance of gendered divisions of public and private institutionalized within and by the state and state-system and, as a result, ignore the political activities and activism of women: whether they are mobilizing for war, protesting state abrogation of their rights or organizing for the international recognition of women's human rights. Moreover, the objectivist approach of much International Relations theory produces relatively superficial knowledge and tends to reproduce the dichotomies which have come to demarcate the field. These dichotomies are gendered: they define power as power-over 'others', autonomy as reaction rather than relational, international politics as the negation of domestic, 'soft' politics and the absence of women, and objectivity as the lack of (feminized) subjectivity. In sum, approaches to international relations that fail to take gender seriously overlook critical aspects of world order and abandon a crucial opening for effecting change.

Feminist International Relations contributes to expanding and strengthening existing theories and analyses including liberal, critical theory, postmodern, constructivist and green theories of international relations. For example, International Relations feminists advance constructivist International Relations approaches by uncovering the processes through which identities and interests, not merely of states but of *key social constituencies*, are shaped at the global level. Elisabeth Prugl (2000) exemplifies this feminist constructivist approach in her study of home-workers in the global political economy (see also Locher and Prugl 2001; Kardam 2004). Prugl (2000) shows how transnational rules and regimes of gender in international organizations such as the ILO and global solidarity networks have been powerful forces in determining the plight of these workers around the world. Similarly, feminist perspectives deepen the neo-Gramscian international political economy (IPE) stress placed on culture and ideology as an integral part of the global political economy (Chin 1998; Ling 2001; True 2003).

Integrating feminist perspectives with postmodern, critical theory and constructivist approaches, represents an important strategy for engaging with other International Relations scholars. Once we recognize the close connections between gender, ideas, identities and norms and aspects of international politics and economics, this becomes a relatively straightforward exercise. Nonetheless, it is an exercise that can have important payoffs in terms of generating new insights into the processes associated with local and global transformations. Yet an even more daunting task involves finding ways to alert proponents of mainstream International Relations to the illuminating effects that can come from viewing social and political processes from a gender perspective. To do this successfully, feminist scholars must be prepared to bring their theoretical and empirical strengths to bear on the study of a full range of issues, and definitely not cede key areas of study to scholars working in the realist and neo-liberal institutionalist paradigms. This agenda need not take a rationalist form, but rather, in line with feminism's reconstructive purposes, it calls for theory-driven empirical studies and more empirically grounded normative theory that reflexively explores and defends feminist approaches to international relations.

This chapter began by asking what is distinctive about a feminist perspective on international relations. Although Harding (1987: 258) has argued that no distinctive feminist methodology exists because each methodology can contribute to feminist goals this should not lead us to conclude that there is no distinctive feminist International Relations perspective. The collective contribution of the diverse range of feminist International Relations inquiry – empirical, analytical and normative – is most significantly methodological (Ackerly, Stern and True forthcoming).

Through ongoing collective self-reflection feminists in and outside the field of International Relations are continually adding to our empirical and normative knowledge, while advancing the tools of gender analysis. It this self-reflexivity rather than any substantive approach or theory that makes feminist International Relations distinctive. Efforts to forge a unitary neo-feminist approach (Caprioli 2004) or non-feminist gender standpoint (Carpenter 2002) seek to mainstream empirical gender analysis without this self-reflexive methodology. Removing women from analysis of gender relations and bracketing out the normative perspective that gave rise to feminism in the first place is tantamount to throwing the baby out with the bathwater. It results in a senseless theoretical approach with no *raison d'être*.

International Relations as a discipline is currently in a state where the mainstream has been shown to have major blindspots with respect to social and political change. This conceptual blindness frequently leads to empirical blindness. It is not surprising then that International Relations analysts are often caught off-guard by events in world politics, most tragically those of 'September 11'. Clearly, a re-thinking of the basic assumptions of this discipline remains urgent if scholars want to under-stand global politics in the twenty-first century. Feminist scholarship of the sort reviewed in this chapter offers a way out of the darkness. If scholars want to gain fresh insights into the dynamics of world order, they need to take into account domestic social processes and non-elite subjects. Feminist perspectives reveal that, in many instances, the sites of global power and transformation are not just the domain of political and economic elites; such sites also exist in the invisible, underappreciated nooks and crannies of societies. Realist and liberal expectations about the nature of states and international relations are both disrupted when a feminist perspective is brought to bear. Feminist perspectives help us to recognize power shifts within nation-states that have ramifications for world order. Surely, observing and interpreting such power shifts as they arise in a variety of global and local venues constitute core functions of International Relations scholarship.

Chapter 10

Green Politics*

MATTHEW PATERSON

Of all the perspectives discussed in this book, Green politics is perhaps the newest. Although the 'environmental issues' around which a Green position on global politics has emerged may not be quite so prominent in the public eye as they were in the early 1990s, few serious observers of global politics would suggest that they have returned (or will do so) to their marginal position they occupied before that period. And behind the scenes, the theorization of what global ecological crises portend for global politics has matured. After moving from comparing Green theory to existing theories in International Relations (Laferrière and Stoett 1999; Laferrière 1996; Hovden 1999; Mantle 1999; Helleiner 1996 2000), debates have moved on to envisaging how Green political movements, and more mainstream responses to global ecological challenges themselves are engaged in reconstructing world politics (Eckersley 2004).

Green politics emerged as a significant political force in many countries from the mid-1970s onwards. Many of the writings of Green thinkers, and the practices of Green movements, contain both analyses of the dynamics of global politics, and normative visions concerning the restructuring of world politics. This chapter aims to outline strands of Green political thought which could be used to develop a Green theoretical position on International Relations, and arguments made in the developing literature in the field. This Green position, of course, has features in common with others presented in this volume, and I will highlight these in the Conclusions. The chapter will focus, however, on what is distinctive about a Green position.

The chapter is organized through a discussion of two main sets of literature which can be used to develop a Green position on International Relations/global politics. These are the literature on Green political theory (e.g. Dobson 1990; Eckersley 1992) and that on 'global ecology' (e.g. The Ecologist 1993; Sachs 1993a; Chatterjee and Finger

* I am grateful to John Barry, Scott Burchill, Richard Devetak, Andrew Linklater, Peter Newell, Ben Seel and Richard Shapcott for helpful comments on earlier versions of this chapter, and to Eric Helleiner for comments on the chapter in the first edition of this volume.

1994). I will outline the general arguments that these writers make in this introductory section. The chapter will then draw out the themes from both which help us construct a Green position in International Relations. I will do this through what I argue are the key strands of Green politics – ecocentric ethics, limits to growth and decentralization of power. Together, these two literatures provide an *explanation* of the destruction of the rest of nature by human societies, and a *normative* foundation for resisting this destruction and creating sustainable societies.

First it is necessary to make an important distinction, between Green politics and *environmentalism* (e.g. Dobson 1990). Broadly speaking, environmentalists accept the framework of the existing political, social, economic and normative structures of world politics, and seek to ameliorate environmental problems within those structures, while Greens regard those structures as the main origin of the environmental crisis and therefore contend that they are structures which need to be challenged and transcended. Although obviously a crude simplification of the variety of positions adopted by those in the Green, and broader environmental, movement it serves a useful function here as a representation of ideal-types. This is the case because it becomes clear that there is no distinctive *environmentalist* position on International Relations. As is obvious from even the most cursory literature survey of the mainstream International Relations literature on environmental problems, the environmentalist position is easily compatible with the liberal institutionalist position outlined most clearly by Keohane (1989a). In fact most writers within International Relations who write on environmental problems, and who are clearly motivated by the normative concerns adopted by environmentalists, adopt liberal institutionalist positions. (Haas, Keohane and Levy 1993; Haas 1990; Young 1989, 1994; Hurrell and Kingsbury 1992; Porter and Brown 1991; Vogler 1995). The analytic concern is with the response of the states-system to environmental problems, focusing on the emergence of 'international environmental regimes', while the underlying assumption is that the states-system can respond effectively to those problems. The theoretical assumptions underpinning these analyses can be found in Chapter 2 in this volume. By contrast, Green politics is far more sceptical about the claim that the states-system, and other structures of world politics, can provide such a response. The contrast between Green politics and environmentalism neatly mirrors one between critical and problem-solving theory (see Chapter 1 in this volume), with Greens focusing on the need for global-scale political transformation rather than institutional tinkering. This chapter will not therefore discuss the mainstream International Relations literature on environmental problems.

After establishing this distinctiveness of the Green position on global politics, what the chapter does is to discuss how Greens have recently re-engaged with mainstream debates in International Relations and, more broadly, to explore how contemporary trends in global politics might be utilized to 'green global politics'. This entails to an extent questioning the crude dichotomy outlined above, and enables a more productive debate between Green politics and both conventional theories of International Relations and practices in global politics.

Green political theory

There is now a well-developed literature on Green political theory (GPT), which gives a useful base for Green ideas about International Relations. Eckersley (1992) suggests that the defining characteristic is *ecocentrism* – the rejection of an anthropocentric world-view which places moral value only on humans in favour of one which places independent value also on ecosystems and all living beings (Eckersley 1992). In addition to this rejection of anthropocentrism, Dobson (1990) suggests that a second key feature of Green politics is the 'limits to growth' argument about the nature of the *environmental crisis*. Greens suggest that it is the exponential economic growth experienced during the last two centuries which is at the root cause of the current environmental crisis. Thus it is not the belief in an environmental crisis which is defining, but the particular understanding which Greens have of the nature of that crisis which makes them distinctive.

Dobson's addition is important, in my view. A reduction of the Green position to an ethical stance towards non-human nature, without a set of arguments about why the environment is being destroyed by humans, seems to me to lose much of what is central to Greens' beliefs. It is also highly indeterminate politically, as I will show later on. However, I would also argue that a third key plank of Green politics can also be identified, that of *decentralization*. There is an ongoing debate both about whether this is a key and necessary part of Green politics at all, but also whether it is something which is derived from the arguments about ecocentric ethics and limits to growth, or is something which can be regarded as a Green principle in its own right (Dobson 1990; Goodin 1992; Helleiner 2000). I do not propose to answer the second of these debates directly, but against writers like Goodin and Eckersley, I will try to show that decentralization is a key plank of Green politics. It is also worth a good deal of space here, principally because it is where the implications for International Relations are most tangible.

Global ecology

In the early 1990s a literature emerged which builds on the basic Green principles outlined above and provides an analysis of the present situation which is consistent with them. In other words, while GPT provides a normative foundation for a Green view of global politics, 'global ecology' provides an explanatory foundation. This literature can be associated most centrally with the writings of Wolfgang Sachs, Pratap Chatterjee and Matthias Finger, Vandana Shiva and magazines such as *The Ecologist* and *Third World Resurgence*. This literature has two central themes – development as the root cause of environmental problems, and the protection and reclamation of 'commons' as central to the Green vision.

Much of these ideas emerged out of critiques of UNCED, or the 'Earth Summit', held in 1992. Mainstream environmentalist accounts of UNCED usually regard the conference as having been a tremendous success for environmentalists and for the environment, marking the culmination of years of effort in getting politicians to take environmental problems seriously. By contrast, Chatterjee and Finger see it rather differently, suggesting that UNCED was a failure for the environmental movement, since it marked the final cooptation of environmentalism by ruling elites (1994; see also Doran 1993; Hildyard 1993; Sachs 1993a).

The concern of these writers therefore is to reclaim a set of beliefs about the nature of the ecological crisis which emphasize that radical social and political changes are necessary in order to respond to those problems. The analysis is again that it is not possible simply to adapt existing social institutions to deal with environmental problems – entirely new ones will have to be developed. There is a lineage back to Green writers of the early 1970s, such as Schumacher, which is clearly intended.

Ecocentrism

A central tenet of Green thought is the rejection of anthropocentric ethics in favour of an ecocentric approach. For Eckersley, ecocentrism has a number of central features. Empirically, it involves a view of the world as ontologically composed of *inter-relations* rather than individual entities (1992: 49). All beings are fundamentally 'embedded in ecological relationships' (1992: 53). Consequently, there are no convincing criteria which can be used to make a hard and fast distinction between humans and non-humans (1992: 49–51). Ethically, therefore, since there is no convincing reason to make rigid distinctions between humans and the rest of nature, a broad emancipatory project, to which Eckersley allies herself, ought to be extended to non-human nature. Ecocentrism is about 'emancipation writ large' (1992: 53). All entities are endowed with a relative autonomy, within the ecological relationships in which they are embedded, and therefore humans are not free to dominate the rest of nature.

Ecocentrism therefore has four central ethical features which collectively distinguish it from other possible ethical positions towards the environment (namely, resource conservation, human welfare ecology, preservationism and animal liberation; see 1992: Chapter 2). First, it recognizes the full range of human interests in the non-human world, as opposed simply to narrow, instrumental, economic interests in resource use. Secondly, it recognizes the interests of the non-human community. Thirdly, it recognizes the interests of future generations of humans and non-humans. Finally it adopts a holistic rather than an atomistic perspective – that is, it values populations, species, ecosystems and the ecosphere as a whole, as well as organisms individually (1992: 46).

Many challenge both whether ecocentrism is descriptively a necessary component of Green ideology, or whether it is an adequate or desirable basis for a political theory. Normatively, for example, both Barry (1999) and Hayward (1995, 1998) question both the intellectual coherence and strategic viability of ecocentrism, and argue for a 'soft' anthropocentrism as the basis for Green politics. Hayward (1995), for example, argues that the rejection of anthropocentrism in much Green thought is misplaced – what Greens seek typically to criticize should more accurately be thought of as either speciesism (arbitrary and unjustifiable discrimination against or oppression of organisms by species) or human chauvinism (attempts to specify the relevant criteria of ethical judgement which invariably benefit humans at the expense of other species). Anthropocentrism is not necessarily the problem in either of these cases, and in fact a proper respect for humanity may in fact itself lead to respect for other species as well (Hayward 1998: 46–9). Nevertheless, despite the details of their arguments, Hayward and Barry both agree that a radical thinking of the ethical relationship between humans and the rest of 'nature' is a fundamental part of Green politics.

Limits to growth, post-development

A second plank of a Green position is the belief in limits to the growth of human societies. Although the idea has a long lineage, the immediate impetus for arguments concerning limits to growth came from an influential, controversial and very well-known book, *The Limits to Growth* (Meadows *et al.*, 1972). That book argued that the exponential economic and population growth of human societies was producing an interrelated series of crises. Exponential growth was producing a situation where the world was rapidly running out of resources to feed people or to provide raw material for continued industrial growth (exceeding *carrying capacity* and *productive capacity*), and simultaneously exceeding the *absorptive capacity* of the environment to assimilate the waste products of industrial production (Dobson 1990: 15; Meadows *et al.* 1972). Meadows *et al.* produced their arguments based on computer simulations of the trajectory of industrial societies. They predicted that, at current rates of growth, many raw materials would rapidly run out, pollution would quickly exceed the absorptive capacity of the environment, and human societies would experience 'overshoot and collapse' some time before 2100.

The details of their predictions have been fairly easily refuted. However, Greens have taken their central conclusion – that exponential growth is impossible in a finite system – to be a central plank of their position (e.g. Spretnak and Capra 1984; Trainer 1985; Porritt 1986; Bunyard and Morgan-Grenville 1987). Dobson suggests there are three arguments which are important here (1990: 74–80). First, technological solutions will not work – they may postpone the crisis but cannot prevent it occurring at some point. Secondly, the exponential nature of growth means that 'dangers stored up over a relatively long period of time can very suddenly have a catastrophic effect' (1990: 74). Finally, the problems associated with growth are all inter-related. Simply dealing with them issue by issue will mean that there are important knock-on effects from issue to issue; solving one pollution problem alone may simply change the medium through which pollution is carried, not reduce pollution overall.

From this, Greens get their notions of *sustainability*. Environmentalism concentrates on 'sustainable development', a concept originally used in the *World Conservation Strategy* (IUCN 1980) and popularized by the World Commission on Environment and Development (WCED 1987). Sustainable development presumes the compatibility of growth with responding successfully to environmental problems. Greens reject this, arguing that sustainability explicitly requires stabilizing and, in the industrialized countries almost certainly reducing, throughputs of materials and energy, and thus economic output (Lee 1993).

As the notion of sustainable development became fashionable in the 1980s, and as the specific predictions of Meadows *et al.* concerning resource exhaustion proved inaccurate, belief in limits subsided. But in the 1990s a politics rejecting economic growth as the primary purpose of governments and societies re-emerged. It came, however, less out of the computer-modelling methods of Meadows *et al.* (although her team did produce a twenty-year-on book *Beyond the Limits*, Meadows and Randers 1992) than out of emerging critiques of development in the South from the 1980s onwards. Such 'post-development' perspectives draw heavily on postmodernism and feminism (e.g. Escobar 1995; Shiva 1988), and have been used by Greens in the North to develop the 'global ecology' perspective. Through the critique of 'development', economic growth again became the subject of critique, although in this vein critics made much closer connections between its ecological and its social consequences. Through the critique of 'development', economic growth became again the subject of critique, although in this vein critics made much closer connections between its ecological consequences and its social consequences (Douthwaite 1992; Wackernagel and Rees 1996; Booth 1998).

One of the reasons why the 'global ecology' writers object to development is the limits to growth arguments, abandoned by much of the environmental movement during the 1980s. Implicit throughout their work is a need to accept the limits imposed by a finite planet, an acceptance which is ignored by the planet's managers and mainstream environmentalists (e.g Sachs 1993a). They are also sceptical of the idea that it is possible to decouple the concept of development from that of growth. While many environmentalists try to distinguish the two by stating that 'growth is quantitative increase in physical scale while development is qualitative improvement or unfolding of potentialities' (Daly 1990; Ekins 1993), others would suggest that in practice it is impossible to make such neat distinctions. For the practitioners of sustainable development, 'sustainable growth' and 'sustainable development' are in practice usually conflated, and certainly the Brundtland Commission regarded the pursuit of economic growth as essential for sustainable development (WCED 1987).

However, their arguments are more subtle than simply re-asserting limits to growth arguments. They focus on a number of *anti-ecological* elements of development. One of the central features of development is the enclosure of commons in order to expand the realm of commodity production and thus the expansion of material throughput (*The Ecologist* 1993). A second is the way such enclosure redistributes and concentrates resources, which has direct ecological consequences and creates a growth-supporting dynamic as growth mitigates the effects of enhanced inequality. A third is the concentrations of power which are involved in enclosure, as smaller numbers of people are able to control the way that land is used (and often able to insulate themselves from the ecological effects of the way land is used, for example by reserving for themselves privileged access to uncontaminated water sources). A fourth is the way such enclosure and the concentrations of power and wealth it effects produce shifts in knowledge relations and systems, typically involving the marginalization of 'indigenous knowledges' and the empowerment of 'experts' (*The Ecologist* 1993: 67–70; Appfel-Marglin and Marglin 1990). Finally, such a set of shifts in property systems, distribution of resources and power–knowledge relations entrenches the world-view which regards the non-human world in purely instrumental terms, thus legitimizing the destructive use of non-human nature.

The global ecology writers therefore present a powerful set of arguments as to how development is inherently anti-ecological. This is not only because of abstract limits to growth-type arguments, but because they show in a more subtle fashion how development in practice undermines sustainable practices. It takes control over resources away from those living sustainably in order to organize commodity production, it empowers experts with knowledge based on instrumental reason, it increases inequality which produces social conflicts and so on.

Green rejections of the state-system

A central question for the present purposes is the position which Green politics has concerning questions of world order. Although some arguments made by environmentalists concerning such institutional reform have clear connections to other traditions, what I argue is the most plausible and representative account of what Greens believe provides a distinctive account of what forms of global political restructuring are required. This is therefore the third plank of a Green politics – *decentralism*. However, whether this is a key principle of Green politics or not is certainly contested, as will be obvious below.

The implications for global political structures of Green arguments are clearly considerable. O'Riordan (1981) presents a useful typology of positions which emerge from the limits to growth account of sustainability which Greens adopt (1981: 303–7; Dobson 1990: 82–3). The first that the nation-state is both too big and too small to deal effectively with sustainability, and new regional and global structures (alongside decentralization within the state) are needed to coordinate effective responses. I will revisit this argument later in a discussion of Eckersley's work.

A second interpretation, prevalent in the 1970s but virtually absent from discussions in the 1980s, is what O'Riordan calls 'centralised authoritarianism'. This generally follows the logic of Garrett Hardin's 'tragedy of the commons' (1968), which suggested that resources held in common would be overused. This metaphor led to the argument that centralized global political structures would be needed to force changes in behaviour to reach sustainability (e.g. Hardin 1974; Ophuls 1977). In some versions, this involved the adoption of what were called 'lifeboat ethics' (Hardin 1974), where ecological scarcity meant that rich countries would have to practise triage on a global scale – to 'pull up the ladder behind them'. This argument, largely an ecological version of the world government proposals of 'Idealist' versions of liberal internationalism (see Chapter 2 in this volume) has, however, been rejected by Greens.

The third position is similar to the above in that it suggests that authoritarianism may be required, but rejects the idea that this can be on a global scale. The vision here is for small-scale, tightly knit communities run on hierarchical, conservative lines with self-sufficiency in their use of resources (*The Ecologist* 1972; Heilbroner 1974). It shares with the above position the idea that it is freedom and egoism which has caused the environmental crisis, and that these tendencies need to be curbed to produce sustainable societies.

The final position which O'Riordan outlines is termed by him the 'anarchist solution'. This has become the position adopted by Greens as the best interpretation of the implications of limits to growth. For many, it is also regarded as a principle of Green politics in its own right (e.g., decentralization is a one of the four principles of Green politics in the widely cited *Programme of the German Green Party* 1983). The term 'anarchist' is used loosely in this typology. It means that Greens envisage global networks of small-scale self-reliant communities. This position would for example be associated with people like E. F. Schumacher (1976), as well as bioregionalists such as Kirkpatrick Sale (1980). (Bioregionalists argue that ecological societies should be organized with natural environmental features such as watersheds forming the boundaries between communities.) It shares the focus on small-scale communities with the previous position, but has two crucial differences. First, relations within communities would be libertarian, egalitarian and participatory. This reflects a very different set of assumptions about the origins of the environmental crisis; rather than being about the 'tragedy of the commons' (which naturalizes human greed), it is seen to be about the emergence of hierarchical social relations and the channelling of human energies into productivism and consumerism (Bookchin 1982). Participatory societies should provide means for human fulfilment which do not depend on high levels of material consumption. Secondly, these communities, while self-reliant, are seen to be internationalist in orientation. They are not cut off from other communities, but in many ways conceived of as embedded in networks of relations of obligations, cultural exchanges and so on.

Greens also often object to the state for anarchist reasons. For example, Spretnak and Capra (1984) suggest that it is the features identified by Weber as central to statehood which are the problem from a Green point of view (1984: 177). Bookchin (1980) gives similar arguments, suggesting that the state is the ultimate hierarchical institution which consolidates all other hierarchical institutions. Carter (1993) suggests that the state is part of the dynamic of modern society which has caused the present environmental crisis. He outlines a 'environmentally hazardous dynamic', where '[a] centralized, pseudo-representative, quasi-democratic state stabilizes competitive, inegalitarian economic relations that develop "non-convivial", environmentally damaging "hard" technologies whose productivity supports the (nationalistic and militaristic) coercive forces that empower the state' (Carter 1993: 45; see also Wall 1994). Thus the state is not only unnecessary from a Green point of view, it is positively undesirable.

However, whether or not one subscribes to this anarchist interpretation, the decentralist impulse is nevertheless the most important theme coming out of Green politics for International Relations. One of the best-known Green political slogans is 'think globally, act locally'. While obviously also fulfilling rhetorical purposes, it is often seen to follow from the two above principles. It stems from a sense that while that global environmental and social/economic problems operate on a global scale, they can be successfully responded to only by breaking down the global power structures which generate them through local action and the construction of smaller-scale political communities and self-reliant economies.

One of the best-developed arguments for decentralization within GPT is given in John Dryzek's *Rational Ecology* (1987). Dryzek summarizes the advantages of decentralization thus; small-scale communities are more reliant on the environmental support services in their immediate locality and therefore more responsive to disruptions in that environment (1987: Chapter 16). Self-reliance and smallness shortens feedback channels, so it is easier to respond quickly before disruptions become severe. Dryzek also suggests that they are more likely to develop a social ontology which undermines pure instrumental ways of dealing with the rest of nature, commonly identified by Greens (and others) as a cause of environmental problems (1987: 219; see also *The Ecologist* 1993 for extended discussions of similar arguments).

The 'global ecology' writers also reinforce this GPT argument for decentralization of power. At the same time, they give this argument a political economy, by which I mean they make it so that it is not only a question of the scale of political organization but also a reorganization of the structural form of political institutions, and in particular a reconceptualization of how economic production, distribution and exchange – the direct way in which human societies transform 'nature' – is integrated into political life. Their positive argument is that the most plausibly Green form of political economy is the 'commons'. This argument is most fully developed by the editors of *The Ecologist* magazine in their book *Whose Common Future? Reclaiming the Commons* (1993).

The argument is essentially that common spaces are sites of the most sustainable practices currently operating. They are under threat from development which continuously tries to enclose them in order to turn them into commodities. Therefore a central part of Green politics is resistance to this enclosure. But it is also a (re)constructive project – creating commons where they do not exist.

Commons regimes are difficult to define, as *The Ecologist* suggests. In fact the book suggests that precise definitions are impossible, as the variety of commons around the world defy clear description in language. The first point of definition is a negative one however. The commons is not the commons as referred to by Garrett Hardin (1968). His 'tragedy of the commons', where the archetypal English medieval common gets overgrazed as each herder tries to maximize the number of sheep they graze on it, is in practice not a commons, but an 'open access' resource (*The Ecologist* 1993: 13).

Commons, therefore, are not 'anarchic' in the sense of having no rules governing them. They are spaces whose use is closely governed, often by informally defined rules, by the communities which depend on them. They depend for their successful operation on a rough equality between the members of the community, as imbalances in power would make some able to ignore the rules of the community. They also depend on particular social and cultural norms prevailing – for example, the priority of common safety over accumulation, or distinctions between members and non-members (although not necessarily in a hostile sense, or one which is rigid and unchanging over time) (*The Ecologist* 1993: 9).

Commons are therefore clearly different from private property systems. However, commons are also not 'public' spaces in the modern sense. 'Public' connotes open access under control by the state, while commons are often not open to all, and the rules governing them do not depend on the hierarchy and formality of state institutions. A further difference from 'modern' institutions is that they are typically organized for the production of use values rather than exchange values – that is, they are not geared to commodity production and are not susceptible to the pressures for accumulation or growth inherent in capitalist market systems.

Commons are therefore held to produce sustainable practices, for a number of reasons. First, the rough equality in income and power means that none can usurp or dominate the system (*The Ecologist* 1993: 5).

Second, the local scale at which they work means that the patterns of mutual dependence make cooperation easier to achieve. Third, this also means that the culture of recognizing one's dependence on others, and therefore having obligations, is easily entrenched. Finally, commons make practices based on accumulation difficult to adopt, usufruct being more likely.

The idea of the commons is clearly very consistent with the arguments from GPT about the necessity of decentralization of power, and grassroots democracy. It should of course be clear that from this perspective the term 'global commons', in widespread use in mainstream environmental discussions to refer to problems such as global warming or ozone depletion (e.g. Vogler 1995; Buck 1998) is literally nonsensical. However it supplements it by showing how small-scale democratic communities are the most likely to produce sustainable practices within the limits set by a finite planet.

Objections to Green arguments for decentralization

Much of the academic literature on Green politics in the 1990s questioned the Green commitment to decentralization (e.g. Goodin 1992; de Geus 1995). In addition, Doherty and de Geus (1995: 4) suggest that Green parties scaled back their commitments during the 1990s in response to electoral success and the corresponding need for 'realism'. Objections to decentralization tend to come in three forms; the first two will be treated here, while the third forms part of the following section.

First is the claim that small-scale anarchistic communities would be too parochial and potentially self-interested to provide atmospheres conducive to cross-community cooperation. 'One of the major fears of observers outside the Green movement is that its picture of localized politics smacks of a petty parochialism, which would be both undesirable and unpleasant to live with', writes Dobson (1990: 101, 124). Part of this argument is therefore that it would be stultifying or oppressive for those within the community, but it also suggests that they would be unconcerned with effects across their borders. This argument is generally empirical in character; that in human societies (historical and present) organized on such a small scale such a parochial character is pervasive, and that a universalistic ethics which Greens also espouse only emerged in modernity, with its nation-states, cities and so on. It does not necessarily follow that this would happen when modern societies with modern universalistic sensibilities try to reorganize themselves along ecoanarchist lines.

Whether or not Greens have an adequate answer to this problem, this objection to the anti-statist position is very odd. The objection that small-scale communities may be too parochial could just as easily be a charge levelled against sovereign states. It is the practice of sovereignty which enables states to be primarily self-regarding, and avoid any sense that they have fundamental obligations to the rest of the world. And the sorts of communities Greens envisage are *post-sovereign* communities. Confederations of small-scale communities could be organized in such a way that effects on other communities would have to be taken into account in decisions. But even if this is rejected as naïve, the point that is missed in this objection is that no particular political form (arguably excepting world government, but that has its own problems) could *guarantee* that communities would be concerned with effects on other communities. Solving that problem is a question of political *culture*, not political structure.

A second objection is that while Greens' advocacy of decentralization clearly involves an explicit rejection of the contemporary sovereign states-system, this undermines Greens' claims to global relevance. Decentralized small-scale communities, it is claimed, will have little chance of developing effective mechanisms for resolving global environmental problems. The clearest argument of this sort is put by Goodin (1992).

Goodin argues (as do others) that since many environmental problems are transnational or even global in scope, global cooperation to respond to these problems is necessary. This is a reasonable enough argument. But he then goes on to argue that the state, with sovereign rights intact, is a necessary political form to procure this cooperation. This turn in the argument is perhaps less convincing.

Goodin outlines four well-known games which could be said to model cooperation between small-scale anarchistic communities: Prisoners' Dilemma (re-interpreted here as Polluters' Dilemma), Chicken, Assurance and Altruism. His concern is to try to show that, for each of these, substantial powers may have to be transferred to institutions well beyond the local level, right up to the global level. The problem gets less acute as we move through his four models towards Altruism (which he reasonably suggests approximates the Green utopia), but he argues that it applies there also. This model assumes that all the communities have a fully 'green' culture, in that they follow Green ethical norms as he outlines them, and base their decisions on norms which are global in orientation – they are not purely interested in the quality of their own environment.

Goodin argues that even in this scenario there will still be a significant need for coordinating mechanisms among communities. In particular, even if Green communities abided by Green norms, they would still need information about what other communities were doing on a particular problem in order to find out what precisely they needed to do about a problem. Thus 'there will still be a need for a central coordinating mechanism to collate everyone's action plans' (Goodin 1992: 166).

Goodin then argues that 'the role [of centralized agencies] will be greater, the need for sanctioning powers more urgent, the more the situation resembles the Polluters'-cum-Prisoners' Dilemma' (Goodin 1992: 167). There are two major flaws in his argument here. First, there is a great difference between 'organized information-pooling' and 'sanctioning powers' which, although Goodin is obviously aware of it, glosses over its importance for Green conceptions of the location and nature of political authority (Goodin 1992: 167). If the state is the focus of the discussion, then only where sanctioning powers are concerned would we be fully talking about something resembling a state. While most Greens reject the idea of global political authorities, there is no reason why they should have any problem with institutions concerned with information-pooling across communities, and these arguments are strengthened by the focus in debates in the 1990s on the increasing predominance of network forms of organization globally (on which more later).

Secondly, Goodin makes much too much of the need for *sanctioning* powers in the Prisoners' Dilemma situation. Much theorizing about international cooperation has highlighted how extensive cooperation can be produced despite the lack of enforcement powers in international agencies, relying on the sort of information-pooling which Goodin highlights would be necessary 'even' in the altruist case (e.g. Chayes and Chayes 1993). This undermines his case that institutions with effective authority beyond the local level would be required.

Furthermore, this problem of coordination is not one to which Green positions are uniquely vulnerable. All political arrangements, including the present one, require some form of coordination of action between political units to respond to transboundary environmental problems. Of course, Greens are arguing for a system where power is decentralized as much as possible, so they may be seen to be especially vulnerable to this problem. However, if Goodin has failed to show that Greens need envisage anything more than information-pooling institutions, then Green proposals are left with the advantage that radical decentralization makes environmental management on the ground more practicable, using many of the arguments given by Dryzek earlier.

Greening global politics?

A third objection to the Green argument I have outlined is rather different. Rather than arguing that Greens' attempts to abandon sovereignty and decentralize power means that there is insufficient coordinating capacity, much of the recent literature on Green politics in International Relations has argued that Green politics remains overly committed to a sovereign model of politics. Kuehls (1996), Dalby (1998) and Stewart (1997), and from a different theoretical background, Wapner (1996), all advance such an argument. Dalby suggests, while agreeing with Green critiques of 'global environmental management', that:

> The political dilemma and the irony here is that the alternative to global management efforts – that of political decentralization and local control, which is often posited as the political alternative by green theory – remains largely in thrall to the same limited political imaginary of the domestic analogy. (1998: 13)

Dalby's critique is that Greens remain committed to a sovereign model of politics, the 'domestic analogy'. In a different theoretical context, Wapner makes the same form of critique in his account of 'world civic politics' (1996), or in Kuehls' critique of Bookchin (1996: esp. 106). Decentralization of power, as Wapner or Dalby read the Green decentralist position, is simply a matter of recreating existing political institutions, sovereign states, at much more local, 'human scale' levels. But this is a misreading. Green decentralists do base much of their arguments on questions of scale. But they are also clear that such decentralization for ecological purposes involves creating fundamentally different political institutions. That is clear by the way that many such writers are explicitly opposed to institutions and practices of sovereignty; as Helleiner (1996) points out, this has always been an intended implication of the slogan 'Think Globally, Act Locally'. It is also clear that such decentralization also arises from Green concerns with hierarchy and domination. So the state is not simply about the scale of political institutions, but also their form.

Both sets of writers – Kuehls (1996), Stewart (1997) and Dalby (1998) from poststructuralist frameworks, and Wapner (1996) and Lipschutz (1997) from liberal-pluralist ones – suggest that a more appropriate way to understand forms of governance in relation to environmental politics is to abandon spatial–territorial conceptions of politics totally. In an age of globalization, they both suggest, transnational network forms of governance are emerging, not least to deal with ecological problems, which make possible an alternative form of politics. But much of the problem with this formulation is it takes as given the political–economically driven processes of globalization which undermine traditional forms of politics, and fails to imagine the possibility of resisting globalization, not in order (as social democrats such as Hirst and Thompson 1996, or

Weiss 1998, want) to revitalize the national state, but to make possible a more thoroughgoing decentralization of political life. The 'networks' of global civil society as envisaged by Wapner and Lipschutz may be appropriate modes of facilitating inter-community cooperation to get round the problems discussed above, or appropriate tactical or transitional modes of organization enabling political change to occur. But it does not follow that they provide a model of a sustainable polity.

There are therefore good reasons to be sceptical of critics of Green politics who focus on the inadequacies of Greens' proposed restructuring of global politics. This is strengthened by some of the arguments made by the 'global ecology' writers, who focus on how the 'commons' are a form of political and social space which are the most conducive to sustainable practices (contrary to the suggestions of Garrett Hardin and others), a position which strengthens arguments for decentralization. Despite some challenges in the 1990s, it certainly still remains the case that, for most writers on the subject from diverse perspectives, the political implications of Green politics are in the direction of radical decentralization of power (e.g. Bryant and Bailey 1997; Luke 1997; Helleiner 2000).

But at the same time, what is important about this critique of Green positions is the way it draws attention to the contemporary strategic situation facing Greens, and at the same time to the way that ecological challenges and the political responses to them are themselves engendering changes in global political structures in ways whose potential are missed by the abstract nature of the Green critique of the states-system. Put differently, they enable us to ask a question of what an immanent Green critique of global politics might look like, as opposed to a transcendental Green critique of the (reified) states system, as in Bookchin's anarchist arguments, for example.

It is in this light that Eckersley's *The Green State* (2004) comes to the fore. Eckersley's earlier book (1992) contained an explicit rejection of eco-anarchism and the decentralist emphasis in much Green thought. On the basis of her reading of the implications of ecocentrism, she develops a political argument from this which is statist in orientation. Although she does not adopt the position of the 'eco-authoritarians' such as Hardin (1974), Heilbroner (1974), or Ophuls (1977), she suggests, in direct contradiction to the eco-anarchism which is widespread in Green political thought, that the modern state is a necessary political institution from a Green point of view. She suggests that ecocentrism requires that we both decentralize power down within the state, but also centralize power up to the regional and global levels. In line with O'Riordan's first type of Green world order reform (see p. 10) she argues that a 'multitiered' political system, with dispersal of power both down to local communities and up to the regional and global levels is the approach which is most consistent with ecocentrism (Eckersley 1992: 144, 175, 178).

This position could be developed within a conventional perspective on international relations (such as liberal institutionalism, see Chapter 2 in this volume) to look at the character of a wide variety of inter-state treaties and practices. The most obvious would be those regarding biodiversity, acid rain, or climate change. But it could also be developed for global economic institutions such as the World Bank, or the military practices of states.

But Eckersley's account could also be developed in the context of the literature on 'global environmental governance', which implies forms of governance emerging which do not rely solely on sovereign states (Paterson 1999; Humphreys, Paterson and Pettiford 2003). One view of this is that we are currently witnessing a simultaneous shift of authority up to international/transnational institutions, and down to local organizations (Rosenau 1992; Hempel 1996). Rosenau makes this claim concerning patterns of authority in global politics in general, but also specifically in relation to global environmental politics (Rosenau 1993). For Hempel, such forms of global environmental governance are emerging because the spatial scale of the state is inadequate for dealing with the scales of environmental change. The state is simultaneously too small and too big to deal effectively with such change, and thus practices of governance move towards regional and global levels and at the same time towards local levels, in response. Eckersley's position in her (1992) book is a normative claim justifying such shifts in authority.

A core problem with this argument is that the interpretation of ecocentrism, which underpins Eckersley's (1992) book, is challengeable. Ecocentrism is in itself politically indeterminate. It can have many variants, ranging from anarchist to authoritarian, with Eckersley's version in the middle of the continuum. The predominant alternative interpretation within Green thought suggests that it is the emergence of modern modes of thought which is the problem from an ecocentric point of view. The rationality inherent in modern Western science is an instrumental one, where the domination of the rest of nature (and of women by men) and its use for human instrumental purposes have historically at least been integral to the scientific project on which industrial capitalism is built (e.g. Merchant 1980). In other words, environmental ethics are given a historical specificity and material base – the emergence of modern forms of anthropocentrism is located in the emergence of modernity in all its aspects.

This interpretation argues therefore that since modern science is inextricably bound up with other modern institutions such as capitalism, the nation-state and modern forms of patriarchy, it is inappropriate to respond by developing those institutions further, centralizing power through the development of global and regional institutions. Such a response will further entrench instrumental rationality which will undermine the possibility for developing an ecocentric ethic. An ecocentric position therefore leads to arguments for scaling down human communities, and in particular for challenging trends towards globalization and homogenization, since it is only by celebrating diversity that it will be possible to create spaces for ecocentric ethics to emerge. The 'global ecology' writers outlined already develop this argument.

In *The Green State* (2004), Eckersley develops an argument with similar conclusions, but in much greater detail, and based not on the transcendental claims of ecocentric ethics but on the importance of an immanent critique of contemporary global politics. That is, she starts from an analysis both of the contemporary anti-ecological tendencies and structures within global politics (for her, these are inter-state anarchy, global capitalism, the limits of liberal democracy) *and* the contemporary trends which create the possibility of countering these tendencies (environmental multilateralism, ecological modernization, deliberative/discursive democracy).

Collectively, Eckersley argues that these three elements create the possibility of an ecological world order which works from existing practices, rather than having to develop a world order anew. Thus she draws heavily on constructivist accounts of international politics (see also Reus-Smit, Chapter 8 in this volume), particularly on the notion of 'cultures of anarchy' (Wendt 1999) to argue that sovereignty need not simply mean relentless hostility and competition between states (as assumed in both ecoauthoritarian arguments for world government and in ecoanarchist arguments against the state), but can entail the development of mutual obligations and extensive cooperation, and suggests that the development of environmental multilateralism to date (as discussed by the mainstream literature on international environmental regimes, as mentioned on p. 10) is evidence for the possibilities here. Eckersley draws on accounts of ecological modernization (e.g. Hajer 1995; Christoff 1996; Mol 1996) to suggest that the growth and globalization dynamic of global capitalism is only one possible future for the world economy, while remaining highly critical of the 'weak' nature of most actually existing ecological modernization. Finally, she draws on work on deliberative and transnational democracy (Held 1995; Dryzek 1990, 1992, 1999; Linklater 1998) and implicitly at least on ecological citizenship (Dobson 2003) both to suggest that the former would enable the move to 'strong' ecological modernization which would properly ecologize economic processes, and the latter could embed properly the transformations of sovereignty away from the Hobbesian image.

Once Green conceptions of critiques of international politics are understood this way, this then opens the door for a critical but constructive re-engagement with other International Relations traditions thinking similarly about the way that the states-system is undergoing transformation and how such transformations might be pushed in a radical direction. In the environmental sphere, work such as that by Hurrell on challenges to sovereignty and the states-system (1994), Shue on global justice and global environmental politics (1992, 1995, 1999), or Dobson on ecological citizenship (2003). All of these suggest, in differing ways, how Green conceptions of necessary global political reforms could fruitfully engage with specific existing elements of global politics in the manner indicated at a more general level by Eckersley. Outside the environmental sphere, Linklater's account of critical theory (see Chapter 4 in this volume; Linklater 1998) in terms of the possible transformations of forms of political community, or related debates about cosmopolitan or transnational democracy (Held 1995; Dryzek 1999) would be obvious sites of potential engagement.

An objection to this argument would be to question the focus on democratic deliberation in Eckersley's arguments. Fundamentally, she assumes that it is the character of *democratic deliberation* which underpins (un) sustainable polities. That is, while in *Environmentalism and Political Theory* (1992), it was her ecocentric ethics which underpin political claims about sustainability, in *The Green State* (2004) what sustainability requires politically is that 'all those potentially affected by ecological risks ought to have some meaningful opportunity to participate, or be represented, in the determination of policies or decisions that may generate risks' (2004: 243). This assumption generates the focus both on the weak nature of deliberative processes in liberal democracy, and the need to enable deliberative processes which do not exclude those beyond the borders of individual states. The main Green criticism here could come from the lines of argument developed by the 'global ecology' writers. Eckersley's account of democratic deliberation rightly questions the uncritical nature of 'individual preferences' as invoked by liberal democratic rhetoric – or, if you like, the separation of public and private, but fails to question also its (related) separation of politics and economics. Thus in the 'reclaiming the commons' literature, what is evident is that it is the embeddedness of political institutions in concrete socio-economic forms which engenders sustainable practices, whereas in Eckersley's account of ecological democracy it is clear that the practices of democratic deliberation and the practices of the production of daily life are much more clearly removed from each other, disembodied if you will. However, what is at the same time clear is that Eckersley's arguments concerning ecological democracy, if given a 'decentralist' twist – that is, if her insistence on the national state as the starting point for thinking about the site of political activity is dropped – then become significantly more attractive for most Greens, and an enormously sophisticated and valuable addition to Green arguments.

What is perhaps also therefore at stake is Eckersley's account of contemporary global political developments which inform therefore the 'limits of the possible' out of which her immanent critique can then be developed. To repeat, this is for her the emergent potential of environmental multilateralism, ecological modernization and deliberative democracy arising out of inter-state anarchy, global capitalism and liberal democracy. What is interesting in this context is perhaps the lack of a discussion of 'anti-globalization' movements, in which Greens have played prominent roles, as well as an acknowledgement that the commons as a form of political economy which Greens want to promote already exists in many areas around the world, as noted already. If one adds this dimension to contemporary global developments to those Eckersley discusses, then this perhaps transforms what one thinks of the potential by decentralism as argued by Greens. These movements can, of course, be analysed as pressures which support (while keeping radical pressure on) more reformist movements developing environmental multilateralism, ecological modernization and discursive democracy. But they can also be analysed as movements generating political change in their own right, embedded in a broader pattern of Green/left social and political change which challenge (rather than just shape) the power of global capital, the centralization of power and so on, and act as the agents which help to forge and sustain ecological democracy and citizenship.

Conclusions

The central point of this chapter has concerned the particular way in which most Greens reject the states-system, arguing primarily for decentralizing political communities below the nation-state, rather than for new forms of global political authority. This involves decentralization not only of political organization, but economic and social organization as well. They also argue for abandoning traditional sovereign systems and practices in favour of more mixed locations of authority. Global ecology complements this by suggesting in rich detail how contemporary political–economic practices undermine the sustainability of human societies, and how those power structures need to be challenged to create sustainable societies. Their focus on 'reclaiming the commons' supports the decentralization argument in GPT.

The Introduction to the book (Chapter 1) outlined some of the central questions and distinctions concerning theoretical traditions in International Relations. Green politics should clearly be regarded as a critical rather than problem-solving theory. It is one, however, which aims to be both explanatory and normative – it tries both to explain a certain range of phenomena and problems in global politics and provide a set of normative claims about the sorts of global political changes necessary to respond to such problems. Writers within this tradition have to date spent less time engaging in constitutive–theoretical activity – reflecting on the nature of their theorizing *per se*, although there is attention, in particular among the writers in what I have called the 'global ecology' school to power/knowledge questions (but cf. Doran 1995).

For Greens, the central object of analysis and scope of enquiry is the way in which contemporary human societies are *ecologically unsustainable*. Such a destructive mode of existence is deplored both because of the independent ethical value held to reside in organisms and ecosystems, and because human society ultimately depends on the successful function of the biosphere as a whole for its own survival. Regarding International Relations specifically, Greens focus on the way in which prevailing political structures and processes contribute to this destruction. The purpose of enquiry is thus explicitly normative – to understand how global political structures can be reformed to prevent such destruction and provide for a sustainable human relationship to the planet and the rest of its inhabitants. Like idealism (see Chapter 2 in this volume), the normative imperative is the original impulse in Green politics – the explanation of environmental destruction comes later. Methodologically, while Greens are hostile to positivism, not least because of its historical connection to the treating of 'nature' (including humans) as objects, purely instrumentally, there is no clearly identifiable 'Green' methodology. Eckersley (2004: 8–10) proposes 'critical political ecology' as a method for Green politics. But this turns out to be the method of immanent critique of Frankfurt School critical theory, with an ecological focus. Finally, Greens share with many other perspectives a rejection of any claimed separation of International Relations from other disciplines. As Chapter 1 suggests, the possibility of the emergence of a distinct Green perspective in International Relations has seen the breaking down of disciplinary boundaries.

Regarding other International Relations traditions, Green politics has a number of features in common with many other critical approaches. First, it shares the rejection of a hard and fast fact/value distinction with feminism, critical theory and poststructuralism, by making clear attempts to integrate normative and explanatory concerns. Its conception of theory is clearly incompatible with positivist conceptions which have such a clear distinction. Secondly, it shares an interest in resisting the concentration of power, the homogenizing forces in contemporary world politics and the preservation of difference and diversity with poststructuralism and feminism. Thirdly, it shares a critique of the states-system with critical theory and others, although it adopts a position which rejects the idea of global power structures emerging in correspondence with some idea of a 'global community' in favour of decentralizing power away from nation-states to more local levels. (For an account with many similarities to that of Linklater in relation to environmental politics, see Low and Gleeson 1998: Chapter 7. For a critique of such universalist thinking along the lines of the 'global ecology' writers discussed above, see Esteva and Prakash 1997.) While for critical theorists such as Linklater (1998), the idea of community at the global level is about balancing unity and diversity rather than one which wishes to create a homogeneous global identity, there is a much stronger sense in Green politics that community only makes sense at the very local level – the idea of a 'global community' is for Greens nonsensical, if not potentially totalitarian (Esteva and Prakash 1997). Nevertheless, there is a shared sense that the purpose of theory is to promote emancipation (Laferrière 1996; Laferrière and Stoett 1999). Allied to this normative rejection of the states-system is a rejection of a clear empirical split between domestic and international politics shared in particular with pluralists such as John Burton, but also with Marxists, critical theorists and feminists. Greens would not think it useful therefore to think for example in terms of 'levels of analysis', a form of thinking still prevalent in realism, as it arbitrarily divides up arenas of political action which should be seen as fundamentally interconnected. Finally, there is a clear focus on political economy, and the structural inequality inherent in modern capitalist economies also focused on by Marxists and dependency theorists.

However, in contrast in particular to poststructuralism, it shares to an extent an element of modernist theorizing, in the sense that Greens are clearly trying to understand the world in order to make it possible to improve it. For Hovden (1999), this makes it more compatible with Frankfurt School-type critical theory and feminism than with poststructuralism, as these both have a clear emancipatory normative goal, and in particular a clearer sense that their explanations or interpretations of the world are connected to a clear political project. This is linked to poststructuralism's rejection of foundationalism, which marks a clear difference from Green politics which necessarily relies on fairly strong foundational claims, of both the epistemological and ethical variety. However, this argument should not be pushed too far, as there are also tensions with the way in which critical theory tries to reconstruct Enlightenment rationality. Eckersley, for example (1992: Chapter 5), makes much of attempts by Habermas in particular (she contrasts Habermas to Marcuse) to reclaim science for radical political purposes, suggesting that it necessarily ends up justifying human domination of nature. I would ultimately concur with Mantle (1999), who argues that the closest connections which Green theory has to other approaches in International Relations are to feminism.

Green theory therefore clearly has its own distinctive perspective. The focus on humanity–nature relations and the adoption of an ecocentric ethic with regard to those relations, the focus on limits to growth, the particular perspective on the destructive side of development and the focus on decentralization away from the nation-state are all unique to Green politics. This chapter has illustrated how the purpose of Green theory within International Relations is to provide an explanation of the ecological crisis facing humanity, to focus on that crisis as possibly the most important issue for human societies to deal with, and to provide a normative basis for dealing with it.

Bibliography

Ackerly, B. A. (2001a) *Political Theory and Feminist Social Criticism* (Cambridge).
———— (2001b) 'Women's Human Rights Activists as Cross-Cultural Theorists', *International Journal of Feminist Politics*, 3(3).
Ackerly, A. and Okin, S. M. (1999) 'Feminist Social Criticism and the International Movement for Women's Rights as Human Rights', in I. Shapiro and C. Hacker-Cordon (eds), *Democracy's Edges* (Cambridge).
Ackerly, B., Stern, M. and True, J. (eds) (2006) *Feminist Methodologies for International Relations* (Cambridge).
Ackerly, B. and True, J. (2006) 'Studying the Struggles and Wishes of the Age: Feminist Theoretical Methodology and Feminist Theoretical Methods', in B. Ackerly, M. Stern and J. True (eds), *Feminist Methodologies for International Relations* (Cambridge).
Adler, E. and Barnett, M. (1998) *Security Communities* (Cambridge).
Afshar, H. and Dennis, C. (1992) *Women and Adjustment in the Third World* (London).
Agamben, G. (1998) *Homo Sacer: Sovereign Power and Bare Life* (Stanford).
Agathangelou, A. (2004) *The Global Political Economy of Sex: Desire, Violence and Insecurity in Mediterranean Nation States* (New York).
Amnesty International (1990) *Women in the Front Lines: Human Rights Violations Against Women* (London).
Anderson, P. (1974) *Lineages of the Absolutist State* (London).
———— (1983) *In the Tracks of Historical Materialism* (London).
Apel, K.-O. (1980) *Towards a Transformation of Philosophy* (London).
Appfel-Marglin, F. and Marglin, S. (eds) (1990) *Dominating Knowledge: Development, Culture and Resistance* (Oxford).
Arblaster, A. (1984) *The Rise and Decline of Western Liberalism* (Oxford).
Archibugi, D. (ed.) (1998) *Re-Imagining Political Community: Studies in Cosmopolitan Democracy* (Cambridge).
———— (2002) 'Demos and Cosmopolis', *New Left Review*, 13.
———— (2004a) 'Cosmopolitan Democracy and its Critics: A Review', *European Journal of International Relations*, 10(3).
———— (2004b) 'Cosmopolitan Guidelines for Humanitarian Intervention', *Alternatives*, 29(1).
Archibugi, D. and Held, D. (eds) (1995) *Cosmopolitan Democracy: An Agenda for a New World Order* (Cambridge).
Art, R. J. and Waltz, K. N. (1983) 'Technology, Strategy, and the Uses of Force', in R. J. Art and K. N. Waltz (eds), *The Use of Force* (Lanham).
Ashley, R. K. (1981) 'Political Realism and Human Interests', *International Studies Quarterly*, 25.
———— (1987) 'The Geopolitics of Geopolitical Space: Toward a Critical Social Theory of International Politics', *Alternatives*, 12(4).

———— (1988) 'Untying the Sovereign State: A Double Reading of the Anarchy Problematique', *Millennium*, 17(2).

———— (1989a) 'Living on Border Lines: Man, Poststructuralism and War', in J. Der Derian and M. J. Shapiro (eds), *International/Intertextual Relations: Postmodern Readings of World Politics* (Massachusetts).

———— (1989b) 'Imposing International Purpose: Notes on a Problematic of Governance', in E.-O. Czempiel and J. Rosenau (eds), *Global Changes and Theoretical Challenges: Approaches to World Politics for the 1990s* (Massachusetts).

Ashley, R. K. and. Walker, R. B. J. (1990) 'Speaking the Language of Exile: Dissidence in International Studies', *International Studies Quarterly*, 34(3).

Axelrod, R. (1984) *The Evolution of Cooperation* (New York).

Axelrod, R. and Keohane, R. O. (1986) 'Achieving Cooperation under Anarchy: Strategies and Institutions', in Kenneth A. Oye (ed.), *Cooperation under Anarchy* (Princeton). Reprinted in D. Baldwin (ed.) (1993), *Neorealism and Neoliberalism: The Contemporary Debate* (New York).

Bain, W. (2003) *Between Anarchy and Society* (Oxford).

Baines, E. K. (1999) 'Gender Construction and the Protection Mandate of the UNHCR: Responses from Guatemalan Women', in E. Prugl and M. K. Meyer (eds), *Gender Politics and Global Governance* (Lanham).

Bairoch, P. (1993) *Economic and World History* (Chicago).

Bakker, I. (ed.) (1994) *The Strategic Silence: Gender and Economic Policy* (London).

Banks, M. (1985) 'The Inter-Paradigm Debate', in M. Light and A. J. R. Groom (eds), *International Relations: A Handbook of Current Theory* (London).

Barnett, M. and Duvall, R. D. (2004) 'Power in World Politics', *International Organization*, 59(1).

Barnett, M. and Finnemore. M. (2004) *Rules for the World: International Organizations in Global Politics* (Ithaca).

Bar on, B. (2003) 'Manly After-Effects of 11 September 2001: Reading William J. Bennett's Why We Fight: Moral Clarity and the War on Terrorism', *International Feminist Journal of Politics*, 5(3).

Barry, J. (1995) 'Towards a Theory of the Green State', in S. Elworthy *et al.* (eds), *Perspectives on the Environment* 2 (Aldershot).

———— (1999) *Rethinking Green Politics: Nature, Virtue and Progress* (London).

Baylis, J. and Smith, S. (eds) (2005) *The Globalisation of World Politics* (Oxford).

Beitz, C. (1979) *Political Theory and International Relations* (Princeton).

Beneria, L. (ed.) (1982) *Women and Development: The Sexual Division of Labor in Rural Societies* (New York).

Benhabib, S. (1986) *Critique, Norm and Utopia: A Study of the Foundations of Critical Theory* (New York).

Benner, E. (1995) *Really Existing Nationalisms: A Post-Communist View from Marx and Engels* (Oxford).

Berman, J. (2003) '(Un)popular Strangers and Crises (Un)bounded: Discourses of Sex Trafficking, the European Political Community and the Panicked State of the Modern State', *European Journal of International Relations*, 9(1).

Bleiker, R. (2000) *Popular Dissent, Human Agency and Global Politics* (Cambridge).

Block, F. (1980) 'Beyond State Autonomy: State Managers as Historical Subjects', *Socialist Register*.

Block, F. and Somers, M. (1984) 'Beyond the Economistic Fallacy: The Holistic Social Science of Karl Polanyi', in T. Skocpol (ed.), *Vision and Method in Historical Sociology* (Cambridge).

Bohman, J. (2002) 'How to Make a Social Science Practical: Pragmatism, Critical Social Science and Multiperspectival Theory', *Millennium*, 31(3).

Bohman, J. and Lutz-Bachmann, M. (eds) (1997) *Perpetual Peace: Essays on Kant's Cosmopolitanism* (Cambridge).

Boli, J., Meyer, J. and Thomas, G. (1989) 'Ontology and Rationalization in the Western Cultural Account', in G. Thomas *et al.* (eds), *Institutional Structure: Constituting State, Society, and the Individual* (London).

Bookchin, M. (1980) *Toward an Ecological Society* (Montreal).

————— (1982) *The Ecology of Freedom: The Emergence and Dissolution of Hierarchy* (Palo Alto).

————— (1992) 'Libertarian Municipalism: An Overview', *Society and Nature*, 1(1).

Booth, D. (1998) *The Environmental Consequences of Growth: Steady-State Economics as an Alternative to Ecological Decline* (London).

Booth, K. (1991a) 'Security and Emancipation', *Review of International Studies*, 17(4).

————— (1991b) 'Security in Anarchy: Utopian Realism in Theory and Practice', *International Affairs*, 67(3).

————— (1997) 'A Reply to Wallace', *Review of International Studies*, 22(3).

Booth, K. and Dunne T. (eds) (2002) *Worlds in Collision: Terror and the Future of Global Order* (London).

Boris, E. and Prugl, E. (eds) (1996) *Homeworkers in Global Perspective* (New York).

Bottomore, T. B. and Goode, P. (1978) (eds) *Austro-Marxism* (Oxford).

Brewer, A. (1990) *Marxist Theories of Imperialism: A Survey* (London).

Bromley, S. (1999) 'Marxism and Globalisation', in A. Gamble *et al.* (eds), *Marxism and Social Science* (London).

Brown, C. J. (1988) 'The Modern Requirement: Reflections on Normative International Theory in a Post-European World', *Millennium*, 17(2).

————— (1992) 'Marxism and International Ethics', in T. Nardin and D. R. Napel (eds), *Traditions of International Ethics* (Cambridge).

————— (2002) *Understanding International Relations*, 2nd edition (Basingstoke).

Brunnee, J. and. Toope, S. J. (2000) 'International Law and Constructivism: Elements of an International Theory and of International Law', *Columbia Journal of Transnational Law*, 39(1).

Bryant, R. and Bailey, S. (eds) (1997) *Third World Political Ecology* (London).

Buck, S. J. (1998) *The Global Commons: An Introduction* (London).

Bukharin, N. (1972) *Imperialism and World Economy* (London).

Bull, H. (1966a) 'The Grotian Conception of International Society', in H. Butterfield and M. Wight (eds), *Diplomatic Investigations: Essays in the Theory of International Relations* (London).

———— (1966b) 'International Theory: The Case for a Classical Approach', *World Politics*, 18. Reprinted in K. Knorr and J. N. Rosenau (eds) (1969), *Contending Approaches to International Relations* (Princeton).

———— (1969/1995) 'The Theory of International Politics, 1919–1969', in B. Porter (ed.), *The Aberystwyth Papers* (London). Reprinted in J. Der Derian (ed.) (1995), *International Theory: Critical Investigations* (Basingstoke).

———— (1973) 'Foreign Policy of Australia', *Proceedings of Australian Institute of Political Science* (Sydney).

———— (1977) *The Anarchical Society: A Study of Order in World Politics* (London).

———— (1979a) 'Human Rights and World Politics', in R. Pettman (ed.), *Moral Claims in World Affairs* (London).

———— (1979b) 'The State's Positive Role in World Affairs', *Daedalus*, 108.

———— (1982) 'The West and South Africa', *Daedalus*, 111.

———— (1983) 'The International Anarchy in the 1980s', *Australian Outlook*, 37.

Bull, H. (ed.) (1984) *Intervention in World Politics* (Oxford).

———— (1984a) 'Justice in International Relations', *The Hagey Lectures, The University of Waterloo* (Ontario).

———— (1984b) 'The Revolt Against the West', in H. Bull and A. Watson (eds), *The Expansion of International Society* (Oxford).

Bull, H. and Watson, A. (eds) (1984) *The Expansion of International Society* (Oxford).

Bunyard, P. and Morgan-Grenville, F. (eds) (1987) *The Green Alternative* (London).

Burke, A. (2004) 'Just War or Ethical Peace? Moral Discourses of Strategic Violence After 9/11', *International Affairs*, 80(2).

Butler, J. (1990) *Gender Trouble: Feminist Subversions of Identity* (New York).

———— (2004) *Precarious Life: The Powers of Mourning and Violence* (London).

Butterfield, H. (1949) *Christianity and History* (London).

———— (1953) *Christianity, Diplomacy, and War* (London).

Butterfield, H. and Wight, M. (eds) (1966) *Diplomatic Investigations* (London).

Buzan, B. (2001) 'The English School: An Exploited Resource in IR', *Review of International Studies*, 27.

———— (2003) 'Implications for the Study of International Relations', in M. Buckley and R. Fawn (eds), *Global Responses to Terrorism* (London).

———— (2004) *From International Society to World Society? English School Theory and the Social Structure of Globalisation* (Cambridge).

Buzan, B., Jones, C. A. and Little, R. (1993) *The Logic of Anarchy: Neorealism to Structural Realism* (New York).

Buzan, B. and Little, R. (2000) *International Systems in World History: Remaking the Study of International Relations* (Oxford).

———— (2001) 'Why International Relations has Failed as a Project and What to Do about it', *Millennium*, 31(1).

Buzan, B. and Waever, O. (2003) *Regions and Powers: The Structure of International Security* (Cambridge).

Campbell, D. (1992) *Writing Security: United States Foreign Policy and the Politics of Identity* (Minneapolis).

———— (1994) 'The Deterritorializing of Responsibility: Levinas, Derrida and Ethics after the End of Philosophy', *Alternatives*, 19.

———— (1996) 'Political Prosaics, Transversal Politics, and the Anarchical World', in M. J. Shapiro and H. Alker (eds), *Challenging Boundaries: Global Flows, Territorial Identities* (Minneapolis).

———— (1998a) *National Deconstruction: Violence, Identity, and Justice in Bosnia* (Minneapolis).

———— (1998b) 'Why Fight? Humanitarianism, Principles, and Post-Structuralism', *Millennium*, 27(3).

———— (1999) 'Violence, Justice and Identity in the Bosnian Conflict', in J. Edkins, N. Persram and V. Pin-Fat (eds), *Sovereignty and Subjectivity* (Boulder).

———— (2002a) 'Time is Broken: The Return of the Past in the Response to September 11', *Theory and Event*, 5(4).

———— (2002b) 'Atrocity, Memory, Photography: Imaging the Concentration Camps of Bosnia – The Case of ITN versus Living Marxism, Part 2', *Journal of Human Rights*, 1(2).

Campbell, D. and Dillon, M. (1993) 'Introduction', in D. Campbell and M. Dillon (eds), *The Political Subject of Violence* (Manchester).

Caprioli, M. (2000) 'Gendered Conflict', *Journal of Peace Research*, 37.

———— (2004) 'Feminist IR Theory and Quantitative Methodology', *International Studies Review*, 6(2).

Caprioli, M. and Boyer, M. (2001) 'Gender, Violence, and International Crisis', *Journal of Conflict Resolution*, 45.

Carpenter, R. C. (2002) 'Gender Theory in World Politics: Contributions of a Nonfeminist Standpoint?', *International Studies Review*, 4(3).

Carr, E. H. (1939/1945/1946) *The Twenty Years' Crisis: 1919–1939: An Introduction to the Study of International Relations* (London).

———— (1945) *Nationalism and After* (New York).

———— (1953) 'The Marxist Attitude to War', in E. H. Carr, *A History of Soviet Russia, 3, The Bolshevik Revolution, 1917–23* (London).

Carter, A. (1993) 'Towards a Green Political Theory', in A. Dobson and P. Lucardie (eds), *The Politics of Nature: Explorations in Green Political Theory* (London).

Carver, T. (1998) *The PostModern Marx* (Manchester).

Chan-Tiberghien, J. (2004) 'Gender Scepticism or Gender Boom? Poststructural Feminisms, Transnational Feminisms and the World Conference Against Racism', *International Feminist Journal of Politics*, 6(3).

Chang, K. and Ling, L. H. M. (2000) 'Globalization and its Intimate Other: Filipina Domestic Workers in Hong Kong', in M. Marchand and A. S. Runyan (eds), *Gender and Global Restructuring: Sites, Sightings and Resistances* (New York).

Charlton, S. E., Everett, J. and Staudt, K. (eds) (1989) *Women, the State, and Development* (Albany).

Chatterjee, P. and Finger, M. (1994) *The Earth Brokers: Power, Politics and World Development* (London).

Chayes, A. and Chayes, A. H. (1993) 'On Compliance', *International Organization*, 47(2).

Chin, C. B. (1998) *In Service and Servitude: Foreign Female Domestic Workers and the Malaysian Modernity Project* (New York).

Chomsky, N. (1969) *American Power and the New Mandarins* (Harmondsworth).

———— (1994) *World Orders, Old and New* (London).

———— (1999a) *The New Military Humanism: Lessons from Kosovo* (London).

———— (1999b) *Profit Over People: Neoliberalism and the Global Order* (New York).

Christensen, T. J. and Snyder, J. (1990) 'Chain Gangs and Passed Bucks: Predicting Alliance Patterns in Multipolarity', *International Organization*, 44.

Christoff, P. (1996) 'Ecological Modernisation, Ecological Modernities', *Environmental Politics*, 5(3).

Clairmont, F. F. (1996) *The Rise and Fall of Economic Liberalism* (Penang).

Clark, A. M., Friedman, E. J. and Hochstetler, K. (1998) 'The Sovereign Limits of Global Civil Society: A Comparison of NGO Participation in UN World Conferences on the Environment, Human Rights, and Women', *World Politics*, 51.

Clark, I. (1989) *The Hierarchy of States* (Cambridge).

Cochran, M. (1999) *Normative Theory in International Relations: A Pragmatic Approach* (Cambridge).

Cockburn, C. (1998) *The Space Between Us: Negotiating Gender and National Identity in Conflict Zones* (London).

Cohen, J. (1990) 'Discourse Ethics and Civil Society', in D. Rasmussen (ed.), *Universalism vs Communitarianism* (Massachusetts).

Connell, R. J. (1990) 'The State and Gender Politics', *Theory and Society*, 19.

Connolly, W. (1991) 'Democracy and Territoriality', *Millennium*, 20(3).

———— (1994) 'Tocqueville, Territory and Violence', *Theory, Culture and Society*, 11.

———— (1995) *The Ethos of Pluralization* (Minneapolis).

Copeland, D. C. (1996) 'Neorealism and the Myth of Bipolar Stability: Toward a New Dynamic Realist Theory of Major War', *Security Studies*, 5.

Cox, R. W. (1981) 'Social Forces, States and World Orders: Beyond International Relations Theory', *Millennium*, 10(2).

———— (1983) 'Gramsci, Hegemony and International Relations', *Millennium*, 12(2).

———— (1986) 'Postscript 1985', in R. O. Keohane (ed.), *Neorealism and Its Critics* (New York).

———— (1987) *Production, Power and World Order: Social Forces in the Making of History* (New York).

———— (1989) 'Production, the State, and Change in World Order', in E.-O. Czempiel and J. Rosenau (eds), *Global Change and Theoretical Challenges* (Cambridge).

———— (1992a) 'Towards a Post-Hegemonic Conceptualization of World Order: Reflections on the Relevancy of Ibn Khaldun', in J. N. Rosenau and

E.-O. Czempiel (eds), *Governance Without Government: Order and Change in World Politics* (Cambridge).

———— (1992b) 'Multilateralism and World Order', *Review of International Studies*, 18.

———— (1993) 'Structural Issues of Global Governance: Implications for Europe', in S. Gill (ed.), *Gramsci, Historical Materialism and International Relations* (Cambridge).

———— (1994) 'Global Restructuring: Making Sense of the Changing International Political Economy', in R. Stubbs and G. Underhill (eds), *Political Economy and the Changing Global Order* (London).

———— (1999) 'Civil Society at the Turn of the Millennium: Prospects for an Alternative World Order', *Review of International Studies*, 25(1).

Cronin, B. (1999) *Community under Anarchy: Transnational Identity and the Evolution of Cooperation* (New York).

———— (2001) 'The Paradox of Hegemony: America's Ambiguous Relationship with the United Nations', *European Journal of International Relations*, 7(1).

Cummins, I. (1980) *Marx, Engels and National Movements* (London).

Cusack, T. R. and Stoll, R. J. (1990) *Exploring Realpolitik: Probing International Relations Theory with Computer Simulation* (Boulder).

Dalby, S. (1993) *Creating the Second Cold War: The Discourse of Politics* (London).

———— (1998) 'Ecological Metaphors of Security: World Politics in the Biosphere', *Alternatives*, 23(3).

———— (2004) 'Ecological Politics, Violence, and the Theme of Empire', *Global Environmental Politics*, 4(2).

Daly, H. E. (1990) 'Toward Some Operational Principles of Sustainable Development', *Ecological Economics*, 2(1).

Daly, H. E. and Cobb, J. B., Jr (1989) *For the Common Good* (Boston), 2nd edition (1994).

De Geus, M. (1995) 'The Ecological Restructuring of the State', in B. Doherty and M. de Geus (eds), *Democracy and Green Political Thought* (London).

Deleuze, G. and Guattari, F. (1977) *Anti-Oedipus: Capitalism and Schizophrenia* (New York).

———— (1987) *A Thousand Plateaus: Capitalism and Schizophrenia* (Minneapolis).

Der Derian, J. (1987) *On Diplomacy: A Genealogy of Western Estrangement* (Oxford).

———— (1989) 'The Boundaries of Knowledge and Power in International Relations', in J. Der Derian and M. J. Shapiro (eds), *International/Intertextual Relations: Postmodern Readings of World Politics* (Massachusetts).

———— (2002) 'The War of Networks', *Theory and Event*, 5(4).

Derrida, J. (1974) *Of Grammatology* (Baltimore).

———— (1978) *Writing and Difference* (Henley).

———— (1981) *Positions* (Chicago).

———— (1988) *Limited Inc.* (Evanston).

———— (1994a) 'Spectres of Marx', *New Left Review*, 205.

———— (1994b) *Spectres of Marx: The State of the Debt, the Work of Mourning and the New International* (London).

———— (2003) 'Autoimmunity: Real and Symbolic Suicides – A Dialogue with Jacques Derrida', in G. Borradori (ed.), *Philosophy in a Time of Terror: Dialogues with Jürgen Habermas and Jacques Derrida* (Chicago).

Deutsch, K. W. and Singer, J. D. (1964) 'Multipolar Power Systems and International Stability', *World Politics*, 16.

Devetak, R. (1995a) 'Incomplete States: Theories and Practices of Statecraft', in J. MacMillan and A. Linklater (eds), *Boundaries in Question: New Directions in International Relations* (London).

———— (1995b) 'The Project of Modernity and International Relations Theory', *Millennium*, 24(1).

———— (2002) 'Signs of a New Enlightenment? Concepts of Community and Humanity after the Cold War', in S. Lawson (ed.), *The New Agenda for International Relations: From Polarization to Globalization in World Politics* (Cambridge).

———— (2003) 'Loyalty and Plurality: Images of the Nation in Australia', in M. Waller and A. Linklater (eds), *Political Loyalty and the Nation-State* (London).

———— (2005) 'Violence, Order and Terror', in A. Bellamy (ed.), *International Society and Its Critics* (Oxford).

Devetak, R. and Higgott, R. (1999) 'Justice Unbound? Globalization, States and the Transformation of the Social Bond', *International Affairs*, 75(3).

Dillon, M. (1999) 'The Sovereign and the Stranger', in J. Edkins, N. Persram and V. Pin-Fat (eds), *Sovereignty and Subjectivity* (Boulder).

Dillon, M. and Everard, J. (1992) 'Stat(e)ing Australia: Squid Jigging and the Masque of State', *Alternatives*, 17(3).

Dillon, M. and Reid, J. (2000) 'Global Governance, Liberal Peace, and Complex Emergency', *Alternatives*, 25(1).

Dobson, A. (1990) *Green Political Thought* (London).

———— (2003) *Citizenship and the Environment* (Oxford).

Doherty, B. and de Geus, M. (1994) 'Introduction', in B. Doherty and M. de Geus (eds), *Democracy and Green Political Thought* (London).

Donnelly, J. (1992) 'Twentieth Century Realism', in T. Nardin and D. Mapel (eds), *Traditions of International Ethics* (Cambridge).

———— (1995) 'Realism and the Academic Study of International Relations', in J. Farr, J. S. Dryzek and S. T. Leonard (eds), *Political Science in History: Research Programs and Political Traditions* (Cambridge).

———— (2000) *Realism and International Relations* (Cambridge).

Doran, P. (1993) 'The Earth Summit (UNCED): Ecology as Spectacle', *Paradigms*, 7(1).

———— (1995) 'Earth, Power, Knowledge: Towards a Critical Global Environmental Politics', in J. MacMillan and A. Linklater (eds), *New Directions in International Relations* (London).

Doty, R. L. (1999) 'Racism, Desire, and the Politics of Immigration', *Millennium*, 28(3).

Douthwaite, R. (1992) *The Growth Illusion* (Dublin).

Doyle, M. (1983) 'Kant, Liberal Legacies and Foreign Affairs', *Philosophy and Public Affairs*, 12.

————— (1986) 'Liberalism and World Politics', *American Political Science Review*, 80.

————— (1995) 'Liberalism and World Politics Revisited', in C. W. Kegley Jr (ed.), *Controversies in International Relations Theory* (New York).

————— (1997) *Ways of War and Peace: Realism, Liberalism and Socialism* (New York).

Dryzek, J. (1987) *Rational Ecology: Environment and Political Economy* (Oxford).

————— (1990) *Discursive Democracy: Politics, Policy, and Political Science* (Cambridge).

————— (1992) 'Ecology and Discursive Democracy: Beyond Liberal Capitalism and the Administrative State', *Capitalism, Nature, Socialism*, 3(2).

————— (1999) 'Transnational Democracy', *Journal of Political Philosophy*, 7(1).

Dunne, T. (1998) *Inventing International Society: A History of the English School* (Basingstoke).

————— (2003) 'Society and Hierarchy in International Relations', *International Relations*, 17.

Dunne, T. and Wheeler, N. J. (eds) (1999) *Human Rights in Global Politics* (Cambridge).

Eckersley, R. (1992) *Environmentalism and Political Theory: Towards an Ecocentric Approach* (London).

————— (2004) *The Green State: Rethinking Democracy and Sovereignty* (Massachusetts).

Edkins, J. (2000) 'Sovereign Power, Zones of Indistinction, and the Camp', *Alternatives*, 25(1).

————— (2002) 'Forget Trauma? Responses to September 11', *International Relations*, 16(2).

Edkins, J. and Pin-Fat, V. (1999) 'The Subject of the Political', in J. Edkins, N. Persram and V. Pin-Fat (eds), *Sovereignty and Subjectivity* (Boulder).

Ekins, P. (1983) 'Making Development Sustainable', in W. Sachs (ed.), *Global Ecology* (London).

Elshtain, J. B. (1985) 'Reflections on War and Political Discourse: Realism, Just War, and Feminism in a Nuclear Age', *Political Theory*, 13.

————— (1987) *Women and War* (New York).

————— (1992) 'Sovereignty, Identity, Sacrifice', in V. S. Peterson (ed.), in *Gendered States: Feminist (Re)visions of International Relations Theory* (Boulder).

Emmanuel, A. (1972) *Unequal Exchange: A Study of the Imperialism of Trade* (New York).

Emy, H. V. (1993) *Remaking Australia* (Melbourne).

Enloe, C. (1989) *Bananas, Beaches, and Bases: Making Feminist Sense of International Politics* (London).

————— (1994) *The Morning After: Sexual Politics at the End of the Cold War* (Berkeley).

————— (1997) 'Margins, Silences, and Bottom-Rungs: How to Overcome the Underestimation of Power in the Study of International Relation', in S. Smith, K. Booth and M. Zalewski (eds), *International Theory: Positivism and Beyond* (Cambridge).

————— (2000) *Manoeuvers: The International Politics of Militarizing Women's Lives* (Berkeley).

Eschle, C. and Maiguaschca, B. (eds) (2005) *Critical Theories, World Politics, and the 'Anti-Globalization Movement'* (London).

Escobar, A. (1995) *Encountering Development: The Making and Unmaking of the Third World* (Princeton).

Escudé, C. (1997) *Foreign Policy Theory in Menem's Argentina* (Gainesville).

Esteva, G. and Prakash, M. S. (1997) 'From Global Thinking to Local Thinking', in M. Rahnema (ed.) with V. Bawtree, *The Post-Development Reader* (London), originally in *Interculture*, 29(2) (1996).

Fierke, K. M. (1998) *Changing Games, Changing Strategies: Critical Investigations in Security* (Manchester).

Finger, M. (1993) 'Politics of the UNCED Process', in W. Sachs (ed.), *Global Ecology* (London).

Finnemore, M. (1996) 'Norms, Culture, and World Politics: Insights from Sociology's Institutionalism', *International Organization*, 50(2).

Finnemore, M. and Toope, S. J. (2001) 'Alternatives to "Legalization": Richer Views of Law and Politics', *International Organization*, 55(3).

Forbes, I. and Hoffman, M. (eds) (1993) *Political Theory, International Relations and the Ethics of Intervention* (Basingstoke).

Forde, S. (1992) 'Classical Realism', in T. Nardin and D. Mapel (eds), *Traditions of International Ethics* (Cambridge).

Forum on Chomsky, *Review of International Studies*, 29(4).

Foucault, M. (1977) *Discipline and Punish* (Harmondsworth).

————— (1987) 'Nietzsche, Genealogy, History', in M. T. Gibbons (ed.), *Interpreting Politics* (London).

————— (2003) 'Society Must be Defended': Lectures at the Collège de France, 1975–1976 (New York).

Frank, A. G. (1967) *Capitalism and Underdevelopment in Latin America* (New York).

Friedman, E. (1995) 'Women's Human Rights: The Emergence of a Movement', in J. Peters and A. Wolper (eds), *Women's Rights/Human Rights: International Feminist Perspectives* (New York).

Friedman, G. (1981) *The Political Philosophy of the Frankfurt School* (New York).

Friedman, T. (2000) *The Lexus and the Olive Tree* (London).

Fukuyama, F. (1992) *The End of History and the Last Man* (London).

————— (2002) 'History and September 11', in K. Booth and T. Dunne (eds), *Worlds in Collision* (London).

Gabriel, C. and Macdonald, L. (1994) 'Women's Transnational Organizing in the Context of NAFTA: Forging Feminist Internationality', *Millennium*, 23(3).

Gaddis, J. (1992–3) 'International Relations Theory and the End of the Cold War', *International Security*, 15, 5–53.

Gallie, W. B. (1978) *Philosophers of Peace and War* (Cambridge).

Gamble, A. (1981) *An Introduction to Modern Social and Political Thought* (London).

———— (1999) 'Marxism after Communism: Beyond Realism and Historicism', *Review of International Studies*, 25.

Gardner, R. N. (1990) 'The Comeback of Liberal Internationalism', *The Washington Quarterly*, 13(3).

Garnett, J. C. (1984) *Commonsense and the Theory of International Politics* (London).

Gatens, M. (1991) *Feminism and Philosophy* (Bloomington).

Gellner, E. (1974) *Legitimation of Belief* (Cambridge).

George, J. (1994) *Discourses of Global Politics: A Critical (Re)Introduction* (Boulder).

George, J. and Campbell, D. (1990) 'Patterns of Dissent and the Celebration of Difference: Critical Social Theory and International Relations', *International Studies Quarterly*, 34(3).

Gibson, K., Law, L. and McKay, D. (2001) 'Beyond Heroes and Victims: Filipina Contract Migrants, Economic Activism and Class Transformations', *International Feminist Journal of Politics*, 3(3).

Giddens, A. (1981) *A Contemporary Critique of Historical Materialism* (London).

———— (1985) *The Nation-State and Violence* (Cambridge).

Gill, S. (ed.) (1993a) *Gramsci, Historical Materialism and International Relations* (Cambridge).

———— (1993b) 'Gramsci and Global Politics: Towards a Post-Hegemonic Research Agenda', in S. Gill, *Gramsci, Historical Materialism and International Relations* (Cambridge).

———— (1995) 'Globalisation, Market Civilisation and Disciplinary Neo-Liberalism', *Millennium*, 24(4).

———— (1996) 'Globalization, Democratization, and the Politics of Indifference', in J. Mittelman (ed.), *Globalization: Critical Reflections* (Boulder).

Gilligan, C. (1982) *In a Different Voice: Psychological Theory and Women's Development* (Cambridge).

Gilpin, R. G. (1986) 'The Richness of the Tradition of Political Realism', in R. O. Keohane (ed.), *Neo-Realism and Its Critics* (New York).

———— (1996) 'No One Loves a Political Realist,' *Security Studies*, 5.

Glaser, C. L. (1997) 'The Security Dilemma Revisited,' *World Politics*, 50.

Glaser, C. L. and Kaufmann, C. (1998) 'What is the Offense–Defense Balance and Can We Measure It?', *International Security*, 22.

Goetz, A.-M. (1991) 'Feminism and the Claim to Know: Contradictions in Feminist Approaches to Women in Development', in R. Grant and K. Newland (eds), *Gender and International Relations* (London).

Goldstein, J. (2001) *War and Gender* (Cambridge).

Gong, G. (1984) *The Standard of Civilisation in International Society* (Oxford).

Goodin, R. (1992) *Green Political Theory* (Cambridge).

Gouldner, A. (1980) *The Two Marxisms: Contradictions and Anomalies in the Development of Theory* (New York).

Grant, R. and Newland, K. (eds) (1991) *Gender and International Relations* (London).

Gray, J. (2004) *Al Qaeda and What It Means To Be Modern* (London).

Grieco, J. M. (1988) 'Anarchy and the Limits of Cooperation', *International Organization*, 42(3).

―――― (1997) 'Realist International Theory and the Study of World Politics', in M. W. Doyle and G. J. Ikenberry (eds), *New Thinking in International Relations Theory* (Boulder).

Gulick, E. V. (1967) *Europe's Classical Balance of Power: A Case History of the Theory and Practice of One of the Great Concepts of European Statecraft* (New York).

Guzzini, S. (1998) *Realism in International Relations and International Political Economy: The Continuing Story of a Death Foretold* (London).

Haas, P. M. (1990) *Saving the Mediterranean: The Politics of International Environmental Cooperation* (New York).

Haas, P. M., Keohane, R. O. and Levy, M. A. (1993) *Institutions for the Earth: Sources of Effective Environmental Protection* (Massachusetts).

Habermas, J. (1979) *Communication and the Evolution of Society* (Boston).

―――― (1984) *The Theory of Communicative Action, 1: Reason and the Rationalization of Society* (Cambridge).

―――― (1987) *The Philosophical Discourse of Modernity: Twelve Lectures* (Cambridge).

―――― (1990) *Moral Consciousness and Communicative Action* (Cambridge).

―――― (1993) *Justification and Application: Remarks on Discourse Ethics* (Cambridge).

―――― (1994) *The Past as Future* (Cambridge).

―――― (1997) 'Kant's Idea of Perpetual Peace, with the Benefit of Two Hundred Years' Hindsight', in J. Bohman and M. Lutz-Bachmann (eds), *Perpetual Peace: Essays on Kant's Cosmopolitan Ideal* (London).

―――― (1998) *The Inclusion of the Other: Studies in Political Theory* (Cambridge).

―――― (2003) 'Interpreting the Fall of a Monument', *Constellations*, 10(3).

Habermas, J. and Derrida, J. (2003) 'February 15, or What Binds Europeans Together: A Plea for a Common Foreign Policy, Beginning in the Core of Europe', *Constellations*, 10(3).

Hajer, M. (1995) *The Politics of Environmental Discourse: Ecological Modernisation and the Policy Process* (Oxford).

Hall, R. B. (1999) *National Collective Identity: Social Constructs and International Systems* (New York).

Halliday, F. (1983) *The Making of the Second Cold War* (London).

―――― (1988a) 'Three Concepts of Internationalism', *International Affairs*, 64.

―――― (1988b) 'Hidden from International Relations: Women and the International Arena', *Millennium*, 17(3).

―――― (1990) 'The Pertinence of International Relations', *Political Studies*, 38(1).

Halliday, F. (1994) *Rethinking International Relations* (London).

———— (1999) *Revolution and World Politics: The Rise and Fall of the Fifth Great Power* (Basingstoke).

Hanochi, S. (2003) 'Constitutionalism in a Modern Patriarchal State: Japan, the Sex Sector and Social Reproduction', in I. Bakker and S. Gill (eds), *Power, Production and Social Reproduction* (Basingstoke).

Hardin, G. (1968) 'The Tragedy of the Commons', *Science*, 162.

———— (1974) 'The Ethics of a Lifeboat', *BioScience*.

Harding, S. (1986) *The Science Question in Feminism* (Ithaca).

———— (1987) *Feminism and Methodology* (Bloomington).

Harvey, D. (2003) *The New Imperialism* (Oxford).

Havel, V. (1999) 'Speech on Kosovo', *The New York Review of Books*, June 10.

Hay, C. (1999) 'Marxism and the State', in A. Gamble *et al.* (eds), *Marxism and Social Science* (London).

Hayward, T. (1995) *Ecological Thought: An Introduction* (Cambridge).

———— (1998) *Political Theory and Ecological Values* (Cambridge).

Heilbroner, R. (1974) *An Inquiry into the Human Prospect* (New York).

Held, D. (1995) *Democracy and the Global Order: From the Modern State to Cosmopolitan Democracy* (Cambridge).

Held, D. (ed.) (1993) *Prospects for Democracy: North, South, East, West* (Cambridge).

Held, D. and McGrew, A. (eds), *The Global Transformations Reader* (Cambridge).

Held, D., McGrew, A., Goldblatt, D. and Perraton, J. (1999) *Global Transformations* (Cambridge).

Helleiner, E. (1996) 'International Political Economy and the Greens', *New Political Economy*, 1(1).

———— (2000) 'New Voices in the Globalization Debate: Green Perspectives on the World Economy', in R. Stubbs and G. Underhill (eds), *Political Economy and the Changing Global Order*, 2nd edition (Oxford).

Helman, G. B. and Ratner, S. R. (1992–3) 'Saving Failed States', *Foreign Policy*, 89.

Hempel, L. (1996) *Environmental Governance: The Global Challenge* (Washington).

Herz, J. H. (1976) *The Nation-State and the Crisis of World Politics: Essays on International Politics in the Twentieth Century* (New York).

Hildyard, N. (1993) 'Foxes in Charge of the Chickens', in W. Sachs (ed.), *Global Ecology* (London).

Hill, C. J. (1999) 'Where are we Going? International Relations, the Voice from Below', *Review of International Studies*, 25(1).

———— (2003) *The Changing Politics of Foreign Policy* (Basingstoke).

Hirst, P. and Thompson, G. (1996) *Globalisation in Question: The International Economy and the Possibilities of Governance* (Cambridge).

Hobsbawm, E. (2000) *The New Century* (London).

———— (2002) The Observer, 22 September, http://www.observer.co.uk/comment/story/0,6903,796531,00.html

Hoffman, M. (1987) 'Critical Theory and the Inter-Paradigm Debate', *Millennium*, 16(2).

———— (1991) 'Restructuring, Reconstruction, Reinscription, Rearticulation: Four Voices in Critical International Theory', *Millennium*, 20(2).

———— (1992) 'Third-Party Mediation and Conflict-Resolution in the Post-Cold War World', in J. Baylis and N. Rengger (eds), *Dilemmas of World Politics* (Oxford).

———— (1993) 'Agency, Identity and Intervention', in I. Forbes and M. Hoffman (eds), *Political Theory, International Relations and the Ethics of Intervention* (London).

Hoffmann, S. (1990) 'International Society', in J. D. B. Miller and R. J. Vincent (eds), *Order and Violence: Hedley Bull and International Relations* (Oxford).

———— (1995) 'The Crisis of Liberal Internationalism', *Foreign Policy*, 98.

Hollis, M. and Smith S. (1990) *Explaining and Understanding International Relations* (Oxford).

Holsti, K. (1985) *The Dividing Discipline: Hegemony and Diversity in International Theory* (Boston).

Hooper, C. (2000) *Manly States: Masculinities, International Relations, and Gender Politics* (New York).

Hopf, T. (1998) 'The Promise of Constructivism in International Relations Theory', *International Security*, 23(1).

Horkheimer, M. (1972) *Critical Theory* (New York).

Horkheimer, M. and Adorno, T. (1972) *Dialectic of Enlightenment* (New York).

Hoskyns, C. (1996) *Integrating Gender: Women, Law and Politics in the European Union* (London).

Hovden, E. (1999) 'As if Nature doesn't Matter: Ecology, Regime Theory and International Relations', *Environmental Politics*, 8(2).

Howard, M. (1978) *War and the Liberal Conscience* (Oxford).

Humphreys, D., Paterson, M. and Pettiford, L. (eds) (2003) 'Global Environmental Governance for the 21st Century', *Global Environmental Politics*, Special Issue, 3(2).

Huntington, S. (1993) 'The Clash of Civilisations', *Foreign Affairs*, 72.

Hurrell, A. (1994) 'A Crisis of Ecological Viability – Global Environmental Change and the Nation-State', *Political Studies*, Special Issue, 42.

———— (2002) 'There are no Rules (George W. Bush): International Order after September 11', *International Relations*, 16.

Hurrell, A. and Kingsbury, B. (1992) *The International Politics of the Environment* (Oxford).

Hutchings, K. (1999) *International Political Theory: Rethinking Ethics in a Global Era* (London).

———— (2000) 'Towards a Feminist International Ethics', *Review of International Studies*, Special Issue, 26.

Ikenberry, J. G. (2000) *After Victory* (Princeton).

IUCN (1980) *World Conservation Strategy* (Gland).

Jackson, R. (1990) *Quasi-States: Sovereignty, International Relations and the Third World* (Cambridge).

Jackson, R. (2000) *The Global Covenant: Human Conduct in a World of States* (Oxford).

Jacoby, T. (1999) 'Feminism, Nationalism and Difference: Reflections on the Palestinian Women's Movement', *Women's Studies International Forum*, 22(5).

Jaquette, J. (1984) 'Power as Ideology: A Feminist Analysis', in J. H. Stiehm (ed.), *Women's Views of the Political World of Men* (Dobbs Ferry).

Jay, M. (1973) *The Dialectical Imagination* (Boston).

Jeffery, L. A. (2002) *Sex and Borders: Gender, National Identity and Prostitution Policy in Thailand* (Basingstoke).

Jepperson, R., Wendt, A. and Katzenstein, P. J. (1996) 'Norms, Identity, and Culture in National Security', in Peter J. Katzenstein (ed.), *The Culture of National Security: Norms and Identity in World Politics* (New York).

Jervis, R. (1978) 'Cooperation under the Security Dilemma,' *World Politics*, 30.

———— (1998) 'Realism in the Study of World Politics,' *International Organization*, 52.

Johnson, C. (2002) *Blowback*, 2nd edition (London).

Johnston, A. I. (1995) *Cultural Realism: Strategic Culture and Grand Strategy in Chinese History* (Princeton).

Jones, D. (1999) *Cosmopolitan Mediation? Conflict Resolution and the Oslo Accords* (Manchester).

———— (2001) 'Creating Cosmopolitan Power: International Mediation as Communicative Action', in R. Wyn Jones (ed.), *Critical Theory and World Politics* (Boulder).

Jones, R. E. (1981) 'The English School of International Relations: A Case for Closure', *Review of International Studies*, 7(1).

Kabeer, N. (1994) *Reversed Realities: Gender Hierarchies in Development Thought* (London).

Kahler, M. (1997) 'Inventing International Relations: International Relations Theory After 1945', in M. W. Doyle and G. J. Ikenberry (eds), *New Thinking in International Relations Theory* (Boulder).

Kant, I. (1970) *Kant's Political Writings*, ed. H. Reiss, trans H. Nisbet (Cambridge).

Kapstein, E. and Mastanduno, M. (eds) (1999) *Unipolar Politics: Realism and State Strategies after the Cold War* (New York).

Kardam, N. (1991) *Bringing Women in: Women's Issues in International Development Programs* (Boulder).

———— (2004) 'The Emerging Global Gender Equality Regime from Neoliberal and Constructivist Perspectives in International Relations', *International Feminist Journal of Politics*, 6(1).

Kassiola, J. J. (2003) 'Afterword: The Surprising Value of Despair and the Aftermath of September 11th', in Jo. J. Kassiola (ed.), *Explorations in Environmental Political Theory* (Armonk).

Katzenstein, P. J. (1996) *Cultural Norms and National Security: Police and Military in Postwar Japan* (Ithaca).

———— (1999) *Tamed Power: Germany in Europe* (Ithaca).

Katzenstein, P. J. and Okawara, N. (2001/2) 'Japan, Asian-Pacific Security, and the Case for Analytical Eclecticism', *International Security*, 26(3).

Keal, P. (1983) *Unspoken Rules and Superpower Dominance* (London).

———— (2003) *European Conquest and the Rights of Indigenous Peoples: The Moral Backwardness of International Society* (Cambridge).

Keck, M. and Sikkink, K. (1998) *Activist Beyond Borders* (Ithaca).

Keene, E. (2005) *International Political Thought: An Historical Introduction* (Cambridge).

Kennan, G. F. (1954) *Realities of American Foreign Policy* (Princeton).

———— (1985/6) 'Morality and Foreign Policy,' *Foreign Affairs*, 63.

Keohane, R. O. (1984) *After Hegemony: Cooperation and Discord in the World Political Economy* (Princeton).

———— (1986) 'Theory of World Politics: Structural Realism and Beyond', in R. O. Keohane (ed.), *Neo-Realism and Its Critics* (New York).

———— (1988) 'International Institutions: Two Approaches', *International Studies Quarterly*, 32(4).

———— (1989a) *International Institutions and State Power: Essays in International Relations Theory* (Boulder).

———— (1989b) 'International Relations Theory: Contributions of a Feminist Standpoint', *Millennium*, 18(2).

Keohane, R. O. and Nye, J. (eds) (1972) *Transnationalism and World Politics* (Massachusetts).

———— (1977) *Power and Interdependence: World Politics in Transition* (Boston).

Kier, E. (1997) *Imagining War: French and British Military Doctrine Between the Wars* (Princeton).

Kissinger, H. A. (1957) *A World Restored: Metternich, Castlereagh and the Problems of Peace, 1812–22* (Boston).

———— (1977) *American Foreign Policy* (New York).

Klein, B. (1994) *Strategic Studies and World Order: The Global Politics of Deterrence* (Cambridge).

Klotz, A. (1995) *Norms in International Relations: The Struggle Against Apartheid* (Ithaca).

Knei-Paz, B. (1978) *The Social and Political Thought of Leon Trotsky* (Oxford).

Korac, M. (1998) 'Ethnic Nationalism, War and the Patterns of Social, Political and Sexual Violence against Women: The Case of Post-Yugoslav Countries', *Identities*, 5(2).

Koslowski, R. and Kratochwil, F. (1995) 'Understanding Change in International Politics: The Soviet Empire's Demise and the International System', in R. N. Lebow and T. Risse-Kappen (eds), *International Relations Theory after the Cold War* (New York).

Kothari, A. (1992) 'The Politics of the Biodiversity Convention', *Economic and Political Weekly*, 27.

Krasner, S. D. (1999) *Sovereignty: Organized Hypocrisy* (Princeton).

Kratochwil, F. (1988/9) 'Regimes, Interpretation and the "Science" of Politics: A Reappraisal', *Millennium*, 17(2).

———— (1993) 'The Embarrassment of Changes: Neo-realism as the Science of Realpolitik Without Politics', *Review of International Studies*, 19(1).

Kratochwil, F. (2000) 'Constructing a New Orthodoxy? Wendt's' "Social Theory of International Politics and the Constructivionist Challenge",' *Millennium: Journal of International Studies*, 29(1).

Kratochwil, F. and Ruggie, J. G. (1986) 'International Organization: A State of the Art on an Art of the State?', *International Organization* 40(4).

Krippendorff, E. (1982) *International Relations as a Social Science* (Brighton).

Kubalkova, V. and Cruickshank, A. (1980) *Marxism–Leninism and the Theory of International Relations* (London).

Kuehls, T. (1996) *Beyond Sovereign Territory: The Space of Ecopolitics* (Minneapolis).

Labs, E. J. (1997) 'Beyond Victory: Offensive Realism and the Expansion of War Aims', *Security Studies* 6.

Laferrière, E. (1996) 'Emancipating International Relations Theory: An Ecological Perspective', *Millennium*, 25(1).

Laferrière, E. and Stoett, P. (1999) *Ecological Thought and International Relations Theory* (London).

Laffey, M. and Weldes, J. (1997) 'Beyond Belief: Ideas and Symbolic Technologies in the Study of International Relations', *European Journal of International Relations*, 3(2).

Layne, C. (1993) 'The Unipolar Illusion: Why New Great Powers Will Arise', *International Security*, 17.

Lee, K. (1993) 'To De-Industrialize – Is it so Irrational?', in A. Dobson and P. Lucardie (eds), *The Politics of Nature: Explorations in Green Political Theory* (London).

Lenin, V. (1964) *Collected Works*, 20 (Moscow).

———— (1968) *Imperialism: The Highest Stage of Capitalism* (Moscow).

Levinas, E. (1969) *Totality and Infinity: An Essay on Exteriority* (Pittsburgh).

Levy, J. S. (1989) The Causes of War: A Review of Theories and Evidence, in P. E. Tetlock (ed.) (1989), *Behaviour, Society and Nuclear War* (New York).

Ling, L. H. (2001) *Post-colonial IR: Conquest and Desire between Asia and the West* (London).

Linklater, A. (1990a) *Men and Citizens in the Theory of International Relations*, 2nd edition (London).

———— (1990b) *Beyond Realism and Marxism: Critical Theory and International Relations* (London).

———— (1992a) 'The Question of the Next Stage in International Relations Theory: A Critical Theoretical Point of View', *Millennium* 21(1).

———— (1992b) 'What is a Good International Citizen?', in P. Keal, *Ethics and Foreign Policy* (Canberra).

———— (1993) 'Liberal Democracy, Constitutionalism and the New World Order', in R. Leaver and J. L. Richardson (eds), *Charting the Post-Cold War Order* (Colorado).

———— (1997) 'The Achievements of Critical Theory', in S. Smith, K. Booth and M. Zalewski (eds), *International Theory: Positivism and Beyond* (Cambridge).

———— (1998) *The Transformation of Political Community; Ethical Foundations of the Post-Westphalian Era* (Cambridge).

———— (1999) 'Transforming Political Community: A Response to the Critics', *Review of International Studies*, 25(1).

———— (2001) 'Citizenship, Humanity and Cosmopolitan Harm Conventions', *International Political Science Review*, 22(3).

———— (2002a) 'The Problem of Harm in World Politics: Implications for the Sociology of States-Systems', *International Affairs*, 78(8).

———— (2002b) 'Unnecessary Suffering', in K. Booth and T. Dunne (eds), *Worlds in Collision: Terror and the Future of Global Order* (London).

Linklater, A. and Suganami, H. (2006) *The English School of International Relations: A Contemporary Assessment* (Cambridge).

Lipschutz, R. D. (1997) 'From Place to Planet: Local Knowledge and Global Environmental Governance', *Global Governance*, 3(1).

Lisle, D. (2000) 'Consuming Danger: Reimagining the War/Tourism Divide', *Alternatives*, 25(1).

Litfin, (ed.) (1998) *The Greening of Sovereignty in World Politics* (Cambridge, MA).

Little, R. (2000) 'The English School's Contribution to the Study of International Relations', *European Journal of International Relations*, 6.

Locher, B. and Prugl, E. (2001) 'Feminism and Constructivism: Worlds Apart or Sharing the Middle Ground?', *International Studies Quarterly*, 45(1).

Long, D. and Wilson, P. (eds) (1995) *Thinkers of the Twenty Years' Crisis* (Oxford).

Low, N. and Gleeson, B. (1998) *Justice, Nature and Society* (London).

Luke, T. L. (1997) *Ecocritique: Contesting the Politics of Nature, Economy, and Culture* (Minneapolis).

Lukes, S. (1985) *Marxism and Morality* (Oxford).

Lynch, C. (1999) *Beyond Appeasement: Reinterpreting Interwar Peace Movements in World Politics* (Ithaca).

Lynch, M. (1999) *State Interests and Public Spheres: The International Politics of Jordanian Identity* (New York).

———— (2000) 'The Dialogue of Civilisations and International Public Spheres', *Millennium*, 29(2).

Lynn-Jones, S. M. (1995) 'Offense–Defense Theory and Its Critics', *Security Studies*, 4.

Lyotard, J.-F. (1984) *The PostModern Condition: A Report on Knowledge* (Manchester).

———— (1993) 'The Other's Rights', in S. Shute and S. Hurley (eds), *On Human Rights: The Oxford Amnesty Lectures* (New York).

Machiavelli, N. (1970) *The Discourses* (Harmondsworth).

———— (1985) *The Prince* (Chicago).

Mackie, V. (2001) 'The Language of Globalization, Transnationality, and Feminism', *International Feminist Journal of Politics*, 3(2).

Maclean, J. (1981) 'Marxist Epistemology, Explanations of "Change" and the Study of International Relations', in B. Buzan and R. B. Jones (eds), *Change in the Study of International Relations: The Evaded Dimension* (London).

MacMillan, J. (1995) 'A Kantian Protest Against the Peculiar Discourse of Inter-Liberal State Peace', *Millennium*, 24(4).

MacPherson, C. B. (1973) *Democratic Theory* (Oxford).
———— (1977) *The Life and Times of Liberal Democracy* (Oxford).
Magnusson, W. (1996) *The Search for Political Space: Globalization, Social Movements and the Urban Political Experience* (Toronto).
Maiguaschca, B. (2003) 'Introduction: Governance and Resistance in World Politics', *Review of International Studies*, 29.
Mantle, D. (1999) *Critical Green Political Theory and International Relations Theory – Compatibility or Conflict*, PhD thesis, Keele University.
Maoz, Z. and Russett, B. (1993) 'Normative and Structural Causes of Democratic Peace, 1946–1986', *American Political Science Review*, 87(3).
Marchand, M. and Runyan, A. S. (eds) (2000) *Gender and Global Restructuring: Sites, Sightings and Resistances* (New York).
Marx, K. (1966) *The Poverty of Philosophy* (Moscow).
———— (1973) *Grundrisse* (Harmondsworth).
———— (1977a) 'Capital', 1, in D. McLellan (ed.), *Karl Marx: Selected Writings* (Oxford).
———— (1977b) 'Theses on Feuerbach', in D. McLellan (ed.), *Karl Marx: Selected Writings* (Oxford).
———— (1977c) 'Towards A Critique of Hegel's Philosophy of Right: Introduction', in D. McLellan (ed.), *Karl Marx: Selected Writings* (Oxford).
———— (1977d) 'Economic and Philosophical Manuscripts', in D. McLellan (ed.), *Karl Marx: Selected Writings* (Oxford).
———— (1977e) 'The Eighteenth Brumaire of Louis Bonaparte', in D. McLellan (ed.), *Karl Marx: Selected Writings* (Oxford).
Marx, K. and Engels, F. (1971) *Ireland and the Irish Question* (London).
———— (1977) 'The Communist Manifesto', in D. McLellan (ed.), *Karl Marx: Selected Writings* (Oxford).
Mastanduno, M. (1991) 'Do Relative Gains Matter? America's Response to Japanese Industrial Policy,' *International Security*, 16.
———— (1997) 'Preserving the Unipolar Moment: Realist Theories and US Grand Strategy after the Cold War,' *International Security*, 21.
Mayall, J. (ed.) (1996) *The New Interventionism 1991–1994: United Nations Experience in Cambodia, former Yugoslavia and Somalia* (Cambridge).
———— (2000) *World Politics: Progress and its Limits* (Cambridge).
McClure, K. (1992) 'The Issue of Foundations: Scientized Politics, Politicized Science and Feminist Critical Practice', in J. W. Scott and J. Butler (eds), *Feminists Theorize the Political* (New York).
McGlen, N. E. and Sarkees, M. R. (eds) (1993) *Women in Foreign Policy: The Insiders* (New York).
McIntire, C. T. (ed.) (1979) *Herbert Butterfield: Writings on Christianity and History* (New York).
Meadows, D. and Randers, J. (1992) *Beyond the Limits* (London).
Meadows, D., Randers, J. and Behrens, W. (1972) *The Limits to Growth* (London).
Mearsheimer, J. (1990) ' "Back to the Future": Instability in Europe After the Cold War', *International Security*, 15(1).

———— (1994/5) 'The False Promise of International Institutions', *International Security*, 19.

———— (1995) 'A Realist Reply', *International Security*, 20.

———— (2001) *The Tragedy of Great Power Politics* (New York).

Mearsheimer, J. and Walt, S. M. (2002) *Can Saddam Be Contained? History Says Yes*, Belfer Centre for Science and International Affairs, Harvard University (Massachusetts).

Merchant, C. (1980) *The Death of Nature: Women, Ecology and the Scientific Revolution* (San Francisco).

Micklewait, J. and Wooldridge, A. (2000) *A Future Perfect: The Challenge and Hidden Promise of Globalisation* (New York).

Miller, F. (1998) 'Feminisms and Transnationalism', *Gender and History*, 10(3).

Mitrany, D. (1948) 'The Functional Approach to World Organisation', *International Affairs*, 24.

Mitter, S. (1986) *Common Fate, Common Bond: Women in the Global Economy* (London).

Mohanty, C. (1991) 'Under Western Eyes: Feminist Scholarship and Colonial Discourses', in C. Mohanty, T. A. Russo and L. Torres (eds), *Third World Women and the Politics of Feminism* (Bloomington).

Mol, A. (1996) 'Ecological Modernisation and Institutional Reflexivity: Environmental Reform in the Late Modern Age', *Environmental Politics*, 5(2).

Moon, K. (1997) *Sex Among Allies: Military Prostitution in US–Korea Relations* (New York).

Morgenthau, H. (1948/54/73) *Politics Among Nations: The Struggle for Power and Peace* (New York).

———— (1951) *In Defense of the National Interest: A Critical Examination of American Foreign Policy* (New York).

———— (1962) *Politics in the Twentieth Century, I: The Decline of Democratic Politics* (Chicago).

———— (1970) *Truth and Power: Essays of a Decade, 1960–70* (New York).

Mueller, J. (1989) *Retreat From Doomsday* (New York).

Nagel, T. (1986) *The View from Nowhere* (Oxford).

Nairn, T. (1981) *The Break-up of Britain* (London).

Nederveen Pieterse, J. (2004) *Globalization or Empire?* (London).

Neufeld, M. (1993) 'Interpretation and the "Science" of International Relations', *Review of International Studies*, 19(1).

———— (1995) *The Restructuring of International Relations Theory* (Cambridge).

———— (2000) 'Thinking Ethically – Thinking Critically: International Ethics as Critique', in M. Lensu and J.-S. Fritz (eds), *Value Pluralism, Normative Theory and International Relations* (London).

Newland, K. (1988) 'From Transnational Relationships to International Relations: Women in Development and the International Decade for Women', *Millennium*, 17(3).

Niarchos, C. N. (1995) 'Women, War, and Rape: Challenges Facing the International Tribunal for the Former Yugoslavia', *Human Rights Quarterly*, 17.

Niebuhr, R. (1932) *Moral Man and Immoral Society: A Study in Ethics and Politics* (New York).

———— (1941) *The Nature and Destiny of Man: A Christian Interpretation, I: Human Nature* (New York).

———— (1943) *The Nature and Destiny of Man: A Christian Interpretation, II: Human Destiny* (New York).

Nietzsche, F. (1969) *On the Genealogy of Morals, and Ecce Homo* (New York).

———— (1990) *Twilight of the Idols/The Anti-Christ* (Harmondsworth).

Norris, P. and Ingelhart, R. 2003) *Rising Tide: Gender Equality and Cultural Change Around the World* (Cambridge).

Nye, J. S. (1988) 'Neorealism and Neoliberalism', *World Politics*, 40.

Nyers, P. (1999) 'Emergency or Emerging Identities? Refugees and Transformations in World Order', *Millennium*, 28(1).

Ohmae, K. (1995) *The End of the Nation State* (New York).

Ong, A. (1997) 'The Gender and Labor Politics of Postmodernity', in L. Lowe (ed.), *The Politics of Culture Under the Shadow of Capital* (Durham).

Onuf, N. (1989) *World of Our Making: Rules and Rule in Social Theory and International Relations* (Columbia).

Ophuls, W. (1977) *Ecology and the Politics of Scarcity* (San Francisco).

O'Riordan, T. (1981) *Environmentalism*, 2nd edition (London).

Ostrom, E. (1990) *Governing the Commons: The Evolution of Institutions for Collective Action* (Cambridge).

Ó Tuathail, G. (1996) *Critical Geopolitics: The Politics of Writing Global Space* (Minneapolis).

Owen, J. M. (1994) 'How Liberalism Produces Democratic Peace', *International Security*, 19(2).

Oye, K. (1985) 'Explaining Cooperation Under Anarchy: Hypotheses and Strategies', *World Politics*, 38(1).

Pateman, C. (1986) 'Introduction', in C. Pateman and E. Gross, *Feminist Challenges: Social and Political Thought* (Sydney).

———— (1989) *The Disorder of Women* (Stanford).

Paterson, M. (1999a) 'Overview: Interpreting Trends in Global Environmental Governance', *International Affairs*, 75(4).

———— (1999b) 'Globalisation, Ecology, and Resistance', *New Political Economy*, 4(1).

———— (2000) *Understanding Global Environmental Politics: Domination, Accumulation, Resistance* (Basingstoke).

Patton, P. (2000) *Deleuze and the Political* (London).

Persram, N. (1994) 'Politicizing the Feminine, Globalizing the Feminist', *Alternatives*, 19(3).

Peters, J. and Wolper, A. (eds) (1995) *Women's Rights/Human Rights: International Feminist Perspectives* (New York).

Peterson, V. S. (1992a) 'Transgressing Boundaries: Theories of Gender, Knowledge and International Relations', *Millennium*, 21(2).

———— (1992b) 'Security and Sovereign States: What is at Stake in Taking Feminism Seriously?', in V. S. Peterson (ed.), *Gendered States: Feminist (Re)visions of International Theory* (Boulder).

Peterson, V. S. and Runyan, A. S. (1999) *Global Gender Issues*, 2nd edition (Boulder).

Peterson, V. S. and True, J. (1998) 'New Times and New Conversations', in M. Zalewski and J. Parpart (eds), *The Man Question in International Relations* (Boulder).

Pettman, J. (1996) 'An International Political Economy of Sex', in J. Pettman (ed.), *Worlding Women: Towards a Feminist International Politics* (New York).

Philapose, E. (1996) 'The Laws of War and Women's Human Rights', *Hypatia*, 11(4).

Philpott, D. (2001) *Revolutions in Sovereignty: How Ideas Shaped Modern International Relations* (Princeton).

Pietila, H. and Vickers, J. (1996) *Making Women Matter: The Role of the United Nations*, 3rd edition (London).

Pogge, T. (2002) *World Poverty and Human Rights* (Cambridge).

Polanyi, K. (1944) *The Great Transformation* (Boston).

———— (1968) 'Our Obsolete Market Mentality', in G. Dalton (ed.), *Primitive, Archaic and Modern Economies* (New York).

Porritt, J. (1986) *Seeing Green* (Oxford).

Porter, G. and Brown, J. W. (1991) *Global Environmental Politics* (Boulder).

Porter, M. and Judd, E. (eds) (2000) *Feminists Doing Development: A Practical Critique* (London).

Powell, R. (1994) 'Anarchy in International Relations Theory: The Neorealist–Neoliberal Debate', *International Organization*, 48.

Price, R. (1997) *The Chemical Weapons Taboo* (Ithaca).

Price, R. and Reus-Smit, C. (1998) 'Dangerous Liasions: Critical International Theory and Constructivism', *European Journal of International Relations*, 4(3).

Programme of the German Green Party (1983) (London).

Prugl, E. (2000) *The Global Construction of Gender* (New York).

Prugl, E. and Meyer, M. K. (eds) (1999) *Gender Politics and Global Governance* (Lanham).

Rae, H. (2002) *State Identities and the Homogenization of Peoples* (Cambridge).

Rao, A. (1995) 'Gender and Culture', in J. Peters and A. Wolper (eds), *Women's Rights/Human Rights: International Feminist Perspectives* (New York).

Rathergeber, M. (1995) 'Gender and Development in Action', in M. H. Marchand and J. L. Parpart (eds), *Feminism/Postmodernism/Development* (London).

Rawls, J. (1999) *The Law of Peoples* (Harvard).

Reanda, L. (1999) 'Engendering the United Nations: The Changing International Agenda', *European Journal of Women's Studies*, 6.

Regan, P. M. and Paskeviciute, A. (2003) 'Women's Access to Politics and Peaceful States', *Journal of Peace Research*, 40.

Reid, J. (2003) 'Deleuze's War Machine: Nomadism against the State', *Millennium*, 32(1).

Reus-Smit, C. (1996) 'The Normative Structure of International Society', in F. Osler Hampson and J. Reppy (eds), *Earthly Goods: Environmental Change and Social Justice* (Ithaca).

Reus-Smit, C. (1999) *The Moral Purpose of the State: Culture, Social Identity and Institutional Rationality in International Relations* (Princeton).
———— (2000) 'In Dialogue on the Ethic of Consensus: A Reply to Shapcott', *Pacifica Review*, 12(3).
———— (2002) 'Imagining Society: Constructivism and the English School', *British Journal of Politics and International Relations*, 4(3).
———— (2004a) *American Power and World Order* (Cambridge).
———— (ed.) (2004b) *The Politics of International Law* (Cambridge).
Ricardo, D. (1911) *The Principles of Political Economy and Taxation* (London).
Richardson, J. L. (1997) 'Contending Liberalisms – Past and Present', *European Journal of International Relations*, 3(1).
Risse, T. (2000) ' "Let's Argue!": Communicative Action in World Politics', *International Organization*, 54(1).
———— (2004) 'Global Governance Communication Action', *Government and Opposition*, 39(2).
Roberts, A. (1993) 'Humanitarian War: Military Intervention and Human Rights', *International Affairs*, 69(3).
Roberts, B. (1984) 'The Death of Machothink: Feminist Research and the Transformation of Peace Studies', *Women's Studies International Forum*, 7.
Robinson, F. (1999) *Globalizing Care: Ethics, Feminist Theory, and International Relations* (Boulder).
———— (forthcoming) 'Ethics in International Relations: Feminist Approaches', in B. Ackerly, M. Stern and J. True (eds), *Feminist Methodologies for International Relations* (Cambridge).
Roderick, R. (1986) *Habermas and the Foundations of Critical Theory* (London).
Rose, G. (1998) 'Neoclassical Realism and Theories of Foreign Policy', *World Politics*, 51.
Rosecrance, R. N. (1966) 'Bipolarity, Multipolarity, and the Future', *Journal of Conflict Resolution*, 10.
———— (1986) *The Rise of the Trading State* (New York).
Rosenau, J. (1992) 'Governance, Order, and Change in World Politics', in J. N. Rosenau, and E.-O. Czempiel (eds), *Governance Without Government: Order and Change in World Politics* (Cambridge).
———— (1993) 'Environmental Challenges in a Turbulent World', in K. Conca and R. Lipschutz (eds), *The State and Social Power in Global Environmental Politics* (New York).
Rosenau, J. and Holsti, O. (1982) 'Women Leaders and Foreign Policy Opinions', in E. Boneparth and E. Stoper (eds), *Women, Power, and Politics* (New York).
Rosenberg, J. (1994) *The Empire of Civil Society: A Critique of the Realist Theory of International Relations* (London).
Rosenthal, J. H. (1991) *Righteous Realists: Political Realism, Responsible Power, and American Culture in the Nuclear Age* (Baton Rouge).
Ruggie, J. G. (1986) 'Continuity and Transformation in the World Polity: Toward a Neorealist Synthesis', in R. O. Keohane (ed.), *Neorealism and Its Critics* (New York).

———— (1993) 'Territoriality and Beyond: Problematizing Modernity in International Relations', *International Organization*, 47(1).

Runyan, A. S. and Peterson, V. S. (1991) 'The Radical Future of Realism: Feminist Subversions of IR Theory', *Alternatives*, 16(1).

Rupert, M. (2003) 'Globalising Common Sense: A Marxian–Gramscian (Re-vision) of the Politics of Governance/Resistance', *Review of International Studies*, 29.

Rupp, L. (1997) *Worlds of Women: The Making of an International Women's Movement* (Princeton).

Russett, B. (1993) *Grasping the Democratic Peace* (Princeton).

Rustin, C. (1999) 'Habermas, Discourse Ethics, and International Justice', *Alternatives*, 24(2).

Sachs, W. (ed.) (1992) *The Development Dictionary: A Guide to Knowledge as Power* (London).

———— (1993) 'Global Ecology and the Shadow of "Development" ', in W. Sachs (ed.), *Global Ecology* (London).

———— (ed.) (1993) *Global Ecology* (London).

Sale, K. (1980) *Human Scale* (San Francisco).

Sassen, S. (1991) *The Global City: New York, London, Tokyo* (Princeton).

———— (1998a) 'Notes on the Incorporation of Third World Women into Wage Labor through Immigration and Offshore Production', in S. Sassen, *Globalization and its Discontents* (New York).

———— (1998b) 'Toward a Feminist Analysis of the Global Economy', in S. Sassen, *Globalization and its Discontents* (New York).

Schmidt, B. C. (1998) *The Political Discourse of Anarchy: A Disciplinary History of International Relations* (Albany).

Scholte, J.-A. (2000) *Globalisation: A Critical Introduction* (Basingstoke).

Schumacher, E. F. (1976) *Small is Beautiful* (London).

Schweller, R. L. (1994) 'Bandwagoning for Profit: Bringing the Revisionist State Back In', *International Security*, 19.

———— (1997) 'New Realist Research on Alliances: Refining, Not Refuting, Waltz's Balancing Proposition', *American Political Science Review*, 91.

———— (1998) *Deadly Imbalances: Tripolarity and Hitler's Strategy of World Conquest* (New York).

———— (1999) 'Managing the Rise of Great Powers: History and Theory', in A. I. Jonston and R. S. Ross (eds), *Engaging China: The Management of an Emerging Power* (London).

Schweller, R. L. and Priess, D. (1997) 'A Tale of Two Realisms: Expanding the Institutions Debate', *Mershon International Studies Review*, 41.

Scott, J. W. (1988) *Gender and the Politics of History* (New York).

Sen, A. (2001) *Development as Freedom* (New York).

Shapcott, R. (1994) 'Conversation and Co-Existence: Gadamer and the Interpretation of International Society', *Millennium*, 23(1).

———— (2000a) 'Solidarism and After: Global Governance, International Society and the Normative "Turn" ', *Pacifica Review*, 12(2).

———— (2000b) 'Beyond the Cosmopolitan/Communitarian Divide: Justice, Difference and Community in International Relations', in M. Lensu and

J.-S. Fritz (eds), *Value Pluralism, Normative Theory and International Relations* (London).

———— (2001) *Justice, Community and Dialogue in International Relations* (Cambridge).

Shapiro, M. J. (1988a) *The Politics of Representation* (Madison).

———— (1998) 'The Events of Discourse and the Ethics of Global Hospitality', *Millennium*, 27(3).

Sharoni, S. (1993) 'Middle-East Politics Through Feminist Lenses: Toward Theorizing International Relations from Women's Struggles', *Alternatives*, 18.

Ship, S. J. (1994) 'And What About Gender? Feminism and International Relations Theory's Third Debate', in W. S. Cox and C. T. Sjolander (eds), *Beyond Positivism: Critical International Relations Theory* (Boulder).

Shiva, V. (1988) *Staying Alive: Women, Ecology and Development* (London).

Shue, H. (1992) 'The Unavoidability of Justice', in A. Hurrell and B. Kingsbury (eds), *The International Politics of the Environment* (Oxford).

———— (1995) 'Ethics, the Environment, and the Changing International Order', *International Affairs*, 71(3).

———— (1999) 'Global Environment and International Inequality', *International Affairs*, 75(3).

Simpson, G. (2004) *Great Powers and Outlaw States: Unequal Sovereigns in the International Legal Order* (Cambridge).

Singer, J. D. (1961) 'The Level-of-Analysis Problem in International Relations', *World Politics*, 14(1).

Skocpol, T. (1979) *States and Social Revolutions* (Cambridge).

Smith, M. J. (1986) *Realist Thought from Weber to Kissinger* (Baton Rouge).

Smith, S. (1995) 'The Self-Image of a Discipline: A Genealogy of International Relations Theory', in K. Booth and S. Smith (eds), *International Relations Theory Today* (Cambridge).

———— (1996) 'Positivism and Beyond', in S. Smith, K. Booth and M. Zalewski (eds), *International Theory: Positivism and Beyond* (Cambridge).

———— (1997) 'Power and Truth: A Reply to Wallace', *Review of International Studies*, 22(4).

Smith, S., Booth, K. and Zalewski, M. (eds) (1996) *International Theory: Positivism and Beyond* (Cambridge).

Snyder, G. H. (1996) 'Process Variables in Neorealist Theory', *Security Studies*, 5.

———— (1997) *Alliance Politics* (Ithaca).

———— (2002) 'Mearsheimer's World: Offensive Realism and the Struggle for Security', *International Security*, 27.

Soguk, N. and Whitehall, G. (1999) 'Wandering Grounds: Transversality, Identity, Territoriality, and Movement', *Millennium*, 28(3).

Sparr, P. (ed.) (1994) *Mortgaging Women's Lives: Feminist Critiques of Structural Adjustment* (London).

Spretnak, C. and Capra, F. (1984) *Green Politics: The Global Promise* (London).

Spykman, N. J. (1942) *America's Strategy in World Politics: The United States and the Balance of Power* (New York).

Stalin, J. (1953) 'Marxism and the National Question', *Collected Works* (Moscow).

Standing, G. (1992) 'Global Feminization Through Flexible Labor', in C. K. Wilber and K. P. Jameson (eds), *The Political Economy of Development and Underdevelopment*, 5th edition (New York).

Stasilis, D. and Bakan, A. B. (1997) 'Negotiating Citizenship: The Case of Foreign Domestic Workers in Canada', *Feminist Review*, 57.

Steans, J. (1998) *Gender and International Relations* (Cambridge).

Stern, M. (2005) *Naming Insecurity–Constructing Identity* (Manchester).

Steuernagel, G. A. (1990) 'Men do not do Housework! The Image of Women in Political Science', in M. Paludi and G. A. Steuernagel (eds), *Foundations for a Feminist Restructuring of the Academic Disciplines* (New York).

Stewart, C. (1997) 'Old Wine in Recycled Bottles: The Limitations of Green International Relations Theory', Paper presented to the BISA Annual Conference.

Stienstra, D. (1994) *Women's Movements and International Organizations* (Toronto).

Strange, S. (1985) 'Protectionism and World Politics', *International Organisation*, 39(2).

———— (1991) 'New World Order: Conflict and Co-Operation', *Marxism Today*, January.

———— (1996) *The Retreat of the State* (Cambridge).

———— (1998) *Mad Money* (Michigan).

Suganami, H. (1989) *The Domestic Analogy and World Order Proposals* (Cambridge).

———— (1996) *On the Causes of War* (Oxford).

Suh, J. J., Katzenstein, P. J. and Carlson, A. (2004) *Rethinking Security in East Asia: Identity, Power, and Efficiency* (Palo Alto).

Sylvester, C. (1987) 'The Dangers of Merging Feminist and Peace Projects', *Alternatives*, 8(4).

———— (1990) 'The Emperors' Theories and Transformations: Looking at the Field through Feminist Lens', in D. Pirages and C. Sylvester (eds), *Transformations in the Global Political Economy* (London).

———— (1992) 'Feminist Theory and Gender Studies in International Relations', *International Studies Notes*, 16(1).

———— (1994a) *Feminist Theory and International Relations in a Postmodern Era* (Cambridge).

———— (1994b) 'Empathetic Co-Operation: A Feminist Method for IR', *Millennium*, 23(2).

———— (2002) *Feminist International Relations: An Unfinished Journey* (Cambridge).

Taliaferro, J. W. (2000/1) 'Security Seeking Under Anarchy: Defensive Realism Revisited,' *International Security*, 25.

Tannenwald, N. (1999) 'The Nuclear Taboo: The United States and the Normative Basis of Nuclear Non-Use', *International Organization*, 53(3).

Taylor, A. J. P. (1961) *The Origins of the Second World War* (Harmondsworth).

Taylor, B. (ed.) (1995) *Ecological Resistance Movements: The Global Emergence of Radical and Popular Environmentalism* (Albany).

Taylor, C. (1997) 'Interpretation and the Sciences of Man', in F. Dallmayr and T. McCarthy (eds), *Understanding and Social Inquiry* (Notre Dame).

Taylor, M. (1987) *The Possibility of Co-operation* (Cambridge).

Tellis, A. (1995/6) 'Reconstructing Political Realism: The Long March to Scientific Theory', *Security Studies*, 5.

Teschke, B. (2003) *The Myth of 1648: Class, Geopolitics and the Making of Modern International Relations* (London).

Tessler, M. and Warriner, I. (1997) 'Gender, Feminism and Attitudes toward International Conflict: Exploring Relationships with Survey Data from the Middle East', *World Politics*, 49.

Tessler, M., Nachtwey, J. and Grant, A. (1999) 'Further Tests of the Women and Peace Hypothesis: Evidence from Cross-National Survey Research in the Middle East', *International Studies Quarterly*, 43(3).

The Ecologist (1972) *Blueprint for Survival* (Harmondsworth).

———— (1993) *Whose Common Future? Reclaiming the Commons* (London).

Thomas, C. (1999) 'Where is the Third World Now?', *Review of International Studies*, Special Issue, 25.

Thomson J. E. (1994) *Mercenaries, Pirates and Sovereigns* (Princeton).

Thompson, K. W. (1985) *Moralism and Morality in Politics and Diplomacy* (Lanham).

Thompson, K. W. and Meyers, R. J. (eds) (1977) *Truth and Tragedy: A Tribute to Hans Morgenthau* (Washington).

Thucydides (1982) *The Peloponnesian War* (New York).

Tickner, J. A. (1988) 'Hans Morgenthau's Political Principles of Political Realism: A Feminist Reformulation', *Millennium*, 17(3).

———— (1991) 'On the Fringes of the World Economy: A Feminist Perspective', in C. Murphy and R. Tooze (eds), *The New International Political Economy* (Boulder).

———— (1992) *Gender in International Relations* (New York).

———— (2001) *Gendering World Politics: Issues and Approaches in the Post-Cold War Era* (New York).

———— (2002) 'Feminist Perspectives on 9/11', *International Studies Perspectives*, 3(4).

Trainer, F. E. (1985) *Abandon Affluence!* (London).

Treitschke, H. V. (1916) *Politics* (London).

Tronto, J. (1989) 'Woman, the State and War: What Difference Does Gender Make?', in V. S. Peterson (ed.), *Clarification and Contestation: A Conference Report* (Los Angeles).

True, J. (2003) *Gender, Globalization and Postsocialism: The Czech Republic After Communism* (New York).

———— (2004) 'Feminism', in A. Bellamy (ed.), *International Society and its Critics* (Oxford).

True, J. and Mintrom, M. (2001) 'Transnational Networks and Policy Diffusion: The Case of Gender Mainstreaming', *International Studies Quarterly*, 45(1).

Tuathail, G. Ó. (1996) *Critical Geopolitics: The Politics of Writing Global Space* (Minneapolis).

Tucker, R. W. (1977) *The Inequality of Nations* (New York).

———— (1985) *Intervention and the Reagan Doctrine* (New York).

United Nations (1992) *Framework Convention on Climate Change* (New York).

United Nations (2000) *The World's Women's Progress* (New York).

United Nations Development Programme (UNDP) (1999) *Human Development Report 1999: Globalization with a Human Face* (Oxford).

Van Evera, S. (1998) 'Offense, Defense, and the Causes of War,' *International Security*, 22.

Vasquez, J. A. (1998) *The Power of Power Politics: From Classical Realism to Neotraditionalism* (Cambridge).

Vincent, R. J. (1984a) 'Edmund Burke and the Theory of International Relations', *Review of International Studies*, 10.

———— (1984b) 'Racial Equality', in H. Bull and A. Watson (eds), *The Expansion of International Society* (Oxford).

———— (1986) *Human Rights and International Relations* (Cambridge).

Vincent, R. J. and Wilson, P. (1994) 'Beyond Non-Intervention', in I. Forbes and M. Hoffman (eds), *Political Theory, International Relations and the Ethics of Intervention* (London).

Vogel, U. (2003) 'Cosmopolitan Loyalties and Cosmopolitan Citizenship in the Enlightenment', in M. Waller and A. Linklater (eds), *Political Loyalty and the Nation-State* (London).

Vogler, J. (1995) *The Global Commons: A Regime Analysis* (London).

Wackernagel, M. and Rees, W. (1996) *Our Ecological Footprint: Reducing Human Impact on the Earth* (Gabriola Island).

Walker, R. B. J. (1987) 'Realism, Change and International Political Theory', *International Studies Quarterly*, 31(1).

———— (1989) 'History and Structure in the Theory of International Relations', *Millennium* 18(2).

———— (1992) 'Gender and Critique in the Theory of International Relations', in V. S. Peterson (ed.), *Gendered States: Feminist (Re)visions of International Relations Theory* (Boulder).

———— (1993) *Inside/Outside: International Relations as Political Theory* (Cambridge).

———— (1995a) 'From International Relations to World Politics', in J. Camilleri, A. Jarvis and A. Paolini (eds), *The State in Transition: Reimagining Political Space* (Boulder).

———— (1995b) 'International Relations and the Concept of the Political', in K. Booth and S. Smith (eds), *International Relations Theory Today* (Cambridge).

———— (2000) 'International Relations Theory and the Fate of the Political', in M. Ebata and B. Neufeld (eds), *Confronting the Political in International Relations* (London).

Wall, D. (1994) 'Towards a Green Political Theory – In Defence of the Commons?', in P. Dunleavy and J. Stanyer (eds), *Contemporary Political Studies: Proceedings of the Annual Conference* (Belfast).

Wallace, W. (1996) 'Truth and Power, Monks and Technocrats: Theory and Practice in International Relations', *Review of International Studies*, 22(3).

Waller, M. and Linklater, A. (eds) (2003) *Political Loyalty and the Nation-State* (London).

Wallerstein, I. (1979) *The Capitalist World Economy* (Cambridge).

Walt, S. M. (1987) *The Origins of Alliances* (Ithaca).

Walter, A. (1996) 'Adam Smith and the Liberal Tradition in International Relations', in I. Clark and I. B. Neumann (eds), *Classical Theories of International Relations* (Oxford).

Waltz, K. N. (1959) *Man, the State and War* (New York).

———— (1964) 'The Stability of a Bipolar World', *Daedalus*, 93.

———— (1979) *Theory of International Politics* (Reading).

———— (1986) 'Reflections on Theory of International Politics: A Response to My Critics', in R. O. Keohane (ed.), *Neo-Realism and Its Critics* (New York).

———— (1990) 'Nuclear Myths and Political Realities', *American Political Science Review*, 84.

———— (1991a) 'America as a Model for the World?', *PS: Political Science and Politics*, 24(4).

———— (1991b) 'Realist Thought and Neo-Realist Theory', in R. L. Rothstein (ed.), *The Evolution of Theory in International Relations: Essays in Honor of William T. R. Fox* (Columbia).

———— (1993) 'The Emerging Structure of International Politics', *International Security*, 18.

———— (1996) 'International Politics Is Not Foreign Policy', *Security Studies*, 6.

———— (2002) 'The Continuity of International Politics', in K. Booth and T. Dunne (eds), *Worlds in Collision: Terror and the Future of Global Order* (Basingstoke).

Wapner, P. (1996) *Environmental Activism and World Civic Politics* (Albany).

Warren, B. (1980) *Imperialism: Pioneer of Capitalism* (London).

Watson, A. (1982) *Diplomacy: The Dialogue Between States* (London).

———— (1987) 'Hedley Bull, States Systems and International Societies', *Review of International Studies*, 13.

WCED (1987) *Our Common Future – Report of the World Commission on Environment and Development* (Oxford).

Weber, C. (1994) 'Good Girls, Little Girls, and Bad Girls: Male Paranoia in Robert Keohane's Critique of Feminist International Relations', *Millennium*, 23(2).

———— (1995) *Simulating Sovereignty: Intervention, the State, and Symbolic Exchange* (Cambridge).

———— (1998) 'Performative States', *Millennium*, 27(1).

———— (2002) 'Flying Planes Can be Dangerous', *Millenium*, 31(1).

Weiss, L. (1998) *The Myth of the Powerless State: Governing the Economy in a Global Era* (Cambridge).

Welch, D. (1993) *Justice and the Genesis of War* (Cambridge).

Wendt, A. (1992) 'Anarchy is what States Make of it', *International Organization*, 46.

———— (1994) 'Collective Identity Formation and the International State', *American Political Science Review*, 88(2).

———— (1995) 'Constructing International Politics', *International Security*, 20(1).

———— (1999) *Social Theory of International Politics* (Cambridge).

———— (2003) 'Why a World State is Inevitable', *European Journal of International Relations*, 9(4).

Wendt, A. and Shapiro, I. (1997) 'The Misunderstood Promise of Realist Social Theory', in K. R. Monroe (ed.), *Contemporary Empirical Theory* (Berkeley).

Wheeler, N. J. (2000) *Saving Strangers: Humanitarian Intervention in International Society* (Oxford).

Wheeler, N. J. and Dunne, T. (1996) 'Hedley Bull's Pluralism of the Intellect and Solidarism of the Will', *International Affairs*, 72.

———— (1998) 'Good International Citizenship: A Third Way for British Foreign Policy', *International Affairs*, 74.

Wheen, F. (1999) *Karl Marx* (London).

Whitworth, S. (1994) *Feminism and International Relations: Towards a Political Economy of Gender in Interstate and Non-Governmental Institutions* (London).

———— (2001) 'The Practice, and Praxis, of Feminist Research in International Relations', in R. W. Jones (ed.), *Critical Theory and World Politics* (Boulder).

———— (2004) *Men, Militarism and UN Peacekeeping: A Gendered Analysis* (Boulder).

Wight, M. (1966a) 'Why is there no International Theory?', in H. Butterfield and M. Wight (eds), *Diplomatic Investigations, Essays in the Theory of International Relations* (London). Reprinted in J. Der Derian (ed.) (1995), *International Theory: Critical Investigations* (Basingstoke).

———— (1966b) 'Western Values in International Relations', in H. Butterfield and M. Wight (eds), *Diplomatic Investigations, Essays in the Theory of International Relations* (London).

———— (1977) *Systems of States* (Leicester).

Wight, M. (1991) *International Theory: The Three Traditions* (edited by G. Wight and B. Porter) (Leicester).

Williams, J. and Goose, S. (1998) in A. Maxwell, R. Cameron, J. Lawson and B. W. Tomlin (eds), 'The International Campaign to Ban Land Mines', in *To Walk Without Fear: The Global Movement to Ban Landmines* (Toronto).

Wilson, P. (1998) 'The Myth of the First Great Debate', *Review of International Studies*, Special Issue, 24.

Wohlforth, W. C. (1999) 'The Stability of a Unipolar World', *International Security*, 24.

Wyn Jones, R. (2001) 'Introduction: Locating Critical International Relations Theory', in R. W. Jones (ed.), *Critical Theory and World Politics* (Boulder).

Yergin, D. (1990) *Shattered Peace*, Revised edition (London).

Young, O. R. (1982) 'Regime Dynamics', *International Organization*, 36(2).

Young, O. R. (1989) *International Cooperation: Building Regimes for Natural Resources and the Environment* (Ithaca).

———— (1994) *International Governance: Protecting the Environment in a Stateless Society* (Ithaca).

Zacher, M. W. and Matthew, R. A. (1995) 'Liberal International Theory: Common Threads, Divergent Strands', in C. W. Kegley Jr (ed.), *Controversies in International Relations Theory* (New York).

Zakaria, F. (1998) *From Wealth to Power: The Unusual Origins of America's World Role* (Princeton).

Zalewski, M. (1993) 'Feminist Standpoint Theory Meets International Relations Theory', *The Fletcher Forum for World Affairs*, 75(1).

———— (1995) 'Well, What is the Feminist Perspective on Bosnia?', *International Affairs*, 71(2).

Zalewski, M. and Parpart, J. (eds) (1998) *The 'Man' Question in International Relations* (Boulder).

Zehfuss, M. (2003) 'Forget September 11', *Third World Quarterly*, 24(3).

Index

Notes: n = note; **bold** = extended discussion or item emphasized in main text.

Abyssinia   93
acid rain   157, 251
Ackerly, B.   217
actors, pre-social   **192**
Adler, E.   46
Adorno, T.   22, 26, 133, 138
Afghanistan   60, 61, 79, 102, 229
Africa   56
After Hegemony (Keohane, 1984)   190
Agamben, G.   174–5
Age of Absolutism (1555–1848)   196–7
Al-Qaeda   12, 79, 100, 102, 210
alienation   113, 148
altruism   247, 248
amity/friendship   44–5, 47, 196
Amnesty International   12, 220
Anarchical Society (Bull, 1977)   84, **90–1**, 93, 104
anarchism (Green)   244
'anarchist solution' (O'Riordan)   243
anarchy (international)   8, 19, 20, 23, 26, 30–8, 40, 41, 43, 45, 46, 48, 49, 52, 58, 65, 66, 84, 86, 87, 89, 92, 110, 150, 173, 176, 179, 190, 191, 196, 216, 222, 223, 225, 252, 254
   'absence of international government'   30
   bandwagoning   35–6, 38
   'what states make of it' (Wendt)   107
'anarchy problematique'
   Ashley's double reading   **170–1**, 181
ancien régime   148
Anderson, P.   120
animal liberation   239
Annenkov, G.   117–18
anthropocentrism   237, 238, 239, 251
'anti-foundationalism' (Hoffman)   194, 205
apartheid   96
Apel, K.-O.   132
Archibugi, D.   156, 158
Aristotelianism   53
arms races   37
Ashley, R.K.   26, 142, 145, 179, 185
   double reading of 'anarchy problematique'   **170–1**, 181
   'modern statecraft is modern mancraft'   162

statecraft   **179–81**
Asia-Pacific Economic Cooperation (APEC)   75
Asian model   69
assumptions
   background normative   144
   unexamined   143
Australia   10
Austria   6
Austro-Marxism   119, 122, 123, 134
autonomy   21, 138, 222
'autonomy of politics' (Morgenthau)   50
Axelrod, R.   190

Bailey, S.   250
balance of power   7, 11, 19–20, 30, 47, 93, 110, 121, 134, 206, 209, 225
   military   152, 196
balance of threat theory (Walt)   42
balancing   **35–7**, 38, 41, 44
Bali bombing (2002)   80
Balkans   61, 102
Bananas, Beaches and Bases (Enloe, 1989)   214
bandwagoners   35–6, 38
Bangladesh   218
banks   77, 78
'bare life'   174, 175
Barnett, M.   46, 210
Barry, J.   235n, 239
Bauer, O.   119
'becoming-state' (Doty)   181
Benjamin, W.   138
Benner, E.   118
Berlin, Treaty of (1878)   70
Berlin Wall   208
Berman, J.   214
Beslan (2004)   80
Beyond the Limits (Meadows and Randers, 1992)   241
Beyond Realism and Marxism (Linklater, 1990)   150–1, 154
'bi-multipolarity'   39
Bill of Rights (1689)   67
binary opposition   184, 222
biology   221–2, 227

bipolarity   36, 39, 40, 61, 96, 109, 111,
    128, 134, 225
Blair, A.C.L.   94, 103
Bleiker, R.   163, 182
Bloch, C.   6
Bohman, J.   142, 143
Bookchin, M.   244, 249, 250
Booth, K.   26, 145
Bosnia   164, 174, 177, 180
Boulainvilliers, H., Comte de   165
boundaries (of state)
    postmodernism   **175–6**, 181–2, 185
'bounded communities'   150
boundedness   187
'boundedness of identity'   **149**
bourgeoisie   110, 113, 114, 115, 121
    globalization   116–17
    national   117
Brandenburg, E.   6
Bretton Woods system   72, 76
Britain   *see* United Kingdom
Brown, C.J.   101
Brundtland Commission (WCED)   240, 241
Bryant, R.   250
Bukharin, N.I.   120, 121
Bull, H.   2, 3, 8, 16, 22, 25, 64, 69, 84, 87,
    90–1, 211–12
    order and justice in IR   **93–8**
    progress in IR   **103–8**
    protégé of Wight   90
    revolt against West   **98–102**
Bunyard, P.   240
Burchill, S.   x, **25**, 222, 235n
Burke, A.   187
Burton, J.   256
Bush, G.W.   81, 103, 161, 167
'business civilization', neo-liberal (Cox and
    Gill)   152–3
Butler, J.   174–5, 222
Butterfield, Sir Herbert   11, 37, 41, 53
Buzan, B.   22, 23, 46, 84, 94

Cambodia   69
    Vietnamese invasion (1978)   50, 70, 125
Campaign for Nuclear Disarmament (CND)
    220
Campbell, D.   164, 165, 172, 173–4,
    176–8, 180–2, 185, 186
    'writing' security   168
Canada   10, 196
capabilities   38, 41, 42, 45, 53, 170
capital   121, 152
    'desperate need for new outlets'   120
    foreign   78
    'international unity' (Lenin)   122
    transnational   76, 77

capital markets   69, 74, 82
capital mobility   72, 74
capital movements   76
    national controls   73
capitalism   15, 19, 26, 27, 72, 110, 111,
    113, 114, 116, 118–19, 125–9, 133,
    148, 153
    'combined and uneven development'
        (Trotsky)   122, 123
    core societies   122
    early   120
    evolution   132, 135
    free-market/laissez-faire   55, 56, 58,
        70–1, 148, 197
    global   123, 252, 254
    industrial   251
    late   121
    laws modelled on physical sciences   115
    Western   214
Capra, F.   240, 244
Caprioli, M.   217
Carr, E.H.   1, 4, 7, 8–9, 25, 30, 32, 48, 51,
    58, 62, 108, 118, 189, 207
    critique of liberal utopianism   58
Carter, A.   244
Carthage-Rome (bipolar system)   39
Central America   36
Central Asia   60, 61
Central and Eastern Europe   36
'centralised authoritarianism' (O'Riordan)
    242
Chatterjee, P.   237
Chayes, A.   248
Chayes, A.H.   248
children   13, 220, 226
    disease   50
Chin, C.B.   218
China   42, 80, 99–100
    Ancient Chinese   89
    war with Vietnam (1979)   125
Chinese walls   111, 116, 121
choice-theoretic assumptions   192
Chomsky, N.   2, 14
Christianity
    Augustinian Christians   53
    Christian minorities   70
Christoff, P.   252
cinema   29
citizens   91, 147, 148, 154, 156
citizenship   155
civil liberties   79, 81, 167
civil society   4, 12, 79, 151–2, 153, 166, 250
civil war   61, 101–2, 165
civilization   98, 99, 129–30
'clash of civilizations' (Huntington)   98,
    100–1, 164, 211

Claude, I. 189
Clausewitz, K.M. von 100, 166
climate change 27, 251
Cobden, R. 58
coexistence 42, 85, 98, 155, 205, 210
Cohen, J. 132
Coke, Sir Edward 165
Cold War 9, 14, 16, 36, 45, 88, 109, 128,
    147, 165, 178, 194
  end of 38, 80, 188, 194, 195–6, 201,
      206, 207, 208, 229
  post-Cold War liberalism 55–6, 57
  post-Cold War era 61, 69, 70, 75, 156
  realism's failure to account for end of 48
collective security 86
Collège de France 165
colonialism 20, 63
  economic competition 15
  'greatly admired' by Marx 124
colonies 95, 99, 100, 102
commerce 89, 114
  spirit of 62–4
commodities 76
commodity production 242
commons 242–3, 245–6, 250
  enclosure 241
  reclamation 238, 253, 254
communication 199
communism 55, 56, 68, 111
  collapse 81, 218
Communist Manifesto (Marx and Engels,
    1848) 116–17
  Derrida's analysis 133–4
communitarians 149
comparative advantage 63
  relevance in era of globalization (three
      difficulties) 73–6
competition, diffidence, and glory (Hobbes)
    32–3, 34
'complex interdependence' (Keohane and
    Nye) 189
concentration camps 173, 174
conceptual opposition (Derrida) 168
conditionality 127, 179
conflict groups (Gilpin) 30
Confucianism 69
Connolly, W. 176, 186
  state sovereignty and democracy 184–5
consensus 131, 133
constitutive theory 12, 17–18
constructivism viii, 5, 11, 19, 26, 188–212,
    233
  'Atlantic divide' 212
  challenge of critical theory 193–4
  characteristics 188
  contribution 205–7

'conventional' versus 'critical' (Hopf)
    205
critical 21, 205
debates 188, 207, 212
dichotomy between the international and
    the domestic (bridged) 201
differentiated from critical theory 195
differentiated from rationalism 199
discontents 201–5, 207
'English School' characteristics 211, 212
English School 'natural ally' 92
forms (1990s-) 199–201
holistic 26, 201
influence on GPT 252
meta-theoretical level 195, 201–2
modernist versus postmodernist 196
moves away from Wendtian-style
    theorizing 208
normative theorizing 207
'not a theory, but an analytical
    framework' 202
outgrowth of critical theory 204
post-Cold War phenomenon 208
post-11 September (2001) 207–11
rationalist theory 189–93
relationship with rationalism 202, **203**,
    205, 208
research needed 211
rise 194–201, 208
sociological inquiry 206, 211, 212
state interests 107
strengths 209–11
systemic 26, 199–200, 202
'thin form' 203
unit-level 200
US mainstream 188, 205, 206, 208, 212
containment policy (Cold War) 178
cooperation 33, 37–8, 210
  inter-community 250
  international 64, 65, 107, 188, 190–1,
      205, 248
  local 246
'cooperation under anarchy' 25
coordination 248, 249
corporate mercantilism 74–5
Cosmopolitan 214
'cosmopolitan conversations' 108
'cosmopolitan harm conventions' (Linklater)
    153
cosmopolitanism 94, 97, 119, 121, 124,
    131, **154–9**, 160
  'dialogical' (Linklater and Shapcott) 156
  'thin' (Linklater and Shapcott) 156
Cox, R.W. 13–14, **20–1**, 26, 150, **151–3**
  'hegemonic nature of world order'
      126–7

Cox, R.W. – *continued*
  'problem-solving' versus 'critical theory'
    129
  problem-solving theory 141–2
  state and civil society 151–2
  'theory always for someone and some
    purpose' 141
  theory of state 152–3
credit (bonds and loans) 76
crime, transnational 13, 80
crimes against humanity 69
criteria of significance 16
'critical interpretivism' 193–4
critical theorists 188, 256
critical theory 11, 18, 21, 22, **26**, 107,
  125, 129, 131, 132, **137–60**, 174, 212,
  233, 253, 255
  challenge to rationalism **193–4**
  constructivism 'outgrowth of' 204
  contribution of constructivism
    (constructivist discontent) 202,
    204–5, 208
  emancipatory 145–6
  first-wave 195
  Green politics 236
  impact of Marxism 111
  influence of English School 107
  'method of immanent critique' 138, 144
  origins 137–40
  origins in failings of Marxism 136
  politics of knowledge in IR theory 140–6
  rethinking political community 146–59
  Reus-Smit 188
  self-reflective 139, 140, 143
  supersedes classical Marxism 132–3
  task 142
  see also Frankfurt School
Cronin, B. 47
Cuba 196
cultural differentiation 89, 90
cultural imperialism 100
culture 17, 101, 107, 119, 130, 149, 154,
  230, 233
  constructivism 209, **210–11**
  Marxism 124
  pan-Arabic 228
'cultures of anarchy' (Wendt) 252
currency 77, 78
Cusack, T.R. 30
Czech Republic 218

Dalby, S. 177, 249
Dar al Harb (House of War) 99
Dar al Islam (House of Islam) 99
Dar al Suhl (temporary truce) 99
Darfur 49

de Geus, M. 246
De Jure Belli ac Pacis (Grotius, 1625) 85
de-regulation
  finance and currency markets 72
  financial 76
decentralism/decentralization **242**, 243,
  244, 249, 250–1, 254, 256, 257
  GPT **237**
  objections to Green arguments **246–8**
decision-making 159, 171, 191
Declaration of Independence (USA, 1776) 67
Declaration of Rights of Man and Citizen
  (France, 1789) 67
deconstruction 161, **168–9**, 172, 183, 187
deconstructionism (Derrida) 133
Deleuze, G. 181–2
democracy 8, 50, **59**, 92, 138, 219, 246
  cosmopolitan/transnational 133, **156**,
    253
  ecological 253–4
  'incompatible with state sovereignty'
    (Connolly) **184–5**
  radical 131–2
democratic deficit 78
democratic deliberation 253
dependency theory 123, 126, 256
Der Derian, J. 161
Derrida, J. 26, **133–4**, 140, 164, 167,
  168–9, 177, 186, 193
  redefinition of 'text' 168
destabilization (Derrida) 169
Deutsch, K.W. 39, 106
development
  'inherently anti-ecological' 242
  'root cause of environmental problems'
    238
development and underdevelopment 123
Devetak, R. x, **26**, 155, 156, 188, 235n
devolution 79
dialogue 131, 155, 156, 158, 159, 204
dictatorship of proletariat 134
Dillon, M. 172, 174, 175, 183
diplomacy 30, 95, 103, 110, 125, 134
  central task 91–2
  classical 7
  open 86
  secret 7
diplomatic culture (Bull) 90
'diplomatic dialogue' (English School) 108
diplomatic wives 214
'disciplinary neo-liberalism' 127
Discipline and Punish (Foucault, 1977)
  162
'discourse ethics' (Habermas) 130–1, 133,
  156–9
  democratic 157

'discourse ethics' – *continued*
  'inclusionary' 157
  moral-practical reasoning 157
'discourse theory of morality' (Habermas)
  130–1
disinvestment threat 78
dissent, internal 171, 177
division of labour 118
  gendered 218
  international 113, 218, 227
Dobson, A. 235, 237, 240, 246, 253
Doherty, B. 246
'domestic analogy' 249
  rejected by Bull 91
domestic servants 218
dominant actors **12**
dominant relationships **12**
domination 21, 43, 146–7, 193, 249
  forms 137, 138
Donnelly, J. viii, x, **25**, 29n, 30, 189
Doran, P. 238, 255
double exclusion (Ashley) 171
double reading **169–70**
  '*anarchy problematique*' (Ashley) **170–1**,
    181
Doyle, M. 11, 16, 22, 29n, 56, 58, 59,
  60, 92
Dryzek, J. 244, 248
Dunne, T. 84, 85, 88, 96, 103, 106

East Asia 56, 62, 68, 69, 71
East Timor 49, 69, 102
Eastern Europe 125
Eckersley, R. 235, 237–9, 242, **250–7**
ecoanarchism 250, 251, 252
ecoauthoritarianism 250, 251, 252
ecocentricity 252
ecocentrism (GPT) **237, 238–9**, 250–1
ecological
  citizenship 252, 253
  crises 257
  modernization 252, 254
  movement 12
Ecologist (magazine) 235, 238, 244, 245
economic
  base 118
  deregulation 127
  development 66, 71
  growth 27, 123, 241, 252
  independence 82
economic reductionism 117–18, 120, 126,
  129
economics 1, 13, 23, 83, 233
economy and terrorism **70–81**
  liberalism and globalization 71–2
  nature of 'free trade' 72–6

non-state terrorism 79–81
  sovereignty and foreign investment 76–9
ecosystems 237, 255
Edkins, J. 163, 165, 173
education 126, 217
egoism 30, 31, 33, 34, 243
egoists 41, 107, 199
Egypt 100
Eighteenth Brumaire of Louis Bonaparte
  (Marx, 1852) 115, 143
Eleventh of September (2001) viii, 57, 79,
  80–1, 100, 111, 128, 137, 153, 171,
  187, 189, 213, 215, 227, 234
  postmodernism 161, 164–5, 166–7
  'relative autonomy' (constructivism)
    208–9
  Zehfuss 166–7
elites 59, 66, 90, 97, 102, 127, 218, 238
Elshtain, J.B. 223, 224
emancipation 26, 140, 143, 145–6, 147,
  256
  'counter-hegemonic forces' 153
  universal 124–5, 131, 132–3, 140
empire 99
'empirical idealism' 207
empiricism 4, 5, 11, **12–13**, 14, 23, 39, 46,
  52, 53, 126, 135, 136, 150, 179, 186,
  188, 189, 193, 194, 201, 204, 207,
  208, 211, 213, 246, 256
  constructivism **195**
  ecocentrism 238
  feminism **214, 216–21**, 228, 229, 232,
    233, 234
empowerment 217, 218
enclosure 241–2, 245
endogenous versus exogenous
  variables 34, 40
enforcement procedures (international) 65
Engels, F. 110, 111, 114–15, 118–21,
  124, 133
  'The General' 116
English Common Law 67
English School viii, 10, 11, 18, 19, **25**, 30,
  64, **84–109**, 211, 212
  assessment of 'revolutionism' 104
  'British variant on realism' 85, 91
  central purpose 85
  complemented by work of constructivists
    206
  distinguished from 'neo-realism' 92
  expansion of international society
    98–103
  influence on other schools of IR thought
    107
  international society (from power to
    order) 89–92

English School – *continued*
  on Lenin   110
  'natural ally of constructivism'   92
  order and justice in IR   93–8
  progress in IR   103–8
  revolt against West   98–103
Enlightenment   55, 67, 146, 148, 155, 256
  'disparaging about non-Western societies'
    133
  ideals   110
  Marxist origins   124
  origins of critical theory   137–8
Enlightenment project   26, 131, 145
Enloe, C.   27, 214, 216, 220, 223, 226, 229
  'personal is international'   214
enmity   32–3, 44–5, 46, 196
  'structurally induced'   36
environmental
  conservation   13
  crisis   237
  damage   128
  degradation   27, 65, 157
  injustice   216–17
  multilateralism   252, 254
  problems   247, 248
environmentalism
  'compatible with liberal institutionalism'
    236
  'cooptation by ruling elites'   238
  distinguished from 'Green politics'   236
Environmentalism and Political Theory
    (Eckersley, 1992)   253
epistemology   5, 12, 13, 22, 27, 140–1,
    161, 162, 167, 187, 188, 193, 194,
    201, 202, 205, 214, 215, 228, 231–2,
    256
equal opportunities   219
equality   100, 148
Escobar, A.   241
Esteva, G.   256
ethical particularism   147–9
ethics   13, 14, 16, 23, 49, 50, 115, 135,
    144, 193, 208
  ecocentric   236, 238, 252, 257
  environmental   251
  international   12
  postmodern   185–7
  universalistic   246
ethnic cleansing   102, 177
ethnicity   17, 122, 132, 154, 231
Eurocentrism   132
Europe   23, 89, 99, 120, 214
  expansion   98, 99
  international society   196–7
  'neo-mediaevalist'   104
European integration   44

European Union   46, 64, 75, 219
Everard, J.   175
exclusion   163, 174, 175, 182, 184, 185–6,
    187
experts, empowerment of   242
explanatory theory   3, 15–17
exploitation   100, 112, 113, 148
exports   62, 218
extra-territoriality   100

factory production   113
failed states   61, 101, 102, 179
'False Promise of International Institutions'
    (Mearsheimer, 1994/5)   47
Fay, S.B.   6
fear   33, 44
  'Hobbesian'   37
Federalist Papers (1788)   223
femininity   221–2, 223, 229, 230
feminism   viii, 4, 11, 15, 18, 19, 21, 23,
    27, 30, 129, 155, 213–34, 241, 255,
    256, 257
  analytical   214, 221–8, 232, 233, 234
  dichotomies problematized   229
  empirical   214, 216–21, 228, 229, 232,
    233, 234
  first and second generation   215–16
  internal debates   231
  journals   215–16
  meta theory   215
  normative   214, 228–32, 233, 234
  self-reflexivity   234
  'Western ideology'   132
feminist *praxis*   228
feudalism   114, 201
Feuerbach, L.A. (1804–72)   138
Fierke, K.M.   143, 159
finance   121, 157
financial institutions   77, 127
financial markets   66, 76, 127, 218
Finger, M.   235, 238
Finnemore, M.   194, 210
foedus pacificum (Kant, 'pacific federation')
    59
Forde, S.   29n
Foreign Direct Investment (FDI)   76–9
foreign exchange   76, 77, 218
foreign policy   57, 77, 80, 219, 220
  liberal thinking   67
  morality   48–52
foreign policy elites   8
Foucault, M.   21, 26, 165–6, 167, 172, 193
  knowledge and power   162
foundationalism   256
fragmentation   121, 122, 123
  national   119

France 6, 38, 42, 64, 93
Frankfurt School 20, 26, 107, 112, 133, 138, 140, 188, 193, 255, 256
free trade 25, **59**, 63, 64, 71, 77, 121, 198
nature **72–6**
freedom 100, 148, 243
Marx 115–16
socially-produced constraints 145, 146
freedom from starvation (Vincent) 68, 95, 106
Fromm, E., 138
Fukuyama, F. 55–8, 60–1, 70, 81, 100
challenges for orthodoxy within IR 56
thesis challenged 69
full employment 71, 218
function 45
future generations 13

Gabriel, C. 231
Gadamer, H.-G. 149
Gaddis, J. 23
Gallie, W.B. 118
game theory 22, 65, 107
Gandhi, M.K. 105
Gatens, M. 222
Gellner, E. 17
gender 13, 17, 23, 27, 32, 119, 154, **213**
criticisms of concept 230
feminist concept 221
'necessary analytical category' **228**
Third World challenge 230
transformative category **228–9**
Western assumptions 230
see also feminism
gender and development (GAD) 217
gender equality 228
likelihood of war reduced 219–20
gender hierarchy 223, 231
gender persecution 220
'genealogy' **163–7**, 172, 179, 187
Geneva Convention Against War Crimes, 1949 220
genocide 68, 96, 102
geo-politics 17, 116, 118, 124, 125, 126, 134, 151, 152, 177
geography: 'is about power' (Ó'Tuathail) 175
George, J. 4
Germany 6, 36, 64, 93
unit-level constructivism 200
Giddens, A. 61, 111, 150
Gill, S. 152–3
Gilpin, R.G. 30, 53
Gladstone, W.E. 70
Glaser, C.L. 45
Gleeson, B. 256

'global business civilization' 128
global cities 218
'global citizens' 158
'global commons' 246
'global community' 256
global ecology 235, **238**, 241, 244, 250, 252, 253, 254, 255, 256
global economy/world economy 27, 80, 82, 152
anarchic 78
capitalist 126, 132, 142, 196
global environmental governance/management 249 251
'global ethics of care' (Robinson) 144
global politics/world politics 12, 20, 26, 86, 87, 107, 109, 110, 135, 145, 226, 229, 256
constructivism 195–6, 198
continuity versus transformation (constructivist debate) 202
greening? **248–54**
immanent Green critique 250
implications of discourse ethics **157–9**
normative foundations/structures 160, 236
transversal nature 181, 182, 183, 187
'global speech community' (Lyotard) 133
global space 168, 176
global warming 246
globalization 12, 23, 26, 55, 56, 70, 73, 74, 76, 78, 79, 81, 82, 97, 111, 127, 134, 152, 153, 157–8, 181, 182, 184, 206, 207, 217, 249, 252, 254
capitalist 135, 136
Communist Manifesto (Marx and Engels, 1848) **116–17**
early twentieth century 119–20, 122
liberalism and **71–2**
nineteenth century 110, 112, 115–18, 121, 124–5, 128
Gooch, G.P. 6
'good faith with heretics' 105
Goodin, R. 237, 246, 247–8
Gouldner, A. 119
governance 56, 155
cosmopolitan 155
global institutions 158
government 74, 77, 78, 101–2, 125
autocratic government 19
dynastic principle 92
neo-liberal 80
Gramsci, A. 127
neo-Gramscian school 127, 128, 233
Grant, R. 216, 224
great powers 12, 34, 35, 36, 44, 47, 61, 66, 97, 128, 129, 225

great powers – *continued*
  grand coalitions (against hegemon)   38
  'revisionist'/'revolutionary'   39, 43, 47
  'satisfied'/'status quo'   7, 39, 43, 47
  tripolar systems   39
Greece (classical)   89, 138
  Athenian envoys to Melos   31, 46, 48
  Athens-Sparta (bipolar system)   39
  Graeco-Roman international society   89
'Green global politics'   237
Green political theory (GPT)   11, 21, **27**,
    233, 235, **237–8**, 244, 246, 254
Green politics   viii, **27**, **235–57**
  characteristics   237–8
  distinguished from 'environmentalism'   236
  global ecology   238–9
  greening global politics?   248–54
  limits to growth, post-development
    239–42
  literature   235
  objections to Green arguments for
    decentralization   246–8
  rejection of state-system   242–6
Green State (Eckersley, 2004)   250, 252, 253
Grieco, J.M.   29n, 43
Grotius, H.   67, 85
  Grotian community   200
  Grotian tradition/Grotianism   10, 93
Group of Eight (G8)   75
Guantánamo Bay   175
Guattari, F.   181–2
Guzzini, S.   29n

Habermas, J.   26, 106, 112, **130–1**, 133,
    138, 140, 149, 257
  'committed to Western conception of
    society'   131–2
  discourse ethics   **156–9**
Hagey Lectures (1983)   104
Hajer, M.   252
Halliday, F.   16, 125, 127
Hamilton, A.   223
Hapsburg-Bourbon rivalry (bipolar
    system)   39
Hardin, G.   242–3, 245, 250
Harding, S.   233
Harvey, D.   79
Hayward, T.   239
Hegel, G.W.F.   113, 115, 137, 144
Hegelianism   139
hegemony   20, 30, 38, 66, 128, 135, 194,
    209
  Ashley   179
  counter-hegemonic forces/movements
    13, 153
  Gramsci   127

USA   88, 109
  Western brand of masculinity   222, 224
Heilbroner, R.   250
Held, D.   78–9, 156, 157, 158
Helleiner, E.   235n, 249, 250
Helman, G.B.   102
Hempel, L.   251
hermeneutics   145, 150
Herz, J.   31
hierarchy   249
  political rule   31, 34
Hildyard, N.   238
Hirst, P.   249
historical materialism   110, 113–14, 118
  Cox   **126–7**, **128–30**
  current use   128
  reconstruction   **129–32**
  reconstruction by Austro-Marxists   119
  'reconstruction' (Habermas)   112, **130–1**,
    132
  see also Marxism
historical narrative   164
history   22, 209, 211, 230
  counter-histories   163
  international   **206–7**
  'not made under conditions of humans'
    own choosing' (Marx)   115, 143
  'history of present' (Foucault)   167
Hitler, A.   36
HIV/AIDS   13, 157
Hobbes, T.   30, 206
  assumptions   32, 34
  classical realism   **32–4**
  'Hobbesian anarchy of enemies' (Wendt)   47
  Hobbesian state of nature   **32–3**, 200
Hobsbawm, E.   80
Hoffman, M.   11, 145, 158, 159, 194
Hoffmann, S.   105
holistic constructivism   **201**
Hollis, M.   8, 11
Holsti, K.   4
homo economicus   41
homo sacer (sacred man)   174
Homo Sacer: Sovereign Power and Bare Life
    (Agamben, 1998)   174
Honneth, A.   26
Hooper, C.   229
Hopf, T.   205
Horkheimer, M.   22, 26, 112, 133, 138, 141
  two conceptions of theory   139
Hoskyns, C.   219
Hovden, E.   256
human community (Stoic-Christian)   148
human life (Hobbes)   33
human nature   19, 30, 31, 32, 34, 222, 223
  continuous transformation (Marx)   114

human race 110, 113
  directed by capitalism into single historical stream (Marx) 114
  economic and social unification 124
human rights 12, 13, 16, 25, 60, 77, 87, 88, 92, 95–6, 100, 103, 106, 107, 108, 109, 196, 198, 210, 219, 225
  abuses in time of war 96
  gender specificity 220
  liberalism **66–70**
  universal 67, 68–9, 79, 94, 101
  violations 101–2
  women 232
Human Rights and International Relations (Vincent, 1986) 95
human species 121, 140
humanism 53
humanitarian intervention 13, 25, 82, 88, 93, 96, 156, 158, 219
  permissible circumstances 69–70, 95–6, 102–3, 108
humanitarianism 49, 79, 173–4
humanity 51, 148, 153, 154, 156, 159, 184, 239
  duties to 102–3
humanity-nature relations 257
Huntington, S. 100–1, 211
Hurrell, A. 253
Hutchings, K. 141, 144, 148–9
hypotheses 11

idealism 10, 85, 103, 108
idealists 7, 8, 51, 212
ideas 203, 205, 206, 207, 216, 233
identity 23, **45–7**, 129, 150, 155, 166, 179, 182, 184, 186, 187, 200, 203, 226, 233
  'basis of interests' (Wendt) 197–8, 199
  'boundedness' **149**
  'defined through difference' 178
  feminist (Czech Republic) 218
  postmodernism **176–8**
identity politics 129
Ideologiekritik 145
ideology 17, 36, 92, 105, 128, 152, 196, 233
  Fukuyama 46
  horizontal conflict (Kant) 104–5
  militarist 121
immanent critique
  phenomenological version (Hegel) 144
imperialism 15, 94, 114, 116, 133, 152, 186, 230
  nationalism and **120–4**
  new 101
  theory 120–1, 123

Imperialism: Highest Stage of Capitalism (Lenin, 1916) 110, 121
'Indefinite Detention' (Butler, 2004) 174–5
independence 99, 122, 126
India 42, 99
indigenous peoples 67, 129
individuals 136, 148–9, 192, 223
Indonesia 61, 218
inequalities 17, 27, 72, 100, 124, 126, 127, 128, 129, 133, 134, 135, 136, 142, 146–7, 154, 217, 241, 242
  market relations 75–6
  power and opportunities 14
  structural 256
Inside/Outside (Walker, 1993) 183–4
institutions 20, **45–7**, 52, 64, 191
  intergovernmental 49
  political 249
inter-war era (1918–39) 6, 85, 86–7, 208, 213
  peace activists 51
inter-war crisis (1918–39) 1
interdependence 10, 153, 189, 190, 191
  liberal institutionalism **64–6**
  local 246
interest-formation 203
interest-satisfaction 203
interests 90, 155, 162, 170, 192–3, 199, 200, 203
  'identities basis of' (Wendt) 197–8, 199
International Court of Justice (ICJ) 68, 69
international courts 79
International Covenant on Civil and Political Rights (1966) 67
International Covenant on Economic, Social and Cultural Rights (1966) 67–8
International Criminal Court (ICC) 69, 221
'international environmental regimes' 236
International Feminist Journal of Politics (1999-) 216
International Labour Organization (ILO) 68, 219
international law 1, 13, 49, 51, 62, 69, 82, 84, 91–3, 95, 96, 110, 134–5, 151, 154, 158, 209
  criminal 25, 106
  incorporation of non-Western ideas 97
International Monetary Fund (IMF) 75
international order 87, 88, 99, 146, 201
international organizations (IOs) 158, 210
  gendered construction 218–19
'international political culture' (Bull) 90
international political economy (IPE) 111, 128, 233
international relations (IR) **1–28**, 93–8
  contested nature 5–6, 24

international relations – *continued*
  'contingent generalizations'
    (constructivism)   202
  dialogue/debate needed   6, 24, 28
  distinct area of intellectual endeavour
    22–3
  failure of discipline   48
  foundation as separate discipline   6–9
  foundational texts   1
  frameworks of analysis   1–2
  general theory   106
  general theory (rejected by constructivists)
    202, 205
  guiding questions   7
  Marx's writings   **112–20**
  methodology   **21–2**
  object of analysis and scope of enquiry
    18–19
  order and justice   **93–8**
  points of contention   **18–23**
  politicized discipline   15
  popular dissent   182
  postmodernist contribution   187
  progress   **103–8**
  purpose of social and political enquiry
    19–21
  purpose of studying   134–5
  rapid development of discipline (1960s,
    1970s)   10
  social dimensions   205–6
  theories and disciplines   **9–15**
international relations: power and
    knowledge   **162–7**
  genealogy   163–7
international relations theory
  diversity   **2–4**
  evaluation   **23–8**
  explanatory and constitutive   **15–18**
  general   106, 202, 205
  importance   viii
  'itself political' (Hutchings)   141
  Marxism today   **132–5**
  need   16–17
  'no obviously correct'   28
  normative   142
  politics of knowledge   **140–6**
  purpose   **11–12**
  test   108
international society   30, 95, 98, 101, 102,
    104–7, 109, 196, 200, 205, 206
  Bull   93
  conceptions   93
  constructivism   209, **210**
  distinguished from 'international
    systems'   93
  European principles   99

'functional' (Vincent)   90
'hegemonial' conception   99
mediaeval   104
moral consensus   96–7
'normative' and 'institutional' factors   92
overlapping forms (Linklater)   155–6
post-colonial era   97
from power to order   **89–92**
primary goals   93
'real foundation'   91
relationship with 'world society'
    (Buzan)   94
international studies (academic discipline)
    29n
international systems   19, 93, 223
  neo-realism   192
International Theory: Three Traditions
    (Wight, 1991)   107
internationalism   26, 120, 121, 122, 124,
    125
  socialist   134
'internationalization of state' (Cox)   152
'interpretive methodology'   204
Iraq   60, 79, 102, 103, 108, 158, 209
  'realist' opposition to war in   15, 37, 81
Ireland   118
Islam   53, 62, 98, 99, 100, 164–5, 197,
    210, 211, 227–8
  militancy/terrorism   57, 62, 70, 79, 82–3
Israel   42, 80, 100, 220
Italy   93

Jackson, R.   84, 96, 97, 102, 108
Japan   99–100, 200
Jervis, R.   29n
Jews   70, 122
Jones, C.A.   46
Jones, D.   159
just war theory   187
justice   87, 88, 89, 93, 107, 109, 138, 149
  conflicting ideas   94
  economic and social (global)   12, 126
  global   12, 108, 126, 253
  international   90

Kabeer, N.   218
Kahler, M.   29n
Kant, I.   58, 59, 63, 92, 106, 115, 137,
    138, 139–40, 146, 148, 158
  community of co-legislators   159
  ethic of hospitality   187
  horizontal conflict of ideology   104–5
  'power corrupts reason'   162
  principle of generalizability   157, 186
  theory of IR   146
Kantianism/Kantians   53, 95, 104–5

Kaplan, M. 22
Kapstein, E. 38
Kardam, N. 233
Katzenstein, P.J. 208
  unit-level constructivism 200
Kaufmann, C. 45
Keal, P. 88
Keck, M., 210
Keene, E. 47
Kennan, G.F. 30, 50, 52
Kennedy, S. viii
Keohane, R.O. 3–4, 22, 30, 64, 189, 229, 236
  neo-liberal institutionalism 142
'key social constituencies' **233**
Keynesianism 71
kijich'on (prostitutes) 220
Kissinger, H.A. 14, 39
Klein, B. 173
Klotz, A. 203
knowledge 142, 194
  forms (Foucault) 21
  hegemonic 231
  indigenous 242
  link with politics 160
  'never unconditioned' 163
  politics of 229
  postmodernism **162–7**
knowledge claims 2–3, 161, 187
  political nature 139, 146
Kosovo 49, 102, 158
Kratochwil, F. 204
  holistic constructivism 201
Kucuk-Kainardji, Treaty of (1774) 70
Kuehls, T. 249

labour 72, 131, 152
  cheap 73, 74
labour aristocracy 121
labour costs, comparative 218
labour force 126
labour market 78
labour process 119
  history revolves around (Marx) 115
labour rights 67
Labs, E.J. 43
Lakatos, I. 189, 190
land 241–2
landmines 220
language 17, 32, 130, 203
Latin America 56
law 9, 22, 106, 172, 219
  domestic 49, 100
  enforcement 93
  equality before 59
  see also international law
law of nations 67

'Law of Peoples' (Rawls) 62
Law of Sea 64
League of Nations 7, 8, 93, 99
Left Hegelians 113
legitimacy 172, 209, 210, 227
  domestic 59
  international 92
  Weber 126
Lenin, V.I. 105, 110, 111, 119, 125
  national question 122–3
  theory of imperialism 120, 121
levels of analysis (or 'images') 19, 222, 256
Leviathan (Hobbes, 1651) 32
Levinas, E. 186
Levy, J.S. 22
liberal democracy 56, 57, 69, 79, 81, 82,
    100, 131, 175, 198, 211, 253, 254
  conduct towards non-liberal states 60,
    61–2
  limits 252
liberal institutionalism 251
  'compatible with environmentalism' 236
liberal internationalism 1, 8, 24, 69–70, 86
  'endogenous determines exogenous' 81
  'inside looking out' 57–8, 81, 92
  interdependence **64–6**
liberalism **25**, 55–83, 87, 92, 149, 208, 233
  Kantian 166
  individual 'self' problematized (Hutchings)
    149
  challenges 82–3
  economy and terrorism **70–81**
  globalization **71–2**
  moral decay 69
  'naive belief in global progress' 98
  neo-realist responses 66
  post-Cold War **55–6**
  war, democracy and free trade **58–70**
liberals 19, 135, 189
'lifeboat ethics' (Hardin) 243
Lilburne, J. 165
limited power (notion) 62
limits to growth 236, 237, 241, 243, 257
  computer simulation 240
  post-development **239–42**
Limits to Growth (Meadows *et al.*, 1972)
    240–1
Linklater, A. viii, x, **25–6**, 62, 144, 145–9,
    158, 159, 188, 211, 222, 229, 235n,
    253, 256
  Beyond Realism and Marxism (1990)
    150–1, 154
  on freedom 145–6
  on 'immutability thesis' 145
  Men and Citizens (1990) 147–8, 154
  rethinking political community 146–7

Linklater, A. – *continued*
  'sociology of states-systems' 153–4
  state 'too particularistic and too
    universalistic' 155
  Transformation of Political Community
    (1998) 151, 154
  'triple transformation' 154–5
Lipschutz, R.D. 249, 250
Lisle, D. 176
List, F. 71
Little, R. 22, 23, 46, 84
Locher, B. 233
Locke, J. 67
'Lockean' rivals 47
logic of interaction (Hobbes) **33**
London School of Economics 10, 85
Low, N. 256
Lowenthal, L. 138
Luke, T.L. 250
Lynch, M. 158
Lynn-Jones, S.M. 43
Lyotard, J.-F. 26, 133

Macdonald, L. 231
McGlen, N.E. 219
Machiavelli, N. 30, 48–9, 51, 52, 206
Maclean, J. 153
MacPherson, C.B. 70
Magna Carta (1215) 67
Malaysia 218
'Man' Question in International Relations
    (Zalewski and Parpart, 1998) 229
man/state analogy 223–4, 226
Man, the State and War (Waltz, 1959) 19
Mann, M. 61, 150
Mantle, D. 257
Marcuse, H., 138, 257
market forces 71, 78, 80
  'invisible hand' 73
markets 66, 74
Marx, K.H. 26, **110–36**, 138, 139–40,
    146, 147, 148
  class, production and IR **112–20**
  'little to say about relations between
    states' 116
Marxism 7, 11, 13, 18, 20, **25–6**, 27, 58,
    81, **110–36**
  'central flaw' (economic reductionism)
    117
  central purpose of chapter 111
  changing fortunes in IR 124–32
  classical ('culture-bound view of world')
    124
  fourfold contribution 135–6
  in power 132
  IR theory today 132–5

nationalism and imperialism 120–4
new interpretations (1980s-) 111
normative claims 114–15
revolutionary strategy 117
'second-image' account of IR 110
shortcomings 110, 111–12, 130, 132,
    134–5, 136
'spirit' of 134, 136
theory of state 'flawed' 125
Third World 122, 123–4
'transformed by international system' 125
'virtual absence' (USA) 135
'Western doctrine with roots in
    Enlightenment' 124
see also economic reductionism; historical
    materialism; utopianism
Marxism-Leninism 119–20
Marxists 5, 15, 19, 196, 197, 256
  'bourgeois freedoms' dismissed 68
masculinity 27, 30, 221–2, 223, 224, 229,
    230
mass media 182
Mastanduno, M. 38, 43
materialism 205–6, 243
  'explanatory poverty' 207
Mayall, J. 97
Meadows, D. 241
Meadows, D., *et al.* (1972) **240–1**, 276
means of production 131
  modes of production 126
Mearsheimer, J. 42, 43, 50, 52, 61
Melos/Melian Dialogue 31, 46, 48
men and citizens 184
Men and Citizens (Linklater, 1990) 147–8,
    154
mercantilism 62, 121
Merchant, C. 251
metaBosnia (Campbell) 180
metalepsis (substituting causes for effects)
    166
metaphysics 186
metatheoretical critique 188
'methodological conventionalism' 204, 205
methodology 5, 13, **21–2**, 141, 145, 188,
    193, 194, 195, 201, 210–11, 217, 255
  constructivist discontent 202, **203–4**,
    205, 208
  feminist 233
microeconomic theory 189, 192
Middle East 60, 100, 165
migrants 182, 183
militarization 220
military training 222
military-industrial complex 14
Mill, J.S. 63
Milošević, S. 69, 94

'minimal foundationalism' (Hoffman) 194, 205

Mitrany, D. 64

models of agency 224–5

modernism 193–4, 204, 256

modernity
'cosmopolitan culture' 90, 101

Mohanty, C. 230

Mol, A. 252

money 148, 214

Montaigne, M.E. de 168

Montesquieu, Charles de Secondat, Baron de la Brède et de 148

Moody's 77

Moon, K. 220

'moral cartography' (Campbell) 185

moral capital 154

moral hierarchy 156

moral superiority 99, 178

'moralism' 51–2

morality 84, 88, 109
certitude 161
foreign policy 48–52

More, St Thomas 85

Morgan-Grenville, F. 240

Morgenthau, H. 1, 4, 8, 25, 30, 31, 32, 36, 39, 48, 50, 189, 223
six principles of power politics 225

motives 40–4
abstracting from or assuming 41–2
offensive and defensive realism 43–4

Mueller, J. 60–1

multiculturalism 185

multidisciplinarity 13, 23

Multilateral Agreement on Investments (MAI) 78

multinational companies (MNCs) 74, 106, 189, 218

multipolarity 39, 40

Nagel, T. 4

Napoleonic wars 62

nation/s 148–9, 170, 177

nation-building 61

nation-state/national state 56, 61, 63, 65, 68, 77–8, 81, 83, 86, 87–8, 91, 110, 111, 117, 125, 148, 177, 180, 182, 234, 242, 246, 250, 251, 254, 256, 257
boundaries 181
'defensive positionalists' 43, 190, 192
'not gap maximizers' 43
'offensive positionalists' 43
premature announcement of demise 82

national borders
'increasing irrelevance' 72

National Deconstruction (Campbell, 1998) 164, 177

national fragmentation 111–12

national interests 48, 50, 51, 52, 68, 223

national liberation 124, 133

'national question' 122

national security 36, 79, 111, 118, 128, 134, 135, 136, 154, 178

nationalism 23, 26, 50, 63, 113, 117, 119, 125, 134, 155
and imperialism **120–4**
importance in 1848 revolutions 118

'nationalist imaginary' (Campbell) 176

nationality 231

natural law 53, 67, 90, 148

nature 112, 257

Nazis 93, 173, 174

neo-conservativism 81, 227

neo-imperialism 123

neo-liberalism 127

neo-Kantianism 57

neo-liberal institutionalism 10, 25, 106–7, 190, 233
foremost exponent (Keohane) 142
problem-solving theory 142

neo-liberalism 25, 70, 71, 72, 74, 75, 77, 192, 195, 196, 203
'absolute gains' 65, 191

neo-liberals 191–2, 192–3, 197, 206, 217
debate with neo-realists 188

neo-Marxism 5, 126
dependency theory 123
world-systems theory 123

neo-mercantilism 74

neo-positivism 193, 194, 195, 203, 212

neo-realism 11, 20, 21, 22, 25, 26, 31, 57, 104, 189–90, 192, 195, 196, 203, 222, 223, 224
English School distinguished from 92
fatalism 98
and liberal institutionalism 64–5
'problem-solving' purpose 128–9, 142
responses to liberalism 66

neo-realists 12, 85, 134–5, 173, 191–2, 192–3, 197, 208, 217
debate with neo-liberals 188
general theory of IR 202
materialism 205–6

Neufeld, M. 145

neutrality 44

'new constitutionalism' 127

'new International' (Derrida) 133–4

New Right 71

new social movements 153, 182

new world order 80, 86
Marxist 110

New York   137
Newell, P.   235n
Newland, K.   216, 224
Nicaragua   37
Niebuhr, R.   30, 31, 36, 48, 51, 53, 189
Nietzsche, F.W.   138, 163, 164, 166, 172
'9/11' *see* Eleventh of September (2001)
Nixon Administration (1969–74)   14
Nixon Doctrine   220
Noel-Baker, P.   6–7
non-governmental organizations (NGOs)
   12, 153, 210
non-human species   13, 27
non-intervention principle   94, 95, 98
non-state actors   158, 181, 189, 210,
   213, 220
non-tariff barriers (NTBs)   75
non-violence   105
Nordic countries   46
normative concerns   194
normative challenges   201
normative or ideational structures
   (constructivism)   196–8, 200, 204
normative versus material forces
   (constructivist debate)   202
normative theory   12
norms   45–7, 157, 199, 203, 205, 206,
   207, 210, 216, 233
   social and cultural   245
   social and legal   200, 210–11
North (global)   76, 101, 108, 217, 241
North American Free Trade Agreement
   (NAFTA)   75, 231
North Atlantic Treaty Organization
   (NATO)   94, 96, 102–3, 173
North Korea   42
nuclear age   42, 45, 66, 94, 226
Nye, J.S.   64, 189
Nyers, P.   183

objectivity   141, 143, 160
Of Grammatology (Derrida, 1974)   168
Ohmae, K.   82
Omarska   174
ontology   12, 13, 20, 21–2, 29, 140–1,
   148, 150, 166, 167, 171, 172, 173,
   180, 183, 185, 186, 188, 193, 194,
   195, 199, 201, 212, 215, 222, 231,
   238, 244
'ontopology' (Campbell)   177, 182, 185
Ophuls, W.   243, 250
ordering principles
   anarchy   35, 38
   hierarchy   35
Organization for Economic Cooperation and
   Development (OECD)   78

origins (Nietzsche)   163
O'Riordan, T.   242, 243, 250
Osama Bin Laden   161, 167, 227
other, the   149, 177–8, 184
   rights of   133
otherness/'alterity'   129, 131, 185, 186
Ó'Tuathail, G.   175, 176
   'writing' global space   168
Oye, K.   170
ozone depletion   246

Paine, T.   59, 63, 148
Palestine   220
Papua New Guinea   61
'paradigm of communication' (Habermas)
   130
'paradigm of production'   125, 130, 131,
   132, 136
'paradigm of sovereignty'   162
parochialism   246–7
Parpart, J.   229
particularism   149
   modern state   155
Paterson, M.   x, **27**
patriarchy   23, 30, 129, 132, 218, 224,
   225, 231, 251
Patton, P.   182
pax britannica   152
peace   7, 22, 33, 51, **58–62**, 85, 87, 92, 93,
   105, 115, 214
Pearl Harbour   165
penal system   162
Pentagon   137
people   213
performativity   180
Persian Gulf   61
perspectivism   164
Peterson, V.S.   226–7, 228
phenomenology   172
'phenomenology of ethical life' (Robinson)
   144
Philippines   218
philosophers   105, 113
philosophy   22, 29, 186
Pin-Fat, V.   163
Pinochet Ugarte, A.   69
pluralism   109
   conception of 'international society'   93,
      95, 97, 101, 102, 103
Pokrovsky, B.   6
Pol Pot   50
Poland   93, 118
Polanyi, K.   71, 153
polarity   **38–9**, 43
polis   138
political community   56, **146–59**, 160, 177

political community – *continued*
  cosmopolitanism and discourse ethics
    154–9
  ethical particularism and social exclusion
    147–9
  normative dimension 147–9, 204
  praxeological dimension 154–9, 204
  sociological dimension 150–4, 204
  states, social forces, and changing world
    orders 150–4
political economy 82, 111, 128, 254, 256
  global 70, 230
  see also international political economy
political prosaics (Campbell) 181, 182
politics 83, 138, 173
  constitutional 92
  'deterritorialization' 181–2, 183, 184, 186
  domestic 86
  domestic/international split 256
  international 11, 25, 31, 35
  link with knowledge 160
  national 35
  region of approximation between
    international and domestic (Wight) 92
  'reterritorialization' 182, 187
  spatial-territorial conceptions 249
politics of knowledge in IR theory **140–6**
  critical theory's task as emancipatory
    theory 145–6
  problem-solving and critical theories
    141–4
politics of memory 167
Politics Among Nations (Morgenthau,
    1948) 1
pollution 27, 240
population growth 240
Porritt, J. 240
positivism 2, 17, 141, 143, 145, 150, 188,
    231–2, 255–6
  postpositivism 2, 14, 188, 231–2
post-Cold War era 75, 61, 69, 70, 156
post-colonialism 129
post-sovereign communities **247**
post-war era (1945–) 67, 93, 95, 123, 189,
    190, 191, 215, 220
postmodernism 3–4, 12, 17–18, 20, 21,
    26, 27, 107, 129, 132, 133, 155,
    161–87, 193–4,
    204, 241
  '*anarchy problematique*' (Ashley) 170–1
  beyond paradigm of sovereignty
    (rethinking the political) 181–7
  deconstruction 168–9
  double reading 169–70, 170–1
  feminist 221–2, 229
  international theory 188

  meanings 161
  power and knowledge in IR 162–7
  problematizing sovereign states 171–81
  textual strategies 167–71
postmodernists 17
poststructuralism 161, 214, 249, 255–6
poverty 88, 114, 216
  feminisation 217
power 17, 21, 22, 27, 29, 31, 32, 44, 45,
    46, 52, 63, 66, 93, 95, 135, 136, 146,
    158, 175, 187, 191, 193–4, 198,
    214–15, 222, 228, 245
  absolute 209
  concentration 241, 256
  constructivism **209–10**
  decentralization 236
  gender analysis **225–6**
  global configuration 143
  hierarchy 173
  inequalities 33
  military 91, 190, 207
  non-material factors 209
  postmodernism **162–7**
  realist conceptions 209
  redistribution from North to South 101
  relative 43, 190, 209
  relativity 38
  revolutionary 36
  social 148
  social conception (constructivist) 209
  subordination of morality 48
  unbalanced 61
  Waltzian notion 225
  'power-over' 225–6, 227, 232
power politics 29, 34, 50, 125, 134, 170,
    171, 215, 226
  masculine 228
  Morgenthau's six principles 225
  'textual interplay' 167–8
power relations (global) 146, 213, 231
Prague 70
Prakash, M.S. 256
preservationism 239
Pribram, A.F. 6
Price, R. 194, 204, 215
Priess, D. 47
Prince, The (Machiavelli) 48
prisoners' dilemma **37–8**, 41
  reinterpreted as polluters' dilemma 247,
    248
private property 131, 148, 245
private sphere 222–3
privatization 76
problem-solving 21, **128–9, 141–4**,
    158, 255
  constructivism 208

problem-solving – *continued*
  Cox's definition (1981)   141–2
  environmentalism   236
production   111–12, 135, 152, 157
  forms   26
  GPT   244–5
  Marx's writings   **112–20**
production modes (Marx)   114
productivism   243
Programme of German Green Party (1983)
  243
proletarian internationalism   123
proletariat   110, 113, 114, 115, 117, 118,
  120, 121, 122
  'beneficiaries of neo-imperialism'   123
property rights   91
prostitution   218, 220
protectionism   71, 73, 76
Prugl, E.   233
psychology   19
public opinion   8, 49, 60
public/private spheres   223, 224

Quakers   36
quasi-phenomenology   172
quasi-states   179
Quasi-States (Jackson, 1990)   102

race   96, 98, 100, 119, 132, 177, 230, 231
'radical interpretivism'   193
Randers, J.   241
rape   220, 224
rational choice   2, 22, 37, 65, 188
Rational Ecology (Dryzek, 1987)   244
rationalism   viii, 10, 105, 146, 192, 204,
  206, 212, 232
  challenged by critical theory   **193–4**
  differentiated from constructivism   199
  'realist' and 'idealist' wings   103
  relationship with constructivism   202,
    203, 205, 208
  '*via media*' between realism and
    'revolutionism' (Wight)   85, 94, 98,
    109
rationalist theory   **189–93**
rationalists   197, 205, 208
  constructivist debate with critical
    theorists   188
  constructivist foe   201–2
  debate with constructivists   188
rationality   30, 224, 225, 228, 256
Ratner, S.R.   102
raw materials   74, 240
Rawls, J.   60, 61–2
Reagan Administration (1981–9)   37
real world   164, 168, 188

realism   viii, 7, 9, 10, 14–15, 18, 19, **25**,
  29–54, 88, 103, 104, 105, 108, 125,
  127, 135, 146, 147, 150, 189, 208,
  215, 223, 225, 233, 256
  biological   31
  classical   31, **32–4**, 47
  constancy and change   **47–8**
  definitions   **30–2**
  English school similarities   85
  explanatory power lacking   128
  'failure to account for end of Cold
    War'   48
  'failures of third type'   40
  'hegemonic discourse'   194
  Hobbesian   166
  ideas absorbed by Marxism   126
  Marxist critique   111
  morality and foreign policy   **48–52**
  motives matter   **40–4**, 47
  neo-classical   34, 47
  norms, institutions and identities   **45–7**
  offensive and defensive   **43–4**, 47
  pessimism   25
  'problem-solving' purpose   128–9
  process, institutions and change   **44–8**
  process variables   **44–5**
  'proper questions'   54
  state-centrism   181
  strategic competition   128
  structural   31, **34–5**, 39
  structural predictions   **39–40**
  'theoretical account of how the world
    operates'   36
  thinking about realism and its critics
    52–4
'realistic utopianism' (Carr)   207
realists   9, 10, 12, 24, 82, 110, 134, 173,
  198, 209, 212
  human rights   68
  opposition to Iraq war (2003-)   15, 37, 81
  'strong' versus 'weak'/'hedged'   32
reality   23
  interpretation   16–17
  'knowable'   20, 21–2
  theory and   4
reality-in-itself   164
Realpolitik   29
reason   115, 162, 172
reasons of state (*raison d'état*)   31
reductionism   223
  liberal   57
refugee camps   173
refugees   13, 148, 182, 183
regime change   79
Reid, J.   174, 182
relative gains   **37–8**, 44, 191, 192

religion   17, 100, 113, 122, 133, 165, 197
Renner, K.   119
Renouvin, P.   6
republicanism   59, 105
reputation   33
resource conservation   239
resource exhaustion   240
resources   170
   non-renewable   157
   'open access'   245
Reus-Smit, C.   x, **26**, 47, 107, 195, 203,
      204, 205, 215, 252
Review of International Studies
   Forum on Chomsky (2003)   14
revolt against the West   57, 68–9, 79, 89,
      96, 107, 108
   cultural   124
   expansion of international society
      98–103
   'five main components' (Bull)   **99–100**
revolution
   political   114
   proletarian   118
'revolutionism' (Wight)   85–6, 88
   English School assessment   104–5,
      108–9
'revolutionists' (Wight)   10, 95, 104
revolutions (1848)   118
Ricardo, D.   63, 70, 72–3
Righteous Realists (Rosenthal, 1991)   50
'rights of man'   67
Rights of Man (Paine)   59
risk   39, 51
risk-aversion   37, 39
Risse, T.   158
Roberts, A.   103
Roberts, B.   222
Robinson, F.   144
Rorty, R.M.   144
Rosecrance, R.N.   39, 65
Rosenau, J.   251
Rosenberg, J.   127–8
Rosenthal, J.H.   50
Rousseau, J.J.   58, 67, 148
Ruggie, J.G.   153, 204
   holistic constructivism   201
'rule of immanence' (Foucault)   162
rule of law   7, 60, 62, 66–7, 70, 86, 148,
      156, 175
rule-framing   66
ruling class   118, 120, 126
Runyan, A.S.   228
Rupert, M.   139, 148
Russett, B.   59
Russia   6, 80, 96
Rwanda   69, 96, 102

Sachs, W.   235, 238, 241
Saddam Hussein   69, 81, 94, 102, 134, 209
saints   41
Sale, K.   243
Sarkees, M.R.   219
Sassen, S.   218
Schmidt, B.C.   29n
Schmitt, B.   6
Schmitt, C.   174
Schumacher, E.F.   238, 243
Schumpeter, J.A.   58, 59
Schweller, R.L.   36, 39, 47
science   29, 133, 251, 257
   natural/physical   2, 4, 22, 141
   philosophy of   23
   social   2
scientific approach/predictive accuracy   2,
      4, 23
'scientific realism' (Wendt)   202
Scott, J.W.   222
secession movements   101
secularism   100
security   38, 41, 46, 201, 219, 222, 225,
      226–7, 228
   'must be redefined'   227
   national   180
security discourse   176–7
Seel, B.   235n
self and other   177–8, 183–4, 186
self-determination (normative claims)   149
self-interest   31, 32, 64, 73, 190, 192–3
self-reflexivity   234
self-reliance   244
self-sufficiency   243
Sen, A.   217
Serbia   69, 94, 96
Sex Among Allies (Moon, 1997)   220
sex-trafficking   214, 218, 231
sexuality   227, 231
Shapcott, R.   149, 156, 235n
Shapiro, M.J.   178, 186–7
Shiva, V.   238, 241
Shue, H.   253
Sikkink, K.   210
Singer, J.D.   22, 39
'situated knowledge' (Rupert)   139
slave trade/slavery   67, 100
Smith, A.   63, 70, 72–3
Smith, M.J.   29n
Smith, S.   3, 4, 8, 11, 24, 141
Snyder, G.H.   43, 44, 45, 46
social agency (constructivist debate)   202
social bonds   151, 156, 159
social class   13, 17, 20, 68, 110, 126, 127,
      130, 135, 136, 146, 230, 231
   class conflict   111–12, 117, 118, 121, 125

social class – *continued*
   class domination   119
   class struggle   15, 114
   Marx's writings   **112–20**
social construction   11, 19
social contract (Rousseau)   67
social environment   192, 199
social exclusion   119, **147–9**, 155, 159, 160,
social forces   151–2
social sciences/human sciences   4, 22, 23, 162
   philosophical issues   **13**
   positivist   17
social structures   138, 193, 197–8
social systems   128
social theory (French)   20
Social Theory of International Politics
   (Wendt, 1999)   202–3
socialism   110, 111, 114, 115, 118, 125, 133
'socialism in one country'   115
society
   'constitutive realm' (constructivism)   **199**
   pre-capitalist   127
   primary goals (Bull)   90–1
   'primary' and 'secondary' rules (Bull)   91
   'strategic domain'   **197**
'Society Must be Defended' (Foucault,
   1975–6)   165–6
'Society of Peoples' (Rawls)   61–2
society of states (English School tenet)   84,
   87, 88–9, 92, 93, 95, 97, 100, 103, 104,
   106, 211
   defended by Kant   105
   European   90
   'Hobbesian' view   200
   modern   89–90, 108
   pluralist   155
   universal   96
   see also states-system
sociological institutionalism (Finnemore)   194
sociology   23, 211, 212
   constructivism   206
   historical   22, 207
   states, social forces, and changing world
      orders   **150–4**
Soguk, N.   183
solidarism (Grotianism)
   conception of international society   93,
      95, 96–7, 98, 102, 103, 106, 109,
      155
Somalia   61, 69
South ('developing countries'/'Third World')
   20, 74, 75–6, 96, 97–8, 100, 101, 102,
   108, 153, 218, 225, 228
   debt crises   217
   feminism   230
South Africa   67

South Korea   220
Southern Africa   36, 96
sovereign equality (principle)   99
sovereign immunity   69
sovereign powers   91, 175
sovereign rights   69, 70, 104
sovereign states   12, 74, 84, 106, 147,
   148, 149, 155, 156, 160, 182,
   183, 185, 187, 189, 197, 210, 247,
   251
   democratically-deficient nature   157
   rise (holistic constructivism)   201
sovereign states problematized   **171–81**
   boundaries   175–6
   identity   176–8
   statecraft   178–81
   violence   172–5
sovereignty   47, 82, 86, 96, 98, 104,
   154–5, 162–3, 170–1, 176, 179, 187,
   211, 222, 248, 253
   equal   99–100
   'essence of the political' (Agamben)   174
   ethics of exclusion   **183–5**
   and foreign investment   **76–9**
   Hobbesian image   252
   'master signifier' (Edkins and Pin-Fat)   163
   national   101
   'negative' versus 'positive'   102
   postmodernism   175
   territorial   68
   Weber, C.   205
sovereignty, beyond paradigm of (rethinking
   the political)   **181–7**
   ethics of exclusion   183–5
   postmodern ethics   185–7
Sovereignty: Organized Hypocrisy (Krasner,
   1999)   47
'sovereignty contract' (Peterson)   226
Soviet bloc   101
Soviet Union/USSR   14, 23, 39, 96, 119,
   133, 178, 229
   collapse   111
   resort to traditional diplomacy   125
Soviet-US relations   36
space   175, 183
spatial differentiation   177
spatiality
   'privileged in political thought'   176
speciesism   239
Spretnak, C.   240, 244
Spykman, N.   52
stability-effects (Derrida)   169
Stalin, J.V.D.   119
Stalinism   133
Standard & Poor's   77
starvation   68, 95, 106, 173

state, the   25, 72, 80, 82, 117, 118, 124,
    128, 134, 149, 168, 173, 177, 187,
    202, 209, 223, 224, 245, 248, 249
  behaviour (structural determinants)   190
  bounded entity   162–3
  and civil society   151–2
  Cox's theory   152
  'destructive fusion' (Linklater)   155
  'executive committee of bourgeoisie'   126
  five monopoly powers (Linklater)   151
  Green anarchist objections   244
  historical product (Vico)   152
  intervention (in economy)   71
  Marxist theory 'flawed'   125–6
  'natural form of political community'
      (problematized)   147
  power relations (Foucault)   165
  rethought   160
  social purposes   153
  social theory   150
  'too small, too big'   251
'state of emergency'   175
state interests   205–6
state power   62, 189, 210, 211
  'no longer ignored by Marxism'   128
state socialism   125
state sovereignty   69, 93, 94, 175, 198
  beyond the paradigm   **181–7**
  'incompatible with democracy' (Connolly)
      184–5
  re-thinking the political   **181–7**
state-building   151
state-centrism   30, 181, 183
'state-form' (Deleuze and Guattari)   182
statecraft   216
  definition   180
  postmodernism   **178–81**
states   4, 13, 14, 17, 20, 26, 29, 35, 41, 52,
    69, 106, 136, 170, 171, 175, 190, 192,
    199, 210, 252
  alignment   **44–5**
  authoritarian   60
  Catholic and Protestant   85
  defensive positionalists (neo-realist
      view)   192
  identities and interests   200–1
  interdependence   191
  monopoly on legitimate force   227
  'moral concerns'   48
  non-liberal   92
  post-colonial   46
  'protection racket'   226–7
  republican   105
  social identities   199
  utility-maximizers (neo-liberal view)   192
  weak   36, 46

states-system   92, 93, 111, 125, 128, 132,
    142, 152, 160, 211, 225, 236, 247,
    253, 254, 256
  Green critique   250
  modern   153
  rejection by Greens   **242–6**
  reproduction   216
  'sociology of' (Linklater)   153
  see also society of states
statesmanship   31, 50, 51, 52
Steans, J.   27
Stern, M.   217
Stewart, C.   249
Stoll, R.J.   30
strategic rationality   203
Strategic Studies and World Order (Klein,
    1994)   173
structural adjustment policies (SAPs)   27,
    75, 217
structural modifiers (Snyder)   45
structural parasitism (Derrida)   169
structural predictions   **39–40**
structural realism   189
  see also neo-realism
structuralism (Waltzian)   35
structurationists   197
struggle for power (and security)   1, 11, 13,
    23, 24, 31, 46, 47, 51, 56, 68, 86, 92,
    110, 116, 135, 190, 209
subjectivity   172, 179, 193
subsidies   75, 76, 78
subsistence   217
Sudan   102
'suffering humanity' (Dunne and Wheeler)
    106
Suganami, H.   16
Suharto, T.N.J.   69
superstructure (political and ideological)
    118
'supreme humanitarian emergency'   96, 106
survival motive   9, 41–2, 43, 47, 51, 66,
    125, 191, 206
sustainable development   240, 241, 242,
    243, 245–6, 253, 255
Sylvester, C.   27, 224, 226, 231
systemic constructivism   **199–200**, 202
  'major deficiency'   199–200

Taliaferro, J.W.   43
Taliban   102, 134
taxation   82, 151
technology   74, 113, 133, 240
  military   45
telecommunications   182
Tellis, A.   31
territorial conquest   63, 65, 66

territoriality   153, 187
territory   155, 170, 177
terrorism   61, 62, 65, 102, 153, 200, 210,
    211, 220, 227
  economy and   **70–81**
  non-state   **79–81**
  transnational   215
  see also war on terrorism
Teschke, B.   128
'text'   168
textual interplay   168
textual strategies (postmodernism)   **167–71**
textuality   168
theology (Jewish)   186
'theoretical reflexivity'   143
Theories of International Relations
  editions (first, second, third)   viii
  referencing   viii
theorizing process   2–3
theory
  acquisition of dominance   9, 14
  'artful abstraction'   30
  assumptions   4
  'critical' versus 'traditional' (Horkheimer)
    139
  explanatory versus constitutive   3, **15–18**
  nature (constructivist discontent)   **202–3**,
    205, 208
  'no view from nowhere' (Nagel)   4
  purpose   9
  value-free   139
theory construction (Lakatos)   189, 190, 193
Theory of International Politics (Waltz,
  1979)   19, **189–90**
Thimme, F.   6
'think globally, act locally' (Green slogan)
  244, 249
third debate (positivist and post-positivist)
  188, 215
'third way'   25
Third World Marxism   122, 123–4
Third World Resurgence (magazine)   238
'third-image' perspective   199
third-party facilitation   158–9
Thompson, G.   249
Thucydides   30, 31, 46, 48, 206
Tickner, J.A.   32, 225, 228
Tilly, C.   61
time   48, 183
Todorov, T.   149
Tokyo   77
totalitarianism   133, 186, 256
totality (postmodern critique)   187
totalizing perspectives   26
tourism   176–7, 218
trade   65, 82, 191, 213

intra-firm transactions   74
  relative to size of world economy   72
trade unions   78, 153
trade wars   62
'trading state' (Rosecrance)   65–6
'tragedy of commons' (Hardin)   242–3, 245
Tragedy of Great Power Politics
  (Mearsheimer, 2001)   43–4, 51
Trainer, F.E.   240
transfer pricing   75
Transformation of Political Community
  (Linklater, 1998)   151, 154
transnational corporations (TNCs)   12, 72,
  73, 74, 75, 77, 80, 82, 218
transversal struggles (Ashley)   171
treaties   251
trials   69
Trnopolje   174
Trotsky, L.D.B.   122, 123, 125
True, J.   viii, x, **27**, 217, 218
trust   65, 86, 91
trusteeship   99, 102
truth   164
Truth and Tragedy (Thompson and Meyers,
  1977)   51
Tucker, R.   37
Turkey   100
Twenty Years' Crisis (Carr, 1939)   1, 108

UNCED [UN Conference on Environment
  and Development, 1992]   238
unequal treaties   100
unipolarity   38
unit-level constructivism   **200**
United Kingdom   6, 7, 10, 30, 42, 71, 84,
  93, 102, 109, 158, 166, 206
  decline of hegemony   121
United Nations   79, 81, 99, 158, 180
  author   217
  Charter   102, 103
  General Assembly   102
  High Commissioner for Human Rights
    219
  Office of High Commissioner for Refugees
    219
  Security Council   209
  UNICEF   219
United States of America   1, 2, 6, 7, 8, 22,
  30, 42, 44, 52, 53, 60, 61, 69, 71, 96,
  100, 102, 109, 154, 158, 165, 166,
  178, 196, 220, 227
  absence of countervailing pressures   80–1
  constructivism mainstream   188, 205,
    206, 208, 212
  foreign policy   14–15
  framing the rules   66

United States of America – *continued*
  material preponderance versus political
    influence 209
  relationship with Canada 46
units (Waltz) 30, 41
'universal communication community'
  (Habermas) 131–2
Universal Declaration of Human Rights
  (1948) 67
universalism 146, 228
  moral, political, legal principles 154
universities 212
University of Auckland x
University of Denver (USA) x
University of Ottawa x
University of Wales (Aberystwyth) x
  Chair of International Relations (1919-) 6
University of Waterloo (Canada) 104
USA-USSR (bipolar system) 39
use of force 23, 25, 81–2, 91, 105
usufruct 246
utopianism 78–9, 85, 87, 88, 108–9, 129
  liberal 58
  Marxist 110
utopians 7, 8–9, 10

values 22, 90, 142, 144, 162, 164, 196,
  199, 205, 207, 210
  indigenous 98
  separation from 'fact' 141, 143
  Western 100, 101, 124
Van Evera, S. 45
Vasquez, J.A. 29n, 42
Vattel, E. de 93
'*via media*' (Wight) 85–6, 94, 98
Vico, G.B. 152
Vietnam 36, 50, 125
Vincent, R.J. 25, 68, 84, 90, 95, 96, 103,
  106, 108
violence 33, 84, 85, 86–7, 91, 103, 105,
  171, 177, 187, 200, 210, 219–20, 227,
  229
  ethnic 111
  monopoly of legitimate use 151, 174
  postmodernism **172–5**
  structural 216
  Weber 126
  against women 224
von Wegerer, A. 6

wages 126
Walker, R.B.J. 176, 183, 185
  Inside/Outside (1993) **183–4**
Wall, D. 244
Wall Street 77
Waller, M. 155

Wallerstein, I. 123
Walt, S. 42
Waltz, K.N. 5, 11, **19**, 22–3, 30, 31, 32,
  43, 47, 57, 61–2, 80, **189–90**, 223, 225
  argument rejected by Marxists 128
  contribution of realism 53
  direct competition from Wendt 202
  logical coherence 'fatally undermined'
    41–2
  on Marxism 110, 112, 117, 118, 125
  neo-realism 13, 92, 103
  predictive power lacking 45
  'relative gains' 65
  structural realism **34–5**, 38, 39, 44, 46
Wapner, P. 249, 250
war 10, 17, 27, 36, 46, 106, 114, 116,
  117, 118, 120, 121, 125, 126, 134,
  148, 165, 173, 176, 177, 213, 217,
  223, 226, 229
  absent between liberal-democratic states
    11, 22, 57, 58, 59–60, 81–2, 92
  causes 19, 58–9
  defensive 33
  disincentives 63
  Foucault 166
  gender equality reduces likelihood
    219–20
  just versus unjust 93
  mercantilist goals 62
  occasion of greatest violations of human
    rights 96
  'preventive' 103, 209
  propensity to 45
  see also World War I; World War II
'war of all against all' (Hobbes) 31, 32, 33,
  41, 43
war crimes 69, 96, 108
war, democracy and free trade **58–70**
  human rights 66–70
  interdependence and liberal
    institutionalism 64–6
  prospects for peace 58–62
  spirit of commerce 62–4
war discourse 166
war on terrorism 79, 80, 137, 153–4, 165,
  166–7, 175, 209
Washington Consensus 14, 76
watersheds 243
Watson, A. 84, 87, 90, 96, 97, 107
  revolt against West 98, 101–2
wealth 62, 63, 114, 207
Weapons of Mass Destruction (WMD) 79,
  81, 94, 102, 196
Weber, C. 165, 180, 244, 229, 205
  'writing' the state 168
Weber, M. 126, 138

Weiss, L.   250
Wendt, A.   5, 26, 46–7, 53, 107, 197, 208, 209
   'cultures of anarchy'   252
   social theory of IR   202
   systemic constructivism   **199–200**
West, the   67, 68, 81, 97–8, 124, 166, 210, 211, 227, 228
   'alien and decadent' values   124
   see also 'revolt against the West'
Westphalian state   150, 151, 152, 155
Wheeler, N.J.   84, 85, 88, 96, 97, 106
White, H.   164
white supremacism   67, 96, 100
Whitehall, G.   183
Whitworth, S.   219
Whose Common Future? Reclaiming the Commons (1993)   245
'Why is there no International Theory?' (Wight, 1966)   85
Wight, M.   9–10, 11, 22, 25, 28, 29n, 64, 84, **85–6**, 88, 89–90, 92, 94–5, 96, 103, 105–8
   on Lenin's *Imperialism*   110
   on Marxism   112
will to power (Nietzsche)   41
Wilson, P.   103
Wilson, T.W.   70
'withering away of state' (Marx/Trotsky)   125, 134
women   13, 19, 27, 67, 132
   migrant   218
   see also feminism
'Women in Black'   220
women in international development (WID)   217
women's movement   12
women's rights   228
World Bank   75, 251
'world civic politics' (Wapner)   249
World Commission on Environment and Development (WCED)   240, 241

world community   94
   possibility   11
World Conservation Strategy (IUCN, 1980)   240
world economy   *see* global economy
World Food Programme   219
world government   247
World Health Organization (WHO)   219
world market   25
   deregulation   14
world order   13, 136, 151–2, 154, 215, 234, 242, 252
   liberal capitalist   211
   post-European   129, 131
   post-hegemonic   129–30
world politics   *see* global politics
World Population Fund   219
world society
   constructivism   209, **210**
   relationship with 'international society' (Buzan)   94
World Trade Centre   137
World Trade Organization (WTO)   12, 75
World Values Survey   227
World War I   117, 121, 134, 213, 208
   search for causes   6, 7, 8, 15, 120, 121
World War II   8, 9, 36, 94, 174, 208
world wars   134
world-systems theory (Wallerstein)   123

Yergin, D.   14
Yugoslavia   96, 220

Zakaria, F.   43
Zalewski, M.   229
Zehfuss, M.   166
zero-sum game   65, 190, 226
Zimmern, Sir Alfred   6–7, 10
zone of peace (liberal democratic)   60, 62, 70